The Political Theory of Tyranny in Singapore and Burma

The Political Theory of Tyranny in Singapore and Burma applies classical political theory to modern comparative political analysis in Southeast Asia to examine the role of rhetoric in maintaining or transforming a regime. Drawing from Aristotle to develop the rhetoric of benevolent despotism, McCarthy examines how rhetoric addresses commonly held beliefs and how this informs modern comparative political theory. Using Singapore and Burma as case studies, the book questions the basic assumptions of democratization theory, examining the political science of tyranny and exploring the rhetorical manipulation of religion for the purpose of political legitimacy. McCarthy shows how political leaders in Singapore and Burma have either invented or manipulated traditional beliefs by their selective interpretation of Confucian or Buddhist traditions in their favor, and it is by analyzing the rhetoric of benevolent despotism used in these countries that fundamental similarities between rhetorical strategies undertaken by leaders in both regimes can be seen.

The Political Theory of Tyranny in Singapore and Burma presents the first study to combine the fields of classical rhetoric, political philosophy, and comparative politics, and will be essential reading for scholars working within these fields and the areas of international relations and Southeast Asian studies.

Stephen McCarthy is a Research Fellow at the Griffith Asia Institute, Griffith University, Brisbane.

T0347655

Routledge contemporary Southeast Asia series

The Political Theory of Tyranny in Singapore and Burma

Aristotle and the rhetoric of benevolent despotism

Stephen McCarthy

LONDON AND NEW YORK

First published 2006
by Routledge
2 Park Square, Milton Park, Abingdon, Oxon OX14 4RN

Simultaneously published in the USA and Canada
by Routledge
711 Third Avenue, New York, NY 10017

First issued in paperback 2012
Routledge is an imprint of the Taylor & Francis Group, an informa business

Typeset in Baskerville by Wearset Ltd, Boldon, Tyne and Wear

British Library Cataloguing in Publication Data
A catalogue record for this book is available from the British Library

Library of Congress Cataloging in Publication Data
A catalog record for this book has been requested

ISBN13: 978-0-415-65386-2 (pbk)
ISBN13: 978-0-415-70186-0 (hbk)
ISBN13: 978-0-203-08752-7 (ebk)

Dedicated to Richard W. Staveley

Contents

Illustrations

Figures

Tables

Acknowledgments

This book began as a dissertation proposal at Northern Illinois University several years ago. I was very fortunate during the writing of my dissertation to benefit from the direction of Professor Larry Arnhart and the expertise of Professor M. Ladd Thomas, both of whom guided and supported my efforts. Professor James Schubert also offered suggestions for my early ideas and Professor Gary Glenn made helpful comments on my final draft. I would also like to acknowledge Professor Morton Frisch for his continued support and generosity, and Gustaaf Houtman and Janet Philp for their early comments and suggestions. Many thanks also to James Gomez and Donald Seekins for permitting me to reproduce their tables.

I was fortunate to be able to write part of the dissertation while on a Northern Illinois University Graduate School Dissertation Completion Award, and I wish to thank Ann Sorensen and American Farmland Trust for continuing to support me during my studies. I am very grateful to Stephanie Rogers at Routledge for acting on her belief in my work, two anonymous reviewers for their useful suggestions, and Helen Baker for her editorial advice. Thanks also to William Case, Michael Wesley, and the Griffith Asia Institute for supporting me through the final stages.

Finally, I am grateful for the support of my colleagues during my years in the cornfields. For their comments, advice, and generosity through the writing of my dissertation and beyond, I wish particularly to thank Marlene Sokolon, Andy Schott, Jason Jividen, and Kheang Un. My thanks to my mother for her endless support, and also to Christos Panousis, Simon Hood, and Diane Maslowskyj whose assistance allowed me to work on the final draft of this book. I am especially grateful to Christiane D. Ong for her encouragement, generosity, and for always being there.

1 Introduction

Political scientists have much to learn from Aristotle. In particular, if the field of comparative politics is to be saved from its current intellectual poverty, we will need to revive some ideas from Aristotle. A traditional conflict in political science is the dispute over the relative worth of theoretical generalization and regional, or field, specialization. Bridging the gap between the two has become a perennial problem. This tension surfaces within the field of comparative politics when one attempts to draw general inferences about obstacles to democratization from case studies of very different cultures. In this book, I will show that reviving Aristotelian regime analysis and rhetorical theory would be a good way out of the intellectual crisis facing comparative politics.

Adopting Aristotelian theory to analyze existing regimes improves upon modern political development theory for a number of reasons that will become evident. Most noteworthy among the faults pervading contemporary development theory is a form of democratic determinism that did not exist in the classical account of politics. Modern development theory has been distorted by a bias towards imposing institutions of liberal democracy upon developing nations without first coming to grips with the character of the existing regime, the national character of its people, and the character of their leaders. In his second inaugural address, President Bush for example, having claimed that only one "force of history" could expose the pretensions of tyrants – "the force of human freedom," then declared that "[It] is the policy of the United States to seek and support the growth of democratic movements and institutions in every nation and culture, with the ultimate goal of ending tyranny in our world."[1]

Classical political scientists would have found this to be a surprising statement, not only because of the potentially enormous cultural obstacles facing such a mission, but also because the mission's ultimate goal would have been considered theoretically impossible. In addition, the modern concept of legitimacy – whereby the holding of elections and, to a lesser degree, economic success, serve as primary measures of legitimate government and indicators of democratization – would have seemed strange to the classics. Aristotle, for example, did not believe that legitimacy, or constitutional rule, was as important as examining justice and stability within various types of regimes when it came to comparing and classifying them.

Although the problem of tyranny has been raised and popularized in recent public political rhetoric, serious political science continues to avoid examining the topic in any detail. While much of the work in the political culture area of comparative politics, for example, addresses political elite behavior and the cultural obstacles to democratization, there is clearly an aversion to examining the idea of tyranny per se and the rhetoric produced by tyrannical regimes in modern times. That tyranny may remain a possibility is often overlooked, mitigated, or rejected as mythical by modern political scientists as they invent adjectives to describe behavior that the classics would have commonly understood. Aristotle, for example, not only believed that tyranny was real, but that among the variety of tyrannies was a kind where a tyrant was indeed considered to be legitimate. The democratic determinism found in modern development theory, however, denies such a possibility.

Aristotle's account of tyranny in the *Politics* provides a defensible framework for modern political science and complements the modern comparative politics literature. The *Politics* provides a means by which comparative political scientists may classify various examples of past and existing regimes. While modern political theories aim for scientific precision, they often struggle to identify and characterize a regime's harsher traits. Returning to Aristotle, therefore, is an attempt to unite the sophistication of the ancients with the variety of circumstances that are presently found in many harsh regimes.

To show that classical theory helps to provide a more complete and more reasonable account of these types of regimes, the theoretical framework of this book combines Aristotelian political theory with the more appropriate elements of modern comparative political development theory. Because a key to better understanding a regime is to analyze the political discourse of its leading figures, classical rhetorical theory remains a useful guide for this purpose. Combining Aristotle's account of tyranny in the *Politics* with his account of political rhetoric in the *Rhetoric* provides a useful way to analyze and categorize certain harsh regimes in modern times, many of which are to be found scattered throughout Asia and Africa. Burma and Singapore provide particularly good examples of the former.

In the *Politics*, Aristotle appears to identify three major kinds of tyranny, two of which are regarded as more moderate than the common brutish form, and two modes by which tyranny is preserved. When we read Book 5 of the *Politics*, we are obliged to question Aristotle's motives for providing a detailed examination of the creation of tyranny, the behavior of the tyrant, and the means of preserving his rule. It is not unreasonable to suggest that Aristotle intends to be both descriptive and prescriptive. If we can recognize tyranny where it occurs, then Aristotle may provide the means with which to bring about its downfall, or at least to moderate its consequences.

Of Aristotle's two modes by which tyrannies are preserved, the first applies to the more commonly perceived form of brutish tyranny of which Burma is a particularly good example. The second is a more subtle mode whereby the tyrant appears to make himself look more kingly, thus allowing him to rule over both the willing and the unwilling. Although this mode may seem to be more appropriate for analyzing Singapore, it is also useful to apply the elements of this second mode to a case study of Burma and note the ruling *Tatmadaw*'s (army) transition from the first mode to the second by its promotion of Buddhist political rhetoric.

It is particularly important to analyze this second mode of preserving tyrannies today because of the rise of "soft authoritarianism" in East Asia. This is not to say that the former kind of tyranny does not still exist in Asia. Burma, North Korea, and to some extent, the People's Republic of China are enduring examples. But the brutish variety of tyranny has, in general, managed to manifest itself in longer lasting and less offensive ways. The rise, and demise, of totalitarianism and ideologically based systems of tyranny have, on average, created a need for a more appealing, and more economically viable, form of government. Singapore openly flouts this new form and China has been particularly interested in using Singapore's model as it proceeds along its own path of economic liberalization.

Being a city-state, Singapore is a particularly appealing example for a case study because Aristotle would not have experienced any scope of government larger than this. Aristotle's study of 158 regimes was limited to relatively small city-states or *polieis*, and not empires. Burma, on the other hand, comprises a much larger territory that includes many ethnic minority groups. Nevertheless, the kind of rhetoric that is produced with the aim of preserving Aristotle's second form of tyrannical regime may be reflected in the enthymematic propaganda campaigns pursued in both nations.

Lee Kuan Yew's Asian values rhetoric of the 1980s and 1990s in Singapore is matched by the Buddhist political rhetoric of the *Tatmadaw* generals in Burma today. Both serve a common purpose in preserving the regime, and both are designed to make rulers appear to be acting in a kingly fashion. But whereas Singapore lacks the monarchical heritage, the glory days of past kings and dynasties are interwoven into the history and political culture of the Burmese, and this becomes particularly significant when the political elite interpret history to legitimize their rule. It is necessary when assessing the longevity of this new form of tyranny, therefore, to account for the particular social circumstances in Singapore and Burma and the historical grounds for legitimacy used by the ruling elite.

The enthymeme (or rhetorical syllogism) in classical rhetorical analysis is the body of persuasion, and it assumes a central role in political rhetoric. Successful political rhetoric requires that enthymemes – which are reasonable but inconclusive arguments – must appeal to the commonly held opinions of the people. These common opinions, or *endoxa*, form what is called in the language of modern comparative politics – "the political culture" of a people. Because there is a long theoretical tradition suggesting the use of religion in the service of politics, particularly in tyrannies, then it should not be surprising to discover that enthymemes of tyrannical rhetoric should also appeal to the religious elements in the common opinions of the people, or to an ethical code that is revered as authoritative.

Buddhism assumes this position in Burma, while in Singapore, whose people are predominantly of Chinese origin, political leaders have turned to Confucianism as a means of establishing their Asian identity. While the political rhetoric of potentially benevolent despots may appear to be culturally specific, therefore, by adopting a common strategy with respect to the content and purpose of their enthymemes, they are also generalizeable by being identified as a form of tyrannical rhetoric. In this way, by adopting Aristotle's understanding of kingship, tyranny, and rhetoric, we are able to better understand, and compare, political rhetoric.

Following an historical account of the rise of Lee Kuan Yew, Aristotelian theory will be applied to locate the Singapore regime and to show how Lee's rule conformed to Aristotle's prescriptions in the *Politics* for preserving this kind of regime. Singapore's rapid rate of modernization and, at least until fairly recently, economic growth over the past several decades has sparked off one of the great natural law controversies of modern times. The "Asian values debate" is the phrase most often applied to the body of arguments flowing between Eastern and Western politicians and scholars who either support or oppose the existence of a common set of "shared values" within Asia, and which allow some Asian politicians to defend themselves from Western accusations of human rights violations.

It is possible to assess the merits of Lee's Asian values rhetoric by examining the major Confucian arguments offered in support, by exploring how it attempted to interpret, and circumvent, the Universal Declaration of Human Rights, and by illustrating how Lee selectively interpreted Confucianism and Singaporean history. Lee's rhetoric will be analyzed in accordance with Aristotle's discussion of enthymemes in the *Rhetoric*, keeping in mind the kind of regime which it helps to preserve in the *Politics*. Examining the development and content of Lee's Asian values rhetoric is undertaken with a view to questioning the validity of its implicit enthymeme. To complete our Aristotelian analysis along the lines of the framework suggested, it will be necessary to assess the degree of justice in Singapore and discuss the future possibilities for improving justice, and stability, in the regime.

Aristotle's third kind of tyranny is neither based on law nor a monarchic rule over willing persons, but is a sort of counterpart to absolute king-ship and is most particularly held to be tyranny. Burma lies within Aris-totle's description of rule over the unwilling and it is possible to illustrate how the *Tatmadaw* generals have adopted the brutish tactics required to preserve such a regime. Referring to Aristotle's *Politics* shows how the rhetoric of the *Tatmadaw* conforms to the factors that Aristotle considered to be important for explaining how tyrannies are preserved.

Because both the *Tatmadaw* and the opposition leader, Daw Aung San Suu Kyi, claim to be continuing a legacy of Buddhist traditions – Suu Kyi claiming to continue her father's (Aung San) work and the *Tatmadaw* acting as if they were performing the duties of Burmese kings – it is neces-sary to examine the political rhetoric of the *Tatmadaw* in relation to this theme. The "kingly right to rule" argument, which has been offered as a justification for Burmese military rule in the past, has been resurrected under the current regime to support their Buddhist political rhetoric.

This form of political rhetoric, which appeals to the Buddhist mass political culture of Burma through the common opinions they hold con-cerning kingship and Buddhism – whether it is performed by way of speeches or actions – is directed towards achieving some measure of legiti-macy among the Burmese people. It is performed not only because Bud-dhism is the fundamental characteristic in the political culture of the Burman majority, and hence most revered and understood by the greater part of the population, but also, in the case of the generals, because they have failed to achieve legitimacy during times of relative peace through what today are generally considered to be the sufficient measures of legiti-macy – popular consent and economic stewardship.

Indeed, legitimacy itself appears to become a debatable question in modern political science only if what is currently taken as the primary pre-condition and determining factor of legitimacy, elections, is relaxed. Since the Burmese generals chose to ignore the election results of 1990 and yet scholars still debate the legitimacy of the regime on other grounds, exam-ining these other grounds on their own merits could prove to be a more fruitful exercise. This book will concentrate primarily upon the legitimacy that the *Tatmadaw* has attempted to achieve by portraying themselves as the upholders and preservers of the Buddhist traditions, coming as both a response to Suu Kyi's actions and writings and in support of their own claims to possess an historical "kingly right to rule." Of course, to be suc-cessful, then as in the case of Singapore, such claims require a particular historical interpretation of the *endoxa* to support the generals' perform-ance.

While comparing the political use of Buddhism, or Buddhist political rhetoric, among Aung San, Aung San Suu Kyi, and the *Tatmadaw* is reveal-ing, the primary focus of this book will be the Buddhist rhetoric of the regime's current leaders. Buddhist political rhetoric, as used by the mili-tary elite, is of a very rudimentary form when compared with the Buddhist rhetoric of Aung San Suu Kyi. Well-developed theoretical arguments and mental, or meditational, practices are usually absent from their rhetorical public displays. But what the military lacks in theoretical substance, they make up in show, and there has been a plethora of Buddhist political rhetoric on show recently which is regularly recorded in public newspapers and journals.

The generals' rhetoric may appear either in written form – as speeches, articles, and commentary, or in visual form – as photographic evidence or artistic presentations. The findings of this case study will show that, since the coup of 1988, the *Tatmadaw* generals have not only been promoting Buddhism as part of some kingly duty but have increased this promotion and have responded to Suu Kyi's Buddhist rhetoric with their own version. They have come full circle since 1962 by actively promoting Buddhism as, if not the state religion, then the next closest thing resembling one. As in the Singapore study, applying Aristotelian theory provides a unique assessment of the degree of justice in Burma and allows us to comment upon the possibilities for improving justice and stability in the regime.

While it would be fruitful to analyze in further detail the rhetoric produced in Singapore and Burma according to Aristotelian principles, the objective of this book is not simply to conduct a study in rhetoric per se, but to apply these general principles of rhetorical persuasion in order to show how this particular rhetoric substantiates Aristotle's account of tyranny in the *Politics.* Applying Aristotle's elements of rhetorical logic shows how the rhetoric of these regimes may be understood as conforming to the principles of rhetorical deduction (enthymemes addressing the *endoxa*) and rhetorical induction (manipulating the *endoxa* with selective historical examples). This rhetoric is not randomly contrived but follows a pattern developed by the ruling elite which conforms to their enthymemes and to the general principles of enthymematic reasoning, as understood by Aristotle, and are supported by inductive examples and historical arguments. Based on the nature of the historical arguments or of the argument (*logos*) itself, it is possible to reveal the sophistic character of this rhetoric, as befits one who gives a fine performance in the role of a kingly ruler.

The objective of analyzing the rhetoric of the political elite in Singapore and Burma, therefore, is threefold: to show that by addressing the common opinions of the many, their rhetoric conforms to the principles of enthymematic persuasion in the *Rhetoric*; to challenge the examples used to support their enthymemes and the truth of the common opinions upon which they are based; and to show that their rhetoric conforms with Aristotle's advice for preserving regimes in the *Politics.* While comparativists interested in the procedural formalities associated with modern democratization theory often neglect the rhetoric produced by authoritarian regimes, this rhetoric should be regarded as an important element of regime analysis.

It is also the intention of this book to show that applying Aristotelian practical observations to areas where modern comparative theory remains deficient helps bridge the gap between theoretical generalization and regional specialization. Employing an Aristotelian conceptual framework for examining tyranny and the rhetoric of preservation allows one to examine modern, culturally specific, examples of political rhetoric while supporting general theoretical conclusions concerning politics. Using Singapore and Burma as case studies illustrates how this can be done.

2 The intellectual crisis in comparative politics

Modern comparative development theory suffers from a number of fundamental ills which make a return to the classical study of politics seem an attractive alternative. The subfield of political culture theory attempts to address some of these ills, though it too falls short in many respects. It is revealing to show how modern comparative politics compares with classical comparative politics, as understood in the Aristotelian tradition, and it is timely for political scientists to recognize the inherent defects of modernization theory and appreciate why classical comparative theory continues to offer a useful guide for comparing regimes. To question the fundamental assumption of comparative politics modernization literature – that democracy is the best and only legitimate form of government – requires an appraisal of the universality of such an idea given the global variety of cultural diversity, and especially Asian political culture.

In the process of analyzing the faults and the possible remedies of the modern comparative politics literature, we may discover that every sensible idea in modern comparative theory is already implicit in Aristotle. Modern comparative theory, furthermore, provides an impoverished substitute for Aristotle's cyclical analysis of regimes because it reflects the philosophy of historicism, whereby history follows a linear progression towards democracy, and because modern comparative theory is preoccupied with the construction of institutions per se as distinguished from institutions designed to encourage statesmanship and education towards moral virtue. To what degree social capital theory offers a new paradigm, or approach, to remedy the void created by modern comparative politics' focus on democratic institutional proceduralism may also be ascertained by tracing its classical roots. In order to analyze the field's preoccupation with the topics listed above, it may be useful to begin by surveying the most relevant comparative politics literature on development, or modernization, and political culture.

Comparative politics and development

In the preface to their popular text on comparative politics, editors Lichbach and Zuckerman claim that the field of comparative politics has lost its way. Their reasons for this contention are that "too few studies are nomothetic, creatively combining theory and cases and developing general propositions, [while] too many studies are idiographic, offering no more than a wave to the systematic development and assessment of powerful explanatory arguments."[1] According to the editors, "Unlike students of American politics, comparativists do not draw upon methodological advances to power their scholarship [and] unlike students of international politics, comparativists do not debate grand questions of theory."[2] As a consequence, the editors conclude, the field needs to be discovered yet again.

Rediscovering the field of comparative politics, however, may require more than simply an attempt to understand the "messy eclectic center"[3] towards which the various branches of comparative theory have gravitated. Rediscovering the classical understanding of comparative politics may prove to be just as useful in understanding the ills present in the modern variety as are current attempts to theorize drawing from fields other than political science. Yet before one can compare the modern version of comparative politics with the ancient variety, or see how scholars currently draw from among other fields of the social sciences in order to progress from the messy center of comparative politics, it would be prudent to first trace the theoretical development of the field itself.

Modern comparative politics, as we know it today, did not emerge as a distinct discipline on the intellectual scene in North America until after World War II. A survey of the postwar growth of the comparative politics field reveals that theoretical development in the field cannot be divorced from the political and social history of the period and the ideological currents pervading it. The literature and theoretical focus in the field in the 1950s and 1960s contained both a strong moral sense and an ideological agenda. Associated with the emergence of newly independent countries on the world stage, the dominant paradigm in comparative politics at the time, political development and modernization theory, focused upon the question of how to achieve democracy, and how economic development fostered political pluralism and democratization. Various commentators of comparative politics literature have noted that there has not been such a dominance of one paradigm in the field since.[4]

Indeed, modernization theory dominated the field at a time when intellectual interest was being encouraged in developing areas. Seminal authors of the period included the political scientist and chairman of the Social Science Research Council Committee on Comparative Politics, Gabriel Almond,[5] sociologist Seymour Martin Lipset,[6] and economist Walt Rostow.[7] While Rostow laid out an agenda for achieving political development through stages of economic development, Lipset theorized that economic development was correlated to democracy. Choosing indices of, among others, wealth and education, Lipset's findings substantiated his major hypothesis while, in addition, he also theorized that democracy seemed to arise in the presence of certain civic virtues, such as those embodying the Protestant work ethic.

During the late 1960s and early 1970s, however, empirical evidence pointed to the failure of many less developed countries to achieve modernization, economic and political development, while at the same time, for various reasons, U.S. hegemony on the world stage was beginning to falter. Modernization theory was criticized for being biased, ethnocentric, deterministic, overly selective with respect to case studies and data collection, and in general, failing to account adequately for specific problems encountered in Third-World developing nations. European and U.S. economic development, it was argued, had been achieved under very different conditions in the nineteenth century and attempts to impose the Western development experience on the Third World was often interpreted as a suppression, both of the emergence of the developing country and of its traditional culture.

Samuel Huntington criticized modernization theory for its failure to focus upon political stability, the process of change towards political development, and the possibility of political decay.[8] Huntington separated political development from modernization in order to focus upon the process of change and the political instability that results from having poorly developed political institutions. Adam Przeworski and Fernando Limongi have also criticized modernization theory's basic premise by noting that there is no substantive correlation between economic development and democracy, though if democracy does arise, it is more likely to survive in more wealthy countries.[9] Furthermore, citing Singapore as an example, they believe that there is no reason to believe that rapid growth leads to political destabilization and the overturning of dictatorships, though economic crises may do so. They propose that dictatorships will survive if per capita income lies above US$6,000 or below US$1,000.[10] Both Singapore and Burma would appear to be suitable candidates for this hypothesis.

In addition to Huntington's criticisms, two major responses to the modernization literature were Fernando Cardoso and Enzo Faletto's dependency theory[11] and a revised modernization literature, led by Gabriel Almond, Sidney Verba, and Lucian Pye, that focused upon failed modernization and that promoted political culture, the coexistence of traditional and cultural societal values, and a civic culture.[12] Being heavily influenced by Marxist thought,[13] the dependency theory of Cardoso, and in particular, the variety espoused by the *dependencistas*, appeared to suffer from the same deterministic methodology that plagued early modernization theory. The political culture approach, on the other hand, which attempted to fill the void created by modern political scientists' dogmatic focus on political institutions, at the expense of moral character and the way of life of the people, has recently gained popularity in democratization studies and has led to the creation of social capital theory.

The Bureaucratic–Authoritarian model of Guillermo O'Donnell was similar to dependency theory in purpose, describing how the elites, technocrats, and military forge alliances in support of authoritarian regimes.[14] But like dependency theory, the idea lost plausibility due to the lack of empirical evidence at the time. Corporatism also became a popular framework of analysis in the field until its popularity waned under the impact of globalization studies and the rising dominance of international political economy (IPE) as a framework for analysis. The latter two may provide useful insights for an examination of Singapore. But globalization and IPE studies would not be the most appropriate tools for analyzing Burma because of various factors: over 40 years of isolationism and autarchic economic policies, the current lack of any reliable national accounts, an economy that functions primarily with the support of the country's black markets, and a military regime that finances its endeavors with drug money.

Asian political culture

The political culture approach, with its emphasis on elucidating the cultural elements of political legitimacy, would seem to be the most appropriate comparative politics framework to adopt for our purposes. One of the current leading authors on political culture and democratization is the Stanford political sociologist, senior research fellow at the Hoover Institution, and co-editor of the *Journal of Democracy*, Larry Diamond. Diamond suggests that this approach gained in popularity recently following the rise of democratization studies, legitimacy studies, and the need to focus upon the political culture of a people and their acceptance of liberal values that are conducive to democracy.[15] Drawing primarily from the work of Almond, Verba, and Pye in the 1960s and 1980s,[16] Diamond defines political culture as "a people's predominant beliefs, attitudes, values, ideals, sentiments, and evaluations about the political system of their country and the role of the self in that system."[17]

Almond notes that an analysis of a nation's political culture would have to concern itself with, among other things, the "substantive content" component of political culture and that the "system" culture of a nation is one of the elements of the "substantive culture."[18] Using David Easton's Systems Theory formulation,[19] Almond claims that "the system culture of a nation would consist of the distributions of attitudes toward the national community, the regime, and the authorities. . . . These would include the sense of national identity, attitudes towards the legitimacy of the regime and its various institutions, and attitudes toward the legitimacy and effectiveness of the incumbents of the various political roles."[20]

Muthiah Alagappa, director of the East–West Center in Washington, D.C., believes that despite its centrality, political legitimacy in developing countries has rarely been studied explicitly.[21] Political development theories, modernization theory, and dependency theory, according to

Alagappa, all had deterministic tendencies, and various proponents of each preferred to focus their efforts upon economic growth, political stability, the preconditions for democracy and the transition to democracy, or the replacement of one socio-political order with a more egalitarian one.[22] Political culture per se, was either ignored altogether or downplayed as being too difficult to operationalize and, therefore, shunted to a residual category, only to be considered during the transitory phase towards Lipset's goal of a democracy induced by economic development. Diamond notes Ronald Inglehart's suggestion, for example, that "political culture may be a crucial link between economic development and democracy."[23]

A fundamental question arising from the failure of the development literature's promise to produce democracy in certain parts of Asia is whether Asian political culture necessarily tends to promote a certain kind of government, a peculiar party system, and the presence, or absence, of democratic institutions. And if Asian societies do indeed function more on the basis of personal relationships than institutional procedures, then to what extent are the political cultures within these societies open to change?

Lucian Pye provides a comprehensive account of Burmese political culture[24] and, more generally, Asian political culture.[25] Pye notes that while "Asian cultures have historically had a rich variety of concepts of power, they share . . . the common denominator of idealizing benevolent, paternalistic leadership and of legitimizing dependency."[26] According to Pye, while Europe succeeded in imposing on Asia the concept of a nation-state, Asia responded with a powerful form of nationalism based on paternalistic authority.[27] Moreover, Pye believes that, unlike Huntington and other modern political theorists who conceive of power as a universal phenomenon, operating under the same laws everywhere, political power is sensitive to cultural nuances and, therefore, that cultural variations are decisive in determining the course of political development.[28] The Asian political culture, with its "perpetuation of dependency," thus contributes to, and, for Pye, determines, the perpetuation of authoritarian rulers in Asia.

In *The Third Wave*, Huntington attempts to account for the relative success of the dominant-party system model in some parts of Asia.[29] Through the interaction of economic progress and Asian culture, Huntington believes that a distinct East Asian variety of stable, dominant-party ruled, democratic institutions arises. While these dominant-party systems, such as Singapore and its People's Action Party (PAP), would satisfy the required procedural democratic formalities to avoid being classified as strictly "authoritarian" by many analysts, they lack the civil liberties which would elevate a regime to the status of a "liberal democracy." Diamond, for example, distinguishes between electoral democracy and liberal democracy by claiming that "the latter encompasses not only electoral competition for power but (*inter alia*) basic civil liberties, a rule of law under which all citizens are treated equally, an independent judiciary, other institutions of 'horizontal accountability' that check the abuse of power, an open and pluralistic civil society, and civilian control over the military."[30]

Along the lines of Huntington, Francis Fukuyama describes "soft authoritarianism" as an increasingly popular potential competitor to Western liberal democracy.[31] Among the possible ideological competitors to liberal democracy – extreme nationalism or fascism, Islam, and a revived neo-Bolshevism – he regarded Asian paternalistic authoritarianism as posing the most serious threat.[32] Asian countries, Fukuyama believes, "have found a way to reconcile market economics with a kind of paternalistic authoritarianism that persuades rather than coerces" and emphasizes "conformity to group interests over individual rights."[33] This alternative, according to Fukuyama, resonates with Asian leaders like Singapore's Lee Kuan Yew, who believes that because it builds on Asia's shared Confucian traditions, it comes more naturally to Asian societies than Western liberal democracy.[34] Fukuyama also suggests that "Asia's postwar economic success is the chief factor legitimating Asia's 'soft authoritarianism.'"[35] For Singapore, this thesis may yet hold its ground because, in contrast to Indonesia, Thailand, and the Philippines for example, Singapore, where the per capita income is well above Przeworski and Limongi's US$6,000, remained politically stable throughout the Asian financial crisis of the late 1990s. Indeed, Singapore's per capita income ranks it among the ten richest countries in the world. Diamond claims that "never before in history has there been an authoritarian regime whose population is anywhere near as rich and well educated as Singapore's."[36]

Fukuyama believes that there are four levels on which the consolidation of democracy must occur: ideology, institutions, civil society, and culture.[37] It is not correct, according to Fukuyama, to identify the Asian alternative with a particular set of institutional arrangements, like the presence of a parliament or guarantees of individual rights, because Asian society is built around a deeply ingrained moral code that is the basis for strong social structures and community life.[38] But is it correct for Asian leaders to legitimize their paternalistic authoritarianism on the grounds that the promotion of individualized Western liberal ideology, and institutions, may lead to the deterioration of their own civil society and culture? Fukuyama suggests that the fate of liberal democracy in Asia will depend in large measure upon the degree to which the United States can deal successfully, not with its own minor institutional problems, but with moderating the atomizing individualism inherent in traditional liberal doctrine.[39]

It is interesting to note that Diamond criticizes Pye's analysis of Asian political culture as being culturally deterministic. In contrast to Pye's "remarkably durable and persistent" account of political culture, Diamond claims that empirical evidence supports Almond's idea that political culture is "plastic," capable of dramatic change in response to regime performance, historical experience, political socialization, economic and social structures, and international factors, including colonization.[40] Furthermore, the existence of political subcultures, including a distinct culture for elites and masses, only complicates attempts to generalize a nation's political culture.[41]

While political culture is obviously plastic to some degree over time, Diamond's treatment of Pye raises an important question. Should attempts to identify the presence of some underlying national cultural traits which do happen to endure over time be dismissed as deterministic simply because they may not conform with history's progress towards other, more liberal democratic, values? Diamond believes that the normative reason to avoid cultural determinism is a "bias for hope."[42] If one argues that political culture is not at least somewhat plastic and open to change, then, according to Diamond, many countries will be condemned to indefinite authoritarianism.[43] And yet Alagappa's criticism of the dominant currents in comparative scholarship on Third-World politics for having deterministic tendencies, focusing on universal goals and processes, may equally be applied to Diamond's account of political culture and, more generally, to the study of democratization as it is currently undertaken in the field of comparative politics.

Democrazy – the determinism of democratization studies

Perhaps nowhere else in the field of comparative politics is the determinism of modern democratic theorists displayed more prominently than in the increasingly popular area of democratization studies. To illustrate this problem, in *Developing Democracy: Toward Consolidation*, Diamond, for example, claims "the normative perspective underlying [his] book is that democratization is generally a good thing and that democracy is the best form of government."[44] Being the best form of government evidently implies that democracy is best for all nations and all cultures at all times.

Using Huntington's framework, Diamond believes that there is no sign that the world has entered a "third reverse wave" of democratization, though the 1999 military coup in Pakistan was, for Diamond, the most serious challenge to the third wave thus far.[45] Since 1974, marking the beginning of what Huntington called the third wave of democracy, Diamond claims that there have been only three blatant reversals of democracy in countries with more than 20 million people over the past 25 years. This includes the 1991 military coup in Thailand, which he considers was a major setback for democracy in Southeast Asia, though within 17 months, he claims that popular mobilization brought new elections and the return of a genuine democracy.[46] His reasons for Pakistan's threat to world democracy included Pakistan's strategic influence, its possession of nuclear weapons, its terrorist training and financing, the possibility of soon fighting a major war with its powerful neighbor, and the military leaders in Pakistan being less inclined than the elected civilians they displaced to seek a negotiated solution to the problem of Kashmir.[47] Finally, he suggests that Pakistan will not follow Thailand's path of rapid democratic restoration because of the damage done to democratic institutions and norms, state capacity, public services, and civil society by successive authoritarian regimes and by 11 years of venal misrule under alternating elected governments.[48]

In response to Diamond, it would be possible to argue that apart from Pakistan's display of nuclear capability, none of the reasons he suggests is anything new. Pakistan has already fought, and lost, three wars with the world's largest democracy, India; the Kashmir dispute had continued unresolved for the past 50 years without any realistic corresponding willingness on the part of Indian civilian governments to seek a negotiated solution until only recently; and Pakistan's nuclear testing in 1998 came about as a direct response to India's nuclear testing, carried out only weeks before, under a civilian government led by the religiously intolerant, nationalist, and Hindu fundamentalist Bharatiya Janata Party (BJP). Diamond also overlooks the fact that Pakistan hosts the largest refugee camps in the world, lying along its border with Afghanistan, and that Thailand carried a similar burden during the Burmese conflicts over the past 50 years. If Diamond is willing to criticize the Pakistani government on the grounds that it harbors, trains, and finances terrorism, presumably also inside these refugee camps, then surely the same argument could be made of the activities of Burmese students, members of the former Karen National Liberation Army, and other Burmese insurgent groups living in Burmese refugee camps in Thailand today.

More generally, there have been well in excess of just three cases where democracy, or attempts at democracy, has been blatantly reversed over the past 25 years, particularly if one were to relax the stringent procedural definitions of democracy. Democratic elections were held in Burma in 1992, for example, the outcome of which was ignored by the ruling junta – the State Law and Order Restoration Council (SLORC). In addition, following the Thai coup of 1991, Thailand faced a constitutional crisis, peaking in May 1992, that was brought about by the Parliament's selection of General Suchinda as prime minister and its promise to establish a constitution giving the military bureaucracy extensive powers. However, it was Thailand's King Bhumibol, himself an unelected "actor" in the political process, who brought an end to the political and civil disorder that followed. Prime Minister Suchinda, along with Major-General Chamlong, prostrated before the King while he chided them, publicly on television, and strongly urged an end to the disorder.[49] The King's prestige is so great in Thailand that they obeyed.

According to Hewison, the King regularly intervenes in Thailand's political process, even to the point of consulting MPs beyond the cabinet, as in 1992, when he conferred with the leaders of all political parties during the constitutional crisis. The premier statesman in Thailand, the King, therefore, "often appears to be acting outside the limits usually considered appropriate for a constitutional monarch."[50] It would seem that Thailand's "path of rapid democratic restoration" in 1992 had less to do with the maintenance of democratic institutions and norms, but rather was facilitated by the actions taken by an unelected monarch who may take offense at being considered part of the "popular mobilization process," let alone at being labeled a "civil society actor."

Diamond believes that pragmatism is an important ingredient of liberal democracy. Pragmatism "promotes tolerance by accepting the idea that no one has a monopoly on absolute truth" and "pragmatism restrains the role of ideology in politics and, hence, the danger of conflict polarization."[51] Because the goals and policies of democratic pragmatists are flexible and adaptable to circumstances, Diamond sees them as consistent with a commitment to democratic procedural norms. Indeed, Diamond claims, "this overriding commitment to democratic proceduralism is a critical political cultural condition for democracy."[52] Although his idea of pragmatism is said to restrain the role of ideology in politics, therefore, it would seem that it must, nevertheless, be tied to an overriding, or ideological, commitment to democratic proceduralism and democracy. Diamond's idea of pragmatism thus restrains the role of ideology in politics while pursuing an ideological end.

Diamond's deterministic account of politics would not have been regarded as a good thing by the classics, and in particular, by Aristotle, who believed in a more cyclical analysis of regimes. While Diamond's account reflects the dominant bias in modern development literature that focuses upon the promotion of economic growth and democracy in order to improve a regime along the lines of Western liberalism, Aristotle's account of politics recognizes the natural tendency of all regimes to decay into a worse form. Although Diamond acknowledges that Aristotle believed pure democracy could degenerate into a form of despotism, he is willing, nevertheless, to promote democracy unconditionally. Diamond, it appears, mixes scholarship with political activism, criticizing cultural determinism while progressing along his own deterministic path towards democracy.

Western liberal democracy as the end of history

Diamond's determinism is reflected in Fukuyama's claim in 1989 that the triumph of Western liberal democracy indicates that we have reached the end of history, the end point of man's ideological evolution.[53] Although backtracking somewhat on his original assertions ten years hence, Fukuyama maintained that liberal democracy would triumph over all competitive ideologies, in the long run, because of the three-part democratic syllogism underlying U.S. foreign policy from 1989 to 1999: liberal democracies tend not to fight one another; the best means of promoting democracy is through economic development; and the best way to promote economic growth is to integrate a country into the liberal capitalist trade and investment regime.[54] Fukuyama believes that whereas socialism failed to produce material prosperity and recognition of human dignity, liberal democracy succeeds in providing both.[55]

Fukuyama views his "End of History" argument as an example of weak historicism, whereby an historical mechanism or a series of weak connections have developed from the natural world, to the economic world, to the political world, to the cultural world, that help to explain the process of economic, political, and societal modernization.[56] Modernization is driven by the motor of modern natural science. Unlike Huntington, who believes that there is no potential universalism in Western institutions and values, Fukuyama claims that just as it was no accident that Bacon and Descartes' scientific method became accepted worldwide, Western institutions can break out of their cultural homeland. The development of strong and stable state political institutions are more important today, however, than meeting economic and societal problems in the developing world and this, Fukuyama believes, may also require that the end of history be rewritten.[57]

Two causes of this present need for strong-state expertise in nation-building are: a re-adjustment of the "Washington consensus" that economic development promotes democratic institutions and peace throughout the world – without adequately explaining where economic development originates (i.e. political institutions matter); and the rise of humanitarian intervention in recent years by governments of Europe and the United States, as well as the need to address the consequences of the hijacking of states by non-state actors.[58] Yet Fukuyama also notes that the large perceptional gap that opened between Europe and the United States over the Bush administration's invasion of Iraq means that the institutions and values of both can no longer simply be combined as comprising those of the "West." The norms, mores, and perceptions of Europe and the United States vary considerably over issues concerning the role of the state, sovereignty, the use of military power, and religion.[59] But for Fukuyama, presumably this merely represents another temporary setback or reversal of the historical mechanism underlying his thesis.

The onset of globalization, more that anything else, strengthened Fukuyama's belief in the inevitability of Western liberal democracy's victory over its competitive ideologies. Fukuyama praises globalization, and its accompanying information technology revolution, on the grounds that there remains no viable alternative development model that promises better results.[60] The globalization-induced Asian economic crisis of the late 1990s, according to Fukuyama, has also demonstrated that there is no alternative to democracy as a source of regime legitimacy.[61] It appears, to Fukuyama, that the economic crisis demonstrated the hollowness of its most serious competitor, Asian soft-authoritarianism. Yet he neglects to recognize that among the carnage of Asian economies following the crisis, Singapore's emerged relatively unscathed. If economic cycles are an inevitable feature of any capitalist economy, over the long run, then perhaps Fukuyama would be more prudent not to hinge the bulk of his argument on the inevitable forces of globalization.

Fukuyama writes that the universal and homogeneous state that appears at the end of history rests on the twin pillars of economics and recognition.[62] If this is true, then Fukyama's last man may also face difficulty in explaining Singapore's past economic successes, that is, if as Fukuyama claims, he is also imbued with a desire for universal recognition that is satisfied only in a liberal democracy. For Lee Kuan Yew at least, there is more substance to his Asian values rhetoric than merely an argument over economic performance. Perhaps Asian values are an attempt to substitute one of Fukuyama's twin pillars, universal recognition, with another, cultural destiny. Yet it also appears that the hollowness of Lee's cultural arguments in support of soft authoritarianism is indeed mirrored by the hollowness of the character of Fukuyama's last man who, according to Fukuyama, is far more occupied with economics than politics or strategy.[63]

Fukuyama's thesis illustrates the logical conclusion to modern philosophy's departure from the classical understanding of politics. His description of the end of history is a restatement of Alexandre Kojeve's interpretation of Hegel. In reply to Kojeve's thesis, Leo Strauss asserted that modern philosophy created the idea of the universal and homogenized state as the goal of history, the best social order, and the state in which every human being finds his full satisfaction by universal recognition of his human dignity and equality of opportunity.[64] While Fukuyama's last man occupies himself with economics and is said to be completely satisfied, according to Strauss, the universal and homogeneous state would produce Nietzsche's "last man" who, lacking in *thymos*, or spiritedness, lives a sad and unsatisfactory existence.[65]

Whether it is possible to encourage human aspirations within the context of a modern liberal society – that does not destroy the human spirit on the one hand, nor create violent political movements on the other – is the question now facing Europe and the United States. According to Fukuyama, the Europeans are creating a house for the last man to live in.[66] Robert Kagan goes further:

> The Europeans are the ones who actually believe they are living at the end of history – that is, in a largely peaceful world that to an increasing degree can be governed by law, norms, and international agreements. In this world, power politics and classical realpolitik have become obsolete. Americans, by contrast, think they are still living in history, and need to use traditional power-political means to deal with

threats from Iraq, al-Qaida, North Korea, and other malignant forces... the Europeans are half right: They have indeed created an end-of-history world for themselves within the EU, where sovereignty has given way to supranational organization. What they don't understand, however, is that the peace and safety of their European bubble is guaranteed ultimately by American military power.

(Kagan, R. (2003) in Fukuyama, F. (2004): 116–117)

Since the universal and homogenized state is free of wars and revolutions, it must resemble the state produced by Fukuyama's three-part democratic syllogism – liberal democracies which tend not to fight one another. And since unlimited technological progress is an indispensable condition of the universal and homogenized state,[67] the onset of globalization would hasten its coming into being. Yet while Strauss sided with the classical view that unlimited technological progress and its accompaniment are destructive of humanity,[68] Fukuyama seems to believe that, until recently, technology could not have removed the primary reason for Strauss's disagreement with such a state, that is, the elimination of the natural political distinction between the few who are wise, and the possibility that they could rule, and the many who are not.

A scenario of concern to Fukuyama is the end of human history brought on by biotechnological advances, and the beginning of a new "post-human" history.[69] Fukuyama fears that unregulated biotechnological advances in cloning "designer babies" with high intelligence now make possible a post-human future in which we have the capacity to alter the essence of human nature[70] – the motor behind modernization should not go ahead without political control.[71] Fukuyama believes that history cannot end without an end to science, or at least to science that alters human nature, because biotechnology may cause us to lose our humanity.[72] Reflecting as it does a concession to Strauss's fears concerning the implications of eliminating the classical distinction between men, this poses the only serious challenge that Fukuyama acknowledges to his "End of History" thesis. Yet what is preventing the idea of a globalization-led democratization of the world from being challenged on its own merits? Globalization, after all, would act as a medium for the transmission of any post-human future.

Fukuyama's argument, therefore, is as unnecessarily deterministic, and pessimistic, both at the personal and ideological levels as it is overly optimistic towards the satisfaction that man could derive from universal recognition. While it may be easy to paint a picture of biological and philosophical doom, by drawing logical conclusions from what may prove to be an exaggeration of the degree of advances made in the field of biotechnology, perhaps E. O. Wilson is more sensible when he replies that human beings will never choose to become post-human.[73]

Moreover, as a model of development, globalization may promise better results in a world relatively free from cyclical economic recession. But advocating the promotion of Western liberal democracy through the forces of globalization also raises, or rather, ignores, the theoretical possibility of an international globalization-induced depression. Because Fukuyama believes "it still remains possible that there is another shoe to drop ... a devaluation or an unanticipated blowup in the derivatives market," or "a global economic depression" in which case "all bets will be off,"[74] his thesis does not guarantee anything, least of all the inevitable triumph of Western liberal democracy. By recognizing the cyclical nature of economic behavior, Fukuyama undermines his own argument and urges us to consider the possibility of returning to a cyclical understanding of politics.

Cultural relativism and liberal democratic values: are they reconcilable?

A further problem confronting comparativists goes beyond the theoretical question of whether democracy is the best regime to the practical question of whether democracy has a universal appeal to all human beings. While the conflicting methodologies underlying the work of regionalists and universalists has often provided a source of tension in the field of comparative politics, perhaps nowhere is the tension more apparent than in the subfield of political culture. Universalists may discredit the regionalists' findings for lacking any substantive basis on which to conduct truly universal political comparisons, and regionalists often criticize universalists for their lack of detailed knowledge at the country or local level. In the process of conducting their research at the ground level, regionalists may turn to anthropology, and in particular, to cultural anthropologists like Clifford Geertz, in an attempt to lend theoretical support to their political findings. But cultural anthropology has often been accused of promoting cultural relativism, and herein lies a major source of potential conflict in comparative politics. One of the best examples of this conflict surfacing in recent times has been the promotion of "Asian values" by the leaders of allegedly distinctive Asian cultures while denying the liberal democratic values which are promoted as universal principles by the West.

A brief insight into the writings of Clifford Geertz will illustrate the possible ambiguities that may arise when political scientists delve into the field of cultural anthropology to promote cultural relativism and liberal democratic values simultaneously. It is not easy, nor all that convincing, to promote such an apparent contradiction, for to do so could only come about at the expense of much of the cultural anthropological theory, along with a vast depreciation of the status of both cultural relativism on the one hand and universal solutions on the other.

Clifford Geertz describes his concept of culture as "essentially a semiotic one ... not an experimental science in search of law but an interpretive one in search of meaning."[75] The study of anthropology, or cognitive anthropology, according to Geertz, involves an exercise in ethnography which aims to create "a stratified hierarchy of meaningful structures."[76] He does this by "sorting out the structures of signification ... the established codes [of human behavior] ... and determining their social ground and import."[77] An ethnographer, says Geertz, should compose a "thick description" from his records of a society's culture. The thicker the description, the better because ethnographic research consists of personal experience.[78] He argues that as ethnographers, anthropologists should not be seeking either to become natives or to mimic them, but merely to converse with them.[79] Anthropologists should, therefore, aim to enlarge the universe of human discourse, as well as offer "instruction, amusement, promote practical counsel, moral advance, and the discovery of natural order in human behavior."[80] But according to Geertz, "[A]nthropological writings are themselves interpretations, and second and third order ones to boot."[81] They are "fictions" in the sense that they are "something made" or "fashioned" because only a "native" makes first-order interpretations of his own culture.[82]

Geertz argues that one should not question the objective status of anthropology by discrediting its findings as mere scholarly artifice, totally divorced from reality.[83] This would be a hollow threat, according to Geertz, because the subject matter of ethnography is by its nature subjective, and so the cultural findings should remain as subjective, thick, and open to as many various interpretations as possible. With this kind of methodology then, Geertz leaves himself open to a sharp decline into cultural relativism.

Geertz claims that the anthropologist approaches "abstract analyses from the direction of exceedingly extended acquaintances with extremely small matters. He confronts the same grand realities that ... political scientists ... confront in more fateful settings: Power ... Oppression ... Authority ... Violence ...; but he confronts them in contexts obscure enough ... to take the capital letters off them."[84] Believing that "there are enough profundities in the world already," Geertz claims that the advantage of anthropology is to give a "homely context" to "those big words that make us all afraid."[85] Clearly then, Geertz would seem to be opposed to any notion of a universal application of values or standards across cultures and, it would appear, to the idea of tyranny. Strangely though, Geertz is very careful in avoiding any accusations of cultural relativism.

The important thing about the anthropologist's findings, says Geertz, "is their complex specificness, their circumstantiality.... [T]he kind of material produced by ... fine-comb field studies ... [allows them to give] the sort of sensible actuality ... [to the] mega-concepts [like] legitimacy ... that makes it possible to think not only realistically and concretely *about* them, but, what is more important, creatively and imaginatively *with* them."[86] Yet while thinking *about* them and *with* them, he must necessarily be constrained to the detailed circumstantiality of the subject at hand, the culture in question. In other words, an ethnologist cannot be allowed to investigate such scary words as "legitimacy" with an outsider's perspective. Any claims to universalism must therefore appear in the form of a "parochial universalism"[87] originating from within that culture rather than one which can be applied to all.

Geertz, it appears, seems to believe that cultural anthropologists can mix the universalist realm of political science, and the liberal democratic values pursued within that realm, with his own realm of thick fieldwork observations while restricting the scope of their findings to the mere description of the culture in question. Geertz further claims that anthropological theory should not only avoid abstract treatises, but that it should generalize within cases rather than across them. Rather than attempt to subsume a set of general observations under a governing law, like natural law, Geertz believes that inferences should be drawn from the thick description of these signifiers and placed within an intelligible frame.[88] It is not surprising, therefore, that Geertz claims "anthropology ... is a science whose progress is marked less by a perfection of consensus than by a refinement of debate."[89] Geertz, therefore, seems to consider the establishment of any paradigm within anthropology as completely irrelevant. Any framework which helps classify one's thick descriptions is acceptable.

In his essay, "The Impact of the Concept of Culture on the Concept of Man," Geertz provides us with a clear elucidation of his relativist methodology. The problem with defining a universal aspect of culture, says Geertz, is that it must be defined "in most general terms, indeed so general, in fact, that whatever force it seems to have virtually evaporates."[90] He does not dismiss the ability to make generalizations about man as man, but he believes they should not be discovered through a search for cultural universals because "the attempt to do so leads to precisely the sort of relativism the whole approach was expressly designed to avoid."[91] So what then are the universals, or generalizations, which Geertz is promoting in order to ward off what he calls the "genuine danger" of cultural relativism? They involve "facing directly, and fully, the diversities of human culture ... and embracing them within the body of one's [own] concept of man, not by gliding past them with vague tautologies and forceless banalities."[92]

Geertz claims that "It is not difficult to relate some human institutions to what science (or common sense) tells us are requirements for human existence, but it is very much more difficult to state this relationship in an unequivocal form."[93] Moreover, if one maintains that such universals should be taken as a central defining element of man, as humanity's "lowest-common-denominator," one promotes his own prejudiced view of man across cultures.[94] Presumably then, Geertz would view the cross-cultural promotion of any universal standards on liberal democratic values, like human rights, as a prejudiced attempt to impose Western cultural values upon the rest of humanity.

One of the most striking features of Geertz's writings is his attempt to distance himself, and the field of anthropology, from cultural relativism. He remarks upon how anthropologists "are haunted by a fear of historicism, of becoming lost in a whirl of cultural relativism so convulsive as to deprive them of any fixed bearings at all."[95] And yet at the same time he appears to embrace it whole-heartedly. His concept of culture downplays the empirical commonalities of man's behavior across cultures because, according to Geertz, "there is no such thing as a human nature independent of culture."[96]

In an attempt to assimilate his thesis to Aristotle's work on poetry, Geertz agrees with Northrop Frye's claim that Aristotle believed the poet's job was to describe a typical, recurring, universal human event, and not to make any real, particular, or specific statements at all.[97] Geertz believes that an anthropologist's thick description of an event such as the Balinese cockfight, like poetry, allows them to create something better than a typical or universal description, something that could be called a "paradigmatic human event."[98] This certainly is an interesting claim, given that Geertz dismisses the need for any paradigm at all in cultural anthropology; a "paradigmatic human event" may be constructed within the bounds of a paradigm-less science.

According to Geertz, all judgmental questions on religion, law, rationality, and the like should be properly considered as lying within the realm of art, and nothing more.[99] Anthropology, like poetry, is art, and art as art cannot be trash. Yet if anthropological social judgments should be considered as art, as such, they cannot promote anything – least of all liberal democratic values – with some degree of objectivity untouched by subjective personal interpretations. One may "compare forms from different cultures" (political regimes, for example), "to define their character in reciprocal relief," but woe to anybody who does not believe that the "guiding principle" in all cultural studies is that "societies, like lives, contain their own interpretations."[100] In other words, interpretive cultural relativism remains the guiding principle for Geertz. Simple comparisons may be made across cultures, such as defining cultures in "reciprocal relief," placing a culture and its regime within the context of one's own interpretation of self-conceived universals like liberal democratic values, but ultimately all societies must be interpreted in terms of their own cultures. Parochial universalism rules in the world of Clifford Geertz.

Like Geertz, the historian Michael Aung Thwin believes that "cultural relativism does not, in any case, question the (false) issue regarding the universal *humanity* of peoples; it is instead concerned with the various ways in which that humanity is expressed; namely, in culture."[101] Aung Thwin claims that the promotion of parochial Western, and specifically American, values aims to accomplish both the dismissal of cultural relativism, along with any contrary philosophies such as "Asian values," as inconsequential and the acceptance of Western institutions – legal, social, economic, and political, along with the principles of ownership, individualism, leadership, legitimacy, and authority underlying those institutions – as universal.[102] According to Aung Thwin, "[T]he most destructive aspect of democratization is that it invariably means decentralization,"[103] the breakdown of power structures in society. And decentralization, he believes, inevitably brings social and political anarchy.[104] Aung Thwin believes that economic and political decentralization is driven by the rhetoric of universalism and the ideology of democracy, rather than the former driving the latter. It is further rationalized by the notion of globalization, and it most benefits the strongest economies, academies, and polities.[105] Globalization, he claims, aims to recreate the imperialism and colonialism of the late nineteenth and early twentieth centuries, and the "'globalized economy' today closely resembles the 'colonial export economy' at its height."[106]

The establishment of democracy has become, Aung Thwin believes, "a *sine qua non* for legitimate government per se. It now resembles a *jihad*, a holy war, backed by aggressive and confrontational rhetoric as well as economic sanctions or support."[107] Aung Thwin claims that the propagation of democracy resembles the literature of imperialism and the "white man's burden" of colonial times, but that now the "'superior' religious and racial ideology (Christianity and the white man) has been replaced by equally 'superior' secular political and social ideology (democracy and human rights)."[108] The Burmese opposition leader, Aung San Suu Kyi, on the other hand, believes that universal pronouncements, like the Universal Declaration of Human Rights, should not be rejected merely because the document was not drawn up by the Burmese, especially as Burma voted for its adoption in 1948. Moreover, Suu Kyi believes that "if ideas and beliefs are to be denied validity outside the geographical and cultural bounds of their origin, Buddhism would be confined to north India, Christianity to a narrow tract in the Middle East and Islam to Arabia."[109]

Nevertheless, if the principles espoused by Western liberal democracies, like human rights, are truly universal and are not meant to be restricted to the geographical and cultural bounds of their origin, then it is not unreasonable to ask why the leaders of many nations remain hostile towards them. In his popular work, "The Clash of Civilizations," Huntington describes the emergence of opposition among non-Western civilizations both to the Western promotion of democracy and liberalism and to the idea that they are universals. Huntington forecasts that "governments and groups will increasingly attempt to mobilize support by appealing to common religion and civilization identity" rather than ideology.[110] He believes that although much of Western culture has permeated the rest of the world at a superficial level, at the more basic level, Western concepts differ fundamentally from those prevalent in other civilizations.

> Western ideas of individualism, liberalism, constitutionalism, human
> rights, equality, the rule of law, democracy, free markets, the separa-

tion of church and state, often have little resonance in Islamic, Confucian, Japanese, Hindu, Buddhist or Orthodox cultures. Western efforts to propagate such ideas produce instead a reaction against "human rights imperialism" and a reaffirmation of indigenous values, as can be seen in support for religious fundamentalism by the younger generation in non-Western cultures. The very notion that there could be a "universal civilization" is a Western idea, directly at odds with the particularism of most Asian societies and their emphasis on what distinguishes one people from another.... Modern democratic government originated in the West. When it has developed in non-Western societies it has usually been the product of Western colonialism or imposition.

(Huntington, S. (1993): 40–41)

Huntington is consistent with respect to his claim that human rights are a product of Western culture and, at the superficial, legal, or positive level, their promotion often attracts a hostile response from non-Western cultures. In reply to Huntington's argument, it could be said that the ideas he considers to be Western, like human rights and the notion of a universal civilization, would more appropriately be labeled "modern." Moreover, while human rights cannot be natural rights because natural rights are dependent on natural law and human rights are dependent on convention, human rights, at the more basic level, still appeal to natural law for their universal character. Nations with very different religions may recognize universal propositions of natural law which, at best, may only be imperfectly enunciated, and agreed upon, as a human right. Western ideas may, at the superficial level, mirror the particularism that Huntington believes characterizes most Asian societies. Yet natural law, to which human rights must ultimately resort, transcends all cultures. The fact that modern democratic government, though historically of Western origin, can develop when imposed on non-Western societies, and that it is not rejected, is itself evidence of a Western particularism that resonates among non-Western cultures.

It would seem, therefore, that Huntington, to some degree, supports the Asian values arguments. He ventures further to predict a central focus of future conflict arising between the West and an alliance of Islamic-Confucian states. Huntington replaces the ideological conflict of the cold war with religion and, in so doing, transforms religious arguments into a model of cultural conflict. Yet in reply to Huntington's wisdom, Fouad Ajami provides a good Machiavellian account of national self-interest, or realism in international relations:

Nations "cheat": they juggle identities and interests. Their ways meander. One would think that the traffic of arms from North Korea and China to Libya and Iran shows this – that states will consort with any civilization, however alien, as long as the price is right and the goods are ready. Huntington turns this routine act of selfishness into a sinister "Confucian-Islamic connection" ... let us be clear: civilizations do not control states, states control civilizations. States avert their gaze from blood ties when they need to; they see brotherhood and faith and kin when it is in their interest to do so.

(Fouad Ajami (1993): 6–9)

Disregarding Huntington's dire predictions in the wake of the 11 September 2001 terrorist attacks on the United States, an act which tends to support his "Clash of Civilizations" argument, Fukuyama believed that Western liberal democracy and market-oriented economics remained the superior alternative as a governing ideology for real-world societies in the long run, that Islamism as a governing ideology does not meet the aspirations of the vast majority of Muslims themselves, and, by inference, that Islamic countries must choose the Western model if they wish to modernize.[111] He believes that while there is no fundamental cultural obstacle in Muslim countries that prevents modernization, the onset of modern political-Islam ideology in the post-9/11 world does challenge this assertion.[112]

Fukuyama believes, moreover, that human nature "is not infinitely malleable, and that our underlying shared humanity allows us to rule out certain forms of political order, like tyranny, as unjust."[113] Those human rights, therefore, which reflect the "most deeply felt and universal drives, ambitions and behaviors will be a more solid foundation than those that do not."[114] This, according to Fukuyama, explains why there are many capitalist liberal democracies in the world today and very few socialist dictatorships. Furthermore, "it is impossible to talk about human rights – and therefore justice, politics, and morality more generally – without having some concept of what human beings are like as a species."[115] If one denies even the truth regarding the universal *humanity* of peoples, as do Aung Thwin and Lee Kuan Yew[116] for example, or that there is such a thing as a human nature independent of culture, as does Geertz, then there can exist no standards of justice or morality outside of one's own cultural context or laboratory, nor perhaps even within. Yet ultimately, as Fukuyama says, "there will still be a glimmer of recognition when the tribesman and the Internet maven meet."[117]

In Book 7 of the *Politics*, Aristotle divides the world into three kinds of nations and discusses the nature of the political multitude. The Europeans, according to Aristotle, who come from cold climates, are spirited but lacking in thought and art. They are free, but they lack ideas on political governance. Asians, on the other hand, have souls rich in thought and art but are lacking in spiritedness. Hence they remain ruled and enslaved. Greeks, not surprisingly, stand in the middle, sharing in both traits – spirit and thought. It is evident, Aristotle says, that those who are to be readily guided to virtue by the legislator should be both endowed with thought and spirited in their nature.[118]

Carnes Lord believes that for various reasons, Aristotle was hesitant to elaborate fully his theoretical anthropology – i.e. his views on primitive or prepolitical society and human nature – and his thoughts on the evolution of society and the *polis*.[119] Lord interprets Aristotle's passing references to the spiritedness of Europeans, Asians, and Greeks as an indication that spiritedness is the source of the human impulse to rule or to resist rule in the interests of freedom.[120] Lord believes that "it is not material circumstances as such but rather the interaction between reason and spiritedness in a people that fundamentally determines the pace and character of the development of political structures."[121] For example, while both Singapore and Burma have similar climates, Singaporeans are wealthy, but it could be said that they are lacking in spiritedness. The Burmese, on the other hand, are poor but may not be lacking in spiritedness. Singapore's restrictive political structures have developed without the help of a spirited multitude, while Burma's political structures have failed to develop at all.

Aristotle's reference to the Asian character compared with the Greek is also insightful for modern comparative analysis because the rhetoric espoused by the leaders of some Asian regimes includes certain interpretations of Confucianism and Buddhism which promote order while suppressing individual and political freedom. Yet the presence of conflicting interpretations of these moral codes which promote freedom over order, albeit influenced by Western thought, could suggest more about the political nature of the interpretations themselves, rather than the presence of any inherently slavish character in the people, particularly if such interpretations are preferred by the majority of the people.

Overcoming the problem of applying universal ideas to culturally specific problems and, more generally, disputes over theoretical generalization and regional, or field, specialization[122] also requires a re-examination of the application of practical and theoretical knowledge to the issues under consideration. Perhaps one of the more promising attempts to compromise a solution between these apparent extremes, along these lines, may be found in the work of political scientist James Scott, who draws from the work of cultural anthropologists in attempting to forge a compromise from among the three dominant fields in comparative politics: the rationalists, structuralists, and the culturalists.

In *Weapons of the Weak*, Scott developed his own approach, based upon Geertz's interpretive or thick descriptions theory.[123] Focusing upon the everyday forms of peasant resistance to the imposition of new technologies, Scott creates an interpretation of class order from detailed "thick descriptions" of otherwise seemingly irrational peasant behavior. Like Geertz, Scott believes in the substantial documentation of observations made at the ground level to allow broader generalizations to be made thereafter. Universals may be drawn from these thick descriptions, but they should not impede one's initial search for order and meaning discovered at the ground level. From the detailed study of peasant resistance behavior at the village level, Scott moved on to a literary study of peasant resistance, again applying Geertz's interpretive theory to an analysis of what he calls "hidden transcripts" of resistance from around the world.[124] In *Seeing Like a State*, Scott seeks a genuine compromise between anthropological work and the promotion of universals like liberal democratic values, and not merely a post facto account of parochial universals drawn from interpretive generalizations of detailed behavioral patterns.

Scott notes that the problem, "as Aristotle recognized, is that certain practical choices cannot, even in principle, be adequately and completely captured in a system of universal rules."[125] Scott uses the term *metis* to conceptualize the nature of practical knowledge, which, unlike formal, deductive, epistemic knowledge, or *techne*, can come only from practical experience. In Greek mythology, Metis, the personification of wisdom (prudence) and its goddess, was also regarded as the first wife of Zeus and the mother of Athena.[126] Scott defines *metis* as "cunning intelligence," which represents "a wide array of practical skills and acquired intelligence in responding to a constantly changing natural and human environment."[127] "Where *metis* is contextual and particular," says Scott, "*techne* is universal ... and can be taught more or less completely as a formal discipline."[128] Many of the grand schemes imposed by modernist states have failed because planners failed to appreciate the value, range, and potential achievement of *metis*, whose "'findings' are practical, opportune, and contextual, rather than integrated into the general conventions of scientific discourse."[129] According to Scott, "[T]he power of practical knowledge depends on an exceptionally close and astute observation of the environment."[130]

"*Metis* ... is the mode of reasoning most appropriate to complex material and social tasks where the uncertainties are so daunting that we must trust our (experienced) intuition and feel our way."[131] When one conceptualizes plans in accordance with *metis*, no more is attempted than what Nature has already done in the region.[132] "Each prudent, small step, based on prior experience, yields new and not completely predictable effects that become the point of departure for the next step."[133] Scott wishes to emphasize how important such knowledge is and how difficult it is to translate it into a codified form. Being so implicit and automatic, its bearer is often at a loss to explain it.[134] "*Metis* resists simplification into deductive principles which can be successfully transmitted through book learning, because the environments in which it is exercised are so complex and nonrepeatable that formal procedures of rational decision making are impossible to apply."[135]

Scott agrees with Michael Oakeshott's description of traditional, or practical, knowledge as being "preeminently fluid," although he believes that "traditional" is itself a misnomer because of its changing nature.[136] Scott likens the pursuit of rationalist knowledge to a kind of imperialism. He believes that rationalist knowledge is pursued on the basis of universalist claims, leaving no door through which *metis,* or practical knowledge, could enter on its own terms.[137] Unlike rationalism, which fails to recognize any knowledge other than technical knowledge, "*metis* makes no claim to universality and in this sense is pluralistic."[138] Occasionally, certain structural conditions can thwart the imperialism of epistemic claims, like when democratic pressures oblige agricultural scientists to premise their work on the practical problems defined by farmers, and if they are ignored, their plans are met with resistance coming from outside the paradigm of epistemic knowledge itself.[139] But generally speaking, Scott believes that authoritarian high-modernist states in the grip of a self-evident social theory have done irreparable damage to human communities and individual livelihoods.[140]

Scott criticizes Oakeshott, however, for missing the natural appeal that high modernism has both for the intelligentsia and for the people, who may have ample reason to hold their past in contempt. Revolutionaries and postindependence leaders in the non-industrial world, according to Scott, could not be faulted for despising their feudal and inegalitarian past, their colonial domination and economic stagnation, and perhaps even to fear that immediate democracy would simply bring back the old order.[141] Nor, says Scott, "can they be faulted for wasting no time or democratic sentimentality on creating a people that they could be proud of. Understanding the history and logic of their commitment to high-modernist goals, however, does not permit us to overlook the enormous damage that their convictions entailed when combined with authoritarian state power."[142]

Scott argues, "[D]emocracy itself is based on the assumption that the *metis* of its citizenry should, in mediated form, continually modify the laws and policies of the land."[143] Institutions should follow the example of common law, whose longevity as an institution rests upon "the fact that it is not a final codification of legal rules, but rather a set of procedures for continually adapting some broad principles to novel circumstances."[144] Scott, therefore, endorses *metis*-friendly institutions, "many of which in liberal democracies already take such a form and may serve as exemplars for fashioning new ones."[145]

Scott's interpretation of the failure of modernist schemes imposed by authoritarian states goes further than any prior cultural anthropological theory towards the promotion of liberal democratic values. His account of *metis* approaches Aristotle's understanding of prudence, or practical wisdom. He avoids the promotion of Geertzian-like parochial universalisms which subside into cultural relativism, as well as the overriding commitment to democratic proceduralism that plagues Diamond's deterministic account of pragmatism and that accompanies his political cultural conditions critical for democracy. Scott leaves the door open to the kind of Aristotelian prudence and statesmanship that should, at the state level, mirror the prudence exercised in the daily lives of the villagers.

Scott claims that "*metis* has no doctrine or centralized training; each practitioner has his or her own angle."[146] Because universals cannot be applied unequivocally and rigidly without modification to the specific culture in question, then the most practical and effective application of a universal principle of human nature comes about by appealing to practical wisdom to guide one's actions on each occasion. Statesmen, not "actors," are required at local and higher levels to co-ordinate the best practical solutions, given the circumstances at hand.

What needs to be further developed in Scott's account, however, is the nature of the end to which *metis* aspires. This may involve, for example, the promotion of education concerning local agricultural or environmental projects, or education addressing universal principles like the ideas reflected in the Universal Declaration of Human Rights. Whether the subject of the education be local or universal, it should not be rigidly enforced, but rather, it should be prudently administered, taking into account local, particular, cultural, and religious concerns. If Scott can formulate a virtuous end to his concept of *metis*, either for the individual or the community, then he will have come a long way towards reconciling the apparent contradictions inherent in promoting universal values with what was previously deemed to be cultural relativism.

Modern comparative politics and the Aristotelian tradition

Whereas Plato's Socrates has been accredited with being the discoverer of political philosophy, Aristotle was the founder of political science as a discipline. His study of 158 regimes, being a thorough investigation into man's relation to his fellow citizens in political communities, also makes Aristotle the founder of comparative politics. Because Aristotle believed that man is by nature a political animal, Aristotle's political science was considered to be a natural science.

The subject of Aristotle's inquiries into politics was the variety of *politeiai* in which citizens were said to reflect the objects and aspirations of the ruling part. A *politeia* was not simply a form of political arrangement or government, but loosely translates as a "regime." The concept of a regime involved more than simply the arrangement of the political institutions, as it is commonly understood today, but the form and character of the political community, the way of life of its citizens, and what they viewed as most important to their well-being. Institutions were important only in the sense that they established and secured the rule of the virtuous. They were of secondary importance to education and the formation of moral character.[147] For these reasons, the current usage of "regime" and "regime change" in the political discourse of Western, predominantly Christian nations merely to address the nature of government and powers of the "state" could be understood, or misunderstood, as potentially offensive to nations who view their non-Christian religions as most important to their own well-being.

Aristotle remains attractive to modern political scientists like Almond because Aristotle's account of regimes appears to be empirically based and suitable for the inductive methodology used in certain areas of the field of comparative politics. Almond was also attracted to Aristotle's *Politics* perhaps because it appears to be value free and bereft of normative prescriptions. But Aristotle is both descriptive and prescriptive throughout his account of politics, and this attribute is overlooked by modern political scientists who often cite the classics in their quest for approval and then proceed in the deductive manner of the "new science of politics."

Almond's desire to claim Aristotle as his authority, for example, would not so much reflect any desire on his part to account for the moral character of a country's citizens, but rather their culture. Aristotle, on the other hand, would place greater emphasis on the "political" element in political culture and less on the "culture," as understood in modern social science. Unlike Pye, for example, Aristotle would not have claimed that the modern status of culture, though helpful in describing what could also be called "national character," should be elevated to being the decisive factor determining the course of political development. Nor would Aristotle have argued, like Geertz, that all societies must be interpreted in terms of their own cultures, nor that there is no such thing as a human nature independent of culture. Aristotle did not question the universal humanity of peoples, but rather, he embraced the idea as a foundation for comparing different types of political regimes, in which the citizens reflected the objects and aspirations of the ruling part.

Modern comparative politics provides an impoverished substitute for Aristotle's analysis of regimes for two major reasons. The first, already discussed, is that modern comparative politics reflects the philosophy of historicism by implicitly describing a historical progression towards democracy as the final end. A cursory reading of the arguments of Huntington, Diamond, and Fukuyama illustrates that a kind of Hegelian philosophy of history exists in modern comparative politics that did not exist in the classics.[148] History is following a linear progression towards democracy and those who establish non-democratic governments challenge the movement of History. Lipset, Rostow, and most modernization and democratization theorists assume the merits of Western liberal democracy and modern liberal capitalism. Most comparative politics literature assumes that democracy, and in particular, liberal democracy, is the best form of government, and some believe that its universal acceptance is inevitable. Challenges to this basic assumption, as for example, Huntington's *The Clash of Civilizations*, viewed perhaps in response to Fukuyama's *End of History*, tend to become just as deterministic, and overly pessimistic, to counteract the opposing view's optimism.

In contrast, for Aristotle, there was no natural pattern of regime change and a regime could change in either direction, for better or worse. While Huntington speaks of three waves of democratization and his fear of "reverse waves," and Fukuyama declares that liberal democracy signifies the end of history for man, Aristotle's account of regimes recognizes the possibility that regimes may naturally decay, depending upon the natural tendencies for justice and injustice in the ruler and the citizens.[149] Huntington also believes that stability means order. While his major criticism of modernization theory was that it lacked a focus on order, his understanding of stability lacks any detailed consideration of justice.

Stability, for Aristotle, on the other hand, did not mean the absence of faction or preservation of the status quo, as it does in modern political science. Aristotle's notion of stability maintained a view of justice and the common good that naturally implied a degree of social co-operation and trust among all the classes across the regime. Instability, for Aristotle, was also a sign of injustice, and the longevity of the regime reflects justice within the regime. The brutish form of tyranny, for example, is relatively short lived, but the longer lasting form of tyranny is preserved if the tyrant moderates his desires and plays the part of a kingly ruler. In this way, Aristotle is being prescriptive as well as descriptive, hoping that some semblance of virtue will take root in the tyrant's soul. Moreover, following Aristotle's prescriptions for the preservation of tyranny in a kingly mode is in the interests of both the tyrant and the people. By performing the acts of a kingly ruler, a tyranny becomes more moderate and improves for the better. And at the very least, it will be an improvement over the brutish alternative.

In contrast to comparative politics and democratization theorists, Aristotle merely suggests that as cities become larger, it is perhaps no longer easy for any regime to arise other than a democracy.[150] Aristotle believed that democracy could be a deficient form of government since it could naturally lead to the rise of demagogues. His practically best regime was a mixed regime or polity, incorporating attributes of oligarchy and democracy. This was not the theoretically best regime, rule of the wise or aristocracy, nor perhaps was it meant to embody one particular form of regime but a multiplicity of forms, all of which would require some degree of mixing. It was, however, the best among the deficient alternatives, and certainly the most moderate because the mixed form of regime required a middling element, or class, to maintain its stability.[151]

Among the various types of mixed regimes, then, perhaps it could be said that Aristotle believed that a limited form of democracy with a rule of law was more likely to arise as cities grew larger. This, however, is very different from saying that Aristotle promoted democracy as the best regime. Moreover, for Aristotle, the correct regime must continually adapt to the way of life of the people. This meant changing the mixture of oligarchy and democracy in each deficient regime, with a view to improving justice and stability that took account of a people's national character and cultural differences.

The second major preoccupation of modern comparative politics theory, and of the new science of politics in general, is the construction of institutions per se as distinguished from institutions designed to encourage statesmanship and education towards moral virtue. Institutions are viewed by the moderns as a requirement for limiting vice and not, as the classics had thought, promoting virtue. The restraint of power is more important than the ends, honorable or not, to which power is directed. Power is the primary focus of Thomas Hobbes's doctrine of sovereignty. The modern comparative politics equivalent for the focus on institutions is an attention to the role of the state, behavioralism and systems theory,[152] new institutionalism[153] – which incorporates rational choice methodology,[154] and historical institutionalism.[155] Theories of the state, rather than of regimes, substitute the magnanimity of statesmen exercising prudence with political actors – both within and among political, economic, and social institutions.

Strauss believed that the modern doctrinaire adherence to democracy as the best and only legitimate form of government was a product of a new discipline that emerged in the seventeenth century – natural public law. Prior to Hobbes, classical political philosophy recognized a variety of legitimate regimes, whose legitimacy depended upon the circumstances.[156] Hobbes's doctrine of sovereignty assigned the rights of sovereignty on the basis of natural law and this led to the emergence of the school of natural public law. This school of thought concerned itself with the actualization of the right order of society, possible under all circumstances and in a manner that would no longer depend on chance.[157]

While the classics distinguished between the best regime and legitimate regimes, legitimacy varying according to the practical circumstances, the idea of the best regime was not meant to supply a practical solution to the just social order. Natural public law replaced "the best regime" with the idea of a universally applicable just social order in the guise of "legitimate government," regardless of the circumstances.[158] The practical wisdom of the statesman would no longer be required to supplement political theory because this new political theory solved, for all time, the question of the just social order here and now.[159] At that time, Strauss believes, the sensible flexibility of classical political philosophy gave way to fanatical rigidity or "doctrinarism." It is evident that by espousing the theoretical doctrine that the only legitimate form of government is democracy, modern comparative politics has inherited the natural public law doctrine of the seventeenth century.

By encouraging the empirical doctrine of quantification in its research, it is also evident that modern comparative politics has descended from Hobbes's promotion of mathematics to the position of the "mother of all sciences." Perhaps the Freedom House Country Ratings, which are often relied upon by political commentators like Diamond, are the most obvious example of this phenomenon. Since 1972, the Freedom House organization has produced an annual assessment of the degree of freedom in the world. Freedom House analysts assign a country a numerical ranking from one to seven, reflecting their categorization as "free," "partly free," or "not free," based upon the converted average of raw points awarded for the degree to which that country meets their two checklists for freedom: political rights and civil liberties.[160] However, not only is some discretion allowed in the scoring of raw points for each question on the two checklists (up to four points may be awarded for each of the eight questions on political rights – 32 maximum points, and four points for 14 questions on civil liberties – 56 maximum points), much wider discretion is allowed in Freedom House's classification of electoral democracies, the latter judgment of which is made independent of their checklists and index scales for freedom – political rights and civil liberties.

As a quantitative measure of freedom and, ultimately, democracy, the Freedom House survey and Country Ratings prove to be a highly subjective, internally inconsistent, and haphazard conflation of ideas which lack any relative weighting, nor any rigorous theoretical support. Yet they remain the most widely used source of data for comparativists making judgments, backed by quantitative analysis, on country, regional, or worldwide transitions towards democracy or "democratization" – the process of strengthening such transitions. After analyzing these scales, however, one may find much substance in Aung Thwin's seemingly valid criticism of the notion that anything that is not quantifiable is also not legitimate, which he claims is based upon Marshal Sahlins's "quantification of legitimacy" argument, the "belief that quantification *per se* has now become the ultimate criterion for the legitimacy of virtually everything."[161]

The above discussion suggests that there is much room in modern comparative politics for a realignment with the Aristotelian approach to politics. The modern doctrinaire assertion of democracy as the best form of government, along with the institutionalization of political studies, has left modern comparative politics in an impoverished condition when compared with the Aristotelian tradition. The current popularity of "social capital theory" and the resurgence of political culture studies in general is a reflection of this condition which is in need of the prudent Aristotelian approach to politics. But does social capital theory fill this void and provide the kind of Aristotelian prudence which is lacking in modern comparative politics?

Social capital theory: a new paradigm?

In recent years there has been a surge in the popularity of cultural studies in politics and, in particular, a branch of theory that some purport represents a new paradigm in comparative politics – social capital theory. This approach, rather than a paradigm in the Kuhnian sense, appears to follow in the tradition of prior historical and cultural-based development theories that attempted to fill the ideological void created by the end of the cold war and by the field's overemphasizing the institutional elements of democratization. It encourages a healthy mixing of both cultural and institutional elements by examining the voluntary co-operation in a community through "norms of reciprocity and networks of civic engagement."[162] Social capital refers to "features of social organization, such as trust, norms, and networks, that can improve the efficiency of society by facilitating coordinated actions"[163] and "cooperation for mutual benefit."[164] The political scientist Robert Putnam credits sociologist James Coleman for developing the social capital theoretical framework in 1988 to highlight the social context of education.[165]

To name but a few of its applications, social capital theory has been used to explain the development of Italian democracy, to illuminate social ills in the United States, and to provide an account of stability and change in Asia.[166] The attractiveness of this approach lies in its almost universal applicability to a wide range of social and cultural phenomena because it draws inferences that are based upon a fundamental attribute of human behavior required at all levels of politics – trust. Yet trust may manifest itself in an infinite, and changing, variety of situations and cultural contexts, not all of which are necessarily conducive to the creation of a liberal democratic regime. Social capital theory, however, assumes a connection between trust and a society's desire for a liberal democratic regime. Social capital theorists, furthermore, are unlikely to address statesmanship because their primary focus is to explain the lack of democratic consolidation through the levels of trust placed in society's various institutions.

The basic tenets of social capital theory appear to be no more than a restatement of a common theme in political philosophy. Aristotle's comprehensive account of friendship in the *Nicomachean Ethics* would more than account for the modern notions of trust and social capital offered by Almond, Putnam, Fukuyama, Diamond, and most political culture theorists. Indeed, Fukuyama's refined definition of social capital tends to reinforce this observation. He believes that social capital is an "instantiated" informal norm and that "trust, networks, civil society, and the like, which have been associated with social capital, are all epiphenomenal, arising as a result of social capital but not constituting social capital itself."[167] Norms that constitute social capital range from a norm of reciprocity between two friends to complex doctrines like Christianity or Confucianism. According to Fukuyama, "[T]hey must be instantiated in an actual human relationship: the norm of reciprocity exists *in potentia* in my dealings with all people, but is actualized only in my dealings with *my* friends."[168]

What constitutes social capital, therefore, would seem to be already implicit in Aristotle's account of political friendship. Additionally, Aristotle's idea of stability in a regime maintained a view of justice and the common good which naturally implied some degree of social co-operation and trust among all the classes. Putnam notes that civic associations reinforce Tocqueville's "habits of the heart" that are essential to stable and effective democratic institutions.[169] And Almond notes that Aristotle's conception of mixed government, with a predominant middle class, is related to his own idea of a "civic culture, in which there is a substantial consensus of legitimacy of political institutions and the direction and content of public policy, a widespread tolerance of a plurality of interests and belief in their reconcilability, and a widely distributed sense of political competence and mutual trust in the citizenry."[170] Since the idea appears to re-occur, therefore, then perhaps the arrival of, and need for, social capital theory could be explained by the radical change made by the moderns in their notions of stability, justice, and the common good. A useful beginning for illustrating this point would be to repeat the distinction between the classical and modern understandings of virtue with respect to the role played by institutions: Whereas the classics believed that institutions should make possible the rule of the virtuous and promote virtue in the citizenry of the regime, the moderns believed that institutions were necessary to restrain the abuse of power in the state, and if they promoted virtue at all, it would be of a limited kind that secured personal freedom and universal recognition of personal dignity.

Because man is by nature a political animal, all societies require trust simply to survive. The trust necessary for man's survival in the modern state, however, befits no more than the limited kind of virtue that the modern state promotes. It is a kind of trust that fuels a society founded on the low but solid grounds that nurture John Locke's doctrine of property and the spirit of capitalism. It is also the kind of trust that oils Adam Smith's solution to political economy, a system of natural liberty that satisfies the propensity in human nature to truck, barter, and exchange.[171] Because man should not expect to receive benevolence from anyone other than his friends, according to Smith, he cannot expect his dinner from the benevolence of the butcher, the brewer, or the baker, "but from their regard to their own interest."[172] "In civilized societies, [man] stands at all times in need of the cooperation and assistance of great multitudes, while his whole life is scarce sufficient to gain the friendship of a few persons."[173] Accordingly, he must trust not only the butcher, the brewer, and the baker to meet the minimal standards of fairness in exchange, but also the multitudes. Although Smith remarks that there are some principles in man's nature which render the happiness of others "necessary to him, though he derives nothing from it except the pleasure of seeing it,"[174] his system of natural liberty is built upon the foundations of utilitarian self-interest and a kind of trust which Aristotle would have called political friendship, which is a friendship of utility and not of virtue. This kind of friendship, or association, was of the lowest form and the most easily dissolved, being based more upon expediency or that which is useful, rather than being pleasurable or good in itself.[175]

Putnam, however, while noting Michael Walzer's observation that the trust and tolerance of virtuous citizens resembles Aristotle's account of friendship among members of the same political community,[176] still contends that the most fundamental form of social capital is the family and that the massive evidence of the loosening of the bonds within the family helps to explain "social decapitalization" in the United States.[177] To the extent that he uses the family as an indicator of declining social capital, Putnam, therefore, would appear to disagree with Aristotle's understanding of familial friendship. Aristotle believed that friendship among natural kinsmen, and particularly the family, though containing elements of both the useful and pleasurable, was higher and more lasting and that they should be marked off from other kinds of friendships in an association of fellow-citizens or fellow-tribesmen because friendship among kinsmen depends ultimately on paternal friendship, and parents, or kinsmen, love their children as if they were parts of themselves, or other selves.[178]

Putnam's treatment of the family suggests an implicit measurement problem in social capital theory as it is adopted to explain the strengthening of democracy induced by economic development. That is to say, while the kind of trust promoted by modern capitalism reflects Aristotle's lower, more expedient form of political association or friendship and rests upon a utilitarian system of reciprocity founded by Locke and Smith, one of the indicators for measuring social capital, the family, belongs to what Aristotle believed, and probably most people would agree, to be a higher standard of friendship. Even Smith believed that our moral sentiments are strongest for those nearest to us. Putnam, however, chooses as an indicator of a lower form of trust what tends naturally to belong to a higher form of association, or a friendship of virtue. Thus, tribesmen living in remote parts of the world may exhibit very tightly knit familial bonds, though these bonds may not necessarily promote liberal democracy, liberal capitalism, or market economics.

Putnam fails to explain adequately the connection between familial friendship and political friendship. In certain circumstances, and among certain cultures, familial friendship might actually weaken political friendship. A remote tribe in Papua New Guinea, or a fundamentalist religious group in some remote part of the world, for example, may be very trusting and benevolent within and among their families, but they may lack the kinds of civic engagement and other social capital required for economic development, according to social capital theory. The United States, on the other hand, is said to suffer from a crisis of trust and civic engagement, not because their advanced society may be founded upon a basic respect for utilitarian self-interest, but because their bowling league numbers are down.[179] Trust varies among cultures and not all kinds of trust are the same. While patron–client ties in Southeast Asia, or the OneTalk system in Papua New Guinea, may be considered a sign of strong familial bonds at home, they may be judged as examples of nepotism, tribalism, or factionalism by Western researchers and not conducive to the building of social capital at the national level. Putnam should keep familial trust separate from other kinds of trust when searching for indicators of social capital. Aristotle's account of familial friendship, therefore, would seem to be more reasonable and, unlike social capital theory that implicitly assumes that a liberal democracy is the best regime, Aristotle's multiplicity of regimes allows for cultural differences.

Because social capital theory, like most comparative development theory, assumes that democracy is the best form of government and that it is achieved through economic development, it cannot escape the same problematic dichotomy that Smith labors to create in the *Wealth of Nations* and the *Theory of Moral Sentiments* – benevolence must be downplayed for a capitalist society to be founded upon utilitarian self-interest. Perhaps in Aristotelian terms, this means that for a political regime to function properly, friendships of virtue must ultimately coexist with friendships of utility.

The kind of trust and the kind of virtue that is promoted by the modern liberal state characterize the cultural void that social capital theory, and political culture theory, attempts to fill. It is a theoretical void that Almond and Putnam attempt to address when they claim to be writing in the tradition of Alexis de Tocqueville's "mores" and "habits of the heart."[180] Tocqueville, however, did not write *Democracy in America* in order to fill a void in the literature of comparative political theory or modern sociology. Accordingly, the kind of trust and civic engagement Tocqueville had in mind could be of a different form, serving a different purpose, compared with the baser forms which accompany advanced economic development and modernization in the accounts of Almond and Putnam. It is also not impossible that, unlike Almond and Putnam, Tocqueville's observations of mores and habits of the heart were intended to be peculiarly American and not generally applicable in a universal modernization theory for all nations. Perhaps they simply serve to indicate how the American people could successfully maintain a system of government founded upon the principle of equality by moderating the democratic causes of faction in their own peculiar way.

In addressing the modern unfettered promotion of democracy at the expense of constitutional liberalism, Fareed Zakaria also calls for a return to what Tocqueville called "intermediate associations."[181] He believes that the modern promotion of democracy, where legitimacy is ultimately judged by the holding of elections, may lead to untold damage if little attention is paid to the condition of the rule of law; political institutions and civic associations; courts; political parties; and economic, civil, and religious liberties, all of which are yardsticks related to constitutional liberalism.[182] Zakaria's account, however, would seem to differ from social capital theory by questioning the merits of promoting democracy without recovering the constitutional liberal tradition that was central to the Western experience.[183] He also rises above the institutional level of analysis when he addresses a return to statesmanship within this tradition, by calling for responsible leadership from those who hold power and to set standards that are both legal and moral.[184]

In spite of its shortcomings and lack of originality, social capital theory does serve to remind us that institutions do not, by themselves, increase the levels of trust in a community. Nor too will unlimited technological progress and its accompaniment. The classics would not have thought that it was possible to cultivate moral virtue simply by improving one's computer skills and having access to the Internet. The very instrument which, Fukuyama claims, will transmit globalization and the inevitable universal triumph of liberal democracy, the information technology revolution, is regarded by Putnam as an inhibitor of interpersonal communication and trust.[185] Because social trust is also correlated with education, the overall decrease in social trust that has occurred in the United States, while education levels have risen sharply, is a worrying phenomenon for social capital theorists.[186]

Despite its weaknesses, social capital theory is still valuable because like political culture, social capital theories direct us towards the understanding of a people's lasting cultural traits, which is knowledge that a prudent statesman should have. This includes knowledge of the nature of a people's social relations, norms, and habits. The value of these studies lies in providing the cultural background and the circumstances through which justice and injustice play themselves out in a particular regime. It may be helpful, or problematic, to draw inferences upon the general behavior of Asians as Asians for example, but it is far more useful to analyze the peculiar traits of a particular ethnic group or nation. The former may lead to many of the banal generalities and oversimplifications which are found in the Asian values rhetoric, whereas the latter may be undertaken, for example, by more detailed comparisons of the civility, social capital, and civil society that exists among particular countries in Asia.[187]

Framing an examination of political rhetoric within the patterns of social behavior, norms, habits, and beliefs of the people should be considered an important element when considering justice in a regime. But since justice must also exist among a band of thieves who have their own stated and unstated rules of conduct,[188] civility alone is not an adequate measure of virtue and does not suffice when comparing justice among regimes. The ends pursued by the regime reveal its justice and the political rhetoric of its ruling part helps to reveal these ends.

Conclusion

When analyzing regimes we are often drawn into using modern theoretical tools without questioning the assumptions that limit their usefulness. Yet there are alternatives to thinking about regimes beyond the limits imposed by modern comparative theory. These alternatives do not lose sight of the fundamental question posed of every regime, justice. A better understanding of political friendship and the cultivation of virtue among the middling elements of any regime, taking into account their lasting cultural traits, may be a better prescription than the unconditional promotion of universal and deterministic goals and processes like democratic proceduralism and electoral democracy. Political culture and social capital theories serve to remind us that a people's cultural traits should never be overlooked in comparing regimes.

If we seek universal solutions to political questions without having a prudent regard to particular circumstances, the possibility of achieving that aim may only come about through a lowering of the standards of justice in a particular regime. In contrast to modern comparative theorists, perhaps the best solution that Aristotle would prescribe is a better mixing of the democratic elements with the oligarchic to improve justice in that particular regime. This does not imply that the classics would not have chosen liberal democracy by default, however, and Strauss notes that liberal or constitutional democracy does come closer to what the classics demanded than any alternative that is viable in our age.[189]

In their quest to promote democracy as the best regime, however, the moderns either ignore, or make redundant, the classical reasons for it falling short of the best regime. Since the wise do not wish to rule, modern political science offers institutional analysis as a replacement, and as a guarantee of success, for the study and promotion of statesmanship. In addition, statesmanship becomes less important when the fruits of modern science, including the possible advances in biotechnology, combine to remove the "accident of birth" factor that accompanies the fortune of being born into aristocracy, or perhaps even of being born wise. But while humans still maintain a say in their destiny and, assuming that they will never choose to become "post-human," classical political science remains a viable alternative to modern comparative theory.

Central to the classical analysis of regimes was an understanding of tyranny, justice, and stability. We need to examine how this understanding compares with the modern account and, by focusing upon the rhetoric of tyranny, discover how we may put the best features of modern comparative theory to use in classifying and analyzing regimes without having to succumb to the determinism that plagues the modern treatment of democracy.

3   The political science of tyranny

The modern comparative method of regime classification can often become a confusing and problematic exercise in precising definitions to account for a multitude of exceptions. Since the classification of the worst regimes is often conducted with a view to their inevitable transformation into a better form, or the best, modern political scientists are reluctant to call the worst regimes what they are. Instead, they are often assigned labels to signify their distance from the best or adjectives to modify what elements of the best they are lacking. It is possible to illustrate how a return to the classical analysis of regimes, and tyranny in particular, provides not only a more practical way to think about regimes but also offers insights into practical ways to improve the worst regimes. Yet before any improvement can be made in the worst, political scientists should be able to call them for what they are and not what they wish them to become.

Since the transformation of a brutish tyranny into a more moderate regime is a common policy goal among foreign strategists in Western liberal democracies, Aristotle's prescriptions for improving the stability and justice in a regime remain a useful practical guide and, unlike the targets set for less developed countries in much of the modern political analysis, not a practical impossibility. It is timely, therefore, to analyze Aristotle's and Machiavelli's prescriptions for transforming tyranny into a more lasting form of regime, that is, by the tyrant playing a fine performance of the part of a kingly ruler. Because rhetoric plays an important role in maintaining or transforming a regime, it is also fitting to draw from Aristotle to develop the rhetoric of tyranny. That rhetoric addresses the common opinions of the masses conforms with the modern comparative analysis of mass political culture. After examining the common elements of persuasion in rhetorical analysis, we may develop enthymemes of tyrannical rhetoric for the purpose of undertaking empirical case studies.

Tyranny, ancient and modern

Sixty years have passed since World War II came to an end. During those 60 years the world has experienced a succession of minor conflicts, insurgencies, and terrorist activity while the most serious threat to liberal democracy, communism, has been all but silenced. It is not surprising, therefore, that today modern political scientists have difficulty seeing tyranny for what it is.[1] Perhaps 60 years of relative peace, coupled with economic development and technological advances, has bred a complacency among political scientists who continue to invent new adjectives for the less than perfect regimes that ride the wave of democratization. Among the plethora of adjectives used to describe the variants of democratic aspirants one may find "authoritarian democracy," "autocratic democracy," "military-dominated democracy," "neopatrimonial democracy," "protodemocracy," "pseudodemocracy," "virtual democracy," "limited-suffrage democracy," "tutelage democracy," "illiberal democracy," "consociational democracy," "democratizing regimes," "semi-authoritarian regimes," "soft authoritarian regimes," "inclusionary authoritarian regimes," "bureaucratic authoritarianism," "electoral authoritarianism," "competitive authoritarianism," "postauthoritarian regimes," and perhaps the most puzzling of all, "facade democracy."[2]

While research on democratization often degenerates into what Collier and Levitsky call "a competition to see who can come up with the next famous concept,"[3] Boesche claims that the liberal democratic prejudices of the late twentieth century are a major reason for the hopelessly muddled modern vocabulary of tyranny.[4] Today it is often difficult to distinguish between the adjectives that are coupled to democracy when precising its definition, the adjectives used to help classify a subtype of regime, and the modern terms that are applied to describe what the ancients would have called tyranny. "Despotism," "dictatorship," and "totalitarianism," according to Boesche, are only varieties of the familiar theme of tyrannical government which reoccurs like a very frightful melody throughout history, undergoing frequent variations and considerable innovation.[5]

Boesche suggests that most modern commentators would claim that freedom or democracy, or both, are the opposite of tyranny.[6] Neither Plato nor Aristotle, according to Boesche, "saw tyranny as the opposite of freedom – at least not freedom in some Lockean sense – but rather regarded tyrannical government as the opposite of a government that cultivates justice, virtue, excellence, and human greatness."[7] Likewise, Lilla believes that the slogan "totalitarianism or democracy" has captured the political problem of our time for as long as anyone living can remember, and that while such a distinction was once thought useful for the purposes of serious political analysis and public rhetoric alike, that age has definitely passed.[8]

Modern tyranny may indeed be no more than a familiar theme which reoccurs throughout history, with variations and innovations unforeseen by the classics. Nevertheless, while the technological advances produced by modern science have allowed tyranny to adopt many new forms, the classics could still have understood the behavior of present-day common tyrants on their own terms. Despotism and dictatorship are not new ideas comprehensible only to the moderns. Totalitarianism, ideologies, revolutionary, and party-based tyranny may be modern phenomena, but the behavior associated with tyrannical regimes, coupled with the ends towards which their ruling parts direct themselves, was fundamental to classical comparative politics. According to Strauss, the fact that the classics did not even dream of present-day tyranny is not a good or sufficient reason for abandoning the classical frame of reference because present-day tyranny cannot be understood except within the classical framework.[9] The classics did not dream of new forms of tyranny, influenced by technological advances, because they turned their imagination in entirely different directions,[10] namely, human things.[11]

Cicero writes that while "the Romans have always given the name of king to all who exercise for life sole authority over a nation," "tyrant … is the title given by the Greeks to an unjust king."[12] A king is transformed into a despot, and a good form of government is changed into the worst possible form, when a king becomes a master over the people.[13] According to Cicero, the Greeks "maintain that the title of king should be given only to a ruler who is as solicitous for the welfare of his people as is a father for his children, and maintains in the best possible conditions of life those over whom he is set." While such a government is truly a good one, according to Cicero, it nevertheless inclines, and almost naturally tends, toward the most depraved condition of all. "For as soon as this king turned to a mastery less just than before, he instantly becomes a tyrant."[14]

Lilla believes that while the Greeks distinguished despotism (*despoteia*) from kingship and tyranny, to describe non-Greek regimes they considered to be unpolitical and under a kind of household rule, there is a continuous tradition of political theory from the Greeks to the Enlightenment that took the phenomenon of tyranny as its theoretical starting point and the establishment of barriers against tyrannical rule as its practical aim.[15] Because the main focus of Western political thinking up to the French Revolution had been on tyrannical kingship, little thought had been given to the tyrannical propensities of political arrangements other than kingship.[16] Europeans were at a loss to explain the rise of communism and fascism in the twentieth century because, according to Lilla, for a century and a half serious thought about political tyranny had ceased in Europe. Those addressing the question of tyranny today confront what Lilla calls "the paradox of Western political discourse ever since the Second World War: the more sensitive we became to the horrors brought on by the totalitarian tyrannies, the less sensitive we became to tyranny in its more moderate forms."[17] Lilla believes that sooner or later the language of antitotalitarianism must be abandoned and the classic problem of tyranny revisited:

The democratic West does not face an "axis of evil" today, it faces the
geography of a new age of tyranny. That means we live in a world
where we will be forced to distinguish, strategically and rhetorically,
among different species of tyranny, and among different sorts of mini-
mally decent political regimes that might not be modern or democratic, but would be a definite improvement over tyranny.... It will
take more than a generation, apparently, before two centuries of for-
getfulness about tyranny can themselves be forgotten.

(Lilla, M. (2002): 29)

Tyranny then, as understood by the classics, was generally seen as being
the opposite of the best regime, or rule by the best, kingship or aristocracy.[18] Kingship and despotism were both forms of government, but they
differed. Xenophon writes: "For government of men with their consent
and in accordance with the laws of the state was kingship; while government of unwilling subjects and not controlled by laws, but imposed by the
will of the ruler, was despotism."[19] According to Strauss's interpretation of
Xenophon, while kingship involved rule over willing subjects, being based
on law, tyranny was rule over unwilling subjects in accordance not with
laws but with the will of the ruler.[20] Strauss notes that Xenophon's,
or Socrates', definition of this common variety of tyranny excluded
Simonides' description of "tyranny at its best." Tyranny at its best, according to Simonides' suggestions, would become rule over willing subjects,
but would remain "not according to laws."[21] Strauss concludes, "[T]yranny
is essentially rule without laws, or, more precisely, monarchic rule without
laws."[22]

While Aristotle seems to concur with Xenophon on this assessment of
the common variety of tyranny, being a counterpart to absolute kingship,
he clearly distinguishes two varieties of monarchic rule which are tyrannical, and which are based on law:

We distinguished two kinds of tyranny while investigating kingship, as
their power in a sense overlaps with kingship as well on account of the
fact that both of these sorts of rule are based on law ... both were
kingly by the fact of being based on law and a monarchic rule over
willing subjects, and at the same time tyrannical by the rule being
characteristic of a master and in accordance with their own will.

(Aristotle, *Politics*, 1295a7–17)

This discrepancy between Strauss's Xenophon and Aristotle could be
attributed both to Aristotle's thoroughness and to Strauss's agreement
with Xenophon's skepticism towards the possibility of tyranny at its best –
a benevolent despot. Aristotle, it seems, is more hopeful in this regard,
and the fact remains that Aristotle chose to distinguish certain kinds of
monarchical regimes as tyrannies while refraining from classifying them as

absolute monarchies, absolute government, or common tyranny. The distinguishing feature of these lesser forms of tyranny was that their rule was based on law. Among them were the kingships that existed among some of the barbarians (non-Greeks) because

> [B]arbarians are more slavish in their characters than Greeks (those in Asia being more so than those in Europe) that they put up with a master's rule without making any difficulties. They are tyrannical, then, through being of this sort; but they are stable because they are hereditary and based on law.
>
> (Aristotle, *Politics*, 1285a19–24)

Another kind was that which existed among the ancient Greeks – an elective tyranny, or rule by dictators – which differed from barbarian kingships by not being hereditary. Like the barbarian kingships, rule by dictators was also like a rule by a tyrannical master, but on account of their being elective and over willing persons, they too were based on law.[23] Aristotle writes,

> The tyrant, however, arises from the people or the multitude against the notables, in order that the people not be done injustice by them. This is evident from events: most tyrants arose from popular leaders who were trusted because of their slanders of the notables ... some from persons who were elected to authoritative offices ... and some in oligarchies that elected a single person with authority over the greatest offices.... It was easy for them to work their will in all of these modes if only they wanted to do so, on account of the power they already had, whether through kingly office or the power of their prerogative.
>
> (Aristotle, *Politics*, 1310b14–26)

These passages indicate that Aristotle believed it possible for a tyranny to be based upon a rule by law, whether because an elected dictator acted tyrannically for his own advantage or because a hereditary ruler imposed his will over slavish subjects. From his *Politics* then, it is possible to chart Aristotle's classification of tyrannies into three forms, as in Table 3.1.

While a common thread in Aristotle's three varieties of tyranny appears to be rule by the will of a master whose power is comparable with that of kingship, within the context of these observations Aristotle's understanding of a valid or justified title to rule may, under certain circumstances, stand in stark contrast to the modern concept of legitimacy. Unlike modern comparativists, many of whom hold that elections more or less determine legitimacy, for the classics, any idea of a valid title to rule varied according to the practical circumstances and some understanding of justice. The classics played down the importance of constitutional rule in

Table 3.1 Aristotle's classification of tyrannies

Hereditary tyranny
- Power overlaps with kingship
- Rule over willing subjects
- Rule by the will of the master
- Hereditary ruler – plenipotentiary monarch
- Rule based on law
- Characteristic of slavish barbarians (non-Greeks)
- Stable

Elective tyranny
- Power overlaps with kingship
- Rule over willing persons
- Rule by the will of the master
- Elective dictator (rule in office for life, or for a fixed period of time, or for certain actions)
- Rule based on law
- Existed among ancient Greeks[24]

Common brutish tyranny
- Counterpart to absolute kingship
- Rule over the unwilling
- Rule by the will of the master
- Unelected, non-hereditary
- Rule not based on law
- Most particularly held to be tyranny

---

favor of rule by the wise, or a ruler having counsel from the wise. For Aristotle, constitutional rule was only one sign of a ruler's bona fide title and justification to rule, and it was also possible for the rule of a tyrant, if it was based on law, to be deemed warranted and considered justified. Elections per se did not prevent tyranny. Justice, or the appearance of justice, seems to have been a far more important factor in maintaining what today would be called "legitimacy." Thus, while hereditary and elective tyrannies might be called more lawful than common brutish tyrannies, rulers in all tyrannies must, as we shall see, maintain the appearance of justice in order to preserve their rule.

Although the classical distinction between king and tyrant may not be altogether as clear as Strauss suggests, there appears to be some consensus on identifying the common tyrant whose rule over the unwilling is not based on law. The only case in which the classical distinction between a common tyrant and a king becomes somewhat blurred occurs in Xenophon's *Hiero* and Aristotle's *Politics*, where a tyrant is advised to adopt the virtue of a king. Machiavelli, on the other hand, deliberately makes no distinction at all between tyrant and king in the *Prince*, and because of this, Strauss believes, he broke away from the whole tradition of political science.[25] If "the *Hiero* marks the point of closest contact between premodern and modern political science,"[26] and because Aristotle's prescriptions mirror those of Xenophon's Simonides, we are obliged to question whether, and for what purpose, their teaching on tyranny was Machiavellian.

Aristotle on the preservation of tyranny

In Book 5 of the *Politics*, Aristotle discusses the modes by which all tyrannies are destroyed and preserved. Of the two modes by which preservation is made possible, one is particularly brutal, making the tyranny short lived. The other is a more lasting technique which may lead to a transformation of the nature of the tyranny itself. The first method involves simply "lopping off the preeminent and eliminating those with high thoughts ... guarding against anything that customarily gives rise to two things, high thoughts and trust ... everything is done to make all as ignorant of one another as possible, since knowledge tends to create trust of one another."[27] The other mode involves "a sort of superintendence that is *practically* the opposite" of the first.[28] It is the opposite of the first mode because it reflects what must be done in order to prevent the destruction of kingships. But whereas kingship accords with aristocracy, tyranny is composed of the ultimate sort of oligarchy and of democracy.[29] Because kingship does not equate simply with tyranny then, we may glimpse Aristotle's purpose in describing a sort of superintendence that is not *theoretically* the opposite of the first.

Aristotle, like Simonides in Xenophon's *Hiero*, may be prescribing a practical solution aimed at transforming the tyrant into a respectable king with some semblance of virtue. Because a tyrant arises from among the people, he lacks the respectability accorded to a king "on the basis of his preeminence in virtue or in the actions that come from virtue, or on the basis of preeminence of a family of this sort."[30] Like Simonides, Aristotle appeals to the tyrant's self-interest by prescribing the actions which would make him more respected and honored by his people, because by making the city he rules the happiest, he "will be declared by herald the victor in the most noble and magnificent contest among human beings."[31] There is a major difference, however, between Aristotle's transformed tyrant and the respectable king who is preeminent in virtue. This is the presupposition that, while giving a fine performance as the kingly ruler, the tyrant will always safeguard his power so that he may rule over both the willing and the unwilling.[32] By safeguarding his power, the tyranny is preserved, or is it?

The actions that Aristotle prescribes for this fine kingly performance are designed to make a tyrant appear as a manager or steward of the city. These appear in Book 5 of the *Politics* and briefly include: implementing an accountability of public moneys, a fair and efficient tax system, encouraging people to feel awe rather than fear of him, the avoidance of outrages against women and youth, being careful of bodily gratifications, taking care for the appearance of the city, to appear very religious, to honor merit but delegate punishment, to avoid outrages, and to guard against those who have considered him to act arrogantly.[33] By conducting his affairs in such a way, by pursuing moderation in life, a tyrant's rule is said to be "nobler and more enviable by the fact that he rules over persons who are better and have not been humbled and does so without being hated or feared, but his rule will also be longer lasting."[34]

The particular circumstances, as always, will dictate the longevity of such a disguised form of tyranny. Yet Aristotle leaves open the possibility that the middling element may succeed in transforming a tyranny into a mixed regime. The alternative outcome to Aristotle's prescription is, I believe, far too optimistic to hope for. A tyrant will not acquire virtue merely by playing the part of a kingly ruler while, at the same time, safeguarding his power to rule over unwilling subjects. It would be difficult to find any examples of this occurring in modern times, or perhaps ever occurring at all. A tyrant will always remain a tyrant so long as he secures the ability to flex his muscles when the need arises.

Perhaps one possible example comes through Aristotle's account of Peisistratus in *The Constitution of Athens*, which is one of a man who ran the city more like a citizen than a tyrant. Although Peisistratus seized power by disarming the people, according to Aristotle, he ran the city moderately and governed constitutionally in accordance with the laws, rather than as a tyrant. His rule was unlawful but just. He was benevolent, kind, and forgiving to those who did wrong, advanced money to farmers to keep them busy with their own affairs, taxed their produce fairly to raise revenues, established magistrates, and traveled around the country frequently, inspecting and settling disputes.[35] The most important attribute of Peisistratus was that he was naturally inclined to support the common people and was benevolent, and this is why he remained in power for a long time, by attracting the nobles by his association with them and by the assistance he gave to the common people in their personal affairs.[36] Peisistratus, it seems, conducted a fine performance of the part of a kingly ruler and, growing old in office, fell ill and died naturally, but only after having lived for 33 years since he first set himself up as a tyrant, having ruled for 19 of those years.[37]

While Aristotle provides a flattering account of Peisistratus's Golden Age of reign, he is silent on whether he actually acquired virtue. Strauss believes that a tyrant's performance of mere "objective tasks" is not sufficient to transform radically his desire for honor because praise is most honorable when the tyrant's subjects are free, and to promote freedom among the citizenry is not among the tasks prescribed.[38] Nor, it appears, is the promotion of justice or courage, or at least no more than the appearance of justice in Aristotle's narrow sense – fairness in exchange.[39] Yet perhaps the justice promoted by a benevolent tyrant, being no greater than that which accords with Aristotle's discussion of political associations in the *Ethics*, acts as a restraint and is, therefore, an improvement upon the immoderate and unpredictable behavior of the common brutish tyrant.

The rule of a benevolent despot may be more "legitimate" than constitutional rule in a Socratic sense only if the ruler is wise or takes counsel from those who are wise. Because rule of the wise was Socrates' theoretically best solution to the political question, Xenophon and Aristotle could at least entertain the possibility of this solution entering into the realm of tyranny. Yet the theoretical possibility of this outcome being anything more than very improbable is itself indicated by the classical belief that the wise are unwilling to rule, nor would they actively seek to rule – constitutionally or otherwise. And being virtuous, the wise would certainly not choose the unhappy life of a tyrant.

Entertaining the theoretical possibility of rule by the wise entering into the realm of tyranny causes trouble for those who actively promote this as a possibile solution to tyranny, particularly if it is viewed by some as promoting a practically superior alternative to democracy. Just as Athens condemned Socrates and Xenophon for their "tyrannical" teaching, modern political scientists might condemn any teaching that questions their belief in democracy as the best form of government, whether it be offered as a realistic practical solution or simply to show that such a solution is theoretically highly improbable. Yet it is not altogether unrealistic to compare, at least on theoretical grounds, Diamond's "bias for hope" in reference to the democratization of attributes in a political culture[40] to Aristotle's hope that a benevolent despot acquires virtue.

While there may never have been a case of a benevolent despot actually acquiring the kind of virtue that promotes real justice, courage, and freedom in the citizenry, studying his actions may help draw attention to the fact that he is indeed a tyrant in the classical sense, and not simply an authoritarian, semi-authoritarian, patrimonial, or protodemocratic ruler practicing facade democracy. In studying the kind of tyranny that is preserved through the fine performance of a kingly ruler, then perhaps "the best one could hope for is that the tyranny be improved, i.e. that the tyrannical rule be exercised as little inhumanely or irrationally as possible."[41] Yet before we can nurture such hope, we must first be able to recognize a system of government for what it is, and not for the universal solution we would like it to become.

Machiavelli on the preservation of tyranny

Machiavelli's cyclical account of regimes, the emergence of tyranny, and what a prince should do that he may be esteemed resembles Aristotle's account of regimes, and tyranny, in the *Politics*. But whereas Machiavelli's account of the Prince occupies an entire manuscript without ever mentioning tyranny by name, Aristotle's relatively short account of tyranny takes place within the context of his analysis of regimes and, unlike Machiavelli, Aristotle also wrote a treatise on *Ethics*. This might suggest that tyranny, or at least the importance of how to avoid being seen as a tyrant and the precautions a tyrant should take to secure himself, was a common theme in Machiavelli's understanding of politics. While only briefly mentioning the ordering of a republic or kingdom for the common good, for example, he devotes his longest chapter in the *Discourses* to an account of conspiracies.

In the *Discourses*, Machiavelli says that tyranny arises when a prince becomes hated and begins to fear. Fear soon creates offenses and tyranny, from which arises "the beginnings of ruin and of plots and conspiracies against princes."[42] While he also says in his *Discourses* that the "founders ... of a tyranny are worthy of reproach," and includes the Roman emperor Severus among these,[43] Machiavelli nevertheless praises the "virtue" of the "criminal," Severus, both in the *Discourses* and in his longest chapter in the *Prince*.[44] While Severus possessed the "exceedingly cruel and rapacious" qualities shared by Commodus, Antonius Caracalla, and Maximinus, unlike the other Roman emperors who were killed, he managed to die ordinarily because "he knew how to use the *persona* of the astute fox and the ferocious lion." According to Machiavelli,

> [H]e was always able to rule happily; for his virtues made him so wonderful in the view of the soldiers and of the people that the former remained, in a certain way, astonished and stupefied, and the others reverent and satisfied.... [H]e was elected Emperor by the Senate through fear.... [He was] feared and revered by everyone, and not hated by the armies ... [Severus] was able to keep so much imperium, for his very great reputation always protected him from that hatred which the people might have conceived because of his rapacity.
>
> (Machiavelli, *Prince*, XIX: 117–118)

While a tyrant, therefore, should himself avoid fear, and yet be astute and aware of conspiracies, he should cultivate a reputation of great virtue among the people to ensure that their fear of him does not evolve into contempt and hatred. Machiavelli appears to endorse Aristotle's second mode for preserving tyrannies in the *Prince* and, as in Book 5 of Aristotle's *Politics*, he lays out his own prescription for a prince to maintain his rule in a seemingly kingly fashion. For a prince to be esteemed, according to Machiavelli,

> [H]e should also show himself a lover of virtue, giving welcome to virtuous men, and honoring the excellent in an art. Next, he should encourage his citizens, enabling them quietly to practice their trades in merchandise and in agriculture and in every other trade of men –

so that this one is not afraid to embellish his possessions for fear that these might be taken from him, nor this other to open a traffic for fear of taxes. But he ought to prepare rewards for the one who wants to do these things, and for whoever thinks, in whatever mode, of increasing his city or his state. He should, besides this, at the proper times of the year, keep the people occupied with feasts and spectacles. And because every city is divided into arts and trades, he should take account of these universities, meeting with them sometimes, and making himself an example of humanity and munificence, always keeping firmly, nevertheless, the majesty of his dignity, for this he does not want to be lacking in anything.

(Machiavelli, *Prince*, XXI: 135)

Because both Aristotle and Machiavelli seem to promote the preservation of tyranny in this kingly mode, it could be inferred that both realized how the first mode of brutish tyranny is naturally a relatively short-lived phenomenon, and that encouraging a tyrant to behave as an apparently benevolent king is itself a teaching in moderation. But whether virtue actually arises in the tyrant as an effect of this teaching in moderation, or whether Machiavelli believes that it is possible for virtue to arise at all, could be the main factor distinguishing his account from Aristotle's. While Machiavelli encourages the tyrant to be a lover of virtue for the sake of preserving his tyranny, Aristotle recognizes that tyranny and depravity are at opposite poles to virtue. Moreover, the character of a tyrant who follows Aristotle's advice will only "either be in a state that is fine in relation to virtue or he will be half-decent – not vicious but half-vicious."[45]

In the *Prince*, Machiavelli praises Severus' virtue, the virtue of the fox and the lion, and warns tyrants of the danger in being feared, hated, and held in contempt. In the *Discourses*, he says that men are driven by two principal things, love or fear, and that both allow one to command, but an excess of each may lead a prince to his ruin, "for he who desires too much to be loved becomes despicable, ... [while] the other, who desires too much to be feared, becomes hateful."[46] Yet Machiavelli believes that "it is of little import to a captain whichever of these ways he walks in, provided he is a virtuous man and that the virtue makes him reputed among men."[47] Although Machiavelli claims that our nature does not allow us to "hold exactly to the middle way" between excessive fear and love, he also writes that Hannibal's excessive cruelty in no way hurt him, whereas Scipio's excessive love required an occasional cruelty to remedy his error.[48] Therefore, according to Machiavelli, "the mode in which a captain proceeds is not very important, provided that in it is the great virtue that seasons both modes of life," an "extraordinary virtue" that is able to correct the danger of excess.[49] This is the virtue of Severus, the fox and the lion, which Machiavelli understands and which distances himself from Aristotle.

Because it is his "intention to write a useful thing for him who understands," and since it is "more profitable to go behind to the effectual truth of the thing, than to the imagination thereof," Machiavelli wishes to examine how one lives, and what is done, rather than concern himself with "imagined republics and principates that have never been seen or known to be in truth."[50] Because "there is such a distance between how one lives and how one should live," according to Machiavelli, "he who lets go that which is done for that which ought to be done learns his ruin rather than his preservation."[51] Machiavelli, therefore, will teach "a prince, if he wishes to maintain himself, to learn to be able to be not good, and to use it and not use it according to the necessity."[52]

Machiavelli's prudence is not directed by any Aristotelian sense of moral virtue but rather is concerned with knowing how a prince should oscillate between being good and not good where the occasion demands it, while avoiding "the infamy of those vices which would lose him the state."[53] And since Machiavelli believes that our nature does not consent to a middle way,[54] he cannot teach moderation, and especially not to a tyrant. His extraordinary virtue, or prudence, that seasons both modes of life is the knowledge of a base form of political expediency, void of virtue in the classical sense.

Stability and justice in a regime

In the *Politics*, Aristotle emphasizes the importance of stability to the preservation of existing regimes. Machiavelli, in the *Discourses*, agrees with Aristotle's prescription for a mixed regime that shares the attributes of all, making it firmer and more stable.[55] It is a sign of a well-organized regime, according to Aristotle, if the people voluntarily acquiesce in the arrangement of the regime and if there has never been factional conflict worth mentioning, or a tyrant.[56] The greatest factional split is that between virtue and depravity,[57] and all the characteristics of tyrants that help preserve their rule in no respect fall short in depravity.[58] Nevertheless, all who dispute about regimes speak of some part of justice.[59]

When Aristotle speaks of the stability required for the preservation of regimes, therefore, he does not prescribe imposing the kind of order flaunted by modern soft authoritarian regimes, as described by Huntington[60] and Fukuyama[61] of the Asian variety. This version of political stability lies at the heart of Lee Kuan Yew's promotion of one-party rule in Singapore, just as it does in the State Peace and Development Council's daily publication of its four political objectives in Burmese newspapers. While both set out to oppose the kind of individual freedoms fostered by Western liberalism, they effectively secure the rule of incumbents against any political change at all.

In contrast, for Aristotle, preservation does not imply preserving the regime in its original form, but rather moving the regime in the direction of virtue and justice so as to prevent its degeneration into a worse form of regime. Aristotle did not believe that the stability of a regime was a static concept measurable by the lack of faction, although it certainly helps to avoid factional conflict, but rather, stability sets the parameters within which the regime's natural decay may be prevented by the improvement of justice. Thus, a better regime was considered to be a practical possibility and a consequence of improving justice within the regime.

Aristotle believed that justice is held to be something equal, and equality requires that whatever the multitude resolves is authoritative.[62] However, while democracies are defined by equality – the majority having authority – and freedom, those democracies which are held to be most particularly democratic have established the opposite of what is advantageous because they define freedom badly.[63] Freedom and equality, according to Aristotle, was a poor thing in a democracy if it allowed everyone to live as he wants towards whatever end he happens to crave.[64] Preservation of the regime meant living with a view to the regime, for the common good, rather than living as a slave of one's passions, and the greatest of all the things which make a regime lasting was education relative to the regimes.[65]

Aristotle promoted education, not in the enjoyment of oligarchic and democratic freedoms as such, but in the things that enable a regime to be best run as an oligarchy or democracy. Even the most beneficial laws, according to Aristotle, are useless unless individuals are properly habituated and educated both in the spirit of the regime and in the ends pursued by the regime because "if lack of self-control exists in the case of an individual, it exists also in the case of a city."[66] Aristotle's answer to the ills of Western liberalism, therefore, would not have been to impose draconian laws and prohibitions on the exercise of individual freedoms, but rather to moderate such exercise through education directed towards moral virtue.

One needs ultimately to look at the ends towards which the stability of the regime is directed and if, as is the case with Burma and Singapore, stability merely implies the preservation of the status quo, then we must question the merits of the justice produced by the regime. If the status quo consists of the people who wish to participate in politics having little or no participation in government and no ability to audit the government, but rather the government audits their ability to implement its policies, we are obliged to ask whether Aristotle would have considered that these circumstances could be reflective of a just regime.

The rhetoric of tyranny

Technology has equipped tyrants with the ability to enforce their will on a scale that could not have been foreseen by the classics, and this has played itself out, particularly during the twentieth century, both in terms of the capacity for destruction as well as in more subtle ways. Advances in man's ability to communicate quickly with wider audiences over greater distances, either in printed form, radio broadcasting, or modern telecommunications, have elevated the role of propaganda to a cornerstone of tyrannical rule. While it could be argued that the classics may have believed that as far as tyranny was concerned, actions were more important than speeches, the success of modern tyranny has, to a large degree, been founded upon technologies which place speech and action on an equal footing.

Classical tyrants could have naturally preferred action over speeches, given that the mediums for projecting rhetorical speeches on a grand scale were as yet unavailable. Nor would they have felt pressure to justify their behavior in the face of worldwide criticism, threats of a withdrawal of international funding or trading privileges, and the imposition of sanctions. Modern technology has fundamentally raised the importance of the role played by rhetoric in both modern tyrannies and democracies compared with the ancients. Yet because Aristotle, and Machiavelli, believed that the brutish form of tyranny would always be relatively short lived, the kingly types of actions they prescribed to transform a brutish tyranny into a longer lasting form would themselves involve more symbolism than substance, especially if the tyrant would always maintain his ability to wield power when the need arose. The modern broadcast and publication of speeches, therefore, reinforce the already rhetorical nature of the symbolic actions prescribed by Aristotle for preserving tyranny in a longer lasting form.

Reflecting upon whether it is appropriate to analyze modern tyranny from the standpoint of classical rhetoric obliges us to consider the appropriateness of applying any classical analysis in our modern, technology-ridden times. While the ancients could not have foreseen the unlimited progress of a science based on the conquest of nature and, therefore, could have rejected modern tyranny as unnatural, destructive of humanity, and even preposterous, they could not have foreseen the importance of rhetoric to modern tyranny either, and certainly not in any tyranny larger in size than a *polis*. To dismiss the application of classical rhetoric to modern tyranny, or any form of government, on these grounds would be equivalent to dismissing the importance of Aristotelian principles to the American founding simply because the United States is larger in size than a *polis*.

If modern tyranny cannot be properly understood without having access to the classical framework, then rhetoric, which plays a role in Aristotle's understanding of politics, should play an important role in our understanding of modern tyranny. Aristotle prescribes that a tyrant "should give a fine performance of the part of the kingly ruler,"[67] making his appearance to the ruled and a show of his stewardship both major factors in this performance. Since a fine performance is a successful act of persuasion, then it would not be inconsistent with Aristotle's advice for the tyrant to combine speeches with actions, depending upon his rhetorical abilities to do so. It is not unreasonable to surmise that if modern means of persuading the many had existed in Aristotle's time, then Aristotle would wish to educate both prudent statesmen and the public in the rhetoric of tyranny, among which propaganda would feature prominently.

While modern forms of tyranny have proved to be longer lasting than their ancient equivalents, individual tyrants in the twentieth century have reigned for comparable lengths of time to their earlier counterparts. After monarchs, whose average length of rule in the twentieth century was 22 years, tyrants have averaged between 11 and 21 years of rule, while leaders of emerging democracies averaged ten years' rule, and those of established democracies averaged only six years.[68] Aristotle may offer a means for the tyrant's demise. If it is possible for a tyrant to be overturned by a public who are wise in the ways of rhetoric, then drawing attention to the tyrant's rhetoric may affect the longevity of his rule. But if he succeeds in maintaining their ignorance, his kingly performance may continue indefinitely. Indeed, the tyrant's rhetoric may be needed ultimately to disguise the fact that he has not relinquished the safeguards on his power, nor that he has any intention of doing so. It seems necessary, therefore, to relate Book 5 of the *Politics* to Aristotle's account of *Rhetoric* in order to examine the rhetoric produced by tyrannical regimes. To facilitate this exercise, it would be useful to examine briefly the role of rhetoric in Aristotle's understanding of politics.

Aristotle's treatment of rhetoric appears to counteract Plato's criticisms of the art. While implicitly acknowledging that rhetoric and poetry could be dangerous rivals to philosophy, Aristotle's theoretical and practical account of rhetoric confers an intellectual status for the art of political rhetoric while remaining subordinate to political science proper. While the topic of rhetoric may be political in nature, the art itself may be practiced to inform reasoned deliberation on political matters rather than as an exercise in sophistry. By elevating the art of rhetoric to the level of a quasi-science on par with dialectics, Aristotle attempts to distinguish good rhetoric from bad and to educate both the prudent statesman and the *public* in an art of persuasion that lies above the popular sophistical variety. Indeed, Lord notes that Aristotle's lectures on rhetoric were said to have been given in the afternoon, along with others intended for the public, as distinguished from students of the school.[69]

In the *Rhetoric*, Aristotle defines rhetoric as an ability, in each case, to see the available means of persuasion.[70] Rhetoric is like no other art because it does not include technical knowledge of any particular, but rather it includes the persuasive elements in other arts. There are three elements of the means of persuasion, or proof (*pisteis*), provided through speech: the character of the speaker (*ethos*), the argument itself (*logos*), and the emotion felt by the audience (*pathos*). All speakers produce logical persuasion by means of examples (rhetorical inductions) or enthymemes (deductive, rhetorical syllogisms). Paradigms, in Aristotle's model, are examples derived from rhetorical induction. Enthymemes comprise the body of proof (*pisteis*) or persuasion, through which the *ethos*, *logos*, and *pathos* take effect.

While the formal logic of persuasion is not restricted to speech, Aristotle identifies three forms of rhetoric with regard to the content of the argument, or *logos*: deliberative – which seeks to persuade an audience towards a future course of action; epideictic – which praises and blames the present deeds of men; and forensic – which accuses or defends the past deeds of men. Aristotle considers the character of the speaker (*ethos*) and the passions of the audience (*pathos*) as important as the *logos* itself. Among the elements of rhetorical style, metaphor and amplification are also important aids of persuasion. A good rhetorician will make use of these elements of persuasion if he is to be successful. Alternatively, we may use these elements of persuasion to analyze the rhetoric of the not-so-good rhetoricians when comparing regimes according to Aristotelian theory.

Rhetorical logic differs from scientific logic by the nature of the premises upon which each proceeds. While scientific logic uses demonstrative syllogisms grounded in axioms and scientific truths, rhetoric proceeds deductively by way of rhetorical syllogisms, or enthymemes, and inductively by way of examples. A syllogism is a rational proof or valid inference drawn from true premises and based on substantive knowledge. Irrational persuasion or sophistry, on the other hand, consists of sophistical manipulation through deceptive arguments and emotional appeals.

Being the body of persuasion, or *pisteis*, enthymemes are reasonable but inconclusive arguments that appeal to commonly held opinions (*endoxa*) and appear to take the middle ground between logical syllogisms found in dialectic and sophistical arguments found in sophistry. An enthymeme is a sort of syllogism or rhetorical demonstration that aims at commonly held opinions resembling the truth. Rhetoric addresses opinions rather than truth, and opinions, being formed from both reason and passion, may be prejudiced by falsehoods. While commonly held opinions must be at least partially true, rhetorical arguments or apparent enthymemes aimed at informing false opinions of the truth may themselves be partially false.

If enthymemes are drawn from common opinions rather than scientific truths, then how does one distinguish rhetoric from mere sophistry? Arnhart believes that sophistry "consists either of arguing from what *appear* to be common opinions but are not, or of making something *appear* to follow necessarily from common opinions when it does not."[71] Furthermore, "sophistical politicians can deceive the people by appealing to their passions and prejudices in ways that betray the public interest."[72] Sophistical politicians, then, either invent common opinions or deductively mislead their audience from partially true common opinions by appealing to their passions and prejudices against the common good, presumably for their private benefit. Tyranny also looks to nothing common, unless it is for the sake of private benefit.[73] Tyrannical rhetoric, therefore, should resemble the rhetoric of sophistical politicians, being based on common opinions which are either invented or historical facts poorly understood by the citizens. The problem, for the citizen, is that their understanding of common opinions may be defective because their own direct experience with them may be limited. According to Arnhart, "The mistakes of popular judgment commonly result from the human tendency to make unqualified generalizations on the basis of limited experience, so that what is true in some cases is falsely assumed to be true in all."[74]

Given the defective nature of common opinions, we should not be surprised when a sophistical politician legitimizes his rule with unqualified generalizations drawn from historical political events of which the citizens have had no experience. Justifying one's rule is simplified when the regime's legitimizing principles lie in ancient history and there exist historiographers that are friendly to the regime. The rulers' task, for example, becomes merely one of interpreting, for their own benefit, the modern political realities of Confucian thought or ancient Buddhist teachings and practices.

The serpentine nature of Aristotle's account of rhetoric lends itself to the criticism that the *Rhetoric* is a handbook for sophistical manipulation of the passions. Yet the nature of rhetoric must conform to suit its practical role in politics, a role far removed from the dialectic of the philosopher and scientist – to persuade the many. According to Lord, "Rhetoric is the method of communication of political men. More precisely, it is the method of communication of the political elite with the political mass, 'the many'; its character is determined above all by the requirements of persuading the mass."[75]

If we recognize that rhetoric can become "an instrument of political prudence or of a political science which educates to prudence,"[76] then not only should a prudent statesman use the *Rhetoric* as a handbook on persuading the political mass, but the mass, and especially the "middling element," may also become more critically aware of the rhetoric produced by their political elite. Sound knowledge of the common opinions upon which politicians base their political rhetoric assists in identifying the invention or manipulation of common opinions against the public interest when it occurs. For a statesman to be successful in his persuasion of the political mass, on the other hand, he must have a sound knowledge of the opinions they hold in common, their widely accepted beliefs, their political culture.

Commonly held opinions (*endoxa*) and mass political culture

One definition of political culture stated previously was: "a people's predominant beliefs, attitudes, values, ideals, sentiments, and evaluations about the political system of their country and the role of the self in that system."[77] It was also previously noted that Almond's concept of a nation's political culture includes the attitudes toward the national community, the regime, and the authorities; the sense of national identity; attitudes toward the legitimacy of the regime and its various institutions; and attitudes toward the legitimacy and effectiveness of the incumbents of the various political roles.[78] These predominant beliefs and attitudes that people hold toward the legitimacy of their regime and the political incumbents in the regime, along with the people's own sense of national identity are in Aristotelian terms, *endoxa*, or commonly held opinions. The mass political culture of a nation must be rooted in commonly held opinions. Enthymemes, which are also rooted in commonly held opinions, may be formulated by the political elite of a nation in order to sway the passions of the mass political culture. In this sense, Diamond is correct when he says that elites typically have distinctive values and norms, and they often lead the way in large-scale value change.[79] The elite political culture, therefore, is as crucial to what modern comparativists call the "democratic consolidation process" as it is to the classical idea of preserving tyranny.

Yet understanding the mass political culture is also essential for the rhetoric of the elites to be successful. In formulating and demonstrating their enthymemes, the political elite cannot base their arguments on complete falsehoods, but must appeal to some sense of the truth which is incorporated into the commonly held opinions. Whether this truth is universal or culturally specific, representing the truth about a cultural trait or an historical account of political figures, for example, the important thing is that enthymemes rooted in complete falsehoods will not be successful in the long run because they will run contrary to the commonly held opinions. Lucian Pye claims that "political culture assumes that the attitudes, sentiments, and cognitions that inform and govern political behavior in any society are not just random congeries but represent coherent patterns which fit together and are mutually reinforcing."[80] Likewise, the common opinions of the many cannot be random or even purely mythical if they are to survive over the long run, but must contain some element of truth. For so long as a myth is perceived by the public, for whatever reason, as being true for the most part, then a good rhetorician will not conduct demonstrations which challenge that truth but rather should work within the bounds of what is commonly perceived to be true and construct his enthymemes accordingly. According to Arnhart, "The reputable opinions on any particular subject are usually confused and even apparently contradictory, but in most cases they manifest at least a partial grasp of the truth, and therefore any serious inquiry into moral or political subjects must start from them."[81]

Diamond believes that although elite political culture is crucial to democratic consolidation, the mass level has been neglected in recent democratic theorizing.[82] "Ultimately," says Diamond, "if democracy is to become stable and effective, the bulk of the democratic citizenry must develop a deep and resilient commitment to it."[83] While democratic theorists may ignore the mass political culture, recent experiences in Singapore and Burma would suggest that the political elite themselves take mass political culture seriously. Regardless of whatever else enters the overall makeup of the elite's political culture, be it democratic or tyrannical in nature, elites must address the common opinions which inform the mass political culture in order to earn some degree of acceptability, or legitimacy. The elite must appeal to the mass political culture with rhetoric that is directed towards satisfying the common opinions of the common people. If we can say that the idea of a mass political culture is essentially the same as the common opinions held by the people, then we may apply an Aristotelian framework to analyze the rhetoric of the political elite, as understood in the political culture language of modern comparative politics. Being open to the study of tyranny and, lacking the democratic determinism of the alternative, such an analysis should supplement and improve upon those already undertaken through the lenses of political culture and area studies.

Enthymemes of tyrannical rhetoric

In order to develop enthymemes that conform to the rhetoric being produced in tyrannical regimes, we must proceed inductively on the basis of observations concerning the intent of the ruling elite in each country and on what we know of the common opinions of the masses there. This is because, as Arnhart says, "*[A]ll* reasoning, according to Aristotle, depends *ultimately* on induction, because the first premises of deductive reasoning arise as generalizations from sense experience, and reasoning from common opinions is reasoning from the common experience of human beings."[84] If all reasoning depends on commonsense opinions,[85] then for enthymemes to be successfully argued at the national level, the political elite must address what is most commonly understood and revered as authoritative and influential to the common opinions that comprise the national political culture. Taking this into consideration when developing enthymemes upon which to focus a rhetorical study of Singapore and Burma, one finds that much of the political rhetoric produced by the political elite in these regimes is directed towards, or supports, a certain interpretation of Confucianism and Buddhism. The advantage of basing rhetorical arguments for legitimacy in the religion or spiritual beliefs of the mass is that they address what is perhaps the key element in the political culture of the mass. Because classical theory allows us to analyze these regimes according to their compatibility with the elements common to all types of regimes, including tyranny, then it may be helpful to discuss briefly the long classical tradition of utilizing religion for the purpose of securing political rule, specifically in tyrannies.

Both Aristotle and Machiavelli were well aware of the important role that religion, or spiritual beliefs, played in maintaining a tyrant's rule. In the *Metaphysics*, Aristotle notes that it is constitutionally useful to use myths about the gods for the sake of expediently persuading the masses.

> A tradition has been handed down by the ancient thinkers of very early times, and bequeathed to posterity in the form of a myth, to the effect that these heavenly bodies are gods, and that the Divine pervades the whole of nature. The rest of their tradition has been added later in a mythological form to influence the vulgar and as a constitutional and utilitarian expedient.
>
> (Aristotle, *Metaphysics*, 1074b)

In a similar vein, Cicero writes in the *Laws* and in the *Republic* that the establishment of religion is more important than the magistrates in the formation of a commonwealth, that the establishment of religion most conspicuously contributes to the stability of a State, and that promoting piety towards the gods, and maintaining a monopoly over both private and public worship, are useful to the State:[86]

> I do not follow the view of the Persian magi under whose persuasion Xerxes is said to have burned the temples of Greece because they enclosed within walls gods for whom everything ought to be open and free and whose temple and home is this entire universe. The view of the Greeks and of our own people is better, who wanted the gods to dwell in the same cities as we do in order to increase piety towards the gods. This view supplies a religion useful to states ...
>
> (Cicero, *Laws* (1999), II, 26)

> No one shall have gods to himself, either new gods or alien gods, unless recognized by the State.
>
> (Cicero, *Laws* (1928), II, viii, 19)

> The clause that follows [on augurs], however, is relevant not only to religion but also to the condition of the state: that proper private worship should not be possible without the people who are in charge of public rites. For it sustains the commonwealth to have the people always be in need of the judgment and authority of the nobility, and the organization of the priesthoods omits no type of legitimate religion.
>
> (Cicero, *Laws* (1999), II, 30)

In the *Politics*, Aristotle writes specifically on the tyrant's use of the gods:

> Further, he [the tyrant] must always show himself to be seriously attentive to the things pertaining to the gods. For men are less afraid

of being treated in some respect contrary to the law by such persons, if they consider the ruler a god-fearing sort who takes thought for the gods, and they are less ready to conspire against him as one who has the gods too as allies. In showing himself of this sort, however, he must avoid silliness.

(Aristotle, *Politics*, 1314b38–1315a2)

Likewise, in the *Discourses*, Machiavelli writes:

As the observance of the divine cult is the cause of the greatness of republics, so disdain for it is the cause of their ruin. For where the fear of God fails, it must be either that the kingdom comes to ruin or that it is sustained by the fear of a prince, which supplies the defects of religion.

(Machiavelli, *Discourses*, I, 11, 4)

Machiavelli believes that a prudent man will also make use of religion to persuade the people to accept extraordinary laws.[87] Used well, by interpreting prodigies in his favor and persuading the people of his interpretation, religion will help a prudent dictator carry out his enterprise.[88] And in the *Prince*, Machiavelli notes that while it is not necessary for a prince to have the qualities of pity, faithfulness, humanity, openness, and religion, it is indeed necessary to *appear* to have them.

[H]aving them and observing them always, they are harmful, but in appearing to have them, they are useful – so as to be full of pity, faithful, human, open, and religious, and to be so, but with one's mind constructed in such a mode that when the need not to arises, you can, and know how to, change to the contrary. . . . A prince, then, ought to take great care that nothing goes out of his mouth which is not full of the five qualities written above, and that he appears to be, when one sees and hears him, all pity, all faith, all integrity, all humanity, and all religion. Nothing is more necessary than to have this last quality.

(Machiavelli, *Prince*, XVIII: 108–109)

If Buddhism is the closest Burmese resemblance to Aristotle's idea of the gods in the passages above, then the *Tatmadaw*'s intentions certainly conform with Aristotle's, and Machiavelli's, descriptions. Likewise, in Singapore, Lee Kuan Yew's interpretation of Confucianism to support his promotion of a distinct set of Asian values also appears to be in accordance with Machiavelli's, and with Aristotle's, prescriptions. Buddhism and Confucianism, in particular, lend themselves to such an interpretation of Aristotle and Machiavelli. Buddhism, in other words, lacks one universal theological deity, or first cause. Like the Greeks and Romans who worshipped many gods, there are many manifestations, images, and forms of the Buddha. Buddhism incorporates reverence for past Buddhas, future Buddhas, and Bodhisattvas. While followers of Confucius, on the other hand, may pay homage to their ancestors, the Analects of Confucius befits a society without any notion of a transcendental God. Confucianism itself is more a philosophical moral code rather than a religion with a benevolent, caring, providential God. As such, it closely resembles the kind of natural religion that David Hume may have promoted in his *Dialogues*.[89]

U Nu's promotion of Buddhism as the state religion in Burma during his prime ministership may have been an excessive illustration of Machiavelli's advice, and his intentions may have been far removed from countering threats of conspiracy against his rule. Though U Nu himself would not be judged to have been a tyrant, his personal commitment to his faith was in the end politically harmful.[90] Whether "silliness" in Aristotle's prescription constitutes political naivety on the one hand or sham sophistry on the other, therefore, could depend on the faith of the tyrant, or at least the successful appearance of such faith in the minds of the people. The current military regime's promotion of Buddhism in Burma, however, is a byproduct of their fear of conspiracies and also reflects the seriousness with which Buddhism is held as a fundamental belief by the common people.

In the language of comparative politics, the political culture of the political elite cannot ignore the mass political culture of the Burmese people. To apply Aristotle, the enthymeme central to the *Tatmadaw* generals' rhetoric, for example, must address the common opinions manifested in Buddhism as understood and practiced in the traditions of the Burmese. Because an enthymeme is a sort of syllogism, it is also a sort of hypothesis, not conducive to rational proof but rather a relaxed form of reasoning that appeals to the passions yet must be still grounded in common opinions. In a country whose major ethnic group is Buddhist, the primary method for rhetorically demonstrating an enthymeme that appeals to the passions and the common opinions of the public is to couch one's argument in terms of Buddhist language and symbolism. The use of symbolism in politics has also proved to be a major research agenda for some modern behavioral political scientists.[91]

Enthymemes that appear to have been developed by each of the Burmese political elites, designed to support their own legitimacy, are rhetorically demonstrated in their public speeches, writings, and in the state-controlled newspapers. For the *Tatmadaw*, legitimacy largely appears to be grounded in preserving the Buddhist traditions. The enthymeme for the *Tatmadaw*, therefore, would be that their legitimacy is based on an ancient kingly duty to maintain order through the preservation of Buddhist traditions. This requires an interpretation of Buddhist traditions that is consonant with preserving order. Being based upon the commonly held opinion that past kings were charged with this duty, this enthymeme should be reflected in the rhetoric of the current regime and the inductive examples used to support the enthymeme. Challenges to the substance of this enthymeme can come by way of contrary historical evidence on this theme which questions both the truth of the common opinions upon which it is based and their supporting examples.

In addition, the main opposition political elites have their own enthymemes to oppose the *Tatmadaw*'s which reflect their own concepts of freedom and legitimacy. For Aung San Suu Kyi, freedom and legitimacy are conceptualized within the framework of Buddhist traditions while under military rule. By promoting her own enthymeme – an interpretation of Buddhist traditions that is consonant with democratic government and democratic freedoms – in opposition to the *Tatmadaw*'s, Suu Kyi opposes the truth of the common opinions upon which the *Tatmadaw*'s enthymeme is based. The truth of her own enthymeme may be weighed up against the *Tatmadaw*'s, both on the basis of historical evidence and by having access to Aung San's speeches. For Aung San, freedom meant Burma's national independence, and the legitimacy of his actions was grounded in achieving that purpose.

In comparison with the *Tatmadaw*'s rudimentary rhetoric, Lee Kuan Yew's Asian values rhetoric was sophisticated and seductive. Because the major ethnic group in Singapore is Chinese, Lee chose to demonstrate his enthymeme rhetorically by grounding his Asian values rhetoric within the context of Confucian thought. Lee's enthymeme, therefore, is that his legitimacy is based on a Confucian tradition to preserve order. His arguments for Asian values are the inductive examples used to support his legitimacy and the means with which to preserve that order and so stave off the civil and moral decay of Western liberalism. Because much of the Asian values rhetoric arose in response to Western accusations of human rights violations practiced by some Asian governments, Lee's enthymeme may be challenged by assessing the merits of the Asian values rhetoric, especially as it concerns the issue of human rights. It is also possible to challenge the truth of the common opinions upon which Lee's enthymeme is based, that is, whether Confucian thought promotes the kind of order and the Asian values that Lee claims it does.

To challenge the examples used to support these enthymemes and, by implication, the truth of the common opinions upon which they are based, it is possible to illustrate how, in their mostly deliberative and epideictic rhetorical forms, each of the elites have either couched their arguments in Confucian or Buddhist language and symbolism or have appealed directly to Buddhist or Confucian traditions in order to demonstrate their enthymemes rhetorically. While assuming that there is *some truth* in both Buddhism and Confucianism for their arguments, we may challenge the truth of the common opinions upon which their enthymemes are based and the examples used to support their enthymemes by providing evidence which assesses the merits and the "truths" of both. Where it is particularly significant, we may also take note of the character of the speaker and audience, the emotions the speaker is attempting to arouse, and the delivery, style, and arrangement of the rhetorical demonstration. Finally, we may demonstrate how the rhetoric in each case conforms to Aristotle's prescriptions for preserving tyrannies in the *Politics*. It would be prudent to begin our case studies by providing an account of the tyrannical-like behavior of the political elite in each country and determine whether their behavior conforms to Aristotle's descriptions and prescriptions for preserving their kind of rule. Each case study should include an examination of justice and stability in the regime, along with the prospects for change.

Conclusion

Aristotle's analysis of the preservation of tyranny provides major implications for the political scientist interested in classifying the wide variety of modern regimes and transforming bad regimes into more moderate ones. Interpreting political elite behavior in terms of a fine performance of the part of a kingly ruler allows us to infer political intentions to their speeches and actions. Analyzing the rhetoric of tyranny is useful to the political scientist, the political mass, and the political elite in opposition. Central to this rhetoric is an enthymeme that appeals to a key element in the political culture of the mass and the common opinions of the many – religion or spiritual beliefs.

While the advent of modern technology may facilitate the extension of a tyrant's rule, tyrants cannot preserve their tyranny for long if they do not appear just. To appear just, they must employ a rhetoric that is rooted in the common opinions about justice. But in doing so, they have invoked standards of rhetorical persuasion that can be turned against them. If they appeal to Confucian or Buddhist rhetoric, their opponents may answer by developing their own interpretations of Confucianism or Buddhism.

While Aristotle offers practical prescriptions for moderating tyrannical rule and improving the justice in a regime, analyzing the rhetoric of tyranny makes a transformation in the regime more possible. Such a transformation may not bring about another Western liberal democracy, but nevertheless, the consequence of improving justice in a regime lacking in justice must be an improvement over the alternative. In classifying a regime, recognizing the alternative for what it is and not for what we would like it to become, must be our first step along this path.

4 Tyranny in Singapore?

Of the two modes of preservation discussed by Aristotle, Singapore may offer an example of the more subtle mode whereby the ruler appears to rule in a kingly fashion over willing persons. Singapore is an appealing case for such a study because Aristotle would not have experienced any regime greater in size than a *polis*, or city-state. In order to place Singapore within the context of Aristotle's classification of regimes in the *Politics*, we must briefly examine the rule of Lee Kuan Yew before determining whether he conformed to Aristotle's advice on preserving this kind of regime.

Because political rhetoric plays some part in preserving any regime, Lee's rhetoric of Asian values, supported by his rhetoric of survival, will be analyzed in accordance with Aristotle's discussion of enthymemes in the *Rhetoric*, keeping in mind the kind of regime which they help to preserve in the *Politics*. And because Aristotle's understanding of the preservation of stability and justice in a regime differs from that discussed in modern political science, we must also examine the stability and justice found in the Singapore regime from Aristotle's point of view before assessing the chances of "preserving" such a regime in the future.

Political awakening in Singapore and the rise of Lee Kuan Yew

Singapore returned to civilian rule following World War II as a Crown Colony under a British governor in April 1946. Yet the first elections to the Singapore Legislative Council were not held until March 1948. They, along with the elections held in 1951, attracted little public interest and only British subjects were allowed to vote. While the British had tried to encourage Singaporeans to participate in politics, their interest only grew during the 1950s due primarily to the poor social and economic conditions, the influence of communism through the Malayan Communist Party, and the public's awareness of the growing anticolonial movement in Asia and Africa. Indeed, the minds of the young population – composed primarily of ethnic Chinese, Indians, and Malays – were to be influenced, to a large degree, by the current of world events.

Indonesia's proclamation of independence from the Dutch in 1945 was soon followed by Great Britain's granting of independence to India in 1947. Mao Zedong's defeat of the Kuomintang in 1949 and the Chinese army's successes in Korea further encouraged the political attitudes of the Chinese youth in Singapore. Given the poor educational and civil service prospects of the Chinese youth (English was the only official language recognized in Singapore at that time), the Chinese High School and Nanyang Girls' High School became centers for the promotion of communist activities among the students while trade unions increasingly voiced the opinions of the Malayan Communist Party. Trade union and student-organized boycotts, protests, strikes, and riots were a common feature of life in Singapore in the 1950s. Singapore's political system in the 1950s allowed for various social groups, organized around ethnic and economic identifications, to bargain freely and negotiate with the government on matters of policy.

Lee Kuan Yew gained prominence at the head of a small group of British-educated intellectuals who formed the People's Action Party (PAP) in 1954. Having studied law at Cambridge University, Lee had become a legal advisor to several trade unions in Singapore that were sympathetic to communism and anticolonialism. While securing an end to colonial rule was publicly stated as the PAP's main objective, it was clear that given the economic circumstances and the political climate, a popular political platform would require the forging of an alliance with the Chinese public and the communist trade unions. Despite the presence of communist members in its committee and within its rank and file, Lee maintained that the PAP's objective was to create a non-communist independent state.

Recommendations of the Rendel Constitutional Commission in 1954 led to the creation of a Legislative Assembly in the same year, consisting of 32 members, 25 of whom would be elected by the British subjects of Singapore (Singapore remained a colony of Great Britain). The remaining seven members would comprise three British officials and four non-officials appointed by the governor. While the three British officials would be in charge of finance, the judiciary, and information services, the governor still exercised control over foreign relations, defense, internal security, and the public service while maintaining a veto over all legislation. Elections for the Legislative Assembly were held in 1955 and the PAP won three of the four seats it contested. A larger voter turnout, coupled with a poor performance by the conservative parties, indicated that the people were ready for change.

Internal power struggles among the procommunists and the moderates inside the PAP subsided for the time being, in 1957, when the government arrested 35 procommunists; these included members of PAP's central executive committee. The PAP went on to perform well during the City Council elections held later that year. In 1958, the British government agreed to the writing of a constitution for a State of Singapore. Although the constitution granted powers of self-government to Singapore, the British would maintain control of foreign affairs and defense, while internal security would fall under an Internal Security Council whose ultimate authority would be based in Malaya. Elections were held in 1959 and, following changes to Singapore's citizenship laws that now allowed China-born citizens to vote, along with the introduction of compulsory voting, the PAP won 43 of the 51 seats in the Legislative Assembly.

Lee Kuan Yew became the first prime minister of the city-state of Singapore, his party having been supported on the promise of working towards full independence from Great Britain by a mass following of workers and Chinese students, gained through a tactical alliance with radical left-wing forces, including the Communists. Upon coming to power, Lee distanced himself from his radical supporters and began to seek a new base for his legitimacy by emphasizing the promise of economic performance.[1] Because this required an efficient administration to undertake economic policies, Lee now forged an alliance with the civil service, whose technocrats saw the previous system of political bargaining as irrelevant and a potentially destabilizing influence upon economic growth.[2]

The PAP still believed that independence from Great Britain could only be made possible through Singapore's reunification with Malaya, the latter having gained its independence in 1957. Yet the government of Malaya had resisted the idea of merger with Singapore because of the possible disturbance of the racial balance in Malaya that would follow from a sizable influx of Chinese citizens. Malaya, however, which had also been fighting a communist insurgency led chiefly by the Malayan Communist Party backed by the People's Republic of China, also feared a possible Cuban-style communist takeover of Singapore when the PAP lost the Hong Lim by-election in April 1961, triggering a wide rift between the party's moderates and procommunists. The procommunists struggled to take control of the party and the government in the months that followed. Another by-election loss and the defeat of a vote of no confidence left the PAP with a majority of only one in the Legislative Assembly and led to the expulsion of many assemblymen, political and parliamentary secretaries; the suspension of 14 PAP branches; and the defection of 35 of the 51 PAP branch committees and 19 of the 23 paid organizing secretaries. These PAP dissidents formed the *Barisan Sosialis* (Socialist Front) in August 1961.

The Malayan government had swung to support a merger with Singapore on the proviso that the Muslim British territories of Sabah, Sarawak, and Brunei were included to balance the new racial mix in the proposed Malaysian Federation. While the British government agreed to the terms proposed for federation, the Communists opposed such a move because of the openly anticommunist stance of the government in Kuala Lumpur. But a referendum held in Singapore, in September 1962, showed overwhelming support for the merger on the terms proposed by the PAP. The *Barisan Sosialis* was thus forced to garner foreign support for its antimerger movement from left-wing political groups in Malaya, Borneo, and Brunei, as well as from the Partai Kommunis Indonesia (PKI).

In late 1962, the Indonesian government, influenced as much by the sheer size of the PKI's membership as President Sukarno's anti-British sentiments and territorial ambitions, began openly to oppose the formation of Malaysia and discreetly support a revolt in Borneo. In January 1963, Indonesia launched its confrontation policy (*konfrontasi*) with Malaysia. The leaders of Malaya, Singapore, Sabah, and Sarawak met in London in July to sign the Malaysia Agreement following Brunei's decision not to join the new Federation, and 16 September 1963 was set as the date for Malaysia's inauguration. Lee Kuan Yew, meanwhile, declared Singapore's de facto independence on 31 August 1963 and stated that his government looked upon themselves "as trustees for the Central Government of Malaysia" for the next 15 days until the inauguration on 16 September.[3] But on 14 September, President Sukarno rejected the findings of the United Nations survey mission which reported that the majority of the people in Sabah and Sarawak territories supported joining the Federation. Indonesia severed relations with Malaysia, increased its harassment and armed raids into these territories, and launched insurgency and sabotage operations in Sarawak and Singapore. While the *konfrontasi* was eventually suppressed by British, Australian, New Zealand, Malayan, and Singaporean forces, it did not officially end until President Sukarno was ousted by General Suharto in Jakarta in August 1966.

Singapore had joined the Malaysian Federation on the assurances that the Chinese in Singapore would not threaten Malay rule on the Peninsula. The people of the Malayan Peninsula had traditionally enjoyed more conservative social, economic, and political lives than their island neighbors. Sultans still ruled as the heads of most states and Peninsula Malays enjoyed special privileges. The Malaysian Peninsula was ruled by a coalition of the United Malays National Organization (UMNO), the Malayan Chinese Association (MCA), and the Malayan Indian Congress (MIC). Tensions between the Peninsula and Singapore had already been raised at the time Lee declared Singapore's de facto independence. They increased when, in 1963 and 1964, Lee questioned and criticized the Malaysian budget in Parliament, the lack of progress made towards the creation of a common trading market, the closure of the Bank of China in Singapore, the revenues demanded from Singapore to finance the Federation's defense of the *konfrontasi*, and the developmental loans set for Sabah and Sarawak.

UMNO, furthermore, took exception to the fact that Singaporean Malays did not vote for their candidate in Singapore's general election held in late 1963 and that the PAP ran a token number of candidates in the Malaysian general election of April 1964. Winning an additional seat, the PAP became the leading opposition party in the Malaysian federal legislature and soon announced its intentions to open branches across the

Malay Peninsula. UMNO supporters demanded that Singapore's Malays be given special privileges, and both sides accused each other of unfairness, discrimination, and communalism. Racial rioting broke out in Singapore in July and September 1964, causing many deaths and injuries. The PAP's decision in May 1965 to form an alliance (the Malaysian Solidarity Convention) of opposition parties on the Peninsula and in Sarawak with the aim of creating a multiracial, non-communal Malaysia intensified UMNO's resentment of the PAP to the point where UMNO appeared openly to support the *Barisan Sosialis* candidate running against the PAP in a Singapore by-election held in July.

Finally, and perhaps inevitably, on 6 August 1965 the prime minister of the Federation of Malaysia, Tunku Abdul Rahman, told Lee Kuan Yew that Singapore would have to leave Malaysia immediately. On 9 August 1965, in the absence of all the PAP representatives, the Malaysian legislature unanimously passed a bill of separation and Lee Kuan Yew declared Singapore to be a sovereign, democratic, and independent state. Singapore was now totally independent from both Malaysia and Great Britain. The Singapore government announced on 11 August 1965 that Singapore was to become a republic, the Legislative Assembly would become Parliament, the prime minister would be the head of government, and that a president elected by Parliament would be the head of state.

The rhetoric of survival

Lee's rhetoric of survival leading up to and following independence reflected the sense of vulnerability and isolation of the new city-state. His claim to power was based largely on his ability to convey a shared perception of an external threat to most Singaporeans. And these threats were indeed real. From the early 1950s through much of the 1960s, the public of Singapore had experienced a turbulent political awakening with events that included a communist insurgency backed by the Malaya Communist Party, a confrontation with a much larger Muslim neighbor in Indonesia, and racial rioting inspired by its Muslim neighbor on the Peninsula. As late as 1963, the British government was concerned that if Singapore had become an independent state, the violence on the island could not have been contained and that bringing Sabah and Sarawak into the Federation could help to somewhat balance the racial tension. Nevertheless, the PAP leadership gained enduring political capital from pitching the idea that it was Singapore's sole defense against both external threats and, when it clamped down on communist insurgency and ethnic rioting, domestic violence as well.

Whereas these security concerns dominated Singapore's early years, many of the external threats were no longer real by the early to mid-1970s. Direct confrontation with guerrillas of the Malayan Communist Party was less likely after 1959 when they had crossed into southern Thailand, although some underground activity caused concern in the early to mid-1970s. Additionally, the anticommunist Suharto government ended *konfrontasi* in 1966 and destroyed the PKI. The creation of the Association of Southeast Asian Nations (ASEAN) in 1967 helped further to reduce tensions among Singapore, Indonesia, and Malaysia. The threat of domestic violence had also become less likely over time, due primarily to the government's swift response to sit-ins, strikes, or threats by students and trade unions. The government expelled "communist" students from the Chinese-Nanyang University and Ngee Ann College when they protested changes to the Chinese curriculum; trade unions were deregistered when they went on strike to oppose the National Service Bill in 1967; and although racial rioting occurred again in 1969, it too was dealt with swiftly by the government.

However, the rhetoric of survival that was most common, and most appropriate, to Singapore's early struggles continues to be employed by the PAP today. Yet it has become increasingly difficult to justify the imprisonment of dissidents on the grounds of communist insurgency, communalism, or inciting racial conflict. Singapore's external threats today come by way of China's territorial claims which, though remote, if enforced could possibly lead to a blockade of the Straits of Malacca; and from Islamic terrorists seeking revenge on Western and Israeli embassies, as well as Singaporean targets and American naval assets. But are these relatively recent threats reason enough to justify the harsh laws and regulations that have remained a hallmark of life for the average citizen of Singapore for so long?

Lee Kuan Yew's rule over Singapore

At first glance, Lee's conduct in ruling Singapore may reflect many of the attributes associated with Aristotle's first mode of preserving tyranny in its common or brutish form. In the *Politics*, Aristotle notes that expulsion from town and resettlement of the mass is common to both tyranny as well as oligarchy.[4] Following independence, the PAP had sought to project the appearance of a benevolent, paternalistic government by establishing political order with an efficient administration and by securing the welfare of its citizens. Faced with housing shortages and a pressing need to acquire land for the development of its businesses and industries, Lee's government set out to rehouse much of the city-state's population.

Singapore had traditionally remained a port through which goods could be shipped, with little value-added contribution coming from local industry. Self-sufficiency required that Singapore should refrain from buying foreign goods, save foreign currency, and develop a strong manufacturing base for the production of exports. However, while the government's seizure of land may have occurred partly for development purposes and partly to clean up the slum housing areas in the city, Lee has consistently claimed that Singapore could not survive unless all the major ethnic groups – the Chinese, Malays, and Indians – thought of themselves as Singaporeans. Forcing them to live together was, for Lee, a policy of survival. Scott, on the other hand, believes that the real purpose of this feat was one of political and social engineering.[5]

Aristotle says that if justice is whatever the few decide, it is indistinguishable from tyranny.[6] Lee's principal opposition, the *Barisan Sosialis*, crumbled during the years following independence, and any populist rivals along with them. From that time on, the ruling elite set the goals to be achieved and the means by which they might be pursued, thereby removing any freedom of choice for the citizens and any open negotiation between competing groups in economic, social, and political arenas.[7] Though there were regular elections, honestly reported, and formal electoral rules still allowed most parties to operate (except the Communist Party), the seizure of the social and political agenda by the ruling elite meant that citizens were effectively removed from participating in politics. This state of affairs has continued to the present, with elections merely playing the role of a formal inconvenience in the oligarchic rule of the technocratic elite. Perhaps it also could be an example of the principle that elections per se do not prevent tyranny.

Aristotle notes that a tyrant should take care not to allow social groups to form or meetings to take place outside the ambit of his rule, for these give rise to high thoughts and trust.[8] Additionally, nothing should be said or done which escapes the notice of the tyrant, and this is maintained through operating spies and controlling knowledge.[9] In Singapore, the government has embraced all populist and ethnic groups, as well as the trade union movement, within its own bureaucratic structure. Operating spies and controlling knowledge exist institutionally, to some degree, in both the Singapore civil service and in the government's strict censorship policy.

Although the PAP continues to represent the government in elections, effective power resides in the institutional bureaucracy. The PAP merely represents an administrative body which provides a channel for dispensing government patronage.[10] Moreover, the Singapore army has effectively been integrated into the civil service, and compulsory military service provides an effective means of transmitting the objectives and values of the political leadership to the younger generation of Singaporeans. The dividing lines between the military, the civilian bureaucracy, and the political elite have therefore been erased.[11] Furthermore, the trade union movement, brought together under the umbrella of the National Trades Union Congress, has been closely affiliated with the PAP since its inception and is organized by a technocratic elite ruled by the government.[12]

Because the civil service is accepted by the people as the most suitable group to implement the government's growth policies, the legitimacy of the government has continued to remain strong, although much of this base support could be attributed to Lee himself. Not unlike Ne Win in Burma, Lee's "retirement" into the position of senior minister in 1991, although making way for a well-trained civil servant in Goh Chok Tong (his defense minister), did not mean that he forfeited his dominant role in guiding government policy – he kept his old prime minister's office under Goh's instructions. Lee still exercises enormous influence in his new position as "Minister Mentor" under the prime ministership of his eldest son, Lee Hsien Loong, who has also retained the finance portfolio. This arrangement should ensure that Lee's legacy will continue to be articulated by the ruling technocrats for years to come.

It could also be argued that the political views and actions of Singapore's ruling elite, and more precisely, those of the country's founding father, Lee Kuan Yew, can be interpreted through an application of Machiavellian principles.[13] Lee's words and actions, particularly in his early years, certainly lend themselves to this interpretation. Indeed, Lee remarks:

> Between being loved and being feared, I have always believed Machiavelli was right. If nobody is afraid of me, I'm meaningless. When I say something, to make it easier for me to govern, I have to be taken very seriously. So when I say "please don't do that", you do it, I have to punish you because I was not joking when I said that. And when I punish, it's to punish publicly. And people will know the next time, if you want to do that when he said "no, don't do it", you must be prepared for a brutal encounter. . . . What the crowd thinks of me from time to time, I consider totally irrelevant . . .
>
> (Lee Kuan Yew in Han Fook Kwang *et al.* (1998): 229)

Lee, the founder and lawgiver of a republic, has ensured that a people well ordered "will be stable, prudent, and grateful."[14] His control over all aspects of Singapore's early development, as evidenced in his *Memoirs*,[15] mirrors Machiavelli's observation for ordering a new republic:

> [I]t never or rarely happens that any republic or kingdom is ordered well from the beginning or reformed altogether anew outside its old orders unless it is ordered by one individual. Indeed it is necessary that one alone give the mode and that any such ordering depend on his mind. So a prudent orderer of a republic . . . should contrive to have authority alone.
>
> (Machiavelli, *Discourses*, I, 9)

Gordon argues that Machiavellian principles affect the regime's real-life practices in the everyday management of Singapore. Having assumed office democratically, Lee set about destroying his adversaries and establishing a tight regime of control and violence under the rationale, first, of battling an alleged communist conspiracy, and later in defense of Singapore's economic advancement and independence. In 1963, for example, before the elections, Lee used his power under the British Internal Security Act to imprison 100 key members of the *Barisan Sosialis* party, later releasing them and co-opting them into administrative positions with no real political power.[16]

Machiavelli notes that the ruin of cities arises through not varying the orders of republics with the times.[17] Because it would not, in modern times, be considered proper democratic practice to round up and imprison one's opposition before an election, Lee's regime has resorted to the liberal use of defamation suits to intimidate opponents and secure electoral victories. Operating within the rule of law, and yet tilting the balance of justice towards those who can afford the legal costs involved in contesting a defamation suit, Lee has managed to disguise a regime which rules by brute force with one that rules by subtle, often overt, intimidation, where, according to Gordon, allusions and rumors replace actual threats and bloodshed.

Winborne, on the other hand, prefers to analyze Lee's regime by classifying Singapore as a case of Hobbesian strong liberalism, where obedience to the sovereign produces peace and liberty.[18] Winborne offers many good examples to substantiate his Hobbesian "authoritarian" examination of the highly regulated life in Singapore. Indeed, Lee has certainly acted like a sovereign, and because of this kingly performance, Winborne's examples could also support an Aristotelian interpretation of a tyrant moderating his behavior to extend his rule. It seems that Aristotle could fully account for the examples that Winborne attributes to "Hobbesian liberalism."

Returning to Aristotle's schema, it would be difficult to argue that Lee has been a warmonger, or that he has attempted to make the ruled poor, both of which are attributes of the common brutish form of tyranny.[19] One could, on the other hand, argue that Singaporeans have modest thoughts, that they still somewhat distrust each other (this even after being forced by the government to leave their Chinese, Muslim, and Indian enclaves to live in integrated high-rise housing complexes), that they distrust outsiders, and that they have an incapacity for independent activity in the sense that all economic, military, and political activity is assumed by the state bureaucracy.[20] These are the three defining principles, according to Aristotle, to which the wishes of tyrants may be reduced.[21] Nevertheless, because Lee's regime is lacking in some of the attributes described of common brutish tyranny, and especially since he has made the average Singaporean citizen relatively wealthy and not poor, we should turn to Aristotle for a commentary on the second mode of preservation for this could seem to be more appropriate for characterizing the case of Singapore.

Aristotle on the preservation of Lee's regime

Aristotle's second kind of tyranny, the less common and brutish form, was based on law and could either take the form of an hereditary kingship ruling over willing subjects or an elective dictatorship ruling over willing persons. Of these two forms, from an Aristotelian perspective, the latter seems more appropriate in the context of Singapore. In order to preserve such a rule, Aristotle prescribes a number of measures which, if adopted, combine to present the tyrant as if he were a benevolent, and legitimate, kingly ruler over willing subjects.

Ever since his rise to the prime ministership, Lee has sought to safeguard his power while giving a splendid performance of the part of the kingly ruler of Singapore.[22] His civil service technocrats have ensured that the common funds are accountable and Lee himself has appeared as the chief bureaucrat, Chief Executive Officer, or what Aristotle calls the manager of the city.[23] Lee, the "guardian and treasurer of common funds," has heralded the merits of Singapore's welfare system, making a "show of collecting taxes and public services for the sake of management of the city," as well as his extravagant spending to equip the most modern defense force in Southeast Asia with "something ... for use in times of war."[24] Lee would also appear to be following Simonides' advice, ensuring that his entire city is well armed, making himself appear more formidable to his enemies,[25] both internally and abroad, while he has often used the external threat argument to secure his legitimacy. He is concerned, internally, with "military virtue" and indeed sees the military as an integral part in educating the youth in Singaporean values.[26] His own reputation as father of the country has been built upon a perception of himself as the defender of Singapore against any external threat.[27]

Like Ho Chi Minh, Lee's image among the people has always been one of a paternal nature.[28] Xenophon's Cyrus, whose status as king, tyrant, or sui generis is debatable,[29] was also said to have been called "father" by his people.[30] Lee's appearance has always been "dignified," though often arrogant, while many foreign dignitaries, journalists, and his own citizens have described feeling a sense of awe, rather than fear, in his presence.[31] Though this is reflective of his success, the difference between fear and awe may only be slim when the fear of subtle intimidation is balanced by the economic prosperity enjoyed by Singaporeans.

Aristotle notes that many tyrannies have perished on account of the arrogant behavior of their women.[32] In Singapore, by contrast, it was and perhaps still is deemed a great honor among women, and among the people, to be chosen to represent the national airline. The government held its own graduation ceremony for flight attendants, with a congratulatory speech and certificates awarded by the Deputy Prime Minister himself. Aristotle also claims that the ruler must appear moderate in matters connected with bodily gratifications because "it is the drunkards, not the sober, the drowsy, not the wakeful, who are readily attacked and held in contempt."[33] While Lee himself has always avoided the appearance of immoderation in this respect, the government has enacted harsh laws which discourage drunken and generally immoderate behavior in public. The Singapore civil service, furthermore, sees to it that immoderate behavior is for the most part discouraged altogether.

Aristotle says that the kingly ruler "must furnish and adorn the city as if he were a steward rather than a tyrant."[34] And in the *Hiero*, Simonides is told that "the tyrant is also compelled to be a lover of the city; for without the city he would not be able either to preserve himself or to be happy."[35] Simonides advises Hiero to furnish the whole city with walls, temples, colonnades, market places, and harbors.[36] Singapore is perhaps the cleanest and most efficiently run city in the world. Lee's government has furnished the city with an elaborate transportation system, clean parks and streets, modern high-rise buildings, perhaps the best airport and some of the best harbor facilities in the world, and of course, a national museum with an entire wing devoted to Lee's struggle for independence and his great achievements thereafter.

Giving a fine performance of kingly rule also obliges the ruler personally to "honor those [citizens] who have proven themselves good in some respect."[37] Lee and his government have publicly honored, often personally during award ceremonies, the achievements of model Singaporean citizens. Aristotle further notes that

> [One] precaution common to every sort of monarchy is to make no single person great but [where necessary to elevate] several persons, as they will watch one another. Or if it is necessary after all to make one person great, it should at least not be someone who is of a bold character; such a character is most ready for the attack in connection with every sort of action. And if it is held necessary to remove someone from power, this should be done gradually – his functions should not all be taken away at once.
>
> (Aristotle, *Politics*, 1315a7–13)

When persons are elevated in the Singapore government, they remain tied to the overarching structure of the civil service bureaucracy and the actions of those elevated are always under the close scrutiny of the state bureaucracy. Cho Oon Khong claims that "those of Lee's younger successors who have sought to emulate their master's tough impatient style – without any record of achievement to back them up – have won no popular regard."[38] Promotion in the Singapore government and civil service is, furthermore, based upon the principle of meritocracy, whereby only the best or most senior are said to be appointed or promoted. While the meritocracy principle Lee enunciates is rooted in Confucian teachings and practices, in Lee's case it also incorporates a built-in bias towards those in positions of power replacing themselves. While the PAP take pride in their principles of meritocracy, often those technocrats in close proximity to the elite have risen faster and further through the rank and file of the bureaucracy, and lawsuits have been instigated against newspapers that inferred nepotism in this regard.

In contrast to Lee, the former long-standing Prime Minister of Malaysia, Dr Mahathir, could have prospered by taking heed of Aristotle's advice in late 1998. At that time, Dr Mahathir used Malaysia's Internal Security Act to arrest and detain his outspoken Deputy Prime Minister, Anwar Ibrahim. He was later charged with corruption and sodomy. Anwar had regularly criticized the Malaysian government's economic policies; their lack of transparency and openness, especially to foreigners; their unwillingness to privatize key industries; corruption in the government; and on occasion, the concept of Asian values:

> It is altogether shameful, if ingenious, to cite Asian values as an excuse
> for autocratic practices and denial of basic rights and civil liberties.
> (Anwar Ibrahim (1996): 28)

While not necessarily being indicative of support for any universal liberal democratic values, Anwar's stance illustrates that opposition to the political use of Asian values existed even among Lee's closest rhetorical allies. Dr Mahathir was condemned by the West over Anwar's arrest, his actions arousing mass domestic support for Anwar. The charges laid against Anwar included those "involving bodily abuse" and "taking sexual advantage of youth."[39] Aristotle says that a tyrant "must not engage in such things, or else be seen to administer punishments in a paternal spirit rather than in order to slight."[40] Public opposition to Mahathir's actions arose primarily because of the perception that Anwar's punishment was clearly not administered in a paternal spirit, but rather in order to slight him and the faction he represented. Lee's political judgment would not have allowed a threat such as Anwar to rise through the rank and file of the bureaucracy to begin with, let alone to face charges of sexual abuse aimed at slighting his character.

The relatively high standard of living among most Singaporeans has, in the past, reduced the necessity for Lee's government to be watchful of the perception of the preservation of justice, among the poor and the well off, on account of his rule.[41] Lee appears to most Singaporeans "not as a tyrannical sort but as a manager and a kingly sort, not as an appropriator but as a steward."[42] "As a result of these things ... his rule [has been] longer lasting" than any of his regional contemporaries.[43] Aristotle's second mode of preservation could, therefore, seem to be most applicable for describing the actions which comprise the fine performance of Lee Kuan Yew's rule over the city-state of Singapore. Lee's rule could also appear to vindicate Aristotle's advice favoring the second mode of preservation as being better for the ruler and for his people. What we must now consider in more detail is the verbal and written rhetoric which accompanies Lee's fine performance, for these are common features of modern despotism.

5 The rhetoric of Asian values

The greatest proponent of Asian values, and indeed the architect of a debate that influenced political discourse in the 1980s and 1990s was Singapore's Lee Kuan Yew. His main arguments will be drawn from his autobiography and from a series of interviews undertaken with Western scholars in order to explore the tentative connections he attempted to establish between his idea of Asian values and Confucianism. Because the concept of Asian values allowed some Asian politicians to defend themselves from Western accusations of human rights violations, it is necessary to assess the merits of Lee's Asian values rhetoric and explore how this rhetoric, along with the Bangkok Declaration of Human Rights, attempted to interpret, and circumvent, the Universal Declaration of Human Rights. The rhetoric of Asian values was supported by, and was a development of, an interpretation of history that conformed with the PAP's rhetoric of survival. The creation of the idea of shared Asian values in the 1980s and 1990s represented an invention of the *endoxa*, or common opinions, for political expedience. Throughout their tenure, it may also be possible to illustrate how the PAP have selectively interpreted and manipulated the *endoxa* on Singaporean history for rhetorical effectiveness.

By examining the development and content of Lee's Asian values rhetoric, our aim should be to question the validity of its implicit enthymeme, that his legitimacy is based on a Confucian tradition to preserve order. By offering alternative interpretations, or enthymemes, to the Asian values arguments proposed by Lee since the early 1980s, and the more general survival rhetoric of the regime, supported by inductive observations concerning the content of this rhetoric and the truth of the common opinions upon which his enthymeme is based, Lee's rhetoric may be shown to be sophistry, as befits the rhetoric of despotism.

Asian values – inventing the *endoxa*

Lee Kuan Yew's "Asian values" was the end result of a search for some national survival ideology for Singapore.[1] Having been careful to steer away from radical populist support, an ideology that emphasized discipline and organization was lacking in the technocratic bureaucracy of the Singapore government. The immediate need for this new message of survival arose both as a result of a 1981 by-election loss in the electoral district of Anson and Lee's decision to switch from Chinese to English as the primary medium of instruction in Singapore's schools and universities. In 1981 the PAP nominated CV Devan Nair to the post of president. In order to accept the nomination, Nair resigned his seat in Parliament and a by-election was held at which J. B. (Ben) Jeyaretnam of the Worker's Party defeated the PAP's candidate, Pang Kim Hin, by 653 votes. The Anson by-election loss not only ended the PAP's 13-year monopoly of Parliament, it sent a message within the government that it was under threat of losing power – a threat it took seriously in the following 1984 general election where the PAP's share of the total votes cast fell to 62.9 percent, and two opposition candidates were returned.[2] The very idea of a successful opposition to the PAP was interpreted by the government as a crisis of survival, indicative of a decay in the nation's *asabiyya*, or group solidarity, and the corruption of the nation by the tainted ego of the collective youth.[3]

The PAP dismisses support for the opposition as irrational, it contends that the opposition is not worthy, and that all votes for the opposition are protest votes based on emotions rather than reason.[4] Because the generation of Singaporeans born after 1957 were too young to appreciate the sacrifices of nation building, their critical posture against the authorities meant that they had succumbed to the harmful ideas of Western-style democracy and individualism.[5] Lee's remarks in 1984 are revealing.

[F]rom our perilous years in the 1950s and 60s ... Singaporeans ... were educated in a harsh political school [and] were wise to the ways of an irresponsible opposition, [but now there exists] a younger generation of Singaporeans who, not having experienced the conflicts in this House in the '50s and '60s, harbour myths about the role of the opposition [and] have no idea how destructive opposition can be.

(Lee Kuan Yew in Loh Kah Seng (1998): 4, n.2)

In 1982, the Singapore government moved to equate national survival with national cultural identity by announcing that Confucian Ethics would be offered as an optional subject for moral education in secondary schools. In 1983, the government established an Institute of East Asian Philosophies within the University of Singapore to define Confucianism for the citizens of Singapore. Englehart believes that since there were few Singaporeans who knew much about Confucius, and since there is scarce evidence of Confucianism in Singapore prior to the government's campaign, the PAP had to claim that Singaporeans were implicit Confucians who practiced Confucian principles without recognizing them as such.[6] In promoting a sense of national community by appealing to Confucian

ethics, Lee could reacquaint the predominantly ethnic Chinese popu-
lation with their culture and, at the same time, proudly boast the achieve-
ments of Singapore's economic miracle as being built upon the so-called
Asian values – values which, it was argued, bore a close resemblance to
Weber's Protestant work ethic.[7] The Institute later refocused on studying
Confucian values and the so-called East Asian economic miracle.[8]

In 1991, the Singapore government issued a set of five Shared Values as
a result of its national ideology debate – values which were necessarily
selective and interpreted in such a way to support the government's survival ideology: Nation before community and society above self; The
family as the basic unit of society; Respect and community support for the
individual; Consensus instead of conflict; and Racial and religious
harmony.[9] The idea of shared values helped not only to bridge the gap
between Singapore's rulers and its people, but it also helped to mask the
suspicion among Singapore's Malay and Indian ethnic minorities over the
government's creation of an Asian identity based on Confucian philosophy. If the values were shared, then any ethnic or religious opposition to
the government's policies could be interpreted as illegitimate.[10] Ethnic or
religious groups who wished to oppose a government policy, such as the
forced relocation of Christian churches from particular urban settings,
had to argue their case in line with the national ideology of shared
values.[11] In a proudly secular state, it seems, religious groups are forced to
adopt the political ideology of the PAP in order to survive.

It may be of little consequence to determine whether or not Lee took
these Asian values seriously himself, but what would be far more important, according to Aristotle, is that he showed himself to be seriously attentive to them since the political motive behind showing respect for
Confucianism was akin to Aristotle's advice to show a prudent respect for
the gods. While Confucianism is not a religion as such, and Lee would not
have thought of it as a religion, it is commonly regarded as a philosophy
of how society, government, and the family should be structured and function. The Singapore government accordingly spent a great deal of effort
since the 1980s proselytizing to their regional Asian friends, and to the
Western world, both on the merits of Confucian values for Singapore and
the existence of a common set of shared Asian values.

In 1994, Lee declared that "Westerners have abandoned an ethical
basis for society, believing that all problems are solvable by a good government, which we in the East never believed possible."[12] He condemned the
Western liberal and intellectual tradition that has developed since World
War II, which, according to Lee, claimed that human beings had arrived
at a perfect state where everybody would be better off if they were allowed
to do their own thing and flourish.[13] According to Lee, "Singapore [is] a
Confucian society which place[s] the interests of the community above
those of the individual."[14] The Western idea of the inviolability of the individual, he believed, had been turned into dogma.[15] He found parts of the

American system totally unacceptable: guns, drugs, violent crime, vagrancy, unbecoming behavior in public – in sum the breakdown of civil society.[16] Indeed, in an interview with the political journalist and editor Fareed Zakaria, Lee asserted the following:

> The expansion of the right of the individual [in America] to behave or misbehave as he pleases has come at the expense of orderly society. In the East the main object is to have a well-ordered society so that everybody can have maximum enjoyment of his freedoms. This freedom can only exist in an ordered state and not in a natural state of contention and anarchy.... Asian societies are unlike Western ones. The fundamental difference between Western concepts of society and government and East Asian concepts – when I say East Asians, I mean Korea, Japan, China, Vietnam, as distinct from Southeast Asia, which is a mix of between the Sinic and the Indian, though Indian culture also emphasizes similar values – is that Eastern societies believe that the individual exists in the context of his family. He is not pristine or separate. The family is part of the extended family, and then friends and the wider society. The ruler or the government does not provide for a person what the family best provides.... [T]here is grave disquiet when we break away from tested norms, and the tested norm is the family unit. It is the building brick of society.... [T]he family, the extended family, the clan, has provided a kind of survival raft for the individual. Civilizations have collapsed, dynasties have been swept away by conquering hordes, but this life raft enables the civilization to carry on and get to its next phase.... [T]he family and the way human relationships are structured, do increase the survival chances of its members. That has been tested over thousands of years in many different situations.
>
> (Lee Kuan Yew in Fareed Zakaria (1994): 111–115)

From these remarks, it may not be unreasonable to venture either that Lee has read Book 1 of Aristotle's *Politics*, or if he has not, then what he says resembles Aristotle's observations in the *Politics*, a source that has greatly influenced Western concepts of society and government, although it is doubtful that Aristotle would have believed that a well-ordered society is the same thing as a well-ordered state. In Book 1 of the *Politics*, Aristotle states,

> The household is the partnership constituted by nature for [the needs] of daily life.... The first partnership arising from [the union of] several households and for the sake of nondaily needs is the village.... The partnership arising from [the union of] several villages that is complete is the city.... Every city, therefore, exists by nature, if such also are the first partnerships.... From these things it is evident,

then, that the city belongs among the things that exist by nature, and that man is by nature a political animal. He who is without a city through nature rather than chance is either a mean sort or superior to man; he is "without clan, without law, without hearth", like the person reproved by Homer.... One who is incapable of participating or who is in need of nothing through being self-sufficient is no part of a city, and so is either a beast or a god.... Accordingly, there is in everyone by nature an impulse toward this sort of partnership.

(Aristotle, *Politics*, 1252b13–1253a30)

Aristotle's extensive account of friendship in Book 8 of the *Ethics* also provides examples of natural familial friendship which contradict Lee Kuan Yew's claim that respect for the family is a particularly Asian value.

Zakaria believed that when Lee spoke of East Asian values and the anxious search for religion in the East, he was referring more to his own quest for a Confucian alternative to the West.[17] Yet to say explicitly that Confucianism encompasses all Asian values would deflate his East–West argument. Although he attempted to be diplomatic in order to accommodate and win the support of his ASEAN partners, with their vast array of religions, and where Confucianism has had little to no impact, Lee's examples nevertheless homogenize all of Asia into one Confucian culture, drawing much Western, and Eastern, criticism. Furthermore, Lee was critical of international institutions, like the World Bank, which report their conclusions in terms of American culture. He enjoyed their general praise of the success of East Asian economies but asserted that they are prone to making bland and universal assumptions like – "[A]ll men are equal." According to Lee, they are not:

Groups of people develop different characteristics when they have evolved for thousands of years separately. Genetics and history interact ... two groups may share certain characteristics, for instance, if you measure the shape of their skulls and so on, but if you start testing them, you find that they are different, most particularly in their neurological development, and their cultural values.

(Lee Kuan Yew in Fareed Zakaria (1994): 117)

Forever the pragmatist, Lee concluded many such observations by saying that political correctness requires us to gloss over these kinds of issues rather than see them in their stark reality and, therefore, that we lay land mines for ourselves. He believed that American social policies would always yield meager results because they were too politically correct. Asian societies, particularly the fast-growing countries like South Korea, Thailand, Hong Kong, and Singapore, had, according to Lee, witnessed a rise in the growth of religion. But whether these societies can preserve their core values in their transition towards modernization is a problem they alone can solve – Americans cannot solve it for them. Becoming modernized does not necessitate becoming Westernized.[18] Lee saw this transition, and the rejection of Western values, as a Darwinian struggle in the sense that they would be rejected if they threatened the survival of other self-evident truths found in Asian society.

One interesting vision for Lee's well-ordered state was a restriction on voting. Lee said that he was burdened with the one-man, one-vote system because that is what the British bequeathed to Singapore. His own preference would be to grant two votes for every man over the age of 40 who has a family, because he is likely to be more careful, voting also for his children. He is likely to vote in a more serious way than a capricious man under the age of 30, but once a man reaches the age of 60, he should return to one vote.[19]

By the early 1990s, according to Roy, Singapore and China had become, "in effect, allies in a rhetorical battle with the West," and Singapore had readily come to the defense of China's human rights policy.[20] Several years following the incident in Tiananmen Square in 1988, for example, Lee gradually reversed his earlier criticism of the Chinese authorities and publicly endorsed Deng Xiaoping's handling of the prodemocracy student demonstrators:

> My Cabinet colleagues and I are shocked, horrified and saddened by the disastrous turn of events. We had expected the Chinese Government to apply the doctrine of minimum force when an army is used to quell civil disorder. Instead, the fire-power and violence used caused many deaths and casualties. They were totally disproportionate to the resistance unarmed civilians offered. . . . A China with large sections of her people, including her best educated, at odds with the Government, means trouble, with people resentful, reforms stalled, and economy stagnant. Because of her size, such a China could create problems for herself and her neighbours in Asia. . . . We hope that wiser counsels will prevail to pursue conciliation, so that the Chinese people can resume the progress which the open door policies have brought them.
>
> (Lee Kuan Yew, "Violence Disproportionate to Resistance: Statement by the Prime Minister on the Events in Beijing made on 5 June 1989," in Lianhe Zaobao (ed.) (1991): 1)

I think it was a great tragedy, what took place in Tiananmen, because the students did not remember that this was China. They were not dealing with Marcos in the Philippines, or South Korea against Chun Doo Hwan. Most of them linked closely to America, politically, and therefore, having to take American TV and public opinion and congressional opinion into consideration. . . . This is China. Deng Xiaoping fought with his life to defeat the warlords, and to knock out the

KMT. The students have forgotten that.... He is not interested in what American TV or European TV may think.

> (Lee Kuan Yew, "Students Too Impulsive: Interview by Frankfurter Rundschau, West Germany, on 10 May 1990 in Singapore," in Lianhe Zaobao (ed.) (1991): 64)

I don't think we can speak in terms of just the East Asian order. The question is: Can the world develop a system in which a country the size of China becomes part of the management of international peace and stability? Sometime in the next 20 or 30 years the world, by which I mean the major powers, will have to agree among themselves how to manage peace and stability, how to create a system that is both viable and fair.... The regime in Beijing is more stable than any alternative government that can be formed in China. Let us assume that the students had carried the day at Tiananmen and they had formed a government. The same students who were at Tiananmen went to France and America. They've been quarreling with each other ever since. What kind of China would they have today? Something worse than the Soviet Union. China is a vast, disparate country; there is no alternative to strong central power.

> (Lee Kuan Yew in Fareed Zakaria (1994): 123)

You cannot mock a great leader in an Asian Confucian society. If he allows himself to be mocked, he is finished. There can be only one emperor in China, and Deng understands that.

> (Lee Kuan Yew, "Change Would Come from Within the Communist Party: Answering Questions at a Discussion Organized by the Institute of International Relations of France," Paris, 23 May 1990, in Lianhe Zaobao (ed.) (1991): 78)

So too, it would seem, did Lee. Not surprisingly, the PRC leaders looked favorably upon Lee's rule over Singapore and consulted with him on the future of Hong Kong and how best to retain political control while encouraging economic reforms in the mainland. Fearing a return to the warlordism of past generations if the order sustained under Chinese Communist Party rule should ever break down following economic liberalization, Lee's style of good government promised the right mix of order and reform. Lee was critical of American liberals who criticized Singapore, not because they were concerned about democracy and human rights for his 3 million people, but because they believed that Singapore was setting the wrong example for China.[21]

Zakaria observed that Lee was not a man untouched by the West. In the mid-1960s the British Foreign Secretary could say to him, "Harry (his name until his thirties), you're the best bloody Englishman east of the Suez."[22] Zakaria interpreted Lee's interest in cultural differences as some-

thing more than providing a coherent defense against Western democratic imperialism – it was an attempt to stave off moral decay in the face
of rapid economic growth. While much of what Lee saw in Eastern cultures was once part of the West, 400 years of economic growth changed
things.[23] The economic, technological, and social changes which took
Europe 400 years to manage had occurred throughout much of Asia over
a mere few decades. Lee was unable to accept that cultures change and
that no culture has remained the same under the impact of economic
growth, technological change, and social transformation.[24] In 1994, prior
to the Asian financial and economic crash, Prime Minister Goh, on the
other hand, believed that traditional values, family strength, and social
cohesion were the intangible factors in the success of East Asian
economies and, if lost, then Singapore's economic growth would lose its
vibrancy and decline.[25]

Others interpreted Lee's words as mere pronouncements by Asia's
most articulate authoritarian leader that the Western concept of democracy and human rights were inapplicable to East Asia.[26] Criticizing Lee's
attack on Western universalism as insupportable and self-serving, former
South Korean president, Kim Dae Jung, believed that Asian governments
intrude much farther than Western governments into the daily affairs of
individuals and families. He believed that in Lee's "near-totalitarian" Singapore, for example, the government regulates individual behavior to an
Orwellian extreme of social engineering.[27] Columbia University's Confucian scholar, William Theodore de Bary, remarked that although spokes-
men for authoritarian regimes like to define the human rights problem as
one of the "individualistic West" versus "communitarian Asia," the social
problems attributed to the "individualistic West" attend the modernization process wherever it goes on, in the East or West. Consequently, "it is
less a question of Asian versus Western values than a problem of how the
forces of a runaway economic and technological modernization are
eroding traditional values in both Asia and the West."[28]

While Lee's pragmatism remains seductive, even among Westerners –
because of what they see as a moral breakdown in many advanced democracies, the proper way to prevent the ills of modernization, according to
many Western and Eastern critics, is not to suppress human rights – nor to
impose the terror of a police state, but to emphasize ethical education. We
should now consider whether Lee's interpretation of Confucian values
served to provide the ethical education required to treat the ills of modernization, or whether it served another purpose.

The politics of Confucianism – manipulating the *endoxa*

In the *Politics*, Aristotle writes that one who gives a fine performance of the
part of a kingly ruler must always show himself to be seriously attentive to
the things pertaining to the gods.[29] While Confucianism could be the

closest Chinese resemblance to Aristotle's nontheological understanding of the gods, Lee's intentions regarding Confucianism would appear to conform to Aristotle's reasoning in this respect. Uri Gordon offers an interpretation of Lee that conforms with my own understanding of Lee in light of Aristotle. He argues that Lee's ideology of Asian values underlying the PAP's policies was a form of Machiavellian *virtu*, a new form of Roman *virtu* which Lee had chosen to oppose the contemporary alternative to Christian morality – Western liberal democracy.[30] Lee's application of Confucianism, according to Gordon, was not a direct reflection of his personal perspective, nor of his desire to integrate its principles, but instead was an extension of his desire to utilize religious ideology as a tool for manipulation.[31] Lee's reference to Confucianism may be seen as a form of "resorting to divine authority," adhering, for example, to Machiavelli's dictate that princes of a republic or of a kingdom should maintain, and magnify, the foundations of the religion they hold.[32] Beyond the actual content of Confucianism, Gordon believes, its very antiquity has served as an instrument of legitimization.[33] Precisely the same argument may be made of Buddhism and the Burmese military rulers' attempts at legitimization by Machiavellian actions resembling what Gordon calls "resorting to divine authority."[34] James Cotton, on the other hand, suggested that it was possible to consider the regime's embrace of these core values as a device akin to Plato's "noble lie" – notions philosophically meaningless and politically vacuous, but sufficient to appeal to the understanding of ordinary citizens.[35]

The public promotion of Confucianism in Singapore also arose as a consequence of the promotion of English as the medium most required for international business. In 1978, the Singapore government decided to merge the Chinese-language Nanyang University with the English-language University of Singapore into the National University of Singapore – where all instruction would be provided in English. Believing that graduates of the Nanyang-Nantah campus would be less disadvantaged and more able to contribute to Singapore's economic prosperity if they were trained by English-speaking instructors, Lee soon after made all Chinese schools switch to English, with Chinese-Mandarin as their second language. Yet he also feared that the switch to English meant that Chinese schools could no longer instill the traditions of discipline, self-confidence, and Chinese moral and social values in their students. Unless these same values could be transmitted to students in the new bilingual schools, the students were in danger of being "deculturalized."[36] In his personal history of Singapore, Lee asserted that if English was used as the medium of instruction, Confucian values of the family could not be reinforced in schools because both teachers and students were multiracial and the textbooks were not in Chinese. The traditional moral values of students were being eroded by increasing exposure to the Western media, interaction with foreign tourists in Singapore, overseas travel, younger teachers who were not steeped in traditional (Confucian) values, and the permeation of America's consumer society values faster than the rest of the region because of Singapore's education in the English language.[37]

In line with promoting Confucian Ethics as an optional subject in secondary schools, the Singapore government in 1982 invited eight distinguished Confucian scholars from America and Taiwan to discuss the conceptual framework for a syllabus with faculty from the University of Singapore, business leaders, and members of Parliament. While some, like Harvard's Tu Wei-Ming, were "excited to think that Confucianism might be very much linked to the modernizing spirit,"[38] others told members of Parliament that "a kind of Singaporean ethic or 'Lee Kuan Yewism' should be developed."[39] Tu Wei-Ming, however, warned government ministers that "if Confucianism were to become a state ideology, it would be used to legitimize autocratic rule and to advocate unthinking respect for authority, submissiveness and obedience to the status quo. In this way, it could easily be used by a particular political machinery to enhance its own power and control."[40] While he nevertheless favored the encouragement of Confucianism as a personal ethic,[41] it seems difficult to believe how a system of ethics that was to be introduced, interpreted, and promoted by the government, ostensibly to instill traditions of discipline and moral values in school students, could be detached from political motivations. Perhaps this is also why Aristotle preferred the household as the teacher of right and wrong, rather than government schools.

Xenophon's Cyrus, it could be argued, honored the virtue of obedience yet failed to instill his own great virtue of self-restraint in his followers.[42] If obedience to a ruler fails to encourage self-restraint in his followers, then perhaps this supports Aristotle's contention that a lasting habituation to moral virtue must be freely chosen and not, as in the case of the "Singaporean ethic" or "Lee Kuan Yewism" – imposed by the government. And since Lee demanded obedience from his followers,[43] then it is not unreasonable to question his own motivations for promoting Confucian morals. It is also interesting to note that among the five courses offered in the newly required Religious Knowledge course that was inserted into the Singapore school curriculum, in 1989 the majority of students freely chose to study Buddhist Studies and Bible Knowledge rather than Confucian Ethics. The Religious Knowledge course was abandoned in 1990.[44]

The evidence presented above suggests that Lee Kuan Yew's paternal concern and desire to promote good Confucian values appeared to have arisen partially in response to a PAP by-election loss, a perceived threat of the erosion of cultural and ethical values accompanying modernization, and as a consequence of his desire to further Singapore's economic prosperity in a world where the English language dominates international business.[45] Coupled with the belief in ruling circles that only strong, steady leadership could keep communal peace, and that authoritarian government – providing firm policy direction and social stability – was the necessary

condition for continued economic growth,[46] the Confucian values promoted in Lee's Asian values rhetoric emphasized order and stability above
all else. A good Confucian family, it followed, should provide the kind of
stability whereby its members would not question a leader's authority and
wherein any opposition or questioning would be understood as dangerous
to the well-being of the family and the country. In order to sustain economic growth, it seemed, Lee's good Confucian family should remain
hard working, respectful of authority, and silent.

Asian values, Confucianism, and human rights

Lee's peculiar interpretation of Confucian philosophy follows in a tradition of many, and varied, political interpretations of Confucianism that
have been undertaken throughout the twentieth century. Before Singapore's rise to economic and political prominence, for example, Confucianism had often been considered a drag on economic development and
modernization, a view that prevailed until the 1960s and 1970s when a
revisionist view of East Asia's "post-Confucian" culture emerged, marrying
Confucian values with modernization.[47] According to Pye, Confucian
philosophy traditionally placed the merchant next to the bottom in the
social scale, below the mandarin and the peasant, and the game of the
merchant was to cheat the customer.[48] The fact that Singapore's existence
has always depended upon merchants should, therefore, if traditional
Confucian thought were respected, pose a major obstacle to Lee's re-inter-
pretation.

Prior to revisionist thinking, Confucianism had been identified with
autocratic and authoritarian rule in the imperial dynasties, a view widely
held in both China and the West after the collapse of the Manchu dynasty
in 1911.[49] Pye believes that during the 1920s and 1930s the Chinese overwhelmingly believed that their traditional culture was a curse that had left
China backward and weak. Confucianism, with its emphasis on authority
and ideological conformity, was regarded as fertile soil for Leninist
communism in the 1950s through the 1960s.[50] Yet communist China
developed a hostility towards Confucianism during the Cultural Revolution, which passed with the death of Mao, and Confucianism was discreetly rehabilitated under the more moderate Deng and Jiang regimes as
a better long-term support for an established government than the revolutionary class-struggle morality.[51] In its rehabilitated form, however, a Confucianism that supported authoritarian rule was very different from the
Confucianism of Chinese scholars carrying on Confucian studies abroad,
free from the depredations of the Cultural Revolution.[52] For those knowl-
edgeable in the Confucian tradition and Western human rights, De Bary
claims, the two were not incompatible.[53] Traditionally, Confucianism has
downplayed the importance of non-consensual and non-contractual
formal dynastic law, such as the Great Tang Code of regulations, designed

to assert and preserve the power of the dynastic state.[54] Instead, Confucianism emphasized the practice of civility and mutual respect through the observance of rites, understood as forms of civil decorum or norms of conduct appropriate in given social circumstances, that embody a humane concern and respect for others.[55]

De Bary, however, believes that Confucian scholars in the pre-modern period were coming to the realization that the limiting of imperial rule required greater participation in the political process by way of a constitutional structure and that, therefore, a constitutional order supportive of some liberal democratic values and human rights, though not at all an assured prospect on Confucian grounds, nevertheless was not an idea totally foreign to Confucian thinking nor out of line with the growing critique of dynastic rule.[56] Moreover, the Republic of China's representatives at the adoption of the Universal Declaration of Human Rights in 1948 included Chinese scholars trained in Western law who were disposed to include Confucian humanistic sentiments in the language of the Declaration and, based upon their experiences in China, proposed adding to the list of human rights.[57] Furthermore, the PRC, as well as other East Asian societies sharing in Confucian cultural influences, including Singapore, has formally subscribed to the Universal Declaration, and its constitution makes provision for human rights without any stated reservations as to their compatibility with Confucian values.[58] This, according to De Bary, is a tacit admission of the difficulty of constructing a Confucian or Chinese rationale for opposing them.[59] He believes that "there is little evidence to suggest that an Asian defense against human rights could be mounted on fundamental Confucian grounds, and good reason to believe that the Confucian historical experience would lend positive support to many of the human rights enumerated in the Universal Declaration, as well as negative confirmation of the need for others of them."[60]

Kim Dae Jung claims that Asia has a rich heritage of democracy-oriented philosophy and tradition. Almost two millennia before John Locke, the Chinese philosopher Meng-tzu taught that heaven bestowed upon a king the mandate to rule righteously in order to achieve good government. If he did not rule righteously, the people had the right to rise up and overthrow his government in the name of heaven.[61] Revolt by the people was the final court of appeal, with the people speaking for heaven. Superior virtue was identified with a heaven-ordained moral law and rulers were answerable to this higher law that constituted a moral constraint on the exercise of power.[62] Kim believes that there are no ideas more fundamental to democracy than the teachings of Confucianism, Buddhism, and the native Korean religion – Thonghak. According to Kim, "When Western societies were still being ruled by a succession of feudal lords, China and Korea had already sustained county prefecture systems for about 2,000 years."[63] Unlike European fiefdoms of that time, for nearly 1,000 years in China and Korea the sons of high-ranking officials were required to pass civil-service examinations before being appointed to important official positions. Boards of censors checked against imperial misrule and abuses by government officials, and freedom of speech was highly valued. Confucian scholars were taught that remonstration against an erring monarch was a paramount duty.[64] If the fundamental ideas and traditions necessary for the birth of democratic ideas existed in both Europe and Asia, the fact that Europe formalized them first does not mean that they will not work in Asia. Kim believes that "Asian authoritarians misunderstand the relationship between the rules of effective governance and the concept of legitimacy. Policies that try to protect people from the bad elements of economic and social change will never be effective if imposed without consent."[65] For many, the biggest obstacle to establishing democracy and strengthening human rights in Asia, therefore, is not cultural heritage, but the resistance of authoritarian rulers and their apologists.[66]

Further criticism of Lee's peculiar interpretation of Confucianism comes from academic and religious quarters. While Donald Emmerson, for example, contends that the sheer diversity of cultures, religions, and traditions across Asia makes the idea of having one set of "Asian values" absurd,[67] Nobel Laureate Amartya Sen adds that East Asia itself is remarkably diverse, with many variations to be found not only among Japan, China, Korea, and other countries of the region but also within each country. Confucius is not the only influence in these countries and there is no homogeneous worship of order over freedom in any of these cultures.[68] Eric Jones believes that for Lee's authoritarian argument to be persuasive, safeguards would be needed to ensure a genuine intention of ultimately relaxing his grip on society because, whatever the justifications for control at present, it is disingenuous to imply that Asians positively *like* regimes where political activity takes place beneath the sword.[69] And the fourteenth Dalai Lama of Tibet believes that it is wrong to contend that the standards of human rights laid down in the Universal Declaration of Human Rights are those advocated by the West and cannot be applied to Asia because of the differences in culture and differences in social and economic development. He writes, "I do not share this view and I am convinced that the majority of Asian people do not support this view either, for it is the inherent nature of all human beings to yearn for freedom, equality, and dignity."[70] Indeed, being a Buddhist, the Dalai Lama represents one Asian religion whose means to personal salvation comes via an inherently individualist pursuit of karma throughout one's life, irrespective of one's political system, level of social and economic development, or level of personal freedom.

Lee, on the other hand, suggested that it may be 100 years before Asians may be trusted with individual Western-style freedoms, and that whereas China, India, and Indonesia need 90 years to learn how to handle modernity in a balanced way, South Korea, Taiwan, and Singapore only need 30 years. Universal values may come, though with any luck not yet, and when they do they will not cause Asian society to decay as it has in the West. Western motives for promoting democracy and human rights are dismissed by the Singapore School as commercial, culturally imperialistic, and hypocritical given the West's willingness to indulge similar authoritarian behavior on behalf of the Saudi Arabias of the world.[71] Lee's pragmatism on this last point was well received among most of the representatives at the Asian states meeting in Bangkok in 1993.

The Bangkok Declaration on Human Rights, signed in 1993, was an attempt by various Asian states to forge a compromise on the issue of the universality as opposed to the relativity of human rights. The Declaration was signed in Bangkok by 40 Asian countries, including China but excluding Japan. Signatories to the Declaration included all the ASEAN states and the states which later joined ASEAN in 1995 and 1997 respectively – Vietnam and Burma. In language akin to the Thomistic distinction between the universality of ends but the non-universality of the inferences, deductions, and applications from the ends, the Declaration accepted that although human rights were "universal in nature," they must be considered "in the context of national and regional particularities, and various cultural, historical, and religious backgrounds, and with the understanding that norms and values change over time."[72] So while being universal, according to the Bangkok Declaration, human rights could also be relative.

The Bangkok Declaration stressed that economic, social, and cultural rights should be given equal emphasis to civil and political rights, and it further recognized the right to development as a "universal and integral part of fundamental human rights."[73] While stating that economic and social progress facilitates the growth of democracy and human rights, the delegates also agreed to uphold the principle of sovereignty and non-interference in the internal affairs of states and urged the promotion of human rights by co-operation and consensus, not by confrontation and conditionality. Furthermore, the Asian states declared, "[H]uman rights should not be applied as a pretext for commercial, political or other pressure."[74] Singapore was among the ASEAN member nations that gave their official approval to the Bangkok Declaration at the 26th ASEAN Ministerial Meeting in July 1993, held in Singapore, and agreed to "coordinate a common approach on human rights and actively participate and contribute to the application, promotion, and protection of human rights."[75]

Because the rhetoric of Asian values challenges the applicability and validity of the Universal Declaration of Human Rights to Asian states, and because the Universal Declaration was partially a product of natural law theorists, it is useful to compare Lee Kuan Yew's Asian values with the Universal Declaration and the Bangkok Declaration. While comparing the three, it should be noted that although the Universal Declaration itself is not a law, it is a universal statement. Aristotle mentions universal statements in his discussion of equity. He believes that all laws are universal in statement, but about some things it is not possible for a universal statement to be right.[76]

> So when the law makes a universal statement about a subject but an instance of that subject is not rightly covered by that statement, then it is right to correct the omission made by the legislator when he left some error in his unqualified [universal] statement; for the legislator himself would have made that correction had he been present, or he would have legislated accordingly if he had known.
>
> (Aristotle, *Ethics*, 1137b20–24)

Would Aristotle prescribe that countries legislate for the implementation of this universal statement in such a way as to conform to their particular cultural practices and traditions? And may legislators omit, or add to, the Declaration in order to meet certain political objectives? Would Aristotle disapprove of any political and cultural interpretations, like certain provisions of the Bangkok Declaration that have the effect of denying the essence of the universal statement? Perhaps the pertinent question to be asked, therefore, is just how much flexibility, or mutability, should be permitted in the universal statement and, with this in mind, whether there are any fundamental differences between the Universal Declaration (and the Bangkok Declaration) that cannot be adequately explained on the grounds of economic and cultural differences between the East and the West. If there are differences completely at odds with each other, then perhaps this would indicate that mutability of the universal statement may conceal hidden political agendas, either in the Bangkok Declaration or in Lee Kuan Yew's Asian values.

The Universal Declaration has been branded a Western document by scholars like Samuel Huntington, whose "Clash of Civilizations" thesis tends to support Lee's Asian values. Huntington claims that modern ideas of democracy have only developed in non-Western societies, if at all, as a product of Western colonialism and imposition. It is true that most of the countries in Southeast Asia, and parts of East Asia, were either still under colonial rule or had just gained their independence at the time of the Universal Declaration's writing in 1948. Yet to bundle the entire assortment of European, and American, colonial rulers into one hegemonic grouping under the label "Western" ignores the differences, the particularisms, within and among each of the Western societies themselves. Huntington is fond of noting the particularisms of Asian societies[77] while overlooking the fact that the British, Dutch, French, Portuguese, Spanish, and Germans have been fighting each other for centuries.

Johannes Morsink believes that the lingering allegations of ethnocentrism that surround the Universal Declaration are in part caused by the fact that very few people know what was said and done during the drafting process.[78] He believes that some of the arguments put forward by those drafting the document were based on a natural law approach to human rights and that the majority of the drafters saw the rights as grounded in human nature.[79] When Asian states, however, endorse Asian values and interpret human rights among themselves as fellow-citizens within the umbrella of ASEAN, they assume a position where justice may equate with convention and legal positivism replaces natural law and human nature.

While the West may criticize Asian values, on the other hand, the East may claim in reply that their Bangkok Declaration of 1993 merely represents an alternative rule of action to the Universal Declaration of 1948. It seems that Western criticism of Asian values may hinge upon whether the ends embodied in Asian values promote a universally held standard of justice. The former Prime Minister of Thailand, Chuan Leekpai, in opening the regional meeting at which the Bangkok Declaration was adopted, asserted that the Declaration would promote the universality of human rights. His claim that it is natural for approaches to the implementation of fundamental human rights to vary in accordance with "socioeconomic, historical, cultural backgrounds and conditions" would seem to conform to the flexibility required to implement a universal statement.[80] Yet the ends embodied in the core arguments used to support Asian values, and many of the provisions in the Bangkok Declaration, go well beyond addressing the cultural problems of implementing a universal statement.

Lee Kuan Yew's insistence that the fundamental difference between Eastern and Western values rests upon the East's greater emphasis of the "family" demands that we examine the so-called Western document on human rights, the Universal Declaration, in respect of this claim. If the Universal Declaration embodies particularly Western values, then does it also embrace any notion of that fundamentally "Eastern" idea, according to Lee, the family? Article 16(3) of the Universal Declaration states:

> The family is the natural and fundamental group unit of society and is entitled to protection by society and the State.
>
> (United Nations (1948), Article 16(3))

Articles 23 and 25, furthermore, contain two more explicit and one implicit reference to the family. Using the original documents and transcripts, Morsink shows how keen the drafters were on protecting the family community.[81] While France's Rene Cassin, for example, "did not think it was possible to disregard human groups and to consider each person only as an individual,"[82] Charles Malik of Lebanon believed that "the family was the cradle of all human rights and liberties. It was in the family that everyone learned to know his rights and duties and it would be inexplicable if everything were mentioned except the family's right to existence."[83] Morsink believes that, during the drafting sessions, Malik pleaded for the reinstatement of the words "the natural and fundamental group unit of society" in Article 16(3), which he called "the most essential part of his amendment." According to Morsink, "[T]he fact that he added the words 'natural' and 'Creator' himself suggests that Malik was indeed thinking of a natural law approach to human rights. His use of the phrase 'antecedent to all positive law' in the earliest formulation of the amendment points in the same direction."[84]

Indeed, aside from its reference to the "state," Article 16(3) also reflects Aristotle's account of familial friendship in the *Ethics*. Moreover, Aristotle's notion of natural friendship extends not only to members of the same race but to the extent that each man is a fellow human being.[85] Regarding the idea of *philanthropia*, Aristotle notes, "In travels, too, one may observe how close and dear every man is to another man."[86] Perhaps the most revealing, at least for our purposes, of Aristotle's passages on his idea of philanthropic friendship is the following:

> [F]or there seems to be something just between every man and every one who can participate in an association where there is law or agreement, and hence in a friendship to the extent that each of them is a man.
>
> (Aristotle, *Ethics*, 1161b6–8)

If read in isolation, this passage could provide the basis for some agreement between Aristotle's discussion of universal statements and a universal statement on human rights. Perhaps the notion of human rights could fall within one of his three kinds of friendship – pleasure, utility, or virtue. But Aristotle seems to qualify his account of friendship by requiring that true friendship entails a certain level of recognition, reciprocity, and a feeling of being well disposed between those who call each other friends. The real question for our purposes then becomes how strictly should these conditions be applied to philanthropic friendships? Could such a wide interpretation of friendship, even with other races, be possible according to Aristotle? Or perhaps we should ask whether such a friendship could be practical, given that reciprocity is not always possible.

Philanthropic friendship certainly appears to be natural, but Aristotle does not include it among the more familial kinds and he does not give such an extensive account of it. Is he perhaps acknowledging the possibility of humanitarian sentiment while illustrating the difficulty of transforming such a sentiment into the political realm via the establishment of an international community? Living in a *polis* would not have inspired such grand ideas as a League of Nations or the United Nations, though he would have been familiar with Thucydides and the Delian League. And if we interpret his comment that "there is only one form of government which is by nature the best everywhere"[87] as meaning that each race of people will have by nature a form of government that best suits their particular circumstances, then this would rule out the possibility of any form of global government. But if we were to read the passage with a "dominant end" interpretation, then perhaps it is possible, at least to the extent that the United Nations, on average, tends to promote more liberal democratic ideas over ones that are not.

One wonders what Aristotle may have thought of the ideas of universal responsibility, a global human family, and a global ethic.[88] How seriously would he have taken friendship with people from another race? Could Aristotle have dismissed the possibility that his student, Alexander, could sustain an empire based on philanthropic friendship? Perhaps Aristotle's realism would tell us that he thought there is a natural limit to the extension of philanthropic friendship, or at least to the effectiveness of such modern notions as a global human family. Perhaps these ideas could appear to be vague and unenforceable at the individual level. Yet because the yearning for freedom, equality, and dignity is the nature of all human beings,[89] and responsibility seems to be the contemporary equivalent of moral virtue, Aristotle would more likely promote education in moral virtue.

Natural law seems to indicate that the family is by nature the fundamental unit of society. And although it makes no explicit mention of the family, Article 1 of the Bangkok Declaration reaffirmed the signatories' commitment to the basic principles of the Universal Declaration. Lee's contempt for Western values must therefore have been founded upon what he saw as the modern moral decay of the family in the West and the West's insistence upon a politically correct reading of the Universal Declaration that overemphasizes individual rights, as perhaps illustrated by some modern – or Western – Buddhist and Confucian interpretations of human rights. But to balance this reading, Article 29(1) of the Universal Declaration says "Everyone has *duties* to the community in which alone the free and full development of his personality is possible."[90]

Perhaps Lee's quarrel with the Universal Declaration, therefore, could simply be understood as a criticism of the modern – or Western – elevation of rights over duties. While the Universal Declaration speaks of family and duties, it does indeed emphasize rights. Yet if it had contained an elaboration of duties as well, then would it not appear to be more of a duties straitjacket, limiting an individual's freedom, rather than a declaration of the individual's freedom? In other words, does the Universal Declaration, for the most part, assume the very duties that Lee attempted to identify as Asian values – values which essentially converted all of the Declaration's rights into a monolithic duty called the family?

Lee's attempt to circumvent the Universal Declaration may also be explained by his wish to avoid the limitations imposed by Articles 29(3) and 30. Lee, and leaders of the People's Republic of China, cited the maintenance of morality and public order as the justification for authoritarian rule. Article 29(2) does indeed allow for some flexibility along these lines and, in what seems to be an implicit contradiction, it promotes restrictions on freedom for the common good – an idea that rejects the Western view that the rights and freedoms of some can only be legitimately restricted to protect the rights and freedoms of others.

> In the exercise of his rights and freedoms, everyone shall be subject only to such limitations as are determined by law solely for the purpose of securing due recognition and respect for the rights and freedoms of others and of meeting the just requirements of morality, public order, and the general welfare in a democratic society.
>
> (United Nations (1948), Article 29(2))

But thereafter follows the provisos in Articles 29(3) and 30:

> These rights and freedoms may in no case be exercised contrary to the purposes and principles of the United Nations. . . . Nothing in this Declaration may be interpreted as implying for any State, group, or person any right to engage in any activity or to perform any act aimed at the destruction of any rights and freedoms set forth herein.
>
> (United Nations (1948), Articles 29(3) and 30)

It appears that the only justification for limiting the rights outlined in the Universal Declaration cannot diminish the same rights and freedoms which the Declaration itself guarantees. A strictly legal interpretation of the Universal Declaration, therefore, may help to explain the rights straitjacket embodied in Western values which Lee found to be so uncomfortable.

The Bangkok Declaration, on the other hand, opens with a reaffirmation by the Asian states of their commitment to the principles contained in the Universal Declaration,[91] including the recognition that the family is the natural and fundamental group unit of society and that everyone has duties to the community. Much of the remainder of the Bangkok Declaration, however, includes articles that appear to have been generated more from matters of regional political concern.[92] Indeed, almost one-quarter of the Bangkok Declaration appears to be a direct attack by the Asian states upon the human rights policies of the West. Furthermore, there are three articles which, when read together, appear to justify the use of terrorism in order to secure the right to self-determination. Article 12 reiterates that self-determination is a principle of international law and a universal right recognized by the United Nations for peoples under alien or colonial domination and foreign occupation, while Article 13 stresses that this right to self-determination should not be used to undermine the territorial integrity, national sovereignty, and political independence of states.[93] In other words, "colonial domination and foreign occupation" refer to Western imperialism rather than Eastern because not only must the intruders be alien but the right to self-determination cannot be exercised by the minority groups within a state. Although Article 11 extends a guarantee of human rights to these minority groups, they cannot exercise a right to self-determination. And this is key to understanding the Western response to the Bangkok Declaration, and indeed the Bush administration's alliance with China in the "War on Terrorism." In order for Western governments to engage economically, politically, or diplomatically with countries like the People's Republic of China, they must recognize her sovereignty over the minority peoples living in her autonomous provinces – including the Buddhist Tibetans and the Muslim Uygurs of Xinjiang. Article 21 notes that

> [T]errorism, in all its forms and manifestations, as distinguished from the legitimate struggle of peoples under colonial or alien domination and foreign occupation . . . must be unequivocally condemned by the international community.
>
> (United Nations (1993a), Article 21)

Terrorism aimed against alien domination and foreign occupation is, apparently, justified as part of a legitimate struggle for self-determination. The term "self-determination" is to be found in Ho Chi Minh's 1945 Vietnamese Declaration of Independence and in the 1975 Paris Peace Accords. It is nowhere to be found in the Universal Declaration of 1948, nor in Thomas Jefferson's Declaration of Independence of 1776 for that matter. Article 4 of the Universal Declaration prohibits slavery and servitude, but this hardly promotes self-determination, let alone a right to terrorism. More pertinent is whether natural law embraces a right to civil disobedience, permits sedition, and indeed encourages terrorism. In other words, what are the limits to the natural right of disobedience?

A natural right of disobedience may be very close to Jefferson's formulation in the Declaration of Independence. And like his Declaration of Independence, in which the Laws of Nature and Nature's God bestowed upon the people a right to abolish any form of government which becomes destructive of man's inalienable rights, Confucian ethics bestowed upon the people the right to rise up and overthrow an unrighteous ruler. It would seem, therefore, that both Eastern thought and Western philosophy may ultimately appeal to heaven as the final arbitrator on the question of revolution. But one doubts whether Ho Chi Minh or George Washington spent too much time pondering over these questions at the time of their own revolutions.

A more favorable interpretation of the Bangkok Declaration would emphasize that Article 1 reaffirms the principles contained in the Universal Declaration. Furthermore, the preambles to both the Bangkok and Universal Declarations emphasize that states need to educate the public on a common standard of achievement in human rights in order to overcome the lack of public awareness. While the Universal Declaration goes further in stressing that such education should promote the effective recognition and observance of human rights among the peoples of member states and the territories under their jurisdiction,[94] Article 27 of the Bangkok Declaration reiterates the need to explore ways to generate international co-operation and financial support for education and training in the field of human rights at the national level and for the establishment of national infrastructures to promote and protect human rights.[95]

Both declarations, therefore, appear to acknowledge the importance of education as a cultural means to enforcing a common standard of achievement in human rights. That state education is deemed necessary may also amount to a tacit admission that the moral education provided by the family is insufficient and, by implication, that the household should no longer be the chief educator in right and wrong. Yet perhaps the Universal Declaration's recognition of the family as the natural and fundamental group unit of society, entitled to protection by society and the state, suggests not only that the household remains the primary source for moral education but also that the two modes of education need not be diametrically opposed, nor that government education must necessarily be politically motivated. Indeed, state education in human rights may, in many cases, reinforce the moral education already undertaken by the household.

If a common standard of achievement of human rights for all peoples of all nations is the desired end, the achievement of such rights must imply something common for all men which exists by nature. Education that is guided by a common standard at least provides the opportunity for prudence to emerge in actions concerning human rights. Education then becomes the cultural substitute for the lack of legal enforcement of human rights by the international community. In this sense, education in human rights is more flexible than are attempts to codify the principles of human rights into declarations. Education may overcome the basic problem encountered in formulating and setting down universal ideas as rules and positive rights – an exercise whose very nature is likely to be plagued with cultural discrepancies and disputes over their interpretation, as evidenced by the Bangkok Declaration and its more extreme cousin, Lee Kuan Yew's Asian values.

If we assimilate the Universal and Bangkok Declarations on the grounds that they promote, through education, an understanding of human rights that is more compatible with implementing some basic principles of human nature, then we may also notice that Lee Kuan Yew stood out on a limb. Neither declaration supports the arguments offered by Lee's Asian values. His kind of education essentially comprised his own interpretation of Confucian ethics and was not an education in a "common standard of achievement of human rights for all people of all nations."[96] Moreover, the promotion of education in human rights may indeed be an expression of the duties which Lee found to be so lacking in the Western system. Rather than embracing a monolithic duty to the family, they recognize the importance of the family and yet are expressed in a manner more compatible with philanthropic friendship, human nature, and prudence.

The politics of the Singapore story – manipulating the *endoxa*

Because enthymemes must appeal to some sense of the truth to be found in commonly held opinions, or *endoxa,* good rhetoricians will attempt to mold historical truths to suit their purpose. The perceived truth of a commonly held opinion may be flawed if citizens have little or no direct experience with the historical record themselves. Moreover, when people look for historical analogies to the present, they most often turn to the recent past which lies within the memories of persons still living.[97] In Singapore, the PAP Old Guard have become the principal narrators of the nation's official history, using their experiences to predetermine popular perceptions of recent history.[98] Commonly held opinions in Singapore are heavily influenced by the political elite's treatment of history, both ancient and modern.

Loh Kah Seng argues that when Singapore achieved independence in 1965, the PAP had rejected history as a threat to nation building. In the late 1970s, however, the PAP began constructing a politically expedient narrative of the past. The National Education initiative, launched by then Deputy Prime Minister Lee Hsien Loong in 1997 with the aim of instilling in young Singaporeans a heightened sense of national identity, represents one product of this positive revaluation of history and now constitutes part of the formal school curriculum.[99] Labeled the *Singapore Story* by Lee Hsien Loong, this officially sanctioned history of the nation is said to be the backdrop which makes sense of the present.[100]

Because the PAP has based its legitimacy, to a very large degree, on its rhetoric of survival, using metaphors that project a sense of crisis and vulnerability, the current talk of survival in the context of communitarian sentiments and Confucian values should not be surprising. In 1965, the PAP projected a crisis message which placed the survival of the young nation in the hands of modernization and economic development. Since the principal opposition to modernization arose from older generations at the time, and because racial conflict remained a real threat, it was thought necessary to reject all links to the past and to tradition.[101] Presumably, tradition then would have included any Confucian thought that stood in the way of modernization, including that which promotes the importance of the family.

By the mid-1970s, however, Singapore's economic success meant that metaphors of economic survival were rhetorically less effective. The emergence of an opposition, albeit limited, in the 1980s, therefore, led the PAP to redefine their survival message by emphasizing culture and national identity. Because the presence of political opposition, in the minds of the PAP elite, represented anarchy and corruption in the youth, a new crisis mentality emerged, and history, insofar as it could be used to instill youth with ideas of respect for order and for their political elders, became far more important. Yet it is an official history narrated principally by the PAP Old Guard.[102] Lee insists that the history of the 1950s and 1960s, and presumably that of the recent past as well, cannot be written by academics.[103] "History does not happen in clean cut units.... It is after the forces let loose in tumultuous events have run their course that the historian comes along ... and narrates them in clear cut chapters."[104]

Loh believes that the history derived from the narratives of a privileged group of PAP leaders has been reduced in recent years to one derived from the experiences of Lee Kuan Yew alone. One CD-ROM on Lee, *Lee Kuan Yew 1995*,[105] portrays him as solely responsible for routing the communists and bringing about Singapore's near-miraculous economic development.[106] Indeed, it may be only coincidental that Lee's *Memoirs*, an unofficial history also entitled *The Singapore Story*, was published in 1998, one year after the National Education initiative's official history of the same name was launched by his son.

Focusing upon the past within living memory, the official *Singapore Story* deals with three major periods, the Japanese occupation, the postwar struggle for independence in the 1950s and 1960s, and economic prosperity since independence.[107] For each of these periods, Loh believes, the PAP have selectively interpreted the facts to provide a politically expedient account of events. During Singapore's early independence period, for example, when trade with Japan was vital to Singapore's industrialization and modernization, the PAP leadership deemed it necessary to play down the sensitive issue of wartime occupation, Japanese atrocities, and compensation for war damages. Yet by the 1980s and 1990s, it had become politically expedient to remind Singaporeans of the occupation and of their ongoing vulnerability to divisive forces, both from within and without.[108] Loh believes that Lee's account of his escape from a Japanese guard in 1942, an incident which, according to Lee, forged his desire to free Singapore from colonial rule, has become identified in the popular mind as the single moment of Singapore's inception as a sovereign state.[109]

The PAP's account of its postwar struggle for independence and economic prosperity since independence has been molded by their effective control of history through limiting public access to government records to all but a few sympathetic historians.[110] Their account of the postwar period is designed to remind the public that communist insurgency and communalist factionalism continue to threaten the survival of the nation, while their account of Singapore's postindependence prosperity reminds the public that economic success was achieved in the absence of a Parliamentary opposition.[111]

Loh claims that while the PAP leadership has constantly encouraged Singaporeans to judge for themselves whether its version of the past is truth or propaganda, the *Singapore Story* remains a tactical selection of facts, highlighting those facts that support the party line while marginalizing or silencing others that do not.[112] Although admitting, in his launching speech, that the National Education program was a "process of indoctrination," Lee Hsien Loong denied that it was political propaganda but said that it is based on historical facts.[113] Truth and facts, according to Lee Hsien Loong, are objective and cannot be propaganda.[114]

Loh believes that although the *Story* does indeed contain verifiable, but tactically selective, facts, it is also an interpretation of the past that has been manufactured for political reasons.[115] While denying that their *Story* is propaganda, the PAP also does not perceive history as simple absolute truth but rather as a mode of rhetoric, and as rhetoric, theirs is more pertinent than others since it directly addresses the nation's survival.[116] As "the archives are starting to be opened ... 30 years after our independence ... and the documents for this period are becoming available to historians," Lee Hsien Loong declared in 1997, "progressively, a more complete picture will emerge."[117] Until that time, presumably, Singapore's official history will continue to reflect the rhetoric of the ruling elite. Common opinions will continue to be based upon highly selective facts which, though true, represent only a fraction of the whole truth. Yet "[t]o the extent that they regard the regime's ideas uncritically as 'commonsense' truisms," Loh believes, "they partake in the government's ongoing hegemony."[118]

Conclusion

Analyzing the popular rhetoric of Asian values, an Asian consensus on human rights stated in the Bangkok Declaration, and the Universal Declaration of Human Rights allows one to discern striking discrepancies between the three and determine whether such differences may be adequately explained on the basis of economic and cultural differences between the East and the West. When Asian states express their understanding of human rights via the Bangkok Declaration, legal positivism tends to replace the expression of some basic principles of human nature found in a universal statement. Upon a close examination of the Bangkok Declaration, one discovers more of a partisan statement than an attempt to adapt basic principles of human nature to Asia's religious and cultural particularities. For example, only by suppressing the Universal Declaration could the Bangkok Declaration allow for a universal right to terrorism in the name of self-determination. Perhaps the solution to the problem of modifying a universal statement to suit cultural particularities lies in making the particular conditions that necessitate and justify some flexibility very difficult to achieve. And in the case of Asian values, elegant arguments for survival should be believed only in the presence of a real, immediate, and present danger.

A political end must, by its very nature, be lower than the theoretical end to which it purports to aim. And this is the fundamental problem encountered in codifying universal principles of human nature into human rights declarations, let alone into declarations that allow for cultural, historical, and religious particularities – legal positivism tends to replace expressions of the basic principles of human nature. At their best, they can promote the education of a common standard of achievement in human rights. And at their worst, they can be used to accuse countries of applying double standards and to condemn another race of people for human rights violations. Because education in common human rights standards at least allows for the possibility of their achievement through actions requiring prudence, both the Universal and Bangkok Declarations acknowledge not only that a just standard is possible, but also that their lack of legal enforcement at the international level should not be used as an argument to justify their violation. On this ground, the Bangkok Declaration may be considered more compatible with some basic principles of human nature than Lee's doctrinaire Asian values.

In the absence of a truly moderate Asian consensus on human rights, the Universal Declaration of Human Rights suffices for a statement on the universality of the fundamental principles to be found therein. Thus far, any elaboration of human rights that allows for cultural, historical, and religious particularities seems to be more of an attempt to meet regional political agendas and is an awkward and unnecessary over-specification. Compromises certainly need to be made, and universal principles can still be applied through Asian practices without losing their universal nature. Yet declarations comprising accusations and defensive pronouncements reached by a consensus of anti-Western opinion are not an adequate replacement for a universal statement.

When judicial positivists battle one another to construct the meaning of the words contained in the Universal Declaration, let alone the Bangkok Declaration, it is time to go beyond this construction to examine the regime itself and, in Singapore's case, what its leading man looked up to. That, apparently, is not moral virtue in the Aristotelian sense because prudence, in the sense of practical action, presupposes neither doing your own thing nor having restrictions imposed upon doing your own thing, but a free habituation to moral virtue. Unless Lee's variety of a well-ordered Confucian society encourages such free moral habituation – and from what we have seen it does not – then it would be shallow to focus solely upon the promotion of human rights as a panacea for a faulty regime. On the other hand, if the education of a common standard of human rights emphasizes rights rather than duties, this may be very much at variance with Aristotle if it encourages the freedom to do whatever one's passions crave for.

The fact that the Universal Declaration does refer to duties is insufficient unless the character of the regime is such that its religion, or philosophy, inculcates moral habits. Since the character of the religion in an authoritarian regime is, to a very large degree, molded by its rulers, the promotion of an education towards a common standard in human rights should only be viewed as a first step, albeit partial and conventional, towards improving the regime. Asian values are not Aristotelian virtues – moral or intellectual – but historical, culturally relative sophistry and are not subject to natural law, unless perhaps Hobbes's natural law wherein the means to peace could correspond to Singapore's Asian economic miracle.

Lee Kuan Yew's Asian values claimed for the East what already exists in the Universal Declaration. His argument became a justification for authoritarian rule in an attempt to resist the moral decay that is made possible in the West through more liberal regimes. Lee saw the West's moral decay in the 1980s and 1990s to be as dangerous to Asia as some saw communism in the 1950s was dangerous to America. Yet Asian values were not so much a consistent ideology, nor did they arise in response to an ideological challenge, but were a series of pragmatic rhetorical arguments invented to justify the PAP's ongoing rule. If Lee's interpretation of Confucian values was meant to bear such a close resemblance to the Protestant work ethic, then why were they particularly Eastern?[119] The attractiveness of Lee's rhetoric to certain harsh African regimes further reinforces the fact that they are hardly genuinely pan-Asian in character.[120]

Finally, Lee's education of the citizenry in Singapore was neither directed towards a common standard of achievement in human rights, nor the moral education by Confucian thought for the purpose of improving the regime. The official history promoted by the PAP not only supported the Asian values and survival rhetoric, it was a self-serving account of facts that remained relatively unchallenged by an uncritical public in times of economic prosperity. In the case of Asian values, arguments emerged from what appeared to be common opinions (shared values and Asian values) but were merely invented ideas. And regarding both Asian values and the survival rhetoric, from a highly selective historical account of facts relating to Singapore and a peculiar interpretation of Confucianism, something was made to appear to follow necessarily from partially true common opinions when it did not. Sophistical rhetoric has deductively misled and deceived an audience by appealing to their passions and prejudices, both contrived and real – Confucianism and economic prosperity.

If the effect of Lee's pronouncements, or "Lee Kuan Yewisms," were limited solely to the citizens of Singapore, then one might feel indifferent towards them for they have chosen their economic lot and must endure the consequences. While at the same time, one could note that Singapore's economic prosperity is an anomaly and that economic success need not walk hand in hand with the suppression of civil liberties. But the Asian values style of rhetoric has gained various degrees of popularity throughout Asia and Africa and has been accepted favorably by China's leaders who today place talk of human rights within the realm of human responsibility, as understood to mean loyalty to the state.

The official "factual" account of Singapore's history supports the PAP's ongoing use of metaphors of survival and crisis, in their various manifestations, that has permeated almost 50 years of political discourse. Indeed, it could be argued that since Singapore, being more industrialized than its regional neighbors, was not as badly hit by the Asian financial crisis of the late 1990s, there is little to prevent the PAP returning to the Asian values discourse should its current survivalist claims – most recently, responding to the threat of terrorism – lose relevance. Survivalist rhetoric serves to legitimize the kind of stability and order that has preserved the regime in its original form.

On purely economic grounds, Singaporeans enjoy the highest standard of living, per capita, in Southeast Asia. Singapore was ranked the ninth richest country in the world in 1995, second only to Switzerland in terms of business and investment potential; Singapore's per capita GNP was among the highest in the world in 1999, and Singapore was described as the most global city in the world in 2001.[121] For Singaporeans to question the PAP survival rhetoric, the PAP official history, or to dismiss the possibility that the nation remains racially explosive, therefore means placing their own economic future at risk.[122] It is in their own interests for Singaporeans to perceive of the PAP rhetoric, and the enthymemes allied to such rhetoric, as partially true and, at least in times of economic prosperity, not lying too uncomfortably inconsistent with their own desire for high standards of living. In times of poor economic performance, however, it would not be inconceivable to discover a far more critical citizenry who may find the PAP rhetoric difficult to swallow.

6 Stability and justice in Singapore

In order to examine the kind of stability and justice promoted in Singapore and more generally, the nature of PAP's regime, we must consider how justice is played out among its citizens. If justice is lacking and reform is necessary, then perhaps Aristotle may be summoned to prescribe a transformation. If on the other hand, through acting like a king, Lee acquired the kingly sort of virtue, or if the citizens are indeed happy in their lot, then perhaps we may find that change is not necessary, nor even desired, by the PAP, the citizens, nor perhaps even Aristotle.

In the *Politics*, Aristotle claims that the best and most choice-worthy way of life, for both the city and the individual, is that accompanied by virtue.[1] Happiness must necessarily be present together with virtue, and one cannot call a city happy by looking only at a certain part of it. Rather, all the citizens must be happy for the city to be happy.[2] It follows that all the citizens must, to some degree, take part in politics because it is impossible for one who acts in nothing to act well, and happiness is a sort of action.[3] Happiness will depend upon how men live their lives and on what constitutes pleasure, wealth, and honor.[4] In a well-organized regime, therefore, the people will voluntarily acquiesce in its arrangement.[5] The stability required for the preservation of regimes, according to Aristotle, does not imply simply preserving the regime in its original form, but rather moving the regime in the direction of virtue and justice. Although stability sets the parameters within which justice may be achievable, natural justice is a form of political justice, and the coming to be of justice, or the improvement of justice, depends upon a particular regime or an improvement in the arrangement of the regime.[6] The best practicable regime is judged to be one in which it is possible for most to participate and in which most cities can share.[7]

Stability for the PAP, on the other hand, is a static concept whereby order means preservation of the status quo and justice is understood as merely conventional, as it would be by legal positivists. The kind of political stability which lies at the heart of their regime is preserved by laws that stifle political discourse and discourage citizens from participating in politics. Such laws are maintained primarily by the PAP's parliamentary

Table 6.1   Total seats occupied in the Singapore parliament after a general election

Year	Total seats	Occupied seats		% of seats	
		PAP	Opposition	PAP	Opposition
1959*	51	43	8	84.3	15.7
1963*	51	37	14	72.5	27.5
1968	58	58	0	100.0	0.0
1972	65	65	0	100.0	0.0
1976	69	69	0	100.0	0.0
1980	75	75	0	100.0	0.0
1984	79	77	2	97.5	2.5
1988	81	80	1	98.8	1.2
1991	81	77	4	95.1	4.9
1997	83	81	2	97.6	2.4
2001	84	82	2	97.6	2.4

Sources: JamesGomezNews.com; Gomez, J. (1999). "Politics and Law in Singapore," *The Singapore Legal System* (2nd Edition), Tan, Kevin, Y. L. (Ed.), Singapore University Press, Singapore; Manikas, P., and Jennings, K., (2001), *The Political Process and the 2001 Parliamentary Elections in Singapore*, National Democratic Institute for International Affairs, Washington, D.C., November 2001.

Note
* Legislative Assembly general elections.

dominance and control over the electoral proceedings. Evidence of the PAP's political domination since 1959, particularly since independence in 1965, may be gleaned from Table 6.1.

There are striking similarities between Lee's articulation of stability and justice as order and the reasoning of the leaders of the People's Republic of China. Roy notes that both the PAP leadership and the Beijing government claim that a single party is required to maintain stability and unity. And like the PAP, the Chinese Communist Party claims to have a popular mandate and democratic representation.[8] China's own conception of human rights echoes Lee's emphasis on order and economic prosperity. Indeed, in 1993 Jiang Zemin claimed that without the bias of Western assumptions, China's human rights record was admirable and that China's universally acclaimed achievements had promoted stability not only in China but in Asia and the world at large.[9] Singapore's then Prime Minister Goh added:

> The new generation of Chinese leaders, like the previous generation, will want a strong government that can maintain stability and order. The new leaders are better educated, more market-oriented and pragmatic. But they are not closet democrats. They do not want China to descend into chaos, and neither does the rest of Asia. China will evolve; change is inevitable. As Communist ideology withers away in the consciousness of the Chinese people and leadership, and the

economy becomes more complex, a looser and more differentiated political system may well develop. But it will not be a "democracy" as the West hopes.... Unlike the Russians, East Europeans or Latin Americans, the Chinese have never had any wish to be considered good Westerners.

(Goh Chok Tong (1993))

America believes that the Chinese public desire not only economic liberalization but political liberalization as well, and that democratization will produce political stability both internally and internationally. Aristotle, on the other hand, would have us question whether the West's model of liberal democracy is the most fitting kind of regime for China, given the size of the population, the relatively poor status of the average Chinese, and the enormous institutional obstacles which must be overcome. It may not be an impossible task to institute a liberal democratic regime in China, but it won't happen overnight. Furthermore, Aristotle's own study of 158 regimes was limited to relatively small city-states or *polieis*, and not empires. Perhaps the best solution that Aristotle could hope for then is a more favorable mixing of the democratic elements with the oligarchic to improve justice within the existing regime.

Yet the Singapore government would have us believe that no such democratic element, or pro-democracy movement, exists at all in China. Rather, the Tiananmen Square incident was merely a battle between soft authoritarians and hard authoritarians, and the students only wanted an end to inflation and corruption and a return to the good government which will bring the prosperity so evident in Singapore.[10] A similar interpretation of the 1990 elections in Burma has been offered, whereby economic considerations were said to dominate any concern for political change.[11]

Lee has argued that while democracy and human rights are worthwhile ideas, the real objective should be good government. He identified the socio-economic prerequisites of democracy as political stability, adequate levels of education, and economic development.[12] "Asian democracy" or "soft authoritarianism," rather than Western or "liberal" democracy, according to Singapore officials, combines the best of both the Western and Asian political traditions.[13] They believe that Confucian East Asians are more inclined than liberal Westerners to accept constraints on individual rights in exchange for stability and economic growth in society as a whole.[14] These constraints come primarily in the form of harsh government regulations which appear to cover the whole ambit of life in Singapore, from a ban on chewing gum to Singapore's Internal Security Act.

The art of legislating in Singapore

In 1992, the Singapore government imposed a ban on chewing gum because of the rising costs of removing gum from public places. In 2002, under American pressure to relent on the ban in the face of a new free-trade agreement, the government decided to allow chewing gum in Singapore, provided that it be sugarless, for medicinal purposes, and approved by honest doctors.[15] Other minor indiscretions which can attract large fines in Singapore included smoking duty-free cigarettes, owning a *Playboy* magazine, dropping confetti, forgetting to flush a public toilet, and dancing in public, the last of which was relaxed in August 2003 to allow for pub patrons to dance on bar-tops.[16] For more serious offenses, on the other hand, there is the Internal Security Act that provides for arrest without a charge warrant and indefinite incarceration without a trial – all of which effectively amounts to a permanently available suspension of the writ of habeas corpus. According to Lee Hsien Loong, this is "one reason why our streets are safe and joggers are not subject to mugging."[17]

The Internal Security Act is a cold-war descendant of the Emergency Regulations implemented by the British in 1948 – well before the PAP came to power on the island – as well as the Malaysian Internal Security Act of 1960 that extended to Singapore on 16 September 1963. The Act, and its predecessor regulations, was originally intended to fight the spread of communism and to quell rioting both on the Malayan Peninsula and in Singapore. It creates the authority for the issue of Orders of Detention or Orders of Restriction that prevent any person "from acting in any manner prejudicial to the security of Singapore ... or to the maintenance of public order or essential services."[18] Any person deemed to be a threat may be detained or have restrictions imposed upon them for a period of up to two years, without limitation on the renewal of such orders,[19] and the deliberations of panels constituted to review cases affected by the Act remain confidential. While the rules and place of detention may be directed by the Minister's pleasure, restrictions may include specified activities, places of residence, employment, confinement, notification of movements, prohibitions against addressing public meetings or from holding office, from advising organizations or associations, from taking part in political activities, or from traveling beyond the limits of Singapore.[20]

According to the Minister of Home Affairs in 2002, Wong Kan Seng, the Act is considered preventive in nature rather than punitive – persons are held in preventive detention for so long as they pose a threat to national security and/or investigation requires it, but not any longer.[21] A former *Barisan Sosialis* member of Parliament, Chia Thye Poh, was arrested in 1966, along with 22 others, without a charge. For refusing to confess publicly that he was a communist and to sever his ties with the Communist Party of Malaya, he was imprisoned for 22 years without a trial under the Internal Security Act and was detained for a further ten years, for a time in government half-way houses, with restrictions placed upon his activities.[22] Interestingly, Chia claims that in 1955 the PAP had called for the abolition of the Emergency Regulations when they were the opposition in Parliament because "excessive powers of arrests and detention hinder democracy."[23] In 1978 though, when the U.S. Assistant Secretary of State for Humanitarian Affairs and Human Rights in the Carter administration visited Lee to urge the abolition of detention without trial, Lee replied that the law had been challenged by the opposition at every election and that each time an overwhelming majority had voted for him and for the law.[24]

In 2001, 13 people were arrested under the Internal Security Act for plotting to bomb the U.S. embassy and other diplomatic missions, along with American naval vessels. Eight of these persons were allegedly trained in Afghanistan by al-Qaeda and were suspected of being members of the Jemaah Islamiyah group. In 2002, 21 more persons were detained for allegedly plotting to attack Singaporean targets, 18 of whom were served with Orders of Detention for two years, while the remaining three were served Orders of Restriction.[25] In December 2002, the Singapore-based and government-friendly newspaper, the *Straits Times*, claimed that the United States was using a parallel legal system for handling its terrorist subjects.[26] While it is true that in 2002 the U.S. government began holding persons designated as "enemy combatants" in a military prison at Guantanamo Bay, the U.S. courts, over the objections of the Bush administration, found that detainees may challenge their incarcerations before a judge and the administration decided to prosecute some in the ordinary federal courts. Moreover, to date, the United States Congress, unlike the Singapore Parliament, has not enacted legislation which provides the government with a permanently available positive power to suspend the writ of habeas corpus. Rather, the Constitution of the United States merely provides that the writ of habeas corpus shall not be suspended unless, in cases of rebellion or invasion, public safety requires it.[27] Regarding this provision, Abraham Lincoln believed that "the Constitution is not, in its application, in all respects the same, in cases of rebellion or invasion involving the public safety, as it is in time of profound peace and public security."[28]

Singaporean officials, therefore, would need to argue that Singapore has been in a state of constant rebellion and invasion since, or before, 1955 in order to associate the Singapore government's suspension of the writ of habeas corpus under the Internal Security Act with the American executive's prerogative to do so in times when profound peace or public security are argued to be lacking. Indeed, it could be argued that Lee's rhetoric of survival, which has been a constant theme since 1959, seems to have been required to justify not only the continued operation of certain provisions in the Internal Security Act but also other varieties of harsh legislation, many of whose provisions operate in conjunction with the Internal Security Act.

Lee Hsien Loong believes that, in Singapore, the media's role is "to inform people of government policies" rather than to question these policies.[29] A censorship board controls the inflow of all foreign journals and magazines, and the Undesirable Publications Act allows the government broad discretion in banning written materials, compact discs, sound recordings, pictures, and computer-generated drawings that threaten the stability of the state, are pro-communist, or incite religious, ethnic, or linguistic animosities. Similar provisions are also found in the Films Act and the Internal Security Act for publications which threaten national security or public order. The government strongly influences the print and electronic media through its approval and removal of management shares in Singapore Press Holdings – a private company which owns all general circulation newspapers published in the four official languages, including the *Straits Times*.[30] The government can also punish international publications by restricting their circulation under the Newspaper and Printing Presses Act.[31] And in August 2001, the Singapore Parliament passed legislation to control politically oriented websites on the Internet.[32] Survey findings published in 2001 showed that Singaporeans lead the world in access to Internet usage.[33]

Public gatherings in Singapore are handled with the same degree of paternal suspicion and caution. Under the Public Entertainment and Meetings Act, permission is still required before any public speech may be delivered. Although there has been indication that the government could relax certain provisions of the Act in the future,[34] persons wishing to speak at any public meeting, except one sponsored by the government, must obtain a public entertainment license from the police, and public meetings of more than five persons require a police permit. Under the Societies Act, organizations with ten or more members must register with the government, and political activities – including commentary on matters deemed to be "political" – by organizations other than political parties are prohibited.[35]

While much of the above legislation that has been passed by the PAP-dominated Singapore Parliament may be used at any time effectively to silence criticism of the ruling elite, its significance comes from its mere existence and the threat of its use, rather than its actual use. The Internal Security Act, for example, was not used to detain anyone from 1989 to 1996, and it had been used sparingly until 2001 and 2002.[36] Lee's view of the harsh measures used against the opposition though, is particularly Machiavellian: "[W]e don't have to use it often. Use it once, twice, against big people. The rest will take notice."[37] While the "big people" are outside the jurisdiction of the Singapore courts if they choose to flee the country, they are penalized if they attempt to continue their "anti-nationalistic" activities abroad and return to challenge the government. All Singaporeans who remain abroad for more than ten years automatically have their citizenship revoked.[38]

The role of the opposition

The one-party dominance in Singapore is thought to ensure continued stability because, in the minds of the ruling elite, opposition parties comprised of professionals, lawyers, and accountants would surely appeal to the gut feelings of race, language, religion, and culture, merely creating contention and division among Singapore's multiethnic society.[39] Commenting on the future structure of the party system in Singapore, Lee Hsien Loong claims that "we should try to preserve a certain social and political cohesion, so that there is a dominant mainstream view of the way the country should go."[40]

While it seems, on the one hand, that the ruling elite recognizes that the presence of an opposition is indeed a feature of a democratic parliamentary system of government, a system which it inherited from Great Britain, on the other hand, that an opposition may voice its views is interpreted not merely as a formal institutional check on the government but as the mocking of a great leader in an Asian Confucian society – and this, Lee Kuan Yew believed, should not be allowed.[41] It would appear that, although Singapore has inherited the British parliamentary system, the PAP has applied its own interpretation of the Westminster parliamentary traditions for according to Lee, "If you had plain straight forward Westminster rules ... it would never have worked. You would never have had the self-renewal and a series of good people getting into the government and working Singapore up the ladder."[42]

Criticism of the government, especially by the opposition, is understood as mocking the ruling elite, and those who dare to speak out against the elite must be held accountable. Singapore's opposition leader and leader of the Singapore Democratic Party (SDP), Chee Soon Juan, for example, who claimed that freedom of expression was protected by the Constitution, was charged twice under the Public Entertainment Act for making unlicensed speeches in 1998 and 1999. Both Chee and the Assistant Secretary-General of the SDP, Wong Hong Toy, were sentenced to 12 days' imprisonment but had their fines reduced by the court, thus saving them from a five-year disqualification from seeking political office.[43]

Although intense competition is a hallmark of Singaporean life, the one institution not subject to any serious competition is the PAP itself. While they have rejected a roundtable's suggestions for reforms that establish an independent election commission to draft constituency boundaries, introduce more single-member constituencies, and raise the minimum number of campaign days from nine to 15,[44] the PAP remains wary of criticism about the lack of an effective opposition. In 2002, then Prime Minister Goh proposed establishing an artificial opposition, an alternative policy group within the legislature called the People's Action Forum – comprised of 20 PAP MPs assisted by the Institute of Policy Studies – who would be charged with challenging government policies in

Parliament.[45] While the proposal was eventually shelved, the idea itself suggests that the only opposition the PAP is prepared to tolerate is its own.

The art of defamation

Aristotle says that the one who gives a fine performance of the part of the kingly ruler should ensure that legal punishments are administered through officials and the courts.[46] The use of defamation lawsuits in Singapore politics is legendary. Along with the British parliamentary system, Singapore inherited British statutory and common law. Perhaps influenced by his legal training at Cambridge, the obvious means with which to hold accountable those who mock great leaders in Singapore became, for Lee, the application of defamation law. Since the 1950s, Lee established a political climate under which politicians have to defend any allegation of misconduct or wrongdoing.[47] He saw the use of lawsuits as justified by the need for politicians wrongfully accused of misconduct to respond in a court of law so that the public could see that they were not fearful of standing up to cross-examination.[48] In this way, he believed, PAP ministers have been able to command the respect of people.[49]

Lee claims that he has personally never been sued for defamation because he has not made any false defamatory statements. Rather, when he said something disparaging about his opponents, he had ample evidence to back his statements.[50] Opposition MPs who have sued when they were defamed, on the other hand, have always lost. Lee's first libel action was in 1965, while Singapore was still in the Malaysian Federation, where he was accused of being an agent of the communists. Since then, he has successfully defended himself against numerous accusations made by his political opponents and unfavorable reporting by the foreign press agencies on matters including corruption, nepotism, and cronyism. The PAP's opponents regard the use of defamation suits as yet another weapon in the government's arsenal to stifle criticism. Some go as far as to claim that a form of legal terrorism exists in Singapore.[51] Their claims that a compliant judiciary, which consistently rules in favor of the government, hears the lawsuits have also led to more lawsuits.[52] The opposition's fear of defamation lawsuits – when all decisions go against them and sometimes lead to bankruptcy – is based on their own experience and the experience of others, and inevitably determines the content of political discourse during an election campaign.

During and after the 1997 elections, for example, the secretary general of the Worker's Party and long-time political rival of Lee, J. B. Jeyaretnam,[53] along with a Worker's Party politician, Tang Liang Hong, were sued by then Prime Minister Goh, then Senior Minister Lee, and nine other senior PAP members for remarks Jeyaretnam made to a Worker's Party rally during the campaign. Goh had previously announced that Tang was unsuitable for Parliament because he regarded him to be a

Chinese chauvinist with anti-Christian views. When Goh refused to retract his remarks, which were published in the newspapers, Tang, in an interview with the *Straits Times*, announced his intentions to initiate legal proceedings against Goh and Lee and that he was contemplating filing a police report against them both on the grounds that they had defamed his character. Jeyaretnam, at the urging of Tang, announced at the party rally that Tang had indeed filed police reports against "Mr. Goh Chok Tong and his people."

Goh immediately initiated proceedings for damages against Jeyaretnam on the grounds that such an announcement implied that he was a criminal. Although the judge claimed to be adopting the reasoning of a 1963 British House of Lords case, which found that guilt could not be inferred in such circumstances, he nevertheless ruled that guilt was inferred in the case before him.[54] Damages and full costs were awarded against Jeyaretnam and Tang the following year. Because all parties to the case against Jeyaretnam and Tang had agreed to be bound to the findings of liability in the case, seven additional damage suits were awarded against Jeyaretnam, who was declared bankrupt, thus making him ineligible to sit in Parliament. Lee's lawyers also filed petitions for Tang's bankruptcy.[55] Tang fled the country for Malaysia after receiving death threats and eventually sought refuge in Australia. The PAP filed an injunction restraining Tang and his wife from disposing of their assets, obtained default judgments against Tang in the High Court, with damages assessed at over $8 million, and immigration authorities seized his wife's passport.

In 1999, the PAP also filed a petition to close the Worker's Party because of its inability to pay over $280,000 damages and costs awarded against it in a 1998 defamation case connected with an article published in the party's paper, *The Hammer*, in 1995. The paper ceased publication in 1995 and did not reappear until 2001. Closure of the party would force the resignation of its two parliamentary representatives. The party lost an appeal against the award in 1999 and, while the sum had grown to over half a million dollars, international media attention and criticisms of the PAP's intentions forced the PAP not to proceed with its action.

In another case, Chee Soon Juan, who was threatened with a lawsuit after heckling Prime Minister Goh during the 2001 campaign, faced one after the election for his accusation that the Prime Minister had misused public funds. Since joining the SDP in 1992, Chee has lost his university position and was sued for disputing accusations related to his sacking. The SDP lost an earlier defamation suit just prior to the 1997 elections.[56]

Allegations of nepotism brought against the government are treated in a similar manner. An article published in the American-owned *International Herald Tribune* in 1994 implying that Lee's son owed his position to his father's influence was met with a defamation suit from then Senior Minister Lee, then Prime Minister Goh, and then Deputy Prime Minister Lee Hsien Loong. In the Singapore Supreme Court, Lee defended

Singapore's strict Press laws, accused the American media of "cultural supremacy," and claimed, "I saw it as a vicious, very daring assault on my integrity, my standing and my honor ... he went right overboard to hurt me, my son, the Prime Minister and my government."[57] The High Court awarded a record US$678,000 in damages to the plaintiffs. In 2002, the online news service *Bloomberg* apologized "unreservedly" for any inference of nepotism which they may have made towards Lee and his son following the appointment of Lee Hsien Loong's wife, Ho Ching, to the head of the state-owned investment company, Temesek. Lee's other son was the CEO of Singapore Telecom, and Lee himself was chairman of the Government Investment Corporation.[58]

The inconvenience of elections

The PAP's absolute parliamentary majority since 1963 and dominance since 1968 have ensured that it has total control over the electoral pro-ceedings. Gerrymandering and the short notice given for the redrawing of political boundaries, the timing of the election, and other strategic law-making give the PAP much advantage.[59] For example, in addition to calling the 2001 general election only nine days before it was held – the minimum under Singapore law – the government also announced new constituency boundaries only one day before calling the election.

Singapore's plurality, or first-past-the-post electoral system, ensures that there is a severe discrepancy, as is the case in the United Kingdom, between the ballots cast for the opposition and the number of seats it obtains in parliament. In the last five general elections, from 1984 to 2001, an average of 30 percent of the ballots cast for the opposition in contested seats has only translated to between 1.2 and 4.9 percent in parliamentary seats. In 1988, a constitutional amendment merged some single-member districts into Group Representation Constituencies (GRCs), a move which would further shore up the PAP's parliamentary dominance. These con-stituencies would return "teams" of three Members of Parliament, later increased to four in 1991 and six in 1996, with at least one member to be an ethnic minority. The party with a plurality of votes in a GRC wins all of the seats.[60]

Because the opposition parties have limited resources, they choose to campaign for protest votes in single-seat wards and only some GRCs. Of the 84 seats in the 2001 Parliament, 75 would come from GRCs with five or six members in each. Since only 29 opposition candidates stood for election in 2001 – nine in single-seat wards and 20 in four five-seat GRCs – the PAP had already won its ninth successive election victory before the polls opened as 55 PAP members had retained their seats unopposed.[61] Following the election, Lee Kuan Yew's concern over the results extended only to the 18 new PAP Members of Parliament who had won their seats without a "fight."[62] Victory by the remaining 37 unopposed members must, presumably in the eyes of the PAP elite, reflect a sign of mass approval.

The government also allocates broadcast time to parties in proportion to the number of candidates fielded. Because opposition parties have difficulty in recruiting candidates, they are rarely heard. Each candidate, in addition, is required to make a S$13,000 deposit, a large sum for those already facing the costs of defamation litigation. Another successful electoral tactic of the PAP, and a practice defended by Lee,[63] is to offer benefits, such as upgraded housing, to constituencies who cast votes for the PAP ahead of those who do not. This practice is particularly effective because approximately 85 percent of all Singaporeans live in public housing.[64]

Finally, when elections do arrive, many Singaporeans may fear that their support for the opposition could at least ruin their career prospects or lead to something worse.[65] Commenting on the 1997 elections, Chee Soon Juan notes that "Unfounded or not, fear among the Singaporeans is very significant. . . . [In the elections] the ballot papers were serially numbered and some Singaporeans were absolutely terrified that their vote can be traced back to them. I don't believe the government would do this. But the fear of it affects us in a major way. Right now everyone is so fearful."[66]

The citizen army

Unlike many harsh regimes, the prospects for change in Singapore are unlikely to be influenced by any alteration in the military's perspective because the military establishment in Singapore has been dominated by the civilian sector since its inception. Rather than functioning as an independent entity outside of civilian authority, the Singapore Armed Forces (SAF) – a creation of the PAP government – are regarded as an integral part of the administrative structure, playing an essentially complementary role in the social and economic functions of the state. The military elite has, therefore, not developed an independent identity or political agenda, a distinct corporate culture separate from those of the administrative and political elites, and the line that traditionally separates the military from the civil bureaucracy and the political leadership has all but disappeared.[67]

Because the military's agenda closely reflects the PAP's, it is not surprising to find that the same small-state survival ideology permeates SAF thought. While threats of Indonesian and Malaysian aggression in the 1960s did linger, the military's survival ideology seemed more indicative of support for Lee's rhetoric than a response to any real threats. In a National Day speech in 1982, for example, Lee's greatest concern was to make the young more conscious of security, while Goh, then defense minister, later announced that "conflict, confrontation and war is the order of the day and peace and stability is the exception."[68] This template for SAF thought ensured that the Bush administration's rhetoric surrounding its home-front efforts in the "War on Terror" would be well received in Singapore. Particularly since the arrest of alleged al-Qaeda and Jemaah Islamiyah members in 2001 and 2002, for example, the PAP has reinforced their justification for the Internal Security Act.[69] Noticeably, however, no such endorsement for amending the U.S. constitution along similar lines has been well received in the United States.

Not surprisingly, given the similarities between the two countries' security concerns, the SAF turned to Israel for a model of a citizen army and, in the early 1970s, sought training assistance from the Israeli military. Like Israel, Singapore was convinced that national service suited the country because it was the most efficient and economic means of maintaining an army. A conscript army of reservists with civilian jobs would also foster a national identity among the citizenry. As a consequence, the Singapore soldier feels not so much an attachment to his unit or regiment than to the nation as a whole. The SAF constantly forges partnerships with the community because more than 80 to 85 percent of its troops are part-time national servicemen.[70] The nature of the military structure in Singapore, therefore, acts constantly to reflect and transmit the agendas of the PAP throughout the citizenry.

Because the military comprises mostly working citizens, they are not likely to question the need for, let alone instigate, any political reformation in Singapore. Rather, the military voices the PAP's message throughout society. Yet because the PAP's Asian values rhetoric was also tied to Singapore's economic miracle, then perhaps a working citizen army may, if affected by economic hardship, be more influential than some may think. Others argue that the sheer amount of money spent directly on the SAF "would suggest that such attention and resources would be zealously maintained in times of economic difficulty."[71]

Will economics determine the PAP's fate?

While some commentators have suggested that Asian values fell from being the cause of Asia's success and the chief factor legitimating Asia's soft authoritarianism to being the root of the economic meltdown across nearly the whole region in 1997,[72] Lee believed that Asian values were not the cause of the meltdown because cronyism and corruption have been endemic since the beginning of the "Asian miracle" in the 1960s, more than 30 years ago.[73] Furthermore, if Asian values were to blame, Lee asked, why were Hong Kong and Singapore not affected?[74] Indeed, while economic and political instability spread rapidly throughout the region, as witnessed by the demise of President Soeharto in Indonesia, Singapore remained politically stable throughout the Asian financial crisis.

Lee believed that cronyism and corruption are not the result of Confucianism, but of the debasement of Confucian values. Singapore weathered the crisis better, according to Lee, because no corruption or cronyism distorted the allocation of resources, and public officers were referees, not market participants.[75] He asserts that where there are transparent systems to detect and check abuses of power and privilege, as in Singapore and Hong Kong, both former British colonies, such abuses are rare.[76] It is true that there is very little corruption in Singapore. Yet one of the reasons for this phenomenon, aside from the harsh punishments, is that authorities make it unnecessary for public officials, and especially senior technocrats allied to the PAP, to engage in corruption by paying them what they would earn in the private sector, along with the attractive perks.

While Lee claimed that Asian values would help countries recover from economic recession, just as they encouraged the economic growth of the past,[77] his confidence must be tempered by the fact that in 2001–2002, Singapore was experiencing its worst recession since independence. This recession, however, was caused primarily by external factors rather than internal, namely, a drastic fall in the demand for Singapore's export products in the United States and Japan, the poor performance of regional economies, a loss in world semiconductor sales to their Taiwanese competitors,[78] a loss of shipping revenue to competitive new Malaysian port facilities,[79] and a fall in tourism following the 11 September 2001 terrorist attacks on the United States.[80] Singapore's trade figures in September 2001 were the worst on record, and Singapore's economic growth rate was predicted to fall from one of the world's highest, averaging 8.7 percent since 1965, by 3 percent in 2001, while total lay-offs were forecast to exceed 20,000 in both 2001 and 2002.[81] In 2002, Singapore's growth rate was estimated to have fallen to 2.2 percent following the impact of Severe Acute Respiratory Syndrome (SARS), and 1.1 per cent in 2003.[82] When unemployment rose to 4.8 percent, growing numbers of Singaporeans expressed a wish to emigrate,[83] and it remained at 4.5 percent throughout 2004.[84] Fortunately for the PAP, a recovery in the U.S. and Chinese demand for Singapore's electronic goods in 2004 led the government to upgrade its economic growth predictions from 3–5 percent to 8–9 percent. Fearing the prospects of future drops in demand for their electronic products, the government has also sought to diversify its manufacturing sector and to increase its offshore investments in telecommunications, banking, and utilities.[85]

To the extent that the population realizes that the economic downturn in recent years was externally derived, the PAP hierarchy may not be blamed. Nevertheless, preempting the full effects of the recession may have figured in the PAP's decision to call an election ten months ahead of schedule. While the economic recession could have tested the validity of Lee's claim that Asian values would restore the growth rates of the past, it may have also compelled Singaporeans to question the legitimacy of a regime that prides itself on its economic performance yet failed, for the first time since independence, to deliver results. Case believed that "it would appear that the terms of Singapore's social contract, limiting political rights in return for economic benefits, can no longer be guaranteed."[86]

In his National Day speech, delivered prior to the 2001 election, then Prime Minister Goh announced a "new social compact" aimed at reducing the growing income disparities between Singapore's richest and poorest, often ethnic Malay, citizens.[87] A New Singapore Share scheme would distribute shares, or redeemable government bonds, to the poor while at the same time government ministers, members of Parliament, senior civil servants, and judges would have their salaries cut by 17–20 percent.[88] Such drastic measures, announced as they were before the government called the general election, while aimed at reducing the possibility of class and ethnic conflict, also help to illustrate the PAP's awareness of the shaky ground upon which they stand during times of economic recession.

Conclusion

In analyzing the stability and justice in any regime, we ultimately need to look at the ends towards which the stability of the regime is directed and if, as is the case with Lee's Singapore, stability merely implies the preservation of the status quo, then we must question the merits of the justice produced by the regime. If the status quo consists of the people having little or no participation in government, and no ability to audit the government but rather the government audits their ability to implement its policies, would Aristotle consider this a just regime?

Or are they like the best people, according to Aristotle, the farming sort, who find working more pleasurable than engaging in politics and ruling? Do they strive more for profit than for honor and put up with oligarchies so long as their property is protected, becoming rich before long while others cease to be poor?[89] Does Aristotle truly believe that it is sufficient for people to have authority over deliberation but no share in elections, as in his example of Mantinea, or is he merely inventing this case to illustrate a deficient form of democracy?[90] In Singapore, it would appear that citizens have some, albeit very limited, share in elections but no authority over political deliberations. Could the case of Mantinea, like Singapore, be an illustration of a regime which requires the kind of reform that Aristotle's "preservation" encourages, or can economic security truly satisfy any yearnings for political change?

Zakaria believes that the absence of free and fair elections should be viewed as one flaw, but not the definition of tyranny.[91] He argues that governments should be judged by yardsticks related to constitutional liberalism, and one of these yardsticks is economic liberty. Despite the limited political choice offered in Singapore, according to Zakaria, the country should not be branded a dictatorship so long as it steadily expands economic, civil, and religious freedoms.[92] While Singapore may indeed "provide a better environment for life, liberty, and happiness of their citizens"[93] when compared with harsh dictatorships in other parts of the world, the fact remains that the political involvement of its citizens has remained overly restrictive and that there has been little to no "steady expansion" in their civil and religious freedoms, but in many cases quite the opposite.[94] While Aristotle, unlike many modern democratization theorists, may have agreed with Zakaria that the absence of free and fair elections does not alone define tyranny (or dictatorship or authoritarianism for that matter), he may have rejected the idea that economic liberty was a sufficient replacement for the absence of liberty elsewhere in the regime. Nevertheless, Singapore is a case where the legitimacy of its leadership rests, perhaps more than any other nation in the world, ultimately upon their economic success. Promoting economic success as the flagship of legitimacy in Singapore, however, could lead the PAP to its own downfall. Before the Asian recession of the late 1990s, Fukuyama asked whether Singaporeans would change as their prosperity continues:

> Lee may think that Singaporeans are one happy family, deferential to his wise and benevolent leadership, but they are, so to speak, just off the farm. Will they remain childishly obedient in another generation or two, when prosperity can be more taken for granted and nearly everyone has a college education?
>
> (Fukuyama, F. (1992a): 60)

If, however, their economic security cannot be guaranteed in the future, during possible times of recession, how will this affect Singapore's "farming sort" of citizenry? When they are unable to strive more for profit than for honor, if some become poor while others cease to be rich, then would they not be less likely to put up with an oligarchy? Indeed, Singapore's minister for trade, industry, and foreign affairs has conceded that lifelong employment in government-linked companies or in the civil service can no longer be taken for granted,[95] and Singapore's manufacturing sector is very likely to face increasing competition from emerging markets in China and India in the future.[96]

Aristotle believes that regimes are best preserved when a certain degree of mixing takes place between the oligarchic and democratic elements. This kind of mixing leads to justice, and in the case of Singapore – where politics is ruled by the technocratic oligarchs – justice can only be improved by allowing the people to participate in politics. Whether the people themselves embrace the opportunity to do so is another matter. Yet to date, the PAP government has done its best to stop this from happening. While encouraging the presence of a facade opposition, the PAP has, historically, obliterated any criticism with a barrage of defamation suits, coupled with harsh legislation, using them not once or twice, but many times, against big people and hoping the rest will take notice.

Allowing the people to take part in politics could be interpreted by some that Aristotle endorses a qualified form of democracy and by others that he encourages a liberal democracy. Yet improving the mixing among the ruling elite is also an important factor for Aristotle in preserving any regime, even a tyrannical one. Apart from the various activities Aristotle prescribes to moderate the tyrant's rule, what seems to define the kingly tyrant is that he maintains his ability to use his power when the need arises. If preserving the regime means improving justice within the limits set by the tyrant, then it is in the tyrant's own interests to provide the democratic elements with at least a fair chance of being heard. Whether this would lead to further opportunities for moderating the tyrant's rule would then depend upon the tyrant, and perhaps upon Aristotle's hope that the tyrant acquires virtue rather than that the tyranny becomes a liberal democracy.

In the case of Singapore, that it could have been possible for Aristotle to view Lee Kuan Yew's strategy as the more moderate way of preserving a tyranny suggests a modest endorsement of his rule. This is because it may be at least the most moderate form of tyranny and, given the altern-ative brutish form of tyranny practiced in Burma, the best one could hope for under the circumstances. Yet it is also quite possible that, by Aristotle's definition, Singapore's prosperity disqualifies the city-state from being classified as a tyranny and that it could more appropriately be cited as an example of oligarchic rule. And if so, then the future preservation of this regime would still require the appropriate mixing on the part of the stewards of the city in the manner that Aristotle suggests.

Aristotle claims that the political expert should be able to assist existing regimes as well and introduce an arrangement which allows for the possi-bility that his reforms may lead to what is best, more attainable, and most fitting.[97] Reforming a regime is, according to Aristotle, no lesser task than to institute one from the beginning.[98] Part of the reason for this is that the people must unlearn what they have learned from the beginning.[99] In the case of Singapore, where the people have lived under Lee's rules for the past 40 years, perhaps this requires rhetoric addressing, and opposing, the *endoxa* fostered by Lee, while in the case of China some 50 years of indoctrination must be overcome.

The people of Singapore have learned to accept Lee's policies, from independence onwards, on the basis that they restore ethnic order, secure the state against external threat, and produce economic growth. On com-paring Lee Kuan Yew's authoritarian political structure in Singapore with the more democratic Taiwan, Huntington noted, "The freedom and cre-ativity that President Lee has introduced in Taiwan will survive him. The honesty and efficiency that Senior Minister Lee has brought to Singapore are likely to follow him to his grave."[100] Cho Oon Khong, furthermore, believes, that while Lee's legitimacy among Singaporeans is understand-able, it is also finite:

To them, he has earned the right, through his considerable accomplishments in building the country, to rule by injunction ... [and because] the terms of political discourse in the city-state have been molded from the beginning by Lee Kuan Yew ... fundamental change to the political regime will have to await Lee's demise.... Any legitimacy that Lee has secured through his personal authority will likely pass with him.

(Cho Oon Khong, (1995): 128–129)

While this may be a reasonable assessment, it is also true that Lee's unique accomplishments have provided him with a legitimacy that has proved difficult to bequeath to his second-generation successors. Nevertheless, it is not simply Lee's passing that could precondition any fundamental change in Singapore, but the demise of his legacy. In 2003, Lee himself announced that he had no intention of leaving his Senior Minister's post, despite his age, and that he would serve in cabinet as long as he could contribute and remain as a Member of Parliament while he was fit and able.[101] And on 12 August 2004, Lee Kuan Yew's son, Lee Hsien Loong, succeeded Goh Chok Tong as Singapore's third-ever Prime Minister. The honor bestowed upon him by his People's Action Party (PAP) ensures that the Lee dynasty will continue to guide the city-state. For while Goh was appointed to Senior Minister, Lee Kuan Yew, at 81, remained a key advisor in the cabinet through his newly created title as Mentor Minister.

These appointments, along with various cabinet promotions and the retention of the finance portfolio by the new Prime Minister, reflected not only a consolidation of power by the third-generation leaders, but that Lee Kuan Yew's legacy of ideas should continue to resonate throughout the PAP hierarchy for years to come. Indeed, while Goh has in the past spoken of developing a fourth generation from professionals entering Parliament, it is difficult to foresee that they too would not conform to the party line or that the senior members among them would not have been well screened by their predecessors. Perhaps this is why reforming a regime like Singapore is, in Aristotle's view, no lesser task than to institute a new one.

7   Tyranny in Burma

In his account of tyranny, Aristotle speaks of a third kind which, being neither based on law nor a monarchic rule over willing persons, is a sort of counterpart to absolute kingship and is most particularly held to be tyranny.[1] It is possible to show how Burma lies within Aristotle's description of rule over the unwilling and to illustrate how the Burmese generals have adopted the brutish tactics which Aristotle says are required to preserve such a regime. In their efforts to make their rule longer lasting, more recently the generals have also been assuming the duties of past kings, providing a performance of the part of kingly rulers.

In the case of Burma, where the generals' rule is neither based on law nor a monarchical rule over willing persons, their legitimacy would always be questionable. This reason, as well as the nation's size, ethnic composition, poverty, and relative international isolation, might explain the tendency of the Burmese rulers to pursue the more brutish strategy to preserve their rule, rather than the kingly strategy of Lee Kuan Yew. It is revealing, however, to discover how they have attempted to transform their defective title into a valid one by promoting the duties of kingship. By way of their Buddhist political rhetoric, the promotion of Buddhism to legitimize their rule, the generals are not only appealing to the mass political culture, the *endoxa*, of the Burmese. They are also attempting to transform a brutish tyranny into a more subtle form and, inadvertently, following Aristotle's prescription for its preservation, in much the same way as Lee Kuan Yew's and the PAP's promotion of Confucianism in the Asian values rhetoric of Singapore.

Tracing the roots of the generals' kingly performance to their defective title requires some understanding of the various grounds on which they have attempted to legitimize their rule. Assessing the validity of their performance also requires some historical understanding of the nature of Burmese kingdoms and the political culture of the Burmese. It is necessary, therefore, to examine these topics before analyzing the Buddhist political rhetoric of the Burmese political elite. As in the Singapore case study, examining stability and justice in the Burmese regime allows us to comment on the regime's "preservation," according to Aristotle.

The *Tatmadaw*'s rule over Burma

Aristotle's "third kind of tyranny" is "most particularly held to be tyranny" because the tyrant rules in an "unchallenged fashion over persons who are all similar or better, and with a view to his own advantage and not that of the ruled. Hence [it is rule over persons who are] unwilling; for no free person would willingly tolerate this sort of rule."[2] However, because most tyrants arise from popular leaders who were trusted because of their slanders of the notables,[3] for a free people to tolerate a tyrant willingly, at least initially, they must have developed some degree of trust in him at the beginning of his rule.

Aristotle does not rule out the idea of tyranny being constituted as rule by a group. Indeed, in his discussion of kingship he notes that kingship accords with merit, whether based on individual virtue or the virtue of "family."[4] He also notes that one of the modes in which tyranny is destroyed is from within itself, "when those sharing in the kingship [power] fall into factional conflict," and he provides examples of tyrants and their families who were destroyed in this way.[5] Since his third kind of tyranny is a kind of counterpart to absolute kingship, then for the purpose of classifying the military regime in Burma, it would not be unreasonable to surmise that an army under the tight control of one man or a few generals could constitute such a family who share power and "look to nothing common, unless it is for the sake of private benefit."[6]

Burma gained its independence from Great Britain in 1948 through the political efforts of Aung San. Aung San, however, was assassinated, along with his cabinet, on 19 July 1947, and to this day he is viewed by the Burmese[7] people as the father of the country. Because he was instrumental in creating the Burmese Independence Army during World War II, he is also seen as the father of the army (the *Tatmadaw*). His struggle for independence from Great Britain spawned a military elite that has maintained a tight hold on the reigns of the country since General Ne Win's coup of 1962.

Bogyoke (General) Aung San was also the natural father of the General Secretary of the National League for Democracy (NLD), Aung San Suu Kyi, who, in the general elections held on 27 May 1990, received a popular mandate to rule Burma after winning 59.9 percent of the popular vote and 392 of the 485 contested seats (80.8 percent of the total seats), while the army-backed National Unity Party (NUP) won approximately only 21.2 percent of the popular vote and ten seats (2.1 percent of the total seats).[8] She remains the leader of the only democratically elected opposition in Burma today yet has remained effectively silenced by the generals of the *Tatmadaw* since before the general election.

From 1948 to 1958, Burma adopted a parliamentary system of government, with representation for ethnic minorities. Insurgencies and factional conflict permeated the entire period, both between and within political parties, and their communist movements. Elections held during this period and in 1960 were "deeply flawed," with allegations of widespread intimidation and ballot rigging.[9] In 1958, citing the army's mistaken fear of a communist takeover (arising through the merger of three parliamentary parties: the "Clean" faction of the Anti-Fascist People's Freedom League [AFPFL], the National United Front [NUF], and the People's Volunteer Organization [PVO]), and facing rumors of an imminent military coup, Prime Minister U Nu resigned and invited the army's senior general, Ne Win, to install a "military caretaker" administration.

Ne Win's brief was to prepare the country for elections within six months.[10] Though it took nearly three times as long, Ne Win followed the legalities of resigning as prime minister when after six months the elections had not taken place, until the Constitution could be amended.[11] The *Tatmadaw*'s presence throughout the caretaker administration was pervasive. Though cabinet positions were held by civilians, over 100 military officers, mostly in their 30s or 40s, were appointed to senior executive positions.[12]

Parliamentary democracy returned to Burma in 1960, and U Nu's Clean faction of the AFPFL was elected by the voters with the moral and sometimes public support of the majority of Buddhist monks, though the *Tatmadaw* would have preferred a victory by the rival Stable faction. When serious differences again arose within the AFPFL and between the AFPFL, the *Tatmadaw*, and ethnic minority leaders in 1962, Ne Win, encouraged by the *Tatmadaw*'s achievements under the caretaker administration, seized power in a *coup d'etat*. Ne Win arrested the civilian political leaders, dissolved the national parliament and state legislatures, dismantled the court system, suspended the 1947 Constitution, along with the writ of habeas corpus, and created a Revolutionary Council comprising 17 military officers with himself as chairman.[13]

Learning from their failed attempt to create a mass non-partisan organization during the caretaker government years – the National Solidarity Association – the military's Revolutionary Council created its own cadre party, the Burma Socialist Programme Party (BSPP) in July 1962. The BSPP was modeled along Leninist lines and was intended to become a mass political organization providing social, political, and economic indoctrination. Ne Win was elected as party chairman when the BSPP held its First Party Congress in 1971, and he resigned his army commission in 1972. A draft of a new constitution, creating a single-party system (the BSPP), was presented to the Second Party Congress in 1973; it was approved in a national referendum later that year and came into effect in 1974. From 1962 to 1988, therefore, Burma was ruled by the military, both directly – under the Revolutionary Council, and indirectly – under the BSPP by way of the 1974 Constitution.

Following a popular but abortive uprising on 8 September 1988, a military coup, led by General Saw Maung, under the direction of Ne Win, ended the 14-year period of constitutional military rule since 1974. A 19-member State Law and Order Restoration Council (SLORC) placed Burma once again under direct military rule by assuming comprehensive executive, legislative, and judicial powers. Composed entirely of military officers, SLORC declared martial law and ruled by decree. The military has ruled the country directly under the auspices of the SLORC, from 1988 to 1997, and the State Peace and Development Council (SPDC), from 1997 to the present.

If most tyrants arise from popular leaders who were trusted because of their slanders of the notables, then perhaps the reformist Ne Win's disdain for the traditionalist U Nu and his Clean faction of the AFPFL, as well as for the ethnic minority leaders in 1962, is an illustration of Aristotle's principle. And for the purpose of applying Aristotle, then, unlike some historians who transpose the past into the present while ignoring the in-between, we can assume that under the parliamentary system of government that existed in 1962 the people could still have been considered "free." Perhaps the common Burmese people, therefore, developed some degree of trust in Ne Win, at least at the beginning of his rule, to tolerate willingly his return.

Smith believes that Ne Win's caretaker administration of 1958 to 1960 was, in effect, a trial run.[14] The caretaker administration brought stability to the previously faction-ridden political environment and, with unrestrained military powers, success in the battle against insurgency.[15] Indeed, Smith believes that "in the army's official account of these years, *Is Trust Vindicated?*, Ne Win allowed the *Tatmadaw*'s record to stand or fall more or less entirely on its successes in the battle against insurgency."[16] Yet the *Tatmadaw* also had some economic success as well. The production and export of rice, for example, reached a postwar high that has not been repeated.[17] And since Ne Win had followed the constitutional procedures for conducting elections, having resigned his prime ministership during the administration, his appearance at that time would not have been one of a power-hungry general. There appears to have been good reason, therefore, for the people to trust Ne Win, and his motives, leading up to the coup of 1962.

Huntington believes that the immediate effect of a military coup is to produce a feeling of relief and harmony.[18] Trager suggests that following the 1962 coup, "if anything, there was a feeling of relief; at least, the slide downward would be stopped."[19] Ne Win's brutal rule since then, however, resembled a counterpart to absolute kingship and, being rule over the unwilling, his behavior fell nothing short of that which Aristotle claims is most particularly held to be tyranny. Ne Win used the army to suppress political opponents, protesters, students, monks, ethnic and religious minorities, and other civilians on numerous occasions, though most particularly in 1962, 1974, and 1988, arresting, torturing, and killing thousands. The *Tatmadaw*, under Ne Win, became the corrupt arm of a tyrant, a family whose senior members were fashioned and promoted by Ne Win on the basis of loyalty, brutality, lack of education and idealism, and successful indoctrination.

Ne Win retired as chairman of the BSPP at an extraordinary party congress on 23 July 1988 and the BSPP renamed itself the National Unity Party on 26 September 1988. Though Ne Win distanced himself from the party's new "democratic" political identity, he remained in the shadows well after the SLORC came to power, and it is only comparatively recently that the generals had been distancing themselves from his influence. In December 2002, Ne Win died while under house arrest and his body was cremated within hours, in a private ceremony without military honors. No senior members of the *Tatmadaw* were present, and no local radio, television, or newspapers carried any official announcements of his death.[20] Yet despite his passing, the senior *Tatmadaw* generals of the SPDC today constitute the major part of Ne Win's legacy, and their rule is no less tyrannical than was his. This may be illustrated by returning to Aristotle's account of the preservation of tyranny in its most brutish form.

Aristotle on the preservation of the *Tatmadaw*'s regime

The brutish mode in which most tyrants administer their rule is, according to Aristotle, preserved by adopting the methods established by Periander of Corinth and are seen in the rule of the Persians.[21] These include

> lopping off the preeminent and eliminating those with high thoughts – and also not permitting common messes, clubs, education, or anything of this sort, but guarding against anything that customarily gives rise to two things, high thoughts and trust. Leisured discussions are not allowed, or other meetings connected with leisure, but everything is done to make all as ignorant of one another as possible, since knowledge tends to create trust of one another.
>
> (Aristotle, *Politics*, 1313a40–1313b6)

The elimination of protesters, political opponents, and the like has been a common feature of the *Tatmadaw*'s regime under the auspices of the SLORC and the SPDC. In this respect, they have continued a tradition laid down by Ne Win. Mass arrests, killings, and disappearances followed the democracy demonstrations of 1988 and again in May 1990, when the SLORC refused to honor the results of Burma's first multiparty general election held in thirty years. The results of the May 1990 general election may be found in Table 7.1. Prior to the election, stringent rules were applied to some candidates, whereby it was deemed an offense to hold public gatherings of more than five persons. Political party candidates, members, and party headquarters were monitored and harassed. Before and after the election, the SLORC arrested the NLD party leadership,

Table 7.1   Results of the general election held in Burma on 27 May 1990

Party name	Seats won	% total seats	% popular vote
National League for Democracy	392	80.8	59.9
Shan Nationalities League for Democracy	23	4.7	1.7
Arakan League for Democracy	11	2.3	1.2
National Unity Party (formerly BSPP)	10	2.1	21.2
Union National Democracy Party	1	0.2	1.5
League for Democracy and Peace	0	0.0	1.8
Other parties, independents	48	10.0	12.7
Total	485	100.0	100.0

Source: Seekins, D., (2002). *The Disorder in Order: The Army-State in Burma since 1962*, Bangkok: White Lotus Press, p. 210.

including Aung San Suu Kyi, along with many opposition candidates. The SPDC continues to monitor the movements of the NLD, while many members remain in prison.

High thoughts and trust are both attributes currently lacking in Burmese society. Indeed, Pye believes that Burma suffers from acute problems with social capital because basic distrust is so widespread, being part of Burmese socialization practices and inferiors cannot trust anyone with power.[22] Pye observed that in the education of Burmese children, "nothing is more important than instructing the child to have absolute faith and loyalty in his family and unrestrained suspicion of strangers." Because of this, the Burmese find "it difficult to conceive of themselves in any way associated with objective and regulated systems of human relationships."[23] Huntington believes that because "the presence of distrust in these societies limits individual loyalties to groups that are intimate and familiar ... people are and can be loyal to their clans, perhaps to their tribes, but not to broader political institutions."[24]

According to Pye, Burmese culture, above all, evinces a deep ambivalence about power. "Everybody wants it, but people are too timid to try for it. Nobody wants to be subordinate, because inferiors are vulnerable and cannot trust anyone with power."[25] The idea of power can be understood by the Burmese concepts of *pon*, *awza*, and *ahnadeh*. Any Burmese wishes to be recognized as possessing *pon*, a blend of charisma, presence, grace, dignity, and holiness. *Awza*, or power, is *pon* in a social context, and anyone aspires to it. *Ahnadeh* is a physical sensation which restrains people from asserting their interests and causes them to defer to the interests of others.[26] Thus, any Burmese quest for power, or perhaps even high thoughts, would be restrained by a higher sense of civility that ensures social order. Yet civility, according to Pye, is only the first step towards the development of social capital and civil society. And because the Burmese show little to no trust, their development of social capital has not gone far beyond the realm of civility.[27]

A tyrant, according to Aristotle, should also "attempt to let nothing that is done or said by any of those he rules escape his notice, but to have spies ... for men speak less freely when they fear such persons, and if they do speak freely they are less likely to escape notice."[28] In addition to operating an elaborate intelligence apparatus – the Directorate of Defence Services Intelligence, which came under the directorship of former Prime Minister, General Khin Nyunt – the state controls all major media outlets in Burma, newspapers, television, and radio, and all press is heavily censored. Neither freedom of speech nor the defamation suits so common in Singapore exist in Burma. Criticism of the government can result in imprisonment without trial and without the need for an Internal Security Act.

Aristotle notes that a feature of tyranny is "to slander ... and to set friends at odds with friends, the people with the notables."[29] The state press has regularly slandered the NLD and, on occasion, Suu Kyi, and state-owned newspapers, such as the *New Light of Myanmar*, publish regular reports of party factionalism and the resignations of NLD members who, though they are said to have resigned "of their own accord," presumably are forced to do so if they have resigned at all.[30] Suu Kyi estimates that the government intelligence organizations spend 80 to 90 percent of their time, energy, and money on matters related to NLD activities.[31]

Another feature of tyranny, according to Aristotle, is

> to make the ruled poor, so that they cannot sustain their own defense, and are so occupied with their daily [needs] that they lack the leisure to conspire. Examples of this are the pyramids in Egypt, the monuments of the Cypselids, the construction of the temple of Olympian Zeus by the Pisistratids, and the work done by Polycrates on the [temples] at Samos. All of these things have the same effect – lack of leisure and poverty on the part of the ruled.[32]
>
> (Aristotle, *Politics*, 1313b19–25)

While it could be argued that making the people poor and keeping them occupied had less to do with deliberate actions on the part of the generals than their general ineptitude, it could also be argued that they took no genuine steps to rectify the situation and, in the case of using forced labor for various archeological, religious, and economic projects, actively maintained such a condition. Through economic mismanagement, autarchy, state central planning, and feeble attempts at economic liberalization, the generals in Burma have, for over 40 years, maintained Burma's status as one of the poorest countries in Southeast Asia.[33] Fear of foreign influence, coupled with the personal whims and desires of the generals, permeated both periods of socialist planning and economic liberalization. For example, in late 1987, Ne Win decided to demonetize between 60 and 80 percent of Burma's currency, destroying most people's savings overnight.[34] The people themselves harbor strong memories of the military's suppression of democracy demonstrators and are now too impoverished and incapable of challenging the SPDC. The *Tatmadaw* have regularly conscripted corvee labor, usually villagers or prisoners, as porters during its military operations and for public works projects. These have included the restoration of the Royal Palace in Mandalay, temples and pagodas in Pagan, and the natural gas pipeline to Thailand.[35]

Aristotle believed that the common brutish tyrant's distrust of the multitude requires "the sequestration of [heavy] arms" and that a tyrant is also "a warmonger, so that they [the ruled] will always be kept lacking in leisure and in need of a leader."[36] The *Tatmadaw* have proudly boasted their abilities to fight ethnic insurgency since Burma's independence, and their arms acquisitions, along with troop recruitment over the past decade, have made them the second largest army in Southeast Asia. Small clashes with Thai forces along the Thai–Burma border have been common. Aristotle notes that ill-treatment of the mass, and its expulsion from town and settlement, is common to tyranny.[37] In addition to their ill-treatment of ethnic and religious minorities, the *Tatmadaw* have also resettled entire Burman villages and townships for various reasons – military, population control, restoration, or beautification for tourism, for example, Pagan.

Aristotle says that a tyrant must beware of those who are dignified or free.

> [I]t is also a feature of tyranny not to delight in anyone who is dignified or free; for a tyrant alone claims to merit being such, and one who asserts a rival dignity and a spirit of freedom takes away the pre-eminence and the element of mastery of tyranny; hence these are hated as persons undermining [the tyrant's] rule.
>
> (Aristotle, *Politics*, 1314a5–9)

In her writings, Aung San Suu Kyi encourages a "spirit of freedom" as a way of mastering the harsh realities of *Tatmadaw* rule. Though not free in the real sense, she is dignified and claims to defeat the *Tatmadaw* tyranny with Buddhist *vipassana* contemplation practice. Hence, she is hated by the generals as a person who undermines their rule.

According to Aristotle, the three things which tyranny aims at are:

> [T]hat the ruled only have modest thoughts (for a small-souled person will not conspire against anyone); ... that they distrust one another (for a tyranny will not be overthrown before some persons are able to trust each other ...); ... and ... an incapacity for activity, for no one will undertake something on behalf of those who are

> incapable, so that not even a tyranny will be overthrown where the
> capacity is lacking.
>
> (Aristotle, *Politics*, 1314a15–25)

In Burma, it seems that all three of these "defining principles to which
the wishes of tyrants may be reduced,"[38] are fulfilled under the rule of the
Tatmadaw. Yet in order to make their rule longer lasting and their defective title more legitimate – both domestically and in the eyes of the international community, at least less offensive – the *Tatmadaw* have attempted
to transform their brutish tyranny into a more moderate sort of superintendence that is practically, though not theoretically, the opposite.[39] They
are preserving their tyranny by attempting to make it appear more kingly,
being sure to safeguard their power, so that they may rule over both the
willing and the unwilling.[40]

That only a small minority of the people were willing to be ruled by the
Tatmadaw was evident in the outcome of the May 1990 elections. Improving this imbalance will depend to some degree upon the success of their
kingly performance, and the Buddhist political rhetoric which accompanies this performance. Before examining this rhetoric, both in theory and
in practice, it would be useful to indicate how the *Tatmadaw* came to this
position by tracing the development of their various claims to legitimacy
since 1962.

The legitimacy of the *Tatmadaw*

Since 1962, when General Ne Win and the *Tatmadaw* seized control in a
coup d'etat, among the reasons initially offered to support the *Tatmadaw's*
rule were its claims to possess a unique ability in suppressing communist
and ethnic insurgencies while effectively managing the economy. Within a
decade, however, the communist insurgency had been greatly reduced
and the latter two rationales had become the *Tatmadaw's* pivotal justifications. The *Tatmadaw* have also sought to placate domestic strife since the
1990 elections by proposing constitutional reforms. Indeed, much of the
scholarship on Burmese politics focuses either upon the *Tatmadaw's* military capabilities or provides political economic interpretations of current
events. More elaborate attempts to establish the legitimacy for the continuation of military rule involve historical and cultural interpretations of
the traditional relationship between Burmese rulers and their subjects.
Although the military themselves have historically tended to realign their
focus strategically among these alternatives, depending upon the changing conditions and circumstances, events have transpired which encouraged the generals to play down the former and promote the latter. It
would be helpful briefly to address the major arguments which are often
used by scholars in justifying or questioning the legitimacy of military rule
in Burma, before introducing the ground which is most responsible for

producing the rhetoric promoted by the generals to preserve their regime in a kingly fashion.

Suppress ethnic insurgencies

The question of political autonomy for the minority groups in Burma has proved to be a source of tension and conflict since independence. Under Great Britain's Indian-style divide and rule policy, the political aspirations of ethnic minorities in Burma were quashed while preference was shown to some groups, particularly the Karens, for recruitment into the Burma British Army. Yet rather than displaying preference towards one ethnic group's aspirations and well-being over another, perhaps it would be more accurate to report that the British administration became adept at playing off the competing interests of various ethnic groups against each other in and around the Frontier Areas while maintaining order in Ministerial Burma or Burma Proper. Smith remarks that the British remained "highly inconsistent in their political recognition of ethnicity" and preferred to sanction traditional rulers in Frontier Areas rather than allow the people the freedom to remove poor leaders.[41] Because of their relative isolation, Frontier Areas remained neglected under British rule, both economically and, to a large degree, politically. Resentment fueled by nationalistic missionary activities and the British practice of recruiting Indians into key administrative and financial positions paved the ground for a nationalistic fervor among the ethnic minorities by the late 1930s, and again after the war.

In 1947, Aung San declared that there could only be one nationality in Burma, though there could be distinct races and tribes within the nation. The Shan States could, however, constitute a National Community, yet there was no other in Burma, and whereas a common language was an essential factor in a National Community, it was not so in a Political Community. His preference was for a Union of Burma, with properly regulated provisions to safeguard the rights of national minorities.[42] Much speculation exists over whether Aung San conceded statehood to the Shans, Karens, and the Kachins so that they would agree to throw in their lot with Burma, and the actual concessions made in the tentative discussions held with minority groups in 1947 remain unclear. What is clear, however, is that Aung San preferred not to commit, or finalize, any further concessions.[43] The issue of whether or not he had agreed to statehood would resurface after his death and helped fuel the demands for autonomy and nationhood among various ethnic groups for the next 50 years.

During the parliamentary debate over Burma's independence, Winston Churchill expressed

> grave doubts that the assent of the frontier tribes has been honestly and genuinely given.... About 12,000 murders and dacoities or armed robberies are reported to have taken place in the first seven

months of this year and this is only a prelude ... in my view to the bloody welter which I fear will presently begin, as it has in India.

(Churchill, W. (1947): 1850)

Following independence, a number of ethnic minorities, including the Shans, sought promises of political autonomy from the government. Succumbing to pressure, Prime Minister U Nu's promise to make Burma a federation of ethnic nationalities, with greater autonomy for ethnic minority provinces, became one of the reasons prompting Ne Win's coup of 1962. While much of Burma's post-independence history has been dominated by ethnic insurgency,[44] it is the *Tatmadaw*'s perception of its ability to quash such insurgencies and maintain peace and order that has provided one of their main sources of legitimacy.

Since 1988, the *Tatmadaw* have acquired an arsenal of military hardware from China,[45] worth between US$1 and 4 billion, either through drug money or on non-collateral loan. Singapore also has been a source of ammunition and smaller weapons.[46] With 400,000 troops at their disposal, the *Tatmadaw* managed to quash all ethnic insurgencies by the mid- to late 1990s, relocate a number of religious minorities, and drive some 200,000 Arakanese Muslims into exile in Bangladesh. Most insurgent groups signed cease-fire agreements with the SLORC in return for local business favors or employment from the government. Following the fall of their headquarters in Mannerplaw, most members of the armed wing of the Karen National Union (KNU), one of the only major minority forces that refused to sign a peace agreement, fled to the Thai border and settled in camps inside Thai territory, where they have been prone to raids conducted by Burmese forces. The Shan State Army-South, formerly the Shan United Revolutionary Army, also continues to resist the Burmese government, and since 1996 the Burmese military have been relocating over 300,000 Shan people from over 1,400 villages in the central Shan State to cut off support for its troops.[47]

Economic stewardship

Because the generals were unable to legitimize their rule on the grounds of popular consent, having overwhelmingly lost the 1990 elections, they have for much of the past 12 years, and indeed for most of their rule since 1962, argued that they were the only group capable of implementing successful economic programs. The military take their role as Burma's economic gurus quite seriously.

In modern times, Burma's economic well-being has been allied, to a large degree, with foreign interests. Burma's long association with foreign investment dates back to its early trading relations with China and India. European interests began to appear in Burma in the form of factories for the processing of teak and other natural resources which were operated by the Portuguese in the 1500s, Britain's East India Company in the 1600s, and by the Dutch in the 1700s.[48] Following Great Britain's annexation of Lower Burma in 1852 and the colonization of Upper Burma in 1886, British firms actively invested in the trade of timber, rice, and petroleum.[49] By 1941, one-quarter of Burma's capital stock was owned by foreign investors, Britain, China, and India being the dominant countries of origin.[50] Following the end of World War II, and upon Burma's achieving independence from Great Britain in 1948, foreign companies returned and were permitted to operate through to the early 1960s, receiving official encouragement by way of the Burmese government's 1955 Investment Policy Statement, and the passing of the 1959 Union of Burma Investment Act.[51]

This policy changed following the military coup of 1962, however, and perhaps in capturing the regional mood at that time while reflecting Burma's neutral foreign policy, Ne Win's promotion of *The Burmese Way to Socialism* in the Constitution of 1974 launched the nation upon a tragic program of international isolation and autarchy.[52] Consequences of the nationalization of agriculture and industries, 25 years of central economic planning, and the curtailment of almost all foreign direct investment ensured the destruction of the Burmese economy while its regional neighbors flourished. Although Burma's national economy had not flourished under civilian rule either, Ne Win's *Way to Socialism*, being a perversion of Aung San's ideas on socialism,[53] quashed any hope of economic recovery from the war-time destruction at a time when Burma's neighbors were benefiting from large sums of anticommunist aid. Burma fell from its position of being the world's largest exporter of rice, and the most economically promising of all the former colonial states upon achieving independence, to the backwater state that it remains to this day. Burma today is unable to produce enough rice to feed its own people and, alongside Cambodia, remains one of the poorest countries in Southeast Asia.

In 1988, the SLORC embarked upon a program of economic liberalization involving the deregulation of many key industries and an opening of the economy to foreign investment and trade. While many Western governments withdrew their aid to Burma following the coup, and private businesses grew wary of investing in the country, Singapore's support of SLORC's program during this period is noteworthy. Table 7.2 shows that Singaporean firms led the official "approved" foreign investment figures in Burma in 1996, although most Chinese investment, along with many Japanese interests, remained officially unrecorded.

Unlike most Western governments, the Japanese and Singaporean governments were actively encouraging companies to invest in Burma after 1988, for the purposes of both commercial gain and, later, to counter the growing Chinese influence in the region.[54] While Japanese companies saw Burma as the next site for their labor-intensive manufacturing operations, the Japanese government, under pressure from the Japan–Burma Business

Table 7.2   Total investment in Burma approved by the MIC, by country, for existing and completed projects – 1996 (US$ millions)

Country	Number of projects		Amount approved		
	May '96	Feb '96	May '95	Feb '96	Dec '96
Singapore	27	38	337.16	683.8	1,170
United Kingdom	11	18	634.15	666.22	807.76
France	1	1	465	465	465
Thailand	27	29	418.26	421.12	427.58
Malaysia	7	9	69.57	227.27	420.27
United States	13	14	226.27	241.07	n.a.
Japan	5	6	101.14	118.21	n.a.
The Netherlands	2	2	83	83	83
Austria	1	1	71.5	71.5	71.5
Hong Kong	17	17	64.44	64.44	n.a.
South Korea	9	9	60.59	60.59	60.59
Australia	4	6	28.2	30	n.a.
Canada	1	6	22	25.03	n.a.
The Philippines	1	1	6.67	6.67	6.67
China	4	5	5.5	5.85	n.a
Bangladesh	2	2	2.96	2.96	2.96
Macao	1	1	2.4	2.4	2.4
Sri Lanka	1	1	1	1	1
Total	134	166	2,599.81	3,096.01	5,270

Source: U.S. Dept. of Commerce, *Country Commercial Guides* (August 1995); Myanmar Investment Commission, *Report on Direct Foreign Investments* (February 1996); Mya Maung (1997), *Asian Survey*, Vol. 37, No. 6 (June 1997); Far Eastern Economic Review (1997), *Asia 1997 Yearbook.*

Association whose members stood to lose if Japan's Official Development Assistance (ODA) was withdrawn, decided to "normalize" relations with Burma in March 1989. Since normalization meant that Japan's existing ODA contracts would be met, Seekins believes the Japanese government used its ODA to coerce the SLORC into holding multiparty elections.[55]

According to Seekins, Tokyo has used its existing ODA contracts, along with its humanitarian aid, to pressure and reward the SLORC into granting concessions on several occasions, including in 1994 and 1995, before and after the release of Aung San Suu Kyi from house arrest.[56] Suu Kyi criticized this policy after her release for having failed to produce any lasting political changes and for ultimately serving the interests of private Japanese firms who are influential in the Diet, in the Liberal Democratic Party, and in the various ministries attached to the administration of foreign aid. Throughout the 1990s, Japanese companies tied to ODA contracts had been pressing their government to resume concessionary loans for infrastructure[57] and, following Japan's resumption of limited aid for humanitarian projects, further increases in Japanese investment were expected to occur before the onset of the Asian recession. Japan remains a major exporter to Burma through the investments of influential firms connected with its various aid programs.

The Singapore government, on the other hand, offered tax incentives for companies investing in Burma and, according to Selth, Burmese ministers had been urged by *Tatmadaw* leaders to give preference to projects supported by the Singapore government.[58] Singapore is now Burma's leading source of imports and its largest market after India and China.[59] Foreign investments originating from Singapore amount to over US$1.1 billion, are committed to more than 50 projects, and some of these are directed towards major infrastructure improvements such as the construction of industrial zones and container port facilities.[60] Singaporean firms have also invested heavily in the hotel and airline sectors for tourism. Singapore Technologies, for example, a Singapore government company, owns a Rangoon hotel for businessmen and has completed a US$150 million airport project in Mandalay, while Asian Pacific Breweries of Singapore established a new plant for Tiger Beer, supposedly to replace the departure of Carlsberg and Heineken.

Moreover, there is much evidence to suggest that, following the Western embargo on the sale of arms to Burma since 1988, Singapore was the first country to supply the *Tatmadaw* with small arms. According to Selth, Singaporean companies, with the full knowledge and support of the Singapore government, have since 1988 supplied Burma with military hardware ranging from small arms, ammunition, automatic rifles, assault rifles, mortars, mortar bombs, artillery shells, rockets, grenade launchers, landmines, a wide range of communications and electronic equipment for defense purposes, artillery training, specialist unit training, intelligence training, Burma's first surface-to-air missile system, and a state-of-the-art facility to manufacture small arms and ammunition.[61] Singaporean companies have acted either on their own behalf or as brokers for the sale and final shipment of arms from other countries. And Singaporean banks have acted as a money-laundering point for the payment of early Chinese arms purchases from the sale of narcotics.[62]

While the Singapore government consistently denies these claims, according to Selth, "Singapore can hardly accuse Western countries of interfering in Burma's internal affairs (for example, by condemning the military regime's repressive policies towards the NLD) when it is helping to provide the same regime with the means to retain its firm grip on power."[63] Selth believes that Singapore does not wish to offend Thailand by admitting to increasing the military capabilities of its neighbor, nor does Singapore wish to lose its reputation as an honest dealer in regional affairs and a staunch opponent of narcotics trafficking.[64] Yet Singapore also does not wish to push Burma closer towards the Chinese, either by criticizing its human rights abuses or by ensuring that China becomes the sole supplier of arms to the *Tatmadaw*.

Suu Kyi accuses Singaporeans of Buddhist *moha*, or ignorance, for thinking that the lack of democracy in Burma is not an obstacle in the way of economic success. She believes that their focus on Burma as virgin territory for investments, such as tourism, forces them to overlook important factors, such as the lack of education, let alone political change, without which there cannot be any sustained economic development.[65] Lee Kuan Yew, on the other hand, believed that it is was not possible to "squeeze" Burma, i.e. to refrain from investing, without the country falling to pieces, and America has not made assurances that they would be there to pick up the pieces should Burma break.[66]

By 1998, the transparency of SLORC's economic liberalization policy had become apparent. Any profits being made were of a short-term nature, usually ending up in the hands of the military rather than being distributed among the people. Between 1989 and 1994, 46 percent of SLORC's total expenditures were spent on defense, while spending on social services, including health and education, fell from 32 percent to 23 percent in real terms.[67] Foreign investment over the ten-year period from 1988 to 1998 generally took the form of natural resource extraction, particularly oil, gas, and timber, while other key sectors were ignored altogether. Domestic investment was discouraged by interest rate ceilings and a reluctance to remove tight controls on the investment and banking markets. A ridiculously overvalued Kyat[68] further discouraged investment and encouraged a flourishing black market. Foreign currency reserves have remained low and inflation remains high. Infrastructure problems are enormous and will never be adequately addressed until IMF and World Bank funding resumes – a move which the United States has refused to endorse for the past decade. The only flourishing sectors in Burma today are, therefore, the black market, the drug market, illegal border trade, and sometimes tourism.

In 1998, in an effort to control border trade and stem the outflow of foreign currency, the SPDC reinstated import and export controls on consumer goods and many key commodities, especially sugar and rice.[69] All trade in "non-essential" goods with China was banned[70] and the SPDC reasserted direct control over the economy, thus ending their brief attempt at economic liberalization – a policy that is recommended by most comparative theorists as a necessary stage in any transition towards democracy.[71] The restrictions were largely ineffective, however, because of the wholesale hoarding of consumer goods in urban areas and the continuation of black-market trading along the border. Such border smuggling trade has largely been ignored, being part of the ceasefire accommodations provided to former insurgents, as well as for fear of offending Chinese border communities and simply to maintain harmony among the profiteering *Tatmadaw* border units.

The SPDC's admission to ASEAN in 1997, while viewed by many as an attempt by the generals to gain some regional legitimacy, was proposed and backed by the former Prime Minister of Malaysia, Dr Mahathir Mohamad. It seemed, however, to have had little effect on Burma's trade or economic prospects, nor have the sanctions imposed by the United States in 1997, nor for that matter did the Asian economic crisis of 1998. All evidence indicates that the *Tatmadaw* generals had performed a far better job of ruining the economy from within, before the crisis ever hit Burma. The SPDC's economic liberalization policies from 1988 to 1998 had failed[72] and, by implication, so too had their ability to ground their legitimacy in economic stewardship rather than popular consent.

Constitutional reforms

Since 1993, the *Tatmadaw* have attempted to gain legitimacy by establishing a National Convention with the purpose of writing a new constitution. The origins of the modern National Convention are very different to those sentiments embodied as the "spirit of Panglong" at Aung San's Panglong conference in 1947. The modern spirit may be traced to the election loss suffered by the *Tatmadaw*'s National Unity Party in 1990. Refusing to hand over power, the generals explained that the election was merely a signal for constitutional change and that all major parties, or at least those members not still incarcerated, would be invited to attend a convention designed for that purpose. Because the generals favor a regime which preserves their political power, they have turned to the Indonesian model that secures a permanent allotment for the military in parliament. In 1993, the SLORC also established the Union Solidarity and Development Association (USDA). Modeled on the BSPP, the USDA represents the *Tatmadaw*'s alternative to the NLD. It is a mass organization which fosters patriotism and loyalty to the government. Should a new constitution ever come about, the USDA could assume a prominent role along the lines of the Golkar party in Indonesia. Callahan, however, believes that since the marginalization of the Indonesian armed forces from decision-making in the 1980s and 1990s, Indonesia's constitution would no longer appeal to the *Tatmadaw*.[73]

There is little to indicate that a new constitution will be drafted anytime soon. Despite this, the *New Light of Myanmar* regularly declares that it is the responsibility of all citizens to work towards a new constitution. The NLD walked out of, and were later expelled from, the national convention in 1995, and in 1996 the SLORC issued law 5/96 silencing any criticism of the convention and the constitution after the NLD threatened to write their own constitution. Prior to 2004, the national convention had not convened in seven years. It had become obvious to all, including the generals, that the first step towards power sharing would be a meaningful dialogue between the SPDC, the NLD, and the ethnic minorities. The NLD, however, along with some minority groups, chose to boycott the constitutional convention in May 2004, the NLD citing the continued detention of

Aung San Suu Kyi and the party's vice chairman, Tin Oo. National constitutional conventions provide the generals with a means to placate international pressure by appearing to facilitate the democratic process. They
serve as veiled attempts by the *Tatmadaw* to demonstrate, perhaps for the
foreign media, their willingness to work towards a negotiated resolution
yet they also illustrate their reluctance to implement any lasting solution
involving all parties.

Historical, traditional, or kingly right to rule

Some Burma scholars have developed a legitimacy argument, based upon
the hereditary right of kings, for the SPDC to rule in the same fashion
today. Examining this argument would seem to be most appropriate for
the purpose of applying Aristotle's account of tyranny to Burma. Victor
Lieberman's theory of Burmese power, being centered around a figure
and emanating to the countryside, causing order with rule or disorder
without, was adopted by the political scientist Robert Taylor in describing
the state in Burma following these precolonial lines of authority.[74] Aung
Thwin's elaborate account of society in the medieval kingdom of Pagan
also plays on this theme, with power concentrated at the top, extending
downwards to the lower classes of the population, and obligations returning to the center.[75] It is possible, therefore, that the *Tatmadaw* may use
historical interpretations to justify the forced conscription of labor for
conducting military exercises, public works, and in general, loyalty to the
state. Viewed as such, the SPDC's kingly rule is a reciprocal relationship,
with authority and responsibility, or caring, flowing in return for loyalty
and order from the SPDC to the people.

Among the numerous kings in Burmese history, perhaps the three most
noted for uniting the people were King Anawrahta in the eleventh
century, King Bayinthaun in the sixteenth century, and King Alaung-
phaya, founder of Konbaung, Burma's last dynasty, in 1798. It could also
be argued that Aung San was the fourth person to reunite Burma and,
being the father of both the *Tatmadaw* and Suu Kyi, became the founder
of the current political dynasty. Following in this glorious tradition, it was
not surprising that in 1988, SLORC too claimed to have a government
that reunited Burma. Indeed, the SPDC appears to have indirectly resurrected the "kingly right to rule" argument, partly because of its historical
appeal as a legitimizing factor and, more importantly, because the preservation of Buddhism was considered to lie among the duties of ancient
Burmese kings.

Smith believes that it was the monarch's unique role as defender and
promoter of Buddhist religion which in the final analysis confirmed his
legitimacy.[76] Pye also claims that "the Burmese kings not only became
defenders of the Buddhistic faith, they even claimed as a basis of their
legitimacy the myth of consanguinity to the noble house of Lord

Buddha."[77] And anthropologist Gustaaf Houtman notes that the promotion of Buddhism during times of political crisis is a long-standing cultural tradition in Burmese politics, dating back to the eleventh-century kingdom of Pagan: "Where a government has faced erosion of political legitimacy, whether it be Anawratha, U Nu, or Ne Win, it returns to Buddhism."[78]

Preserve and protect Buddhism

Since the early 1990s, the current generals have promoted their new role as the protectors and preservers of "traditional" Buddhist culture in Burma, a duty formerly adopted by Burmese kings. This redirection also follows, it seems, as a reaction to the publication of offerings made by NLD candidates to the *Sangha* prior to the 1990 elections, the theoretical development of Suu Kyi's Buddhist political rhetoric – much of which took place during her years spent under house arrest from 1990 to 1995, and her subsequent visitations to monasteries following her release. It appears that, since over 80 percent of the Burmese are Buddhist, the military have been forced to respond to the publication of Suu Kyi's actions, speeches, and writings by creating an image of themselves as better Buddhists than Suu Kyi and, more generally, as being responsible for the preservation and promotion of Buddhist traditions in Burma. Since the early to mid-1990s, especially, the generals have made themselves obvious in consecrating Buddhist sites and engaging and inventing roles for themselves in Buddhist ceremonies. Their rhetorical efforts have intrigued local observers.[79] Yet while locals adjust to the generals' new role, their rhetoric is also pitched to the foreign media.

The *endoxa* on kingship and Buddhism

Understanding the SPDC's current fascination with Buddhism requires a brief introduction to the historical importance of the relationship between Buddhism and kingship, both generally in early Indian folklore and history and specifically in Burma. Because the character of any religious or spiritual tradition will be transformed in accordance with the local customs, traditions, and political culture of the people, the successful, though temporary, adoption of Buddhism in India, its export to Ceylon (Sri Lanka), and its eventual spreading by monks and merchants to parts of Southeast Asia, including Burma, required a transformation of the early Buddhist teachings and folklore in line with the wishes of both the people and their rulers. It would be useful, therefore, also to consider the nature of the kingship that ruled Burma from the eleventh to the latter part of the nineteenth centuries before examining how the political elite have interpreted the Burmese monarchy to accommodate their goals.

Central to Buddhism is the *Dhamma* which, from the earliest Buddhist traditions, refers to the sacred reality which the Buddha had discovered at the point of his Enlightenment and is recognized as both the Law which regulates and governs the totality of existence and the Truth which enables men to break free from the limitations which existence imposes.[80] The *Dhamma* is taken to be both the source of order in the world and salvation from it.[81] At the same time, the *Dhamma* also refers to the preaching through which the Buddha taught his discovery, the teachings or gospel through which men's suffering and sense of meaninglessness could be overcome.[82]

Reynolds believes that while the canonical tradition provides some indications that the Buddha himself may have favored the older, tribal forms of republican polity, there is no evidence that the Buddha recognized any basic conflict between the *Dhamma* and monarchical forms of rule.[83] However, "there is considerable evidence to suggest that he and the early community sought royal favor and sympathy even to the extent of adapting the code of discipline in accordance with the wishes of important rulers. Within early Buddhism as a whole there was a basic acceptance of kingship as the normal and appropriate mode of government."[84] Yet there is also an appraisal of the dangers and abuses of royal power within the Buddhist tradition and a general acceptance of the necessity for maintaining minimum standards of order in society and a related acceptance that kingship, despite its dangers, was an indispensable institution.[85] There was a strong interest, therefore, in articulating the implications of *Dhamma* for the ideals and institutions of kingship.[86] According to Reynolds, almost all the relevant passages in the canon and commentaries express or imply that the ruler's primary task is the maintenance of order and justice in society and to rule in accordance with the *Dhamma*.[87]

The three primary early examples promoting kingship and rule by the *Dhamma* to be found in the canon and commentaries are the mythical accounts of the *Mahasammata, Cakkavatti,* and *Dhammaraja*.[88] The *Mahasammata* (the Great Elect) was the title bestowed upon the most kindhearted and authoritative among men, the original sovereign. According to the myth, men appeared in a state of devolution, an original state of nature which, like Thomas Hobbes's account, was a state of want. In need of food, men decided to cultivate and accumulate rice in excess of their immediate needs. Private property soon came into being, along with theft, lying, violence, and punishment. To maintain order, men elected a sovereign and agreed to provide one-sixth of their rice crop as compensation for his protection and guidance.[89] Men's consensus to the sovereign's rule was established along the lines of a social contract, and the sovereign's rule was to be in accordance with *Dhamma*.[90]

The *Cakkavatti* (the Wheel-Turning Universal Monarch, or Ruler of the Universe) was a *Mahapurisa*, a Great Man or Being who had achieved his status through the merit accumulated during many previous lives and was destined to choose either the vocation of a Buddha Teacher or a *Cakka-*

vatti King.[91] *Cakkavatti* kings have appeared in the past and, like the future Buddha *Metteyya*, will appear again in the future to re-establish a society ordered in accordance with *Dhamma*, bringing prosperity and happiness to their subjects.[92] They are charismatic and their rule is seen as paternalistic and benevolent, rather than contractual. Like the *Mahasammata*, the *Cakkavatti* maintains order and justice by ruling in accordance with the *Dhamma*, yet their benevolence is more explicit, and their death is marked by the construction of *stupas*, whose veneration is rewarded by a favorable rebirth.[93]

The *Dhammaraja* (*Dhamma* King or Righteous Ruler) was seen as less mythical and more closely aligned to actual political situations. *Dhammaraja*'s assumed authority simply, through rightful succession, and ruled in accordance with *Dhamma*, maintaining order and justice with benevolence. Yet their death was not marked with the same kind of veneration as a *Cakkavatti* King.[94] In Burma, there is also the tradition of the *min laung* (king in the making), or individual pretenders to the throne who sought to prove that they had the religious merit necessary to be a *Cakkavatti* or *Dhammaraja* and who would claim such a status to legitimize their rebellion.[95]

Reynolds believes that the legends and folklore contained in the stratum of the early Buddhist tradition provided a storehouse of popular wisdom concerning political affairs and came to serve as a source for later Buddhist kings and royal advisors involved in practical political problems. While the amount of early *Dhamma* literature devoted to kingship was modest, their presence was of significant interest, even among the supposedly world-renouncing monks who were responsible for preserving and extending the Buddha's teaching.[96] Moreover, Reynolds claims that "[T]hese elements are of crucial importance because they provided a commonly accepted, orthodox basis for the richer and more complex patterns of royal symbolism and political involvement which were developed during the subsequent periods of Buddhist history."[97] In other words, they provided the foundation for the *endoxa* upon which future political involvement in Buddhist traditions could be addressed.

The most significant event in the development of the early *Sangha*, the permanent religious community in Buddhism, was the conversion of King Asoka Maurya in the middle of the third century BC. While previous kings had favored the Buddhist community, never before had a reigning monarch become a practicing Buddhist, issuing edicts exhorting his subjects to live in accordance with the *Dhamma*.[98] Yet Asoka, according to Reynolds, was selective in his assimilation of Buddhism, expressing his own conception of the "true *Dhamma*" to make the Buddha's words everlasting.

> It was a moral teaching, an intercourse with the gods, and a meditational practice which was encouraged so that all men might benefit in this world and the next. For Asoka, in other words, the true Dhamma

was a goal which could be actualized in the midst of the day to day personal and social life of his subjects.

(Reynolds, F. (1972): 27)

Asoka's edicts referred to his own rule in accordance with *Dhamma*, his restrictions on sacrifice and animal slaughter, his pilgrimage to the place of the Buddha's Enlightenment, his other pious tours, his sponsorship of "festivals of the *Dhamma*," his generous support for religious establishments, his concern for the unity and well-being of the *Sangha*, his appointment of ministers of the *Dhamma* with responsibilities to oversee and encourage the activities of the *Sangha*, and his missionary efforts to spread the *Dhamma* throughout India and the Hellenistic kingdoms.[99] The sacred biography of Asoka reports his simultaneous construction of 84,000 *stupas* throughout his kingdom, in addition to his acts of beneficence to the *Sangha*, and the convening of a Buddhist Council to interpret the orthodox canon.[100]

Asoka is portrayed as a *Dhammaraja* or *Cakkavatti* monarch as well as a devoted Buddhist layman and hence, a model for the life of laymen in general, and for the Buddhist king in particular – a pious monarch governing a Buddhist state.[101] Asoka's legacy, according to Reynolds, is the creation of a dual structure within the Buddhist tradition which can only be understood by taking account of the simultaneous veneration of the Buddha and Asoka, the orthodox canon and the "true *Dhamma*," and the two patterns of community life, the *Sangha* and the Buddhist state.[102] This dual structure, according to Reynolds, became the hallmark of Theravada Buddhism which spread to some parts of Southeast Asia, including Burma. It would appear as seen in Table 7.3.

Along with the traditions laid down by Asoka's example, Burmese kings were morally bound to observe ten moral precepts: "almsgiving, observance of the Buddhist precepts, liberality, rectitude, gentleness, self-restriction, control of anger, avoidance of the use of violence in his relationship with the people or avoidance of maltreatment of the people, forbearance, and 'non-opposition' against the people's will."[103] The last is interpreted by Aung San Suu Kyi as the democratic-Buddhist equivalent to the Confucian "mandate from heaven":

The real duty of non-opposition is a reminder that the legitimacy of government is founded on the consent of the people, who may with-

Table 7.3 Dual structure of the Theravada Buddhist tradition

Buddha	King
Buddhist *Dhamma*	True *Dhamma*
Sangha	Buddhist state

draw their mandate at any time if they lose confidence in the ability of the ruler to serve their best interests.

(Aung San Suu Kyi (1991): 173)

In addition to the ten moral precepts, kings were to observe four kingly laws, or Assistances to the People: to receive not more than a tithe of the produce of the country, to provide his officials and servants with victuals every six months, to provide his subjects with capital and receive back the loan only at the end of three years without charging any interest, and to use courteous and gentle words in his communication with the people.[104] There were also seven kingly rules, or Safeguards against Decline, that a king should follow to make his country prosperous: to hold assembly three times a day, to carry out an order only after full consultation and agreement, to follow the traditions and practices inherited from the past, to respect and obey the counsel of wise men, not to take away by force the womenfolk of the kingdom, to offer food and show respect to the guardian spirits of the kingdom and share the merits of good deeds with all spirits (*nats*), and to protect and promote the rights and welfare of the monks. The king was also expected to be guided by other codes of conduct such as the Twelve Practices of Kings, the Eight Virtues of Kings, the Four Ways to Overcome Peril, and the Six Attributes of Leaders: alertness, dynamism, compassion, patience, judgment, and care for his people.[105]

Maung Maung Gyi believes that while the Burmese kings formally subscribed to these golden rules and may have tried to live up to the moral precepts, they were never consistent, devoted, regular, nor uniform in their efforts. Indeed, "their queer actions and erratic behavior would only confirm the fact that it was their whims rather than the rules that often guided their conduct. In effect, these moral laws turned out to be little more than pious platitudes."[106] Since the king was responsible to himself alone, his conscience alone determined his actions, and the personality of the king determined the character of the government.[107] Because the king could appoint or dismiss his Supreme Court and Administrative Council ministers (*Hluttaw*) at will, the only influence, yet never a formal restraint, over his absolute rule came from the intervention of the *Sangha*.

While promoting and defending Buddhism confirmed a king's legitimacy, protecting the *Sangha* was also a primary religious function of the king.[108] Pye notes that while the structure of government tended to give some structure to the *Sangha*, in return the sanctions of religion tended to encourage support for the secular authority.[109] Maung Maung Gyi adds that "while technically the Buddhist clergy were neutral to politics, in fact, they supported the Burmese monarchy."[110] Yet, on occasion, monks also provided the only check on the tyranny and extortion of powerful officials, obtaining pardons for executions, remission of taxes for people in times of scarcity, temporary relief when crops failed, and intervention for the release of prisoners.[111]

As defender of the faith, the king was bound by his duty to uphold the traditional custom of displaying reverence towards the *Sangha* and concern for their welfare, and as head of state, he had to set an example of good conduct and righteous behavior.[112] Yet, according to Maung Maung Gyi, "his concept of moral duties and public welfare was neither broad in scope nor profound in depth ... the king's concept of national welfare never extended beyond the confines of religion, religious needs, and institutions."[113] Works performed in the interest of the people included the building and repairing of pagodas and other religious edifices; building monasteries and providing them with food and other necessities; feeding the monks and the Brahmin priests; holding monthly feasts according to custom; designating lands and lakes as sanctuaries for animals; digging and repairing tanks, lakes, and canals; and founding capitals.[114]

The rule of the Burmese king was, in the absence of the rule of law and, with responsibility for the executive, legislative, and judicial functions of government resting with the king, a rule of absolute monarchy which lasted unchallenged in Burma until its abolition when King Thibaw surrendered to General Pendergast in 1885. Without any serious thought given to an alternative system of government, and with no alternative neighboring models with which to compare, absolute monarchy was considered to be the only form of government. There was no hereditary aristocratic class in Burma to consider the various forms of government that could best protect their rights in property. Since the local nobility were appointed at the king's favor, and because new kings were known to have purged and slaughtered hundreds in establishing their rule, the ruling class consisted only of the king, his royal family, and his appointed officials. Nor was there any middle class, only the royal family and the common people.

While the people feared the king and his government, a government capable of transporting hundreds of common people from their native districts to a distant region for exploiting their labor or capable of dedicating the common people as slaves to a pagoda, according to Maung Maung Gyi, Burmese society never realized that the unchecked power of a king was the root of all the evils.[115] Without a king, the people believed, their kingdom would be dead,[116] and "by a king they could only think of one exercising absolute power, though they did not mean that he should be tyrannical. They did not see evil in absolutism, and expected him to rule according to the ten royal precepts, four kingly virtues, and seven kingly rules."[117] For his part, "absolute monarchy was the only system of government that the king and his court knew, and cruel punishments, ruthless suppression, and savage reprisals were the only methods they knew by which to uphold such a government."[118]

Nevertheless, many Burmese maintained a belief that supported the authority of the kings, that their kings were *Bodhisattvas*, or future

Buddhas, and the kings, in turn, could easily take advantage of this belief. One king stated in an eighteenth-century inscription, for example, "In virtue of this my good deed, may I become a Buddha ... an omniscient one."[119] Pye notes that the Burmese fantasy about the omnipotent nature of their god-king's powers became a dogma which could not be challenged by anyone in the court or among the local nobility.[120] Paradoxically, it seems that while the people would hope that a king would live in accordance with the *Dhamma* and by the precepts, rules, and laws laid down by tradition, they also "seemed to have lived in mortal fear of the king and his agents for his spite knew no time, location, nor reason."[121] This fear was so great that, according to Maung Maung Gyi, there was an intense desire of the people to avoid any involvement with anything related to his majesty's government because such involvement would likely bring more evil than good. If one were to suggest that political apathy, or lack of political participation in government, may be considered a prominent national trait of the Burmese people today, then they could perhaps trace its roots to a certain historical desire to remain aloof from the government.[122] Given these conditions, it seems doubtful whether, except in remote areas that were beyond the reach of the court, the people lived their lives in peace.[123]

Notwithstanding this sobering account of the absolute power of a Burmese monarch, Pye believes that "the Burmese love kings and princes, and that if they could not be a king themselves, they would like to be a follower to enjoy some of the perquisites of power."[124] As was noted previously, according to Pye, power (*awza*), or influence, is a fundamental trait of the Burmese character and the Burmese place such a value on it that they are capable of genuine emotional appreciation of pure, unadulterated power. For the Burmese, to have power is to experience an inner thrill and to find true happiness.[125] While the Pali word *awza* translates as power, authority, or influence,[126] a similar Pali word, *ana*, denotes full power and authority,[127] which may be interpreted as the power that is recognized as legitimate or authoritative, even constitutional or perhaps kingly.

Houtman distinguishes authority (*ana*), which is centralized, from influence (*awza*), which is distributed, to compare the power and authority of the military regime (*ana*) with Suu Kyi's influence (*awza*).[128] This fine distinction was not made by Pye in his use of *awza*, perhaps because *awza* embodied the idea of *ana* at the time he conducted his research, that is, prior to Ne Win's 1962 coup. Nevertheless, the distinction at least illustrates that because Pali is a Buddhist language, the study of political legitimacy in Burma is deeply rooted in Buddhist traditions, language, and symbolism, both academically and among the political elite themselves.[129]

The above account of the folklore and history of kingship and Buddhism in India and Burma serves to illustrate the source of the orthodox, commonly held beliefs, the *endoxa*, of the people on this subject. It also indicates how important Buddhism is in any government's quest for gaining legitimacy in Burma. The magical properties associated with kingship in Burma were particularly intense because they involved not only the Hindu concepts of court regalia and the cosmology of the capital but also early Buddhist beliefs on ideal kings and their position as the ultimate patron of the *Sangha*.[130] If the people's idealized Burmese king, being a legitimate ruler, was either a *Cakkavatti* or a *Dhammaraja*[131] who ruled in accordance with the moral precepts, rules, and laws laid down by tradition and with reverence for the *Sangha*, then the political rhetoric of the Burmese elite must appeal to this *endoxa*. Their actions, on the other hand, may reflect their genuine beliefs or, like the actions of their royal ancestors towards whom they turn, fall far short of the Burmese ideal.

Addressing the legitimacy of political rule in Burma on the basis of suppressing ethnic insurgency, promoting economic stewardship, or substantiating some historical kingly right has been favored by the SPDC and by much Western scholarship to date with little progress. Moreover, the use of the political economy approach to analyze a government that is mostly financed by the flow of illegal drugs would seem to be a redundant exercise.[132] Examining the role of rhetoric in Burmese politics, coupled with the dominance of Buddhism in the political culture of the Burmese people, is often downplayed by democratic theorists. In light of the signing of peace treaties with most insurgent groups and the continuing poor performance of the Burmese economy, and because the SPDC have been strongly promoting Buddhism in recent years, it is appropriate to examine in greater detail the *Tatmadaw's* role as the protectors and preservers of Buddhist traditions in Burma.

As is the case in Singapore, the Burmese political elite use their experiences to narrate history in accordance with their objectives. They must, in other words, manipulate the *endoxa* on kingship and Buddhism, and to a lesser extent slavery and freedom, to support their opposing positions. Disagreement over the relationship between the idea of freedom in Burmese Buddhism and the political use of this relationship manifests itself in academic work and in the rhetoric of the Burmese elite.[133] Because Burma conforms to Aristotle's description of common brutish tyranny and, since the generals have moved towards preserving their regime through Aristotle's second mode of preservation, in recent times the *endoxa* concerning kingship and Buddhism has fallen under closer scrutiny, and manipulation. Like the PAP's interpretation and use of Confucianism in Singapore, the SPDC's legitimacy must be based upon a certain historical interpretation of Buddhism and order in society that conforms to the rule of kings and kingdoms, like Pagan.[134]

To provide an account of history which appeals to some commonly held truths and, in order to be able to successfully argue their enthymemes, the elite must fashion an historical record that contains at least partial truths. Yet because citizens have no direct experience with ancient history, the perceived truth of their commonly held opinions, their *endoxa*, is influenced by the officially sanctioned history and by historiographers friendly to the government. Those looking for historical analogies to the present will turn to the recent past and the political figure in the recent past who lies within the memory of those still living is Aung San. Historians, interdisciplinary scholars, and socio-political commentators who are critical of the government, on the other hand, though never heard within the regime, are often cited outside the regime. To counter their claims, the government's rhetoric must, therefore, be broadcast both within and outside of the regime – for domestic consumption and for the foreign media. And so it appears in both Burmese and English language newspapers, radio, television, the Internet, and in foreign academic journals. Today, it is particularly important for an authoritarian government that wishes not to be totally cut off from international funding to at least appear to be interested in democracy. "Tyranny" is a bad, almost mythical, word in modern social science. "Authoritarian" provides an empirically useful, amoral substitute although it is hardly an improvement, and no government would wish to be classified as either.

8   Buddhist political rhetoric

Since Buddhism is practiced by the ethnic majority in Burma, the Burmans, and because both the *Tatmadaw* and the NLD see Aung San as their spiritual father, over the past decade or more, both parties have constructed their own interpretations of Aung San's views on and use of Buddhism and Buddhist ideas in order to support their own agendas, and either play down or magnify important elements of his character in their rhetoric. Focusing on the Buddhist rhetoric of the Burmese political elite attempts to address these interpretations of Aung San's politics and the use, or misuse, of his views by his spiritual and natural descendants. It is also an attempt to understand the *Tatmadaw*'s recent behavior which, lacking such an investigation, could be considered as rather odd, incomprehensible, and even beyond reason.

Because Aung San Suu Kyi claims that the *Tatmadaw* have selectively interpreted her father's speeches and distorted his vision for Burma, a vision of freedom which, she believes, was fundamentally entwined with Buddhist principles, an analysis of Aung San's political use of Buddhism may also have implications for Suu Kyi's legitimacy to the extent that she bases her work on her father's beliefs. The *Tatmadaw*, on the other hand, have interpreted Buddhism in Aung San's speeches to support various agendas ranging from socialist government to promoting a respect for the authority and traditional values which they claim to represent. While, in the past, the *Tatmadaw* have claimed to be upholding his beliefs, Suu Kyi's presence and her criticism of their interpretation of her father have led them pragmatically to downplay his pre-eminence as the father of the country. His face no longer appears on Burmese currency, and his status on Martyr's Day is no longer paid the same importance by the military as in the past.[1]

Regardless of recent developments in the respect paid to Aung San by the *Tatmadaw*, Aung San's central role in Burmese politics demands that we address his speeches with the aim of judging the merits of either case for ourselves. Neither the *Tatmadaw* leaders along with their supporters nor Suu Kyi and the NLD are guiltless of selectively interpreting Aung San's thoughts on religion and politics to support their enthymemes and to legitimize their own agendas on Buddhism and freedom in the political realm. This has occurred primarily because, in applying Diamond's definition of political culture again, Buddhism is the dominant element in the political culture of the Burman majority. If Aung San was well aware of Buddhism's importance in the political culture of the masses, it should not surprise that he too used Buddhism rhetorically to advance his ideas on freedom when addressing the people. Based upon an examination of the evidence, it is possible to draw inferences regarding both the use of Buddhist political rhetoric and the purpose of its use, as understood by an application of Aristotelian theory, and by the three major political elites relevant to the current situation – Aung San, Aung San Suu Kyi, and the *Tatmadaw* generals.

The politics of Bogyoke Aung San

Thank God (if there is a God) that there is no man in Burma like Gandhi because he is so unchangeable.

(Aung San, *New Burma*, 19 May 1939)

The words used by Jawaharlal Nehru to describe Mahatma Gandhi could well be applied to Aung San: "The essence of his teaching was fearlessness and truth, and action allied to these, always keeping the welfare of the masses in view." Gandhi, that great apostle of nonviolence, and Aung San, the founder of a national army, were very different personalities, but there is an inevitable sameness about the challenges of authoritarian rule anywhere at any time, so there is a similarity in the intrinsic qualities of those who rise up to meet the challenge.

(Aung San Suu Kyi (1991): 183–184)

U Aung San went over to the Japanese, and raised what we might call a Quisling army to come in at the tail of the Japanese and help conquer the country for Japan. Great cruelties were perpetrated by his army. They were not very effective in fighting, but in the infliction of vengeance upon the loyal Burmese – the Burmese who were patriotically fighting with British and Indian troops to defend the soil of Burma from Japanese conquerors – great cruelties were perpetrated on those men, because they had helped us to resist the Japanese. . . . Of course it is not a very agreeable transaction, when a traitor rebel leader, who has come in with foreign invaders, brings his army over to your side when so many cruelties and outrages have been perpetrated . . . but in the case of U Aung San one has very little choice. Either he was a traitor to Burma when he helped the Japanese to come in, or he was a traitor to the Japanese when he deserted them to join the British. We get him both ways. . . . I certainly did not expect to see U

Aung San, whose hands were dyed with British blood and loyal
Burmese blood, marching up the steps of Buckingham Palace as the
plenipotentiary of the Burmese Government.

(Winston Churchill (1947): 1848–1850, 1953)

Aung San was the most influential Burmese political figure of the
twentieth century, yet he was no Gandhi. His struggle for freedom and
independence from Great Britain spawned a militant movement that has
maintained a tight hold on the political reins of the country since the military coup of 1962. Aung San was a successful political activist who sought
after any means with which to advance his idea of freedom which, simply
stated, meant Burma's national independence. Yet, far from choosing a
non-violent means with which to achieve his goal, Aung San was open to
any tactic which might prove successful.

Aung San's interest in politics developed at an early age when, as a
child, he was told of the exploits of the town's heroes and his great uncle's
resentment of the British invaders and his participation in the nationalist
movement.[2] While his interest in history and politics grew during his
school years, it was not until Aung San entered the Rangoon University
environment at the age of 19 that his ideas and his commitment began to
take shape. There, Aung San immersed himself into student politics and
political debates on various issues, including the participation of monks in
politics. A former student of Rangoon University notes that in those days
"Aung San was a political animal and politics was his sole existence.
Nothing else mattered for him. Not social obligations, not manners, not
art, and not music. Politics was a consuming passion with him, and it
made him, I thought, crude, rude and raw."[3]

In 1931, the Student Union of Rangoon University (RUSU) was created
to allow students to voice their grievances on many issues. Aung San
assumed various posts within the union, including editor of their magazine, *Oway*, president of the RUSU and, eventually, president of the All
Burma Student Union (ABSU). While at Rangoon University, Aung San
resigned as president of the ABSU and joined the recently formed Thakin
Organization.[4] *Thakin* was the popular name given to the membership of
the Dohbama Asi-ayone (DAA), or the "We Burmese" Society, the "only
militant and intensely nationalistic political party in Burma at that time."[5]
He convinced his former ABSU president, U Nu, to join the *thakins* with
him, though Nu was at first hesitant. When Nu said that it was embarrass-
ing to be addressed as *thakin*, or master, Aung San asked Nu whether he
would instead prefer to be called *kyun*, or slave.[6] The *thakin* movement
provided Aung San the means with which to bridge the confines of
student politics and enter the real contest of national politics.

In 1938, Aung San left his law studies and, as general secretary of the
DAA, helped his *thakin* establish a coalition with the Sinyetha, or Peasant
Party, led by Dr Ba Maw, to form the Freedom Bloc, with Ba Maw as

president and Aung San as secretary general. The Freedom Bloc became involved in violent skirmishes with the colonial authorities before the war. It is doubtful, therefore, that while the DAA sent delegations, one led by Aung San himself, to the conferences of the Indian National Congress and developed close links with Gandhi, Nehru, and the Indian Socialist Party, the *thakins* were too influenced by Gandhi's non-violent strategies.[7] According to Naw, Aung San did not seek to imitate them:

> His greatest desire was for the freedom of his country, and he accepted any idea or method which would help him reach this goal. Aung San's political activities and his involvement in each of the organizations was motivated by that perspective.... The common goal of all the organizations to which Aung San belonged was the independence of Burma, and Aung San gave of himself wholeheartedly and without complaint to his chosen life work.
>
> (Naw, A. (2001): 52)

By mid-1940, both Aung San and Ba Maw toured Burma, gaining support for independence and the antiwar stance adopted by the DAA and the Sinyetha Party. The government declared the movements illegal, arrested nearly all *thakin* leaders, and issued an arrest warrant for Aung San on the grounds of sedition. According to Ba Maw, Aung San was insulted by the insignificant reward offered for his capture and swore that he would fight the British to the end.[8]

Fleeing from his British pursuers, Aung San and his associates, Ba Maw and Thakin Mya, actively sought after Japanese assistance in achieving their goal of national independence.[9] In August 1940, Ba Maw arranged a meeting with Aung San and Japanese Vice Consul Fuki to discuss plans of Aung San's escape to Tokyo, via Amoy, China. Later that month, a draft of the Plan for Burma's Independence was completed in Rangoon by Thakin Mya, Dr Thein Maung, and a Japanese agent acting as the secretary general of the Japan–Burma Society, Colonel Keiji Suzuki of the Army Division of the Imperial General Headquarters. The Plan was not a political document as such, but merely a brief sketch of the major details concerning the Japanese invasion of Burma. According to this plan, 30 Burmese nationalists would be smuggled first to Japan and then to Hainan island, where they would undergo military training before returning to Burma to lead an armed uprising against the British.[10] While in Amoy, Aung San also sought contact with the Chinese communists but without success. After two months, illness and poverty led him to contact Rangoon and ask for his immediate Japanese rescue, whereupon Suzuki, also fleeing from the British, arranged for Colonel Kiyoshi Tanaka in Taiwan to find Aung San. Aung San eventually arrived in Tokyo on 12 November 1940.[11]

Aung San returned to Burma in 1941, having allied his cause with one of the most tyrannical armed forces in modern history – the Imperial

Japanese Army. Concerning the idea of co-operating with fascist Japan, Suu Kyi claims that Aung San took the pragmatic view to accept help from any quarter that offered it and to see how the situation developed.[12] "[H]e acknowledged that it was because of his – not just his – but a general political immaturity of the younger people involved in the independence movement that made them look to a fascist military power [Japan] for help."[13]

In Rangoon, he recruited former *thakin* colleagues (the Thirty Comrades) to return to Japan for military training, which he completed in 1941, and for a brief interim was with Suzuki in Saigon and Thailand to co-ordinate with Premier Tojo's overall plans for Pearl Harbor and the invasion of Thailand. He returned with the main Japanese force, marching into Burma in January 1942 with the newly formed Burma Independence Army (BIA). Aung San assumed the rank of Major General in the Japanese Army and Chief of Staff, later Commander-in-Chief, of the BIA.

The BIA, composed of Burmese nationalists and some Japanese officers, was initially led by Col. Suzuki and, armed by the Japanese, was given the responsibility of aiding the Japanese forces by disrupting the enemy, obtaining the co-operation of the Burmese people, and maintaining law and order in the occupied areas.[14] The BIA recruited from among the people as they marched through Thailand and Burma, and the invasion was welcomed by the locals largely due to the successful propaganda efforts of both the Japanese and the BIA. Aung San, for example, had encouraged the belief that Suzuki (Bo Mogyo) was a descendant of Prince Myingun, a Burmese prince in the direct line of succession to the throne who had been exiled in Saigon and was to lead the resistance movement to restore the throne.[15]

By March 1942, when Rangoon fell to the Japanese, the BIA was a force of around 10,000 men, which swelled with volunteers to 23,000 by May.[16] But citing their lack of discipline, and perhaps fearing their strength in numbers should their goal of independence be stalled indefinitely, the Japanese soon after dissolved the BIA and formed the smaller Burma Defense Army (BDA). Indeed, tension was mounting within the BIA ranks when independence was not forthcoming, and Aung San and his comrades soon came to realize that the Japanese were treating their people worse than they had been treated under the British. The nominal granting of sovereign independence in September 1943 did little to quell the misgivings held towards their Japanese liberators.

Under the new administration, Aung San became Minister for War and Burma was granted co-equal member status of the Greater East Asian Co-Prosperity Sphere. The BDA, however, was again transformed into the Burma National Army (BNA) and its forces scattered across the country. By September 1944, resentment towards the Japanese had intensified to the degree that Aung San proposed the creation of the Anti-Fascist Organization (AFO), whose manifesto called for the people to join the BNA in secret resistance.

During the war, the BIA and the Japanese Army not only attacked British forces but, on occasion, ethnic minorities including, among others, the British-supplied Christian Karens in the Salween district and the Irrawaddy Delta. Fearing rumors of the rape and murder of Karens in villages that had surrendered their arms to the BIA following the British retreat in March 1942, other Karens refused to hand in their weapons. Further rumors that the Karens hid British soldiers led to BIA attacks, killings, and the burning of villages.[17] Rumors that all Karens were to be exterminated led to a Karen attack on the delta city of Myaungmya and large-scale racial rioting and retaliation by the Burmans, including the murder of Karens who sought sanctuary in the town's Catholic churches. When a Japanese colonel and friend of Colonel Suzuki was killed by the Karens, Suzuki ordered the extermination of two villages, whereupon the BIA massacred more that 1,000 Karens. Since the Japanese had entrusted the maintenance of civil law and order to the BIA, Gravers suggests that "the Japanese gave the Burmans a free hand to kill – and stopped the bloodbath when the Karens unconditionally threw themselves at their feet."[18]

Towards the end of the war, Aung San realized Japan's misfortunes and was fortunate himself to be accepted by a forgiving British Southeast Asian theater commander, Lord Louis Mountbatten, who, in accepting Aung San's allegiance, upset many from the prewar British administration, now based in India, as well as many parliamentarians in London. They sought to bring Aung San to trial for treason and collaboration with the enemy and to execute other members of the AFO and BIA. Nevertheless, Mountbatten followed the advice of Force 136, which had been operating in Burma, and of his own field commander, General William Slim, to accept the assistance of Aung San's guerrilla forces in routing the Japanese, noting that his action would be taken into account if charges were to be brought against him after the war. On 27 March 1945 Aung San turned his forces against the Japanese and, in late April, Rangoon fell to the British.

While many accused Aung San of turning against the Japanese only when a British victory was secure, Naw believes that the written evidence indicates that Aung San had planned for his resistance long before the British were able to come and that Major Seagrim of Force 136 had reported in November 1943 that "a certain Aung San of the Burma Defense Army was planning to turn his forces against the Japanese when opportunity presented itself."[19] Mountbatten also confirmed that Aung San's forces switched sides before it was clear that the British would, or could, come to their rescue.[20] Yet according to Naw, when General Slim accused him of only coming to the British for help when he saw that they were winning, Aung San replied that it would not have been much good coming to them if they were losing.[21]

Upon Britain's administrative return to Burma, Aung San resumed his peacetime independence activities, and in 1946 the AFO became the

Anti-Fascist People's Freedom League (AFPFL), which ruled Burma for about 12 years after independence under the leadership of U Nu, albeit interrupted by Ne Win's caretaker administration. Aung San eluded war-crimes charges because of his assistance in defeating the Japanese, and perhaps because of his political popularity, supported as he was by the BNA at a time when the British Army was decommissioning its troops and Mountbatten had already declared that Indian troops would not be brought to Burma to quell any further insurrections.

However, though he was not involved in the Myaungmya slaughter – he was in Upper Burma at the time – a substantiated war-time civil murder case was raised against Aung San. This continued to hinder his legitimacy in future negotiations with the governor, Dorman-Smith, and with London until it was decided that to arrest Aung San would incite civil unrest on a scale too unmanageable at the time. Following the arrival of a new governor, Sir Hubert Rance in September 1946, during a climate of ongoing strikes by police, university students, schools, postal and tele-graph workers, railway employees, and government offices, all with the support of the AFPFL, Aung San was invited by Rance to join a new Executive Council as deputy chairman and counselor for defense and external affairs.[22]

In January 1947, Aung San traveled to London to sign the Aung San–Atlee agreement which eventually led to the granting of independence. If Prime Minister Atlee had not granted independence, it is clear that Aung San was prepared to turn his forces against the British, if necessary, once again. He had already created the People's Volunteer Organization (PVO) in December 1945 for this purpose and by mid-1946 there were 10,000 men in the PVO, armed and prepared to resist "external aggres-sors."[23] While he hoped for the best, Aung San said in an Indian press con-ference before London that "he was prepared for the worst."[24] Six months later, at the age of 32, he was assassinated, along with members of his cabinet, by his political rival U Saw.

The Buddhist political rhetoric of Aung San

The development of Aung San's rhetorical style

Aung San's rhetorical style developed from an early age. Coming from a small town called Natmauk, where schools taught only in Burmese, he was at a disadvantage compared with his elder brothers who attended an Anglo-vernacular school in Yenanchaung and could speak English. Deter-mined to learn English, Aung San was eventually enrolled in Yenan-chaung National High School where his favorite subjects were history and literature. In 1930, his academic results placed him first among all stu-dents of both vernacular and Anglo-vernacular schools in Burma, and this helped earn him a scholarship for the remainder of school.[25] He was appointed editor of the school newsletter and took an active interest in international affairs and Burmese politics. His interest in political rhetoric began while he was still at school, where he attended and studied the speeches of Burmese politicians, then reproduced the speeches at home, imitating the orators' gestures and repeating their words.[26] At Rangoon University, Aung San developed a more serious interest in political science and political rhetoric:

> Aung San lived in a notional world, passing most of his time reading books and studying the thoughts and ideas of great philosophers such as Socrates, Plato, and Karl Marx. He attended student functions in order to tell others what he had found in his books or to explain concepts which he considered important. Whenever the master of ceremonies announced that the audience was welcome to join the talk, Aung San always rose from his seat and participated in the discussion.... Outsiders were normally allowed to speak for only five minutes; at the end of that time the master of ceremonies would ring a bell. But Aung San always ignored the bell and kept talking until he had finished his speech.
>
> (Naw, A. (2001): 23; Thein Swe, Bo (ed.) (1951): 41, 48)

Suu Kyi maintains that in debates Aung San would insist on having his say in English, ignoring interjections to stick to Burmese. He recognized the importance of English in the contemporary world and worked hard to improve his command of the language to achieve a proficiency that was unusual for one of his origins.[27] Aung San wrote many of his speeches in English, or mostly in English, before their delivery. According to Suu Kyi, "Although the style of his delivery was uninspiring, his conviction and thoroughness with which he prepared any subject he tackled earned him a reputation for eloquence."[28] Indeed, many observers had difficulty understanding Aung San's English and often interjected, but, unperturbed, he would continue until he was finished. Suu Kyi writes,

> Aung San was not a fine orator; his speeches could be monotonously technical, rambling, and very long, but the people listened with quiet respect, matching their moods to his, delighting as much in his blunt admonitions as in his rare jokes.
>
> (Aung San Suu Kyi (1984): 47)

Aung San also studied and prepared speeches and practiced his English in his spare time. His university room-mate observed that Aung Sang would go into the bushes and talk for hours:

> When asked what he was doing, Aung San would reply that he was practicing giving speeches to the bushes just as the British Parliament

member Mr. Edmund Burke did to the water. During holidays, Aung San would study the speeches given by famous British parliamentary members until he could recite them by heart.

(Naw, A. (2001): 24; Aung Than (1965): 39)

When Aung San became editor of the student union magazine, his interests were channeled into writing articles, often inflammatory, for magazines and newspapers. In 1936, Aung San played a major part in a large student strike based at the Shwedagon pagoda which lasted over two months. Here, he became well known and perhaps it was also around this time that Aung San developed a certain aptitude towards persuasion on a large scale. His writing skills improved during his editorial post and, with a solid work reputation and popular support, his self-confidence and commitment helped him achieve success in student politics.

It is clear that much of Aung San's political success can be traced to the rhetorical skills which he tried hard to develop during his student union days at Rangoon University. His early flair for imitation continued through his political life wherever he sought after models for political change. This included modeling his tactics on the Congress Party of India in challenging the British, observing the Japanese defy the League of Nations by invading Manchuria in 1931 and attacking China in 1937, watching Siam change its name and move closer to the Japanese political model, and observing the humiliating defeats of the colonial powers in Asia over a relatively short period of time.[29] According to Silverstein, Aung San's ideas and tone reflected these important influences:[30]

> Both as a student and political leader he used Marxism as a model for many of his thoughts and speeches. When, in 1940, he came under the influence of the Japanese his rhetoric became harsh, dogmatic, and imitative of his new masters. The ultimate victory of the Allies was accompanied by further change in his style of speech and the adoption of a more reflective approach, combining liberal, democratic, and socialist ideas with the new internationalism of the United Nations.
>
> (Silverstein, J. (ed.) (1993): 8)

Aung San's rhetorical use of Buddhism in his political speeches

The question of Aung San's invocation of Buddhist ideas to support his political ideas on freedom is important because it has been utilized to legitimize the political elite on both sides of the fence, the *Tatmadaw* and the NLD. Aung San's thoughts on the role of religion in politics also has implications for the present strategies of the political elite. Yet even scholars supportive of Suu Kyi disagree in their interpretation of Aung San. It is revealing to contrast differing accounts of Aung San's use of Buddhist ideas on freedom in his political speeches, for while many scholars claim that Aung San Suu Kyi uses Buddhist ideas in her writings, they differ in their opinions on Aung San's treatment of religion. Whereas Silverstein, for example, claims that Aung San maintained a clear separation between religion and politics, Houtman interprets Aung San's speeches in a manner which leads him to conclude that Buddhist ideas were fundamental to his understanding of freedom and that Aung San Suu Kyi has continued her father's tradition in her own work.

Silverstein is well aware of Aung San's pragmatism. As a political activist, he believes, whose immediate concern was to find workable solutions to problems and to persuade others to support his tactics and goals, Aung San demonstrated in his speeches both pragmatism and eclecticism. "Apparent contradictions did not seem to bother him for in his mixture of ideas and tactics he sought answers, not logical symmetry. If Aung San was flexible and pragmatic in his politics, he was firm and unswerving in his twin goals of independence and national unity."[31] Although Silverstein points us towards the need to examine the source of freedom in Buddhist texts and Buddhist political culture,[32] he follows U Maung Maung[33] in claiming that "Buddhism – an integral part of the Burmese tradition – did not provide Aung San with a dominant theme in his political thought, as it did with several of his contemporaries, nor did it provide a basis for his speeches and actions."[34] Silverstein thus overlooks Aung San's ability to invoke Buddhist ideas rhetorically.

According to Silverstein, Aung San believed that religion and politics must be kept separate. Quoting passages from Aung San's address entitled "Problems for Burma's Freedom," delivered to the First National Conference of the AFPFL in 1946 to provide evidence for his assertion, he cites Aung San as saying, "Politics must see that the individual also has his rights, including the right to the freedom of religious worship. [But] here we must stop and draw the line definitely between politics and religion."[35] In this speech, Silverstein believes, Aung San stated that the role of the Buddhist monks should be to purify the religion and carry its message to the rest of the world.[36] On the eve of the meeting of the Constituent Assembly, in 1947, Silverstein says that Aung San restated this view even more emphatically: "In politics there is no room for religion in as much as there should be no insistence that the president of the republic shall be a Buddhist or a minister of religion should be appointed to the cabinet."[37] It follows from this, Silverstein concludes, that Aung San believed that monks should have no political role in Burma.[38]

This account of Aung San is certainly substantiated by others, including Gravers who claims that Aung San preferred the traditional role for monks, to concentrate on the Buddhist message of charity and non-violence, and where the *Sangha* (the monks) looked after religious functions, kept order in its own ranks, and refrained from politicizing.[39] Aung San's rejection of demands for Buddhism to be made the state religion "was clearly addressed to politicized monks and sects – also to politicians who plotted to harness the *Sangha* for their own political ends."[40] It should be noted, however, that such an institutional separation of religion from politics in no way is inconsistent with Aung San deriving his ideas of freedom from Buddhism.

Silverstein notes that Aung San grew up at a time when Buddhist monks like U Ottama and U Wisara were active in the emerging nationalist movement in Burma, and their faith provided an early and continuing unifying theme. Their imprisonment, hunger strikes, and public meetings proved a magnet for rural Burmese support.[41] Yet despite this, Silverstein claims, Aung San never identified with the Buddhist political leaders and did not employ religion in the service of politics. As a believer in religious freedom, Aung San was able to relate to the people of all faiths and win their backing for his political organization and the cause of national independence. Under his leadership, Silverstein claims, the movement was predominantly secular and impartial on the religious issue.[42] Silverstein, therefore, focuses upon Aung San's promise to unite the country into one federation by ignoring religious differences and, in focusing upon Aung San's belief in the institutional separation of religion from politics, he diminishes the possibility that Aung San could have derived his ideas of freedom from Buddhism. More importantly, he effectively ignores Aung San's own rhetorical ability to follow in the footsteps of U Ottama and U Wisara, using Buddhism as a strong magnet to attract Burmese support for national independence.

Von der Mehden believes that while both Aung San and the AFPFL either accepted or were neutral toward Buddhism in their private lives, they rejected any narrow definition of the nationalist movement along religious lines. Aung San was not irreligious, nor did he support what he called "priestcraft," but he favored national unity along the lines of equal treatment for all religions.[43] Before the war, Aung San declared that the *thakin* movement was "the only non-racial, non-religious and impersonal movement that has ever existed in Burma. Formerly and still now among a certain section of the Burmese public, nationalism was conceived in terms of race and religion."[44] After the war, Von der Mehden claims, Aung San denounced religious and racial discrimination and announced, "Any books, songs, signs, symbols, names, etc. which foster such ideas must be officially banned."[45] The AFPFL, furthermore, declared in its original Manifesto, which was later installed in the Burmese Constitution: "Freedom of conscience should be established. The state should remain neutral on religious questions. Religion should not be used as a means to exploit the masses as is being done by the Japanese."[46] Above all, according to Von der Mehden, the political leaders who gained prominence in the nationalist movement were characterized by large doses of opportunism and corruption. The *thakins* were vigorous young university students with something new to offer, who, though secularist, were successful largely because of the political vacuum in Burma at that time.[47] Such a pragmatic portrayal of the *thakin* lends support to the ambiguous nature of Aung San's thoughts on religion and politics.

Aung San Suu Kyi, on the other hand, believes that Buddhism played an important role in the thoughts and works of her father. She claims that "Aung San, whom popular opinion has often cast in the role of a completely political animal, had a deep and abiding interest in religion" and "his preoccupation with spiritual matters did not cease ... even after he had entered the world of student politics."[48] However, Aung San, according to Suu Kyi, was not fanatical in his belief in communism or any rigid ideology; "his real quest was always for ideas and tactics that would bring freedom and unity to his country."[49] Yet at her first mass rally, Suu Kyi would claim to align herself with her father's views and declare that Aung San believed "democracy is the only ideology which is consistent with freedom" and that democracy was "the only ideology we should aim for."[50] Nevertheless, one of Aung San's lasting convictions, according to Suu Kyi, was that monks should not participate in politics and that to mix religion with politics was to go against the spirit of religion itself.[51]

Houtman, however, believes that Aung San's political speeches cannot be fully understood outside of their Buddhist context. Houtman traces the origins of Aung San Suu Kyi's use of Buddhism in her political speeches to Aung San and, ultimately, to Burmese Buddhist "mental culture." Constructing an anthropological account of the Burmese opposition elite's mental culture under conditions of political crisis, he provides examples of both Aung San's and Suu Kyi's use of Buddhist ideas and suggests that Suu Kyi is continuing her father's work by framing arguments for political reform in terms of Buddhist mental culture. Houtman recognizes that in modern Burmese politics, legitimacy is crucially linked to prominent figures engaged in the national independence struggle and, in particular, it is through Aung San that modern Burmese ideas of nation and nationhood have been translated.[52] Furthermore, "it is historically through Buddhism that the arguments for government reform are made," with the opposition to government operating in the shadow of the Buddhist monasteries and pagodas.[53] One observation of Houtman's that seems strikingly similar to the Christian Middle Ages doctrine of the two swords or the two spheres is that "not only does the monastic population provide numerically a counterbalance to the army, but it also provides the transcendental element that places limits on the authority of the king, general and politician to invade people's lives."[54] According to Houtman, the *Sangha* exercise a formidable influence on political opinion, and because they are "custodians of the techniques of mental culture that ... permit liberation from the prison-as-*Samsara*," the *Sangha* provides the "idiom of liberation in terms of which the avenue to freedom may be conceived."[55]

Houtman suggests that political opposition in Burma has, historically, been couched most effectively and most peacefully in terms of Buddhist concepts, rather than in people grouping together under the banner of a party.[56] Although he believes that there is still a role for secular political parties in opposition, he recognizes that the *Tatmadaw* simply provides no effective space for them in Burma today. He attempts to legitimize Suu Kyi's recognition of this observation historically by transplanting her use of Buddhist terminology back some 50 years in time to her father's use of Buddhism in his speeches. While recognizing that Buddhism has always been used as the dialogue for political opposition in Burma, by transplanting his theory of mental culture across time he also effectively equates the nature of British colonial rule with the brutish tyranny of the *Tatmadaw* – a contention that even Suu Kyi denies.[57] And whereas the British did eventually establish a dialogue with Aung San and ultimately concede to his demands for independence, the *Tatmadaw*'s resistance to any serious dialogue with Suu Kyi, their conduct during secret talks with her since October 2001, her re-incarceration in 2003, and their sacking of her dialogue partner, Khin Nyunt, in 2004 would tend to indicate that they have no realistic intentions of relinquishing their power.

Houtman's methodology rests upon his own understanding of Aung San. He notes, "[T]o understand both the army and the NLD, we cannot avoid coming to terms with the spiritual father of them both."[58] Yet his selective, almost enlightened portrayal of Aung San is questionable. Whether or not Aung San had "literally been kidnapped" by the Japanese army, for example, he was not forced to fight alongside Asia's then most tyrannical regime for three years, albeit with subsequent misgivings.[59] Rather, he chose to do so after actively seeking Japanese assistance. Aung San chose a path of armed resistance against both the British and the Japanese and may well have continued doing so if independence had not been granted in 1948. Concerning this last point, while Suu Kyi claims that "by the time he died, [Aung San] understood that the problems of the country should be resolved through democratic politics and not through armed combat,"[60] she also admits that "Aung San and the AFPFL ... had not dismissed the possibility of further armed conflict should the British government fail to give them the independence they wanted on their own terms."[61]

Houtman provides evidence of a number of Aung San's speeches in which he refers to Buddhism, but none are as convincing for him as Aung San's 1946 speech "Problems for Burma's Freedom" where he believes that "Aung San is preparing to locate politics in an ethical system which depends on personal comportment and spiritual attributes."[62] In this speech Aung San refers to politics as meaning "your everyday life. It is You, in fact; for you are a political animal as Aristotle long ago declared ... and as your everyday life changes, so changes your politics."[63] Houtman believes that when Aung San Suu Kyi encourages a "revolution of the spirit,"[64] she is reminding the army that Aung San's spiritual struggle remains unfinished and that she has effectively established an alliance with the *Sangha* in taking up her father's mantle.[65]

Houtman claims that to understand Aung San's politics we must appreciate that he handled two concepts of Buddhism: one which lay in the mundane world of religion and the other, the highest form, which was beyond religion.[66] He develops his theory along these lines and claims that Aung San displayed both forms in his speech "Problems for Burma's Freedom":

Religion is a matter of individual conscience while politics is a social science. Of course, as a social science, politics must see that the individual also has his rights, including the right to freedom of religious worship. Here we must stop and draw the line definitely between politics and religion, because the two are not one and the same thing. If we mix religion with politics, this is against the spirit of religion itself, for religion takes care of our hereafter and usually has not to do with mundane affairs which are the sphere of politics. Politics is frankly a secular science. That is it.

Speaking of Buddhism particularly, which is the religion professed by the greatest bulk of our people, I can say without prejudice to other religions that it is more than a religion itself and has several indications of its becoming the greatest philosophy in the world, if we can help to remove the trash and travesties which antiquity must have doubtless imposed on this great religion.

I wish therefore to address a special appeal to the Buddhist priesthood and say to them: Reverend Sanghas! You are the inheritors of a great religion in the world. Purify it and broadcast it to all the world. . . . You have a tremendous role to play in world history, and if you succeed, you will be revered by the entire mankind for ages to come. This is one of your high functions ordained by your religion; and this is the highest politics which you can do for your country and people. Go amongst our people, preach the doctrine of unity and love; carry the message of higher freedom to every nook and corner of the country, freedom to religious worship, freedom to preach and spread the Dharma anywhere and anytime, freedom from fear, ignorance, superstition, etc., teach our people to rely upon themselves and re-construct themselves materially spiritually and otherwise. . . .

But I must come back to politics. I have not finished talking about it! As a matter of fact, politics knows no end. It is Samsara in operation before our eyes, the Samsara of cause and effect, of past and present, of present and future which goes round and round and never ends.

(Aung San (1946), "Problems for Burma's Freedom,"
Burma's Challenge in Silverstein, J. (ed.) (1993): 96–97)

Whereas Silverstein and most Western scholars conclude from these passages that Aung San intended politics and Buddhism to be kept separate; that he warned against integrating animism, astrology, and alchemy into Buddhism;[67] and that he condemned the exploitation, superstition, injustice, and priestcraft frequently associated with religion,[68] Houtman claims that they illustrate the final development in Aung San's political use of Buddhist ideas. While the Buddhism of the monks is said to play a role in encouraging the "highest political values," politics per se exists in the mundane world of *samsara*, made dirty by the practice of dirty politicians. Among the highest political values is freedom, including "the message of a higher freedom" and "freedom from fear," the latter of which became the title Suu Kyi chose for her 1990 Sakharov Prize-winning article.

While Houtman wishes to reinterpret Aung San in a manner which conforms with his interpretation of Aung San Suu Kyi, he also places a great deal of emphasis on Aung San's personal knowledge, development, and refinement of Buddhism. If Aung San meant by not "mixing religion with politics" only that monks should not participate in politics, then this is different from, and consistent with, finding Buddhism a source of instruction about matters like freedom. It is not, however, consistent with the idea that Suu Kyi has taken up her father's mantle, against his expressed wishes, by establishing an alliance with the *Sangha*. Whatever role Aung San saw for Buddhism in politics, whether it be for personal moral guidance in the earthly or transcendental realms, a source of instruction for his ideas on freedom, or as a means to achieve social goals with higher forms of Buddhist practices, Houtman's theory must overcome its most obvious criticism: that Aung San's use of Buddhist ideas may just as easily be explained by viewing Aung San as most Western scholars already have. That is, as a political opportunist, a pragmatic young leader who, from what speeches we have, appears to have been well versed in rhetorical techniques and very capable of adjusting the content of his speeches to suit his audience.

Silverstein is, therefore, correct in asserting that apparent contradictions did not seem to bother Aung San, who sought answers, not logical symmetry, in his mixture of tactics and ideas.[69] Aung San was a pragmatist and a realist. He was an idealist primarily to the extent that Burma's national independence was his main goal. Yet after witnessing Britain's embarrassment over the handling of Gandhi's non-violent struggle in India, a struggle which could only have ended in India's achieving its independence, Aung San still chose the violent and hasty route to independence. In pointing to Suu Kyi's comparison of Aung San with Gandhi,[70] scholars overlook the fundamental principle which permeated Gandhi's thoughts and actions – *ahimsa* or non-violence. Indeed, Suu Kyi does not think of herself as a Gandhian politician, though she believes the establishment of a strong tradition of democracy should be achieved by peaceful political change, via the ballot box and not, like her father, through force of arms.[71] It would be helpful if Houtman could reconcile Aung San's use of arms while practicing Buddhist meditation techniques in opposition to both the British and the Japanese. Unless Buddhism can be equated with violence, his interpretation of Aung San would seem problematic.

Given Aung San's hectic political agenda, much of which involved military activities, it is doubtful whether he would have had the time to develop a detailed perspective of Buddhism's relation to politics in addition to performing various degrees of synthesizing and redefining Burmese secularism. Aung San was not a trained scholar, nor was he placed under house arrest for many years as was his daughter for that matter. Whatever his personal beliefs may have been, Aung San's public activities were that of a militant political activist whose opportunism should persuade us to interpret his subtle use of Buddhist ideas in his speeches as political rhetoric. And to the extent that they may have been used to incite armed rebellion, then Aung San could also have been a sophistical rhetorician.

Houtman claims that he is not arguing that Aung San was a devout Buddhist, rather, that "he *could not but help* bring Buddhist sentiments into his speeches, *if only* because he was addressing Burmese people, the majority of whom are Buddhist."[72] While Buddhism may have provided a source of instruction for Aung San on matters of freedom, however, it is more likely that he *intentionally* brought Buddhist sentiments into his speeches, *primarily* because he was addressing Burmese people, the majority of whom are Buddhist. Viewed as such, this was an effective rhetorical technique, designed and delivered in such a way as to have the maximum effect on his predominantly Buddhist audience, just as the *Tatmadaw* has done more recently, though less subtly and on an infinitely greater scale, because of the importance attributed by both to Buddhism's role in Burman political culture.

Houtman also claims that whereas Aung San stood for a political model based on attributes of *ana* (authoritarian) and *awza* (democratic), his legacy is one of *awza*. The *Tatmadaw*, on the other hand, which was founded by Aung San, stands only for *ana*. Suu Kyi represents *awza*.[73] Yet as a pragmatic rhetorician, military strategist, and politician, could it not be impossible that Aung San had the capacity to move from *ana* to *awza* at will – from authoritarian to democratic – depending upon his audience, and this is what makes Aung San one of the most successful political activists of the twentieth century, and which also makes his political legacy ambiguous?

Although Silverstein was well aware of Aung San's pragmatism, he nevertheless overlooked Aung San's ability to invoke Buddhist ideas as a rhetorical device used in order to achieve his twin goals of independence and national unity. Houtman, on the other hand, appeared to reinterpret history in order that it synthesize with his parsimonious general theory on Burmese mental culture and, like Silverstein, largely ignores the possibility of a rhetorical interpretation of Aung San's motives. It is nevertheless possible to argue that all three of the elite group in Burmese politics who are relevant to the current situation, Aung San, Aung San Suu Kyi, and the *Tatmadaw* generals, have consciously used Buddhist ideas rhetorically during times of political crisis in order to support their own claims for independence, freedom, and legitimacy, as understood by themselves and by the audience to which their claims are addressed. Their Buddhist political rhetoric became sophistry if, or when, their words or actions contradicted the principles of non-violence embodied in the Buddhist ideals. Thus, appealing to the common opinions on Buddhism to support armed rebellions or to suppress popular uprisings with force would be a sophistical manipulation of the *endoxa* on Buddhism.

In examining Aung San's views on religion, perhaps a great deal of truth lingers from the thought of Von der Mehden, who claimed that Aung San displayed a flexible pragmatism and agnosticism.[74] We are unable to judge the truth of Aung San's intentions because he did not live long enough for us to witness the kind of political regime he would have overseen. Indeed, it is debatable whether Aung San would have fared any better than U Nu, who found no solutions to Burma's problems. As Kane says,

> It is quite probable that death saved his reputation from the erosion that failure would have caused it . . . the leadership of an independent Burma was a test that Aung San never had to meet, and the sorry trajectory of Burmese history thus served only to sanctify his memory the more.
>
> (Kane, J. (2001): 152)

Nevertheless, we do have a wartime record of Aung San's political opportunism, along with other details of his prewar and postwar history, which indicate that Burma's independence from Great Britain was his primary goal and that he would be prepared to do or say almost anything in order to achieve that goal. Having spent a long apprenticeship involved in student politics at Rangoon University, Aung San's rhetorical sensibilities were well developed. He knew the political importance of appealing to the *endoxa* on Buddhism in a Buddhist country and so it is only to be expected that he should invoke Buddhist ideas to arouse emotions for independence from his predominantly Buddhist audience. While he did, though rarely, use Buddhist similes and metaphors (like *samsara*) in describing politics, their purpose was to support his own authority and legitimacy, to persuade his audience of his bona fide concern for their interest and, perhaps with the assistance of those around him, to put his ideas into a language that could be more favorably received. The same may be true for Aung San's choice of the location for delivering his speeches. Important speeches, like his first AFPFL presidential address, required an appropriate platform to maximize their effectiveness. Aung San chose to deliver this speech, therefore, at the most important and largest symbol of Buddhism in Rangoon – the Shwedagon pagoda.

Aung San's appeal to Buddhism may, therefore, be understood largely as a subtle rhetorical technique by a pragmatic, capable, and rising politician. When he consciously used Buddhist concepts in his political writings and public speeches, their primary purpose was to appeal to the *endoxa* of the political mass and arouse support for his idea of freedom in a society that could be independent from Great Britain. It would be hard to argue, let alone prove, that Aung San personally held any Buddhist beliefs – his actions complicate any speculation over beliefs that he may have held privately. What is important is that he used these concepts to gain political support and to bolster his legitimacy because the political culture of the Burmese people is inextricably bound to Buddhism.

The Buddhist political rhetoric of Aung San Suu Kyi

> I could not as my father's daughter remain indifferent to all that was going on. This national crisis could in fact be called the second struggle for national independence.
>
> (Aung San Suu Kyi, speech to a mass rally at the
Shwedagon pagoda, 26 August 1988)

> By invoking the Ten Duties of Kings, the Burmese are not so much indulging in wishful thinking as drawing on time-honoured values to reinforce the validity of the political reforms they consider necessary. It is a strong argument for democracy that governments regulated by principles of accountability, respect for public opinion and the supremacy of just laws are more likely than an all-powerful ruler or ruling class, uninhibited by the need to honour the will of the people, to observe the traditional duties of Buddhist kingship. Traditional values serve both to justify and to decipher popular expectations of democratic government.
>
> (Aung San Suu Kyi (1991), "In Quest of Democracy")

Aung San Suu Kyi reveals her Buddhist political rhetoric of opposition in her writings, some scholars have claimed, primarily because she holds no real power or institutional means of implementing her party's opposition.[75] Indeed, Suu Kyi's own use of Buddhist ideas is undeniable because they appear quite openly in much of her work composed before, and during, her first six years of house arrest and in her publications and speeches thereafter.[76] Her recitation of Buddhist ideas does change noticeably, however, developing during her house arrest into a discourse on the compatibility of Buddhist thought with a democratic society and the attainment of freedom, through Buddhism, under authoritarian rule. The grounding of her legitimacy in the union of Buddhist thought and democratic government comprises the enthymeme of her political rhetoric.

Gravers notes that in presenting her political alternative in terms of Western democracy and liberalism, Aung San Suu Kyi must communicate her model via Buddhist concepts because large sectors of the population have been isolated from international debate and might criticize her for seeking to introduce an alien political system and of undermining the "Burmese way."[77] There is a great deal of substance to this assertion, particularly since the *Tatmadaw*, who have traditionally tied the Burmese Way to socialism – which according to Aung San was compatible with Buddhism, attempted to somewhat liberalize their economy in the late 1980s yet denied the need for any political reform. Much of the population, unfamiliar with democratic government for almost 30 years, had to be sold on the idea by the NLD leading up to the 1990 elections. Suu Kyi proposed that a liberal democratic government was most compatible with Buddhist thought. While this distinguishes her from her father, she goes to great lengths in maintaining that the difference between her ideas and his is not that great. In addition, though an uncommon practice among the Burmese, she had deliberately chosen to keep his name.

Aung San Suu Kyi arrived in Burma to take care of her dying mother in March 1988, at the same time that student protests were becoming more active. While she did not, at first, intend to become involved personally, Ne Win's resignation as chairman of the BSPP at an extraordinary party congress on 23 July 1988 and the violent suppression of demonstrations on 8 August 1988 drew her into the political morass. Suu Kyi's political appeal to the pro-democracy movement leaders was also undeniable.[78]

Suu Kyi delivered her first major speech on 26 August 1988, below a portrait of her father, at the holiest Buddhist site in Rangoon – the Shwedagon pagoda. As was mentioned previously, this was also the site at which Aung San delivered some of his most important speeches, including his first AFPFL presidential address. Addressing a mass rally of around 500,000 people, it was the only public address delivered before her house arrest for which Suu Kyi had a prepared text in hand.[79] In this speech, combining epideictic and deliberative rhetoric, Suu Kyi points out that she is her father's daughter, that she is "participating in this struggle for freedom and democracy in the footsteps and traditions of my father," and that the national crisis is "the second struggle for national independence."[80] While Suu Kyi frequently quoted her father's thoughts in this speech, emphasizing his support for democracy, she does not discuss religion and politics, nor make use of any Buddhist thought, apart from the symbolism of the location itself.

However, in a later essay, "In Quest of Democracy," written before her house arrest, Suu Kyi begins to appeal to the Burmese people's traditional beliefs, their *endoxa*, by invoking ideas which she later claimed to have surfaced from her visit to her father's home town of Natmauk during her first campaign trip. There, the abbot of a monastery gave a sermon on the four causes of decline and decay and explained how traditional Buddhist views should be interpreted to help build a just and prosperous society in the modern age.[81] In her essay, Suu Kyi claims that the chief causes of Burma's decline since 1962 could be correctly and succinctly identified "by turning to the words of the Buddha on the four causes of decline and decay":

> Failure to recover that which had been lost, omission to repair that which had been damaged, disregard of the need for reasonable economy, and the elevation to leadership of men without morality or learning. Translated into contemporary terms, when democratic rights had been lost to military dictatorship sufficient efforts had not been made to regain them, moral and political values had been allowed to deteriorate without concerted attempts to save the situation, the economy had been badly managed, and the country had been ruled by men without integrity or wisdom.
>
> (Aung San Suu Kyi (1991): 168–169)

In the same essay, Suu Kyi also discusses the ten duties of Buddhist kingship and claims that they reinforce the Burmese desire for democratic government. Yet Suu Kyi also provided more subtle references to Buddhist thought in her early writings. In "Freedom from Fear," for example, Suu Kyi speaks of a "revolution of the spirit":

> The quintessential revolution is that of the spirit, born of an intellectual conviction of the need for change in those mental attitudes and values which shape the course of a nation's development. A revolution which aims merely at changing official policies and institutions with a view to an improvement in material conditions has little chance of genuine success. Without a revolution of the spirit, the forces which produced the inequities of the old order would continue to be operative, posing a constant threat to the process of reform and regeneration.
>
> (Aung San Suu Kyi (1991): 183)

It is interesting to note that in the same essay from which Suu Kyi borrowed her father's phrase "freedom from fear," Aung San spoke of "the spirit of religion." While Aung San's views on religion were primarily secular, Suu Kyi's playfulness with her father's phrase points us towards the direction she would take in her later work:

> When I speak about a spiritual revolution, I'm talking about our struggle for democracy. I have always said that a true revolution has to be that of the spirit. You have to be convinced that you need to change and want to change certain things – not just material things. You want a political system that is guided by certain spiritual values – values that are different from those that you've lived by before. . . . Because of the tremendous repression to which we have been subjected it's almost impossible for it to be either a political or a social revolution. We're so hemmed in by all kinds of unjust regulations that we can hardly move as a political or a social movement. So it has had to be a movement very much of the spirit.
>
> (Aung San Suu Kyi (1997b): 75–76)

Suu Kyi's rhetorical style, and appearance, during her campaigning days was direct and simple. Addressing peasants across the country in a straightforward manner, she conveyed her message of democracy quickly and with emotion, while taking time to answer their questions. Kane believes that her simple but compelling oratory proved crucial.[82] Yet Suu Kyi's image was also particularly appealing, perhaps even more so because she was portrayed as "that woman" set against the might of the *Tatmadaw.* "Suu Kyi's physical appearance, enhanced by the trademark flowers in the hair, projected a persona of combined strength and fragility that had charm not just for Burmese people but for the wider world."[83]

Indeed, unlike the *Tatmadaw* at that time, she knew the importance of appealing to the international press and made the most of every opportunity to convey her message in the same simple but effective manner. This continued after her release, when Suu Kyi would deliver her weekly message to large crowds of people across the fence of her own house. While Suu Kyi made use of her own symbolic status to bring international pressure to bear, according to Kane, symbols would not help her to become what she wanted most to be, an effective political leader.[84]

The politics of metta

Aung San Suu Kyi was placed under house arrest on 20 July 1989 and was not released until 15 July 1995. During these years, she developed an interest in Buddhist *vipassana* meditation practice, or insight contemplation, and read many books on the subject, including Sayadaw U Pandita's *In This Very Life.*[85] Her deepening interest in Buddhist thought and her personal commitment to meditation practice were reflected in her writings. In one of her rare speeches composed during this period, delivered by her husband at Oxford University, Suu Kyi refers to the general teachings of Buddhism and, in particular, the principle of *metta,* or loving kindness and compassion, as a state of mind to help alleviate suffering. Her non-provocative language no doubt also reflects her circumstances at that time: "[T]he only way out of an impasse of hate, bloodshed and social and economic chaos created by men is for those men to get together to find a peaceful solution through dialogue and compromise."[86]

By the time of her release, Suu Kyi had developed her own brand of Buddhist political rhetoric, based upon a combination of her genuine beliefs, her Buddhist meditation practice, and the real problem of voicing her opposition in a way that would not overly offend the military yet could successfully resonate among the people. Following her release, Suu Kyi visited the famous Karen monk Sayadaw U Vinaya and Sayadaw U Pandita, whose teachings on meditation she had adopted. Of these teachings, the most important, according to Suu Kyi, relates to a Buddhist attribute prescribing prudence, namely, mindfulness:

> [Y]ou can never be too mindful. He [U Pandita] said you can have too much *panna* – wisdom – or too much *viriya* – effort; but you cannot overdo mindfulness. I have been very mindful of that throughout these last seven years. . . . Also, he advised me to concentrate on saying things that will bring about reconciliation. And that what I should say should be truthful, beneficial, and sweet to the ears of the listener. He said that according to the Buddha's teachings, there were two kinds of speech: one which was truthful, beneficial and acceptable; and the other which was truthful, beneficial but unacceptable, that is to say that does not please the listener.
>
> (Aung San Suu Kyi (1997b): 28)

When compared with her writings before the period of house arrest, Suu Kyi's political rhetoric was now enriched by a greater personal knowledge, and practice, of a subject which would be most pleasing to her listeners – Buddhism. In addition to promoting a deeper marriage of the spiritual with the political life, her opposition tactics now embodied a desire to practice the tools of meditation, particularly *metta*, actively and on a grand scale. And unlike U Nu, who faced a constant moral dilemma by being both a devout Buddhist and a political leader with responsibility over the use of the armed forces, Suu Kyi saw no split or tension between her Buddhist pursuits and her political ones.[87] Indeed, Suu Kyi claims that in their attitudes, no fundamental differences exist between herself and her father:

> I might have taken the same attitude he did, that any means used for gaining Burmese independence was acceptable. That was why he founded the army. At that time he thought that the most important thing was to achieve independence. But by the time he died, he understood that the problems of the country should be resolved through democratic politics and not through armed combat.
>
> (Aung San Suu Kyi (1997b): 78–79)

Of course, by the time Aung San had died, Burma had already been promised its independence. In an earlier essay, Suu Kyi claims that her father also believed in *metta*: "When political power came into his hands he could say with absolute sincerity and a complete lack of self-consciousness that he would govern 'on the basis of loving kindness and truth.'"[88] Yet she also distances herself from Gandhi in the sense that she would, in certain circumstances, condone the use of violence:

> It depends on the situation and I think that in the context of Burma today, nonviolent means are the best way to achieve our goal. But I certainly do not condemn those who fight the "just fight," as it were. My father did, and I admire him greatly for it.... We keep all our options open.
>
> (Aung San Suu Kyi (1997b): 153)

Emerging from her first six years of house arrest, Suu Kyi's political rhetoric, it seems, had developed into her own version of Sulak Sivaraksa's socially engaged Buddhism, or active *metta*.[89] Implementing her new tactics could not occur, however, without attracting criticism from quarters that believed religion was a matter of individual conscience and that mixing religion and politics was against the spirit of religion itself. To these criticisms she replies:

> Some have questioned the appropriateness of talking about such matters as *metta* (loving-kindness) and *thissa* (truth) in the political context. But politics is about people and what we had seen ... proved that love and truth can move people more strongly than any form of coercion.
>
> (Aung San Suu Kyi (1997a): 17)

> Some people might think it is either idealistic or naïve to talk about *metta* in terms of politics, but to me it makes a lot of practical sense ... politics is about people, and you can't separate people from their spiritual values.
>
> (Aung San Suu Kyi (1997b): 39)

> In Burma today, the large portion of monks and nuns see spiritual freedom and socio-political freedom as separate areas. But in truth, *dhamma* and politics are rooted in the same issue – freedom.... I think some people find it embarrassing to think of the spiritual and political life as one. I do not see them as separate. In democracies there is always a drive to separate the spiritual from the secular, but it is not actually required to separate them.
>
> (Aung San Suu Kyi (1997b): 26)

In essence, Suu Kyi and her NLD executive companions, U Tin Oo and U Kyi Maung, both of whom also practiced *vipassana* meditation, had decided to try to feel affection towards their tyrants[90] as a means of persuading the *Tatmadaw* to the bargaining table. In addition, a deeper combination of the spiritual with the political lives also meant that the *Sangha* would have to become more involved in politics, or more specifically, NLD politics:

> I think monks and nuns, like everybody else, have a duty to promote what is good and desirable. And I do think they could be more effective. In fact, they should help as far as they can ... simply by preaching democratic principles, by encouraging everybody to work for democracy and human rights, and by trying to persuade the authorities to begin dialogue. It would be a great thing if every monk and nun in the country were to say, "What we want to see is dialogue." After all, that is the way of the Buddha.
>
> (Aung San Suu Kyi (1997b): 27)

In late 1996, Suu Kyi claimed that the generals were threatening the rights of NLD members to pursue their freedom of worship. In a supplication addressed by the Minister for Religious Affairs to the abbot members of the state *Sangha* organization, the NLD were accused of infiltrating the *Sangha* to promote the cause of the party and to commit subversive acts against the government. The *Sangha* organizations were "instructed to contact and cooperate with the relevant state/division, township and ward authorities and take protective measures against the dangers to religion," i.e. to prevent NLD members from entering the ranks of the *Sangha*.[91] Suu Kyi claimed: "The authorities accuse us of using religion for political purposes, perhaps because this is what they themselves are doing, or perhaps because they cannot recognize the multi-dimensional nature of man as a social being."[92]

Regardless of their political motives, later that year, Suu Kyi and the NLD participated in the *kathina* ceremony, donating new robes to the monks of the Panditarama Monastery, home of Suu Kyi's teacher, U Pandita.[93] She recalls that many of the NLD attending the ceremony gathered together eight years before to commit themselves to the cause of democracy and human rights.[94] Elsewhere, Suu Kyi claims that unlike Christians who develop congregational relationships, Buddhists are not really organized around their monasteries:

> Christian-based political movements tend to take off quickly and efficiently. The organization is already there. Look at Latin America, you'll find that a lot of their political movements against the dictatorships, although they were not non-violent, were church-based, which made them take off rather quickly. Even in the Islamic countries they

have the mosque, which is formally organized, with regular mosque meetings taking place weekly. This sort of formal organization does not exist in Buddhist countries.... [In Burma] if anybody thought of meeting regularly at a monastery in numbers of a hundred or two, there would be serious consequences.

(Aung San Suu Kyi (1997b): 150–151)

It appears, therefore, that while Suu Kyi and the NLD are critical of the authorities' attempts to curtail their freedom to worship and to gather within the walls of the *Sangha*, the authorities' response, though heavy handed as is usually the case in Burma, was not altogether without reason. The consequences of Suu Kyi's brand of socially engaged Buddhism, the politics of active *metta*, do indeed pose a non-violent threat to the generals' legitimacy. Her Buddhist political rhetoric, born of a deeper marriage between the spiritual and the political lives, though based upon her genuine beliefs, would naturally intimidate the generals and provoke the kind of response which has played itself out in recent years. Suu Kyi, furthermore, believes that some of the generals' "actions are not consonant with Buddhist teachings":

There's so little loving-kindness and compassion in what they say, in what they write and what they do. That's totally removed from the Buddhist way . . . [and removed] from the people.

(Aung San Suu Kyi (1997b): 21)

A lot of people give lip-service to their religion. They can recite prayers, attend the ceremonies, perform all the rites, but they may not really absorb anything in their hearts.

(Aung San Suu Kyi (1997b): 210)

Indeed, Suu Kyi says that she has not reached the stage when she can feel *metta* towards everybody, including the generals, though she does not feel hostile towards them either and would be happy to be on friendly terms with them.[95] Active *metta*, however, does not imply that the NLD will sit and wait for change. It includes criticizing the authorities where there is need for criticism and "doing what is necessary at any certain point."[96]

Although Suu Kyi has been referred to as a female *Bodhisattva*, "a being striving for the attainment of Buddhahood – the perfection of wisdom, compassion and love, with the intention of assisting others to attain freedom," unlike U Nu who claimed to be a committed *Bodhisattva*, she denies the comparison and claims to be nowhere near such a state nor in any position to even contemplate taking the *Bodhisattva* vow.[97] However, because of her personal Buddhist beliefs, and her marriage of religion with politics, Suu Kyi's Buddhist political rhetoric does provide us with a good example of Reynold's description of the dual structure within the Therevada Buddhist tradition.

In particular, her promotion of active *metta* follows in "the tradition of the 'true *Dhamma*' which could be actualized within the context of the ordinary structures of social and political life."[98] Also within this dual structure there exists "two intimately interwoven patterns of community life," the *Sangha* and "the ideal of a Buddhist state governed by a pious monarch who modeled his rule after the example of Asoka."[99] While Asoka's "true *Dhamma*," as expressed in the edicts, according to Reynolds, was a moral teaching and meditational practice, Suu Kyi's own political interpretation of the Buddhist *Dhamma*, along with her *vipassana* meditation practice, embodies her own creation of true *Dhamma*. Suu Kyi, in other words, has adopted the persona of a modern-day *min laung*, a king in the making or contender to the throne, seeking to prove that she has the religious merit necessary to claim her legitimate *Cakkavatti* status.[100]

While this may be considered an extremely theoretical persona for a modern-day politician to adopt, it should not be forgotten that practically the NLD wield no effective political power whatsoever within Burma. The NLD executive's decision to pursue their current line of political rhetoric comes as a direct consequence of their being denied political power by the *Tatmadaw*. It is debatable, though unlikely, that their rhetoric would have developed along these lines had they not been silenced by years of imprisonment. Perhaps it is important to note that, unlike U Nu, whose deep Buddhist faith manifests itself while holding political power throughout his administration, the NLD executive's faith deepened through their denial of political power. The most remarkable consequence of these events is that while the NLD is approaching, and in some sense surpassing U Nu's level of commitment, the SPDC, in countering the NLD's Buddhist rhetoric, are themselves appearing more like U Nu.

If Suu Kyi appears idealistic in her speeches and writings when compared with less idealistic politicians who hold power, therefore, perhaps it is the very denial of power which creates this rhetorical trait. While pragmatic leaders maintain their views and develop their rhetoric from positions, in Lee Kuan Yew's case, of nearly four decades of holding power, Suu Kyi's ideals, beliefs, and rhetoric are to a large degree based on and suffused with "notions of empowerment,"[101] i.e. empowering herself, the NLD, and the Burmese people. It is an open question whether this style of rhetoric would perpetuate, to the same degree, in the world of real politik if the NLD's power was not crushed by a tyrannical regime. It is also a reflection of the absolute nature of the *Tatmadaw*'s tyranny that Aung San was not, in his political rhetoric, espousing the virtues of *metta* under the British.

Houtman, on the other hand, suggests that there has been a continuum of *vipassana* practice by opposition elites and monks from Burma's colonial past through to the present example of Aung San Suu Kyi and the NLD. His account of Aung San Suu Kyi's personal *vipassana* practice while in "opposition" is clearly visible in her writings. He also supplies the background for her principles of national unity as outlined in *Freedom from Fear*, namely, *metta* and *brahma-so-taya*, a kind of social meditation required for transcending from the realm of *loka* to *lokuttara*. Houtman concludes that the NLD, rather than the *Tatmadaw*, have mastered the high ground in Burmese politics through their mental practice of *metta* and accumulation of *karma*. Being seen by the people as the true guardians of the transcendent realm of *lokuttara* means that the NLD have become the legitimate rulers of Burma, according to Buddhist traditions.[102] This legitimacy, Houtman believes, augments any already gained at the polls and leaves the *Tatmadaw* wallowing in the mundane realm of *loka*.

While Aung San's political rhetoric developed socially during his student politics days at Rangoon University, Suu Kyi's political rhetoric transformed noticeably while under house arrest in isolation. Because Suu Kyi, like her father, knew the political importance of appealing to the *endoxa* on Buddhism in a Buddhist country, she chose to invoke Buddhist ideas to arouse emotions for Burma's "second struggle for national independence" from her predominantly Buddhist audience. She followed in the footsteps of her father by choosing the same location for delivering her first major political speech, the Shwedagon pagoda. Yet Suu Kyi's fusion of Buddhist meditation practice with her general, more developed Buddhist thought produced her own distinctive form of political rhetoric.

Suu Kyi's Buddhist political rhetoric was a product both of her unique circumstances and her conscious decision to combine Buddhism with politics in a way that her father had not, nor, from the bulk of the available evidence, was he likely to have done so. Yet like her father, who on occasion put his ideas into a language that could be more favorably received, Suu Kyi heeded the advice of her teacher and delivered her message in a medium that could be more easily, and personally, understood while remaining sweet to the ears of her listeners.

The Buddhist political rhetoric of the *Tatmadaw*

The prevailing atmosphere of mutual trust and confidence between our two countries owes much to the wisdom and constructive advice of Senior Minister Lee Kuan Yew whose vision and experience have been invaluable to us.

(Senior General Than Shwe, Chairman of the SPDC,
the *New Light of Myanmar*, 12 June 1995)

If you stay here long enough and you watch television, you will see the generals ... donating things to monasteries, praying at pagodas and behaving very much like good Buddhists. So one wonders why such violence exists. And I think the conclusion one would have to come to is that perhaps they are not practicing Buddhism anything like enough.

(Aung San Suu Kyi in Dreifus, C. (1996): 31–37)

Because the *Tatmadaw*'s search for legitimacy on military or economic grounds failed to repair their defective title since 1962, in the 1990s they returned to what has traditionally provided the greatest source of legitimacy in Burmese politics and adjusted their rhetorical efforts accordingly. As was previously noted, the SPDC's rhetoric must appeal to the traditional *endoxa* on the people's idealized Burmese king even though their actions, like the actions of their royal ancestors towards whom they turn, fall far short of the Burmese ideal. Yet while the Burmese kings were legitimate absolute monarchs, the *Tatmadaw* are one of the few governments to admit openly that they are in fact a dictatorship and not a *de jure* government.[103] The SPDC's rule, being neither based on law nor a monarchic rule over willing persons, remains a sort of counterpart to absolute kingship and, according to Aristotle, this is most particularly held to be tyranny.[104]

Aristotle's and Machiavelli's thoughts on the important role that religion, or spiritual beliefs, played in maintaining a tyrant's rule have already been raised. Cicero also noted how important the establishment and monopolization of religion and of promoting piety towards the gods was to the stability of the State.[105] Aristotle believed that if a tyrant shows himself to be seriously attentive to the gods, to have the gods too as allies, then men will be less likely to conspire against him.[106] Machiavelli noted that while having and always observing religion are harmful, a prince must take great care that nothing leaves his mouth which is not all religion. Indeed, according to Machiavelli, nothing is more necessary than to appear to be full of religion when the people see and hear him because

> men, universally, judge more by the eyes than by the hands, because it is given to everyone that they see, but to few that they can touch. Everyone sees what you seem to be, but few touch what you are, and those few will not dare to oppose themselves to the opinion of the many who have the majesty of the state defending them.
>
> (Machiavelli, *Prince*, XVIII: 109)

Not only, therefore, is it expedient for the state to maintain a monopoly over the performance of religious services, a tyrant, in particular, must produce the kind of rhetoric that shows himself to be seriously attentive to the gods and to sway the opinion of the many towards the majesty of his state as being full of religion. Encouraging this kind of *endoxa* would be more expediently done if it were made to conform with the already established *endoxa* on the subject. If the nature of the SPDC's rule is of a monarchical sort over the unwilling, then their kingly performance follows in a long tradition of Burmese leaders, both rulers and rebels, who, whether or not their status was lawful, turned to the *endoxa* found in folklore and tradition to bolster their popularity, and their legitimacy, among the people.

Kingly performances by Burmese political elite in the twentieth century

The abolition of the Burmese monarchy by the British in 1885 created a wave of resentment and nationalist sentiment among both the Burman people and the *Sangha*. Returning the *Sangha* to their rightful place as a revered, politically influential, and legitimizing authority would only take place if Burmese leaders drew from the traditional *endoxa* and conducted themselves almost as if they were reinstating their monarchy. Accordingly, the political and military elite has adopted the practice of assuming the role, and the duties, of a Burmese monarch on several occasions, both before and during World War II and following independence.

From 1930 to 1932 Saya San, a former monk, for example, led a peasant rebellion against the British imposition of tax collection. The rebellion transformed into a movement to overthrow the British, though Saya San was eventually caught and executed. Born in Shwebo, home of the founder of the Konbaung dynasty, King Alaungpaya, some believed that Saya San was of royal lineage, and his followers proclaimed him to be the new king of Burma, the *thupannaka galon raja*.[107] The Galon, a mythical eagle who conquered the Naga dragon, symbolized the Burmese victory over all foreigners, particularly the British.[108]

Following the Saya San rebellion, the two young independence-minded lawyers, Dr Ba Maw and U Saw, entered politics, and U Saw called himself "Galon" after Saya San.[109] When Aung San marched into Burma alongside the Japanese Army in 1942, songs were composed about the Bogyoke, glorifying him as the great military leader who liberated the country from the British and associating him with ancient Burmese kings, including King Alaungpaya.[110] Yet perhaps it was Dr Ba Maw who set the stage for what was to follow the withdrawal of the British colonial administration after the war when, in 1943, the Japanese granted Burma nominal independence and he was installed as head of state in a grand ceremony which was described by a journalist present:

> Everything in the setting was calculated to recall the old royal tradition. The music played was the customary accompaniment to the entry of the King in *pwes* (i.e. dramas or theatrical performances), the announcer was a dwarf; and Thakin Kodaw Hmine, in administering the oath, addressed Dr. Ba Maw as ministers of old addressed the King. There stood Dr. Ba Maw in the full light of glory he had created for himself.
>
> (Tun Pe (1949): 73, in Maung Maung Gyi (1983): 162)

Following Burma's independence from Great Britain, when U Nu was made Prime Minister of Burma, from 1947–58 and 1960–62, Buddhism and the *Sangha* once again became dominant political influences. Indeed, U Nu himself was at many times a monk, and as a layman, blending Buddhism and his beliefs in spirits (*nats*) with politics in his speeches and ceremonies, his administration could have been criticized as one long Buddhist ceremony.[111] Under U Nu's patronage, the Sixth Great Buddhist World Council was held in 1956, wherein Buddhist texts were translated, Buddhist relics were collected from Ceylon, and U Nu approved the building of a World Peace Pagoda. Under U Nu's administration, Buddhism also became part of the school curriculum, and Ecclesiastical Courts and Pali universities were created. His government also formed the Buddha *Sasana* Council which, headed by the Chief Justice of the Supreme Court, was devoted to the promotion of all aspects of Buddhism.[112]

In 1960, facing pressure from the *Sangha*, U Nu's electoral campaign included a desire to make Buddhism the official state religion and, in 1961, U Nu used his parliamentary majority to do so.[113] This became another factor prompting the military's coup in 1962. Granting the ethnic minorities more independence on the one hand while officially sanctioning the Burman majority's religion would fuel the already widening ethnic and religious divisions across the country. Nevertheless, Smith notes that because the Burmese kings were strongly motivated by the need to acquire sufficient merit to overcome the consequences of their own bloody and ruthless acts, 800 years later U Nu declared that it was the responsibility of the government to look after the welfare of the people, not only in the present existence, but in countless future existences, and that it was therefore necessary to make Buddhism the state religion in Burma.[114] U Nu also saw it as his personal duty to acquire merit in order to help his subjects reach *nirvana*.[115] U Nu's downfall could, therefore, in part be attributed to the fact that he was not a good Machiavellian prince, nor for that matter was he a tyrant wary of conspiracies. While he was seriously attentive to the things pertaining to the gods, his constant observance of religious things became politically harmful, prompting the *Tatmadaw* to conspire against him.

In light of the ethnic, religious, and communist divisions threatening the Union, Gravers believes that Ne Win, in 1962, stood as the nation's savior, almost as a *Cakkavattin* or a *min laung*, the one who had stopped the growing religious and ethnic split and who had stemmed the foreign influence.[116] Chirot notes that by isolating his country in 1962, Ne Win was behaving like a traditional Burmese king. In the mid-1970s, he married a descendant of the last Burmese royal family and began to appear at state functions in full classical regalia, being convinced that the last royal family were among his ancestors.[117] Lintner believes that Ne Win clearly viewed himself as an absolute monarch rather than a military usurper who had overthrown an elected government.[118] Gravers, however, claims that Ne

Win was hated, presumably because he had not openly assumed the guise of a *Cakkavatti* or a *Dhammaraja*, probably intentionally since such claims could have easily backfired and intruded on his exercise of power.[119]

Indeed, it would be hard to argue that for most of his rule Ne Win was at all interested in politicizing Buddhism or the *Sangha*. The BSPP's guiding ideology, for example, was published in January 1963 under the heading *The System of Correlation of Man and His Environment: The Philosophy of the Burma Socialist Programme Party*. This document posited the BSPP's philosophy as "a purely mundane and human doctrine," without any connection to religion.[120] Seekins believes that "despite its use of Buddhist and metaphysical terminology, this statement reflected Ne Win's opinion concerning the relationship of religion and politics, closer to the secularist Aung San than U Nu: that they are separate spheres of life."[121] While the BSPP may have initially used Buddhist and metaphysical terminology for rhetorical reasons, therefore, it would be hard to deny that for most of Ne Win's rule Buddhism was the preserve of the *Sangha* and monks should avoid politics.

In the 1980s, however, Ne Win's attitude towards the *Sangha* softened somewhat when he openly gave gifts to the monks, engaged U Nu to edit Buddhist texts, and began a pagoda-building project behind the Shwedagon pagoda in Rangoon, personally raising the *hti*, or spire, which is a kingly function symbolizing royal power, glory, and religious merit.[122] Speculation over Ne Win's "conversion" includes reports that he wished to avoid going down in history as a tyrant or that he wished to secure the succession of his daughter, Sandar.[123] In March 2001, Ne Win also hosted a luncheon in a Rangoon hotel for an auspicious number of 99 senior monks.[124]

Among other notable *Tatmadaw* generals who have claimed to possess some royal privilege was General Saw Maung. Leader of the coup in 1988 by the military against itself and the first chairman of SLORC, in October 1990 Saw Maung suppressed a rebellion by over 7,000 monks in Mandalay following their senior abbots' decision to discourage the performance of religious services for families of the military. Having ordered the revocation of the religious boycott, the dissolution of Buddhist organizations, the surrounding of monasteries, the arrest of over 400 monks, and the destruction of buildings near the monasteries, Saw Maung claimed in a meeting with the senior abbots that "his regime's actions against the monks was analogous to the action of King Anoryahtah of the thirteenth century in the purification of religion and monks during his reign."[125] Moreover, according to Mya Maung, "quoting the Buddhist scriptures and king's law, *yahzathart*, he claimed the right of the Buddhist rulers to invade and purify the domain of the Buddhist monks."[126] Soon after, the SLORC issued a law stipulating the proper conduct for a Buddhist monk and penalties for their violation by monks or monk organizations.[127] The following year, in December 1991, Saw Maung would pronounce that he was the reincarnation of King Kyanzittha of the Pagan period. According to Chirot, Saw Maung was heard screaming at a golf tournament, "I am the great king Kyanzittha! I am great King Kyanzittha!" and was later observed by foreign diplomats to be incoherent.[128]

More recently though, all of the top SPDC generals have been performing their roles, more coherently, in speeches and public appearances in a manner that could only prompt an observer to question whether they are reinterpreting, and adopting for themselves, the roles and duties of Burmese kings. By promoting Buddhism, the generals are both responding to the political rhetoric of the elected opposition while at the same time assuming the legitimacy of a Burmese monarch for themselves. As for the kind of kingship the generals are assimilating, perhaps Aristotle's discussion of the Spartan kingship in the *Politics* provides a clue. In the Spartan regime, kingship was constituted either on the basis of family or by being elected. A Spartan kingship, according to Aristotle, was a "sort of permanent generalship of plenipotentiaries" and a "permanent generalship based on family."[129] While Spartan kings held generalship for life, meaning leadership in matters relating to war, they were also assigned leadership over matters related to the gods.[130]

It is ironic that, today, the military promotes at a superficial or rhetorical level a similar kind of devotion to the Buddhist traditions that U Nu was advancing in 1962. The same reasons that prompted the unauthorized military intervention then are being adopted by the *Tatmadaw* themselves now to legitimize their rule. For her part, Suu Kyi believes that in one sense the generals do constitute an improvement on the rule of the old Burmese kings:

> They're ashamed to admit atrocities, even though they commit them.... I'm not saying that their instincts are any better or worse than the old kings'. But the kings did not feel the need to temper their feelings of vengeance and cruelty. They felt that they had a perfect right to indulge in these feelings. At least the authorities here do not really think it is their right to torture and to kill. They can do it, and they do it. But they will not admit to it.
>
> (Aung San Suu Kyi (1997b): 171)

A Cakkavatti *must respond to a* min laung

The SPDC's renewed reverence for Buddhist traditions was not chosen voluntarily, but came about as a consequence of their own actions. Aung San Suu Kyi's imprisonment, along with her NLD colleagues, encouraged the kind of rhetoric to which the SPDC has been forced to respond. In terms of Burmese folklore, the generals have been pressured into proving their worthiness to the people, their *Cakkavatti* status as it were, in response to Suu Kyi's *min laung* rhetoric.

According to Kane,

> Leaders generally try to employ effective rhetoric, exhortation and appropriate symbolism to strengthen constituency morale and resolve, and to maintain commitment through setbacks, disappointments or defeats. Those who are gifted in this respect can usually enlarge their own and their cause's moral capital, but even those who are not cannot be indifferent to the symbolic aspects of their leadership.
>
> (Kane, J. (2001): 39)

Unlike Aung San Suu Kyi, the *Tatmadaw* generals are not known for their gifted oratory or literary skills. Yet they could neither ignore Suu Kyi's Buddhist political rhetoric nor fail to take symbolic measures to counter the threat she posed to their leadership. To negate the influence of Suu Kyi and the NLD, the SLORC embarked upon a massive campaign to promote its own version of nationalism and order through Buddhist culture. The USDA, for example, which the *Tatmadaw* uses for mass rallies in support of the government and to attack the NLD, has offered free courses in Buddhist culture since it was established in 1993. According to Steinberg, the USDA was designed "to create civil society in its own manner while suppressing alternative possibilities."[131] In order to carry out this enterprise, the *Tatmadaw* have interpreted Buddhist traditions in a way that conforms to their orderly vision for society and have promoted one monolithic Burmese culture. Gravers believes that today "no political practice is possible without involving Buddhism – and Buddhism has been politicized to a degree where no religious act is apolitical."[132]

As in Singapore, the government's political rhetoric is imbued with a sense of national survival, and any opposition to the government's policies is considered traitorous, unpatriotic, and must surely be backed by a neocolonialist plot to destroy national unity and cause disaster. The *Tatmadaw*'s siege mentality and its distrust of foreigners have, to a large degree, been fostered by Burma's long period of isolation from Western influence following independence. Like Singapore, order is instilled to stave off supposed threats to the very survival of the nation. Yet unlike Singapore, whose economic development was driven by liberal capitalism and tied closely to foreign interests, the Burmese elite do not simply dislike Western liberalism – as reflected in the Asian values style of rhetoric – they exhibit an exaggerated fear of all foreign influence, often to the degree of paranoia.

Political paranoia in Burma, according to Gravers, is based on "a failure of and a seemingly profound distrust in the Western model of modern social order and its plurality of identities."[133] Yet the promotion of an alternative national identity in a way that conforms to the military's strategies and corporate interests requires a particular interpretation of Burmese history and traditions. In this sense, the promotion of a Buddhist cultural and national identity, which began under the rule of the *Tatmadaw* in the early 1990s, has occurred very much along the lines of the Confucian cultural and national identity policy promoted in the *Singapore Story* under Lee Kuan Yew. Although this does not confirm a direct causal connection between the two countries' programs, one cannot help but notice striking similarities between their policies, and their aims.

The SPDC's three main strategies, or "national causes," for promoting national identity often appear in the state's daily publication, the *New Light of Myanmar*. They are the non-disintegration of the Union, the non-disintegration of national solidarity, and the perpetuation of national sovereignty. According to Philp and Mercer, while the first two of these create a sense of shared history and national pride for all ethnic and religious groups, it is a unity predicated on the subordination of all minority interests in the promotion of a Burman Buddhist national identity. The last cause is a response to the perceived threats to the Burmese national identity from "neocolonialists" and "cultural imperialists" and is the military's attempt to preserve its Asian values and cultural identity.[134] The military's attempts to invent connections between themselves and the monarchy and between the NLD and Western powers both serve its nation-building agenda.[135]

Reinterpreting history to accord with orderly visions for society requires that the *Tatmadaw* downplay the importance of certain political figures who inspire the opposition. Houtman argues that the *Tatmadaw* have for the past ten years (since 1989) set about "re-assassinating" Aung San, or at least his image. This is because, according to Houtman, Suu Kyi has become so identified with her father's views that they were left with no option but to practice "Aung San amnesia."[136] Furthermore, Houtman claims that political controversy has been inflamed over the past decade by the *Tatmadaw* abandoning Aung San's views on politics, in which he strongly argued against reserving a central role for either culture or religion.[137] Moreover, because the word "culture" was not in usage in Burma until the mid-twentieth century, and because there is no equivalent word in the Burmese language, the *Tatmadaw* have effectively set about inventing their own culture.[138]

It is certainly true that the generals of the *Tatmadaw* have been meddling in Buddhism, at least to the degree that they are publicly displayed as benefactors to the monasteries and defenders of the "old Buddhist traditions," many of which were either invented or modified by the *Tatmadaw* themselves since the early 1990s. Indeed, an outside observer might conclude that Suu Kyi and the generals have, for the past decade or more, engaged in a race to win the hearts and minds of the Burmese people by attempting to prove themselves as the better Buddhists. Viewed as such, there could be much truth in Aung Thwin's observation that the contest in Burma today is primarily an elite struggle for the throne, in which both sides have harnessed the masses for support.[139]

In this struggle, both Suu Kyi as *min laung* and the SPDC as *Cakkavatti* harness the masses through the medium of Buddhism, using their Buddhist political rhetoric to convey their traditional bona fides and to support their claims, either for democracy or for order. Because Suu Kyi's actions are restricted, she participates by projecting her rhetoric through some actions but mostly through her speeches and writings. Her non-violent tactics prevent her rhetoric from being labeled sophistry. But since the generals control all the media and most public activities in Burma, their sophistical rhetoric knows no bounds. Their conduct not only illustrates the continuation of the historical tradition in Burma of utilizing Buddhist political rhetoric in the service of legitimizing one's rule, but also represents a concerted attempt to annex Buddhism for themselves.

The **Cakkavatti** *rhetoric of the* **Tatmadaw**

While Aung San Suu Kyi maintains that Buddhist traditions are consonant with a democratic form of government, the *Tatmadaw*'s enthymeme is that their legitimacy is based on an ancient kingly duty to maintain order through the preservation of Buddhist traditions. Being based upon the commonly held opinion that past kings were charged with this duty, their enthymeme should be reflected in the rhetoric of the current regime and the inductive examples used to support their enthymeme. Challenges to the substance of their enthymeme come by way of contrary historical evidence on this theme, as was previously discussed, that questions the truth of the common opinions upon which it is based, and by the contrary enthymeme and rhetoric of Aung San Suu Kyi.

In order to substantiate the proposition that the generals of the SPDC have been conducting their religious activities along the lines of the Burmese kings of old, perhaps it would be useful to restate the actions performed by the ideal *Cakkavatti* monarch, Asoka, during his rule in accordance with *Dhamma.* These include his restrictions on sacrifice and animal slaughter, his pilgrimage to the place of the Buddha's Enlightenment and other pious tours, his sponsorship of festivals of the *Dhamma,* his support for religious establishments, his concern for the unity and well-being of the *Sangha,* his acts of beneficence to the *Sangha,* his appointment of ministers of the *Dhamma* with responsibilities to oversee and encourage the activities of the *Sangha,* his missionary efforts to spread the *Dhamma,* his construction of 84,000 *stupas* throughout his kingdom, and the convening of a Buddhist Council to interpret the orthodox canon.[140] While the generals may not have placed restrictions on sacrifice or animal slaughter, Tables Appendix A3 and Appendix B1 respectively illustrate either that they have performed most of these functions or are currently performing them. Unlike Asoka, however, the generals perform them in the presence of the state-owned media.

While the state coverage of U Nu's religious activities in 1962 was modest, and that of Ne Win's government in 1974 was totally absent, the media coverage of the SLORC and the SPDC's religious activities is telling. Analyzing the state media coverage of the generals' performance shows that their activities have generally corresponded in time with, and followed in response to, the Buddhist political rhetoric produced by Aung San Suu Kyi. Beginning from a modest coverage in 1988, the media reportage of the generals' activities rose significantly in 1990 and, following the SLORC's decision to promote Buddhist culture, it had reached staggering levels by the time Suu Kyi was released from house arrest in 1995. Since then, the coverage has been maintained, though it has fluctuated in certain periods due to the coverage of other political events. Appendices A and B show the kinds of activities performed by the generals, the methodology used, and the findings revealed by the content analysis conducted for this study.

According to Edelman, "The settings of formal political acts help 'prove' the integrity and legitimacy of the acts they frame, creating a semblance of reality from which counterevidence is excluded."[141] In addition to their acts of paying obeisance to the *Sangha*, attendance at important Buddhist functions, their state sponsorship of religious activities, and their publication of the military's donations to monasteries, one activity which makes the generals' performance particularly "kingly," is their attempts at merit-making through the construction of pagodas and the intricate ceremonial roles they play in founding and consecrating them. The generals' restoration and construction of pagodas also reflects their concern for restoring their credibility with the *Sangha* following General Than Shwe's activities in 1990.

A pagoda with *hti*, or umbrella spire, symbolizes the accumulated merit of the Buddha, the previous Buddhas, the future Buddha, the *Cakkavatti*, and the *Sangha*, and those who donate pagodas also accumulate merit.[142] The hoisting of the *hti* symbolizes royal power, the crown on the king's head, and was a function previously reserved for a king either at his inauguration or otherwise. Yet Generals Than Shwe and Khin Nyunt performed these duties, with much pomp and ceremony, at numerous occasions and sites including the Shwedagon pagoda.[143] According to Gravers, the future ruler would be the person who put the *hti* on the pagoda: "The same act executed by [then] Secretary-1 Khin Nyunt [who was close to Ne Win] ... can be interpreted to radiate a traditional mixture of prestige (*goun*), glory (*hpon*), and power (*ana*), as well as religious merit (*kutho*)."[144]

In what appears to be an expedient attempt to establish a monopoly over the performance of some private merit-making and the more public religious services, in recent years the *Tatmadaw* have assumed a high profile in the collection and donation of monies for the restoration and construction of pagodas and Buddha images. Their appeals for public donations and their management of these funds now commonly appear in the daily papers, along with the involvement of local *Tatmadaw* units in the renovation of religious sites.

According to Philp and Mercer, state-sponsored ceremonies and rituals associated with the construction of the Lawka Chantha Abhaya Labha Muni image on Mindhamma Hill in Rangoon, for example, illustrate how the traditional merit-making rituals for individual lay patrons have been appropriated by the military regime in favor of state-sponsored religious devotions.[145] The forced relocation of people from Rangoon and Mandalay also serves this purpose as they are denied their traditional places of worship and the opportunity to perform their customary merit-making rituals.[146] The Protection and Preservation of Cultural Heritage Regions Law of 1998 ensures the maintenance of the *Tatmadaw's* monopoly by restricting the independent construction and renovation of Buddhist structures,[147] effectively assigning the accompanying merit-making ability over to the generals.

The SPDC has also used museums to promote their Buddhist political rhetoric. Both the National Museum and the recently opened Historical Museum of Six Buddhist Councils advance Burma's monarchical heritage and its importance in upholding Buddhism and the unification of the country.[148] The generals have constructed statues of monarchs in public places and renamed important streets after Burmese heroes.[149] In addition, the Mandalay Palace, home of the last Burmese monarch, King Thibaw, has undergone a complete reconstruction since 1989, an act interpreted by Philp and Mercer to signify that the rule of kings has been reinstated.[150] In August 2000, General Khin Nyunt was observed standing in front of a large, unfinished Buddha image and chanting out loud: "Victory, Victory, Victory."[151] Could it be possible that the generals believed they had won the rhetorical battle over Buddhism?

It would appear that while the generals have been seriously attentive to the things pertaining to the gods, unlike U Nu their constant observance of religious things could seem to be politically advantageous for them. Given the presence of the NLD's Buddhist political rhetoric, they may not fear any conspiracy directed towards their excessive use of religion, and since they hold both the power and the most public means of persuasion in Burma, it would appear that the generals are, therefore, acting as a good Machiavellian prince should. Yet Aristotle also warns tyrants against "silliness" in their attentiveness towards the gods.[152] While this characteristic could be attributed to political naïvety, it may also reflect Aristotle's desire for real benevolence to develop on the part of the tyrant. That is to say, while the generals may think they have conquered the high ground in the rhetorical battle over Buddhism, not so much through their argument, or *logos*, but by acting out their *pisteis*, or enthymene, to persuade the *pathos*, or emotions, of their audience, their own brutish actions outside of their religious activities affect their *ethos*, or character, and this conditions their credibility in the eyes of the public. Philp and Mercer would appear to agree:

There is no evidence to suggest that the Burmese people are passive consumers of the state-controlled media propaganda. Often this is the only avenue for people to learn of the activities of the military and, in the private space of the home, official media pronouncements frequently provide a rallying-point for critical conversations constituting a form of "resistance."

(Philp, J. and Mercer, D. (2002): 1607)

The generals have attempted to base their Buddhist political rhetoric on the common opinions regarding kingship and Buddhism in Burmese history and, in seeking legitimacy, implicitly argue that their rule follows necessarily from this *endoxa*. Yet their selective interpretation of historical facts reveals their desire for maintaining order and the preservation of their rule. By deductively misleading their audience from partially true common opinions, or from historical facts poorly understood by the citizens, they deceive them by appealing to their passions and prejudices regarding Buddhism in ways that betray the public interest. Coupled with brutal actions that betray the substance of their rhetoric and reveal their true character, the generals have become sophistical rhetoricians, dictators who attempt to persuade the people to accept extraordinary laws by interpreting prodigies in their favor.[153]

Like the Burmese kings of old, the generals attempt to turn their vices into virtues by symbolic, and very visible, acts of piety. Since it could be considered sacrilege to question the intent behind religious acts performed by the military, the regime's appropriation of the Buddhist concept of *cetana* (intent) is an extremely effective means of imposing its power and authority.[154] Despite this, perhaps in the minds of the people, however, what they truly lack is a deep faith because while appearing religious has been useful to them, they certainly know how to change to the contrary.[155] This contributes to making their royal acts of piety, unlike U Nu's, not so much politically naïve actions as sophistical political rhetoric or sham political sophistry. It would also seem that the generals' excessiveness, in showing themselves as seriously attentive to things pertaining to the gods, has not helped them to avoid silliness.

9   Stability and justice in Burma

[I]f I were Aung San Suu Kyi, I think I will rather be behind the fence
and be a symbol than after two or three years out, without a machine,
be discovered and found impotent.

> (Lee Kuan Yew, "Address to the Singapore Press Club,"
> the *New Light of Myanmar*, 15 June 1996)

At the end of the day, the opposition in Burma has to face the realities
of life. The one instrument of effective government there is the army
– the civil service is not effective, the police are part of the army ...
[Aung San Suu Kyi] wins Nobel peace prizes – a shining star. But if
she was given power in Burma tomorrow she would have to depend
on the army, because there is no other instrument. It would take 10
years for the present government to be defeated, and then they would
have to form a new army.... One-track minds believe they can bring
about Utopia, by human rights, by democracy. Once upon a time, it
was unilateral nuclear disarmament or whatever. All believe they have
the answer to the world's problems. But the world's problems are
much more complex than that. We in South-east Asia know what our
problems are.

> (Lee Kuan Yew, "Myanmar opposition must face reality: SM Lee,"
> the *New Light of Myanmar*, 19 June 1996)

Preservation of the *Tatmadaw*'s regime, according to Aristotelian principles, requires a transition from the brutish to a less brutish form of
tyranny. While Aristotle may have hoped that his prescriptions could moderate despotic behavior, the generals' benevolent kingly performance and
their Buddhist rhetoric have not moderated theirs. There is no evidence to
suggest that the generals are acquiring the virtue necessary to transform
their regime into something other than a longer lasting form of tyranny.
Rather, the generals have taken every step to safeguard their power, which
is the only presupposition that Aristotle makes to a tyrant's kingly performance.[1] They grant the occasional concession to placate the international
community and, in return, are rewarded with some international funding.

What is required to improve the stability and justice in the current regime along Aristotelian lines, however, is more than the granting of minor concessions for short-term gains. Yet the problems facing the generals are complex and would no doubt cause strife also for the NLD if they were ever to govern the country. Unlike Singapore, Burma is not a small *polis*, but the second largest country in Southeast Asia and a republic composed of many ethnic minorities. Nevertheless, Aristotle's advice for preserving the regime, in the sense of improving its stability and justice, can be applied to Burma and it would be appropriate to do so given the current political circumstances.

Conventions, talks, and concessions

According to Aristotle, regimes are best preserved when a mixing of the oligarchic and the democratic elements takes place. All citizens must, to some degree, take part in politics, and the people must voluntarily acquiesce in its arrangement. In Burma, this requires that the ruling oligarchs – the *Tatmadaw*, share their political power with the democratic elements – represented largely by the NLD and ethnic minority groups, and that a proper, fully representative convention on a new constitution be initiated with at least the possibility of all parties voluntarily acquiescing in its arrangement. The first step towards power-sharing would be a meaningful dialogue between the SPDC and the NLD. Yet the NLD's expulsion from the National Convention and the SPDC's law silencing any criticism of the convention and the constitution highlight the *Tatmadaw*'s conception of stability as meaning the preservation of order and the status quo, rather than improving justice in the regime. Concessions made when pressured by international concerns also have not translated into any real improvements in justice in the domestic arena.

In October 2001, the SPDC, and then Secretary-1 Khin Nyunt in particular, entered into secret talks with Aung San Suu Kyi that were brokered by the then United Nations Special Envoy for Burma, Rizali Ismail. Their talks remained secret because the content was not published, either by the SPDC or the NLD. Unless they produce tangible commitments for change, however, any future dialogues may simply constitute yet another attempt by the *Tatmadaw* to placate international concerns in return for short-term gains. The signs were not very promising. In 2001, while the SPDC declared that the talks were going well, their neighbors in Thailand reported on the brokerage of power-sharing deals and that Khin Nyunt and Suu Kyi met for dialogue every two weeks. The NLD, on the other hand, denied any such deals, claimed that the two did not meet regularly, and believed that the talks, as such, had not progressed beyond confidence building.[2] Indeed, while some generals have appeared to be more pragmatic than others, the hardliners in charge, and especially Than Shwe, may see to it that it never does. Khin Nyunt's sacking from the prime ministership in October 2004 may raise serious questions as to the future, both of the ceasefire agreements brokered with ethnic insurgents formerly under his watch, and any meaningful future dialogues with Aung San Suu Kyi.

According to Suu Kyi, a dialogue requires confidence on both sides, which requires trust, and with trust, truth and reconciliation naturally follow.[3] Part of this confidence building is tied to Suu Kyi's insistence that all political prisoners be released. Various reports and records place the number of political prisoners in Burma at between 1,300 and 1,400, the majority of whom are NLD members or supporters.[4] While the release of some of these prisoners by the SPDC over the past years[5] marks, in their eyes, a sign of good faith and progress, they continue to retain, and add to, the substantial inventory of prisoners with which to bargain in the foreseeable future. As another sign of good faith, the SPDC have in the past permitted the reopening of NLD offices, though political activities and meetings were still prohibited inside them, and the use of phones and faxes banned. Public meetings of more than five persons still require a permit from the authorities.

Following several visits to Burma by Rizali Ismail, the *Tatmadaw* released Aung San Suu Kyi from a 19-month period of house arrest in May 2002, which began when she attempted to travel outside of Rangoon to meet supporters in September 2000. Four days after Suu Kyi was released, Japan announced that it would resume its Official Development Assistance (ODA) to Burma, which it had withdrawn following the 1988 coup. While Japan had previously resumed the provision of some US$6 million in "humanitarian aid" per year to Burma, along with any ODA funds committed prior to the coup, it now offered to contribute US$5 million towards a power plant in Rangoon, US$28 million towards a power plant in the Kayah State – classified as humanitarian aid – US$7 million for medical equipment, and in July 2002, Japan announced it would contribute more aid to improve the country's information technology sector.[6] This aid could be attributed as a reward to the SPDC, both for releasing Suu Kyi for the second time and for continuing the talks. In July 2002, South Korea also signed an agreement to provide financial and technical assistance towards developing Burma's mobile phone capabilities.[7] Since the peasant poor comprise the overwhelming majority of Burma's population, one might reasonably question what improvements in their justice could arise from improving the country's mobile phone capabilities.

Suu Kyi was arrested again in May 2003, along with members of her entourage, after serious clashes with members of the regime's mass organization – the Union Solidarity and Development Association (USDA) – while visiting her supporters in northern Burma. NLD offices were shut, up to 200 members were arrested along with at least 300 NLD supporters across Burma.[8] At the moment, only the party's headquarters remain open. The arrests followed Suu Kyi's criticism of the *Tatmadaw* for refusing to start serious talks.[9] Although 91 people, who were detained at the same time as Suu Kyi, were released in July 2003, the *Tatmadaw*'s failure to release Suu Kyi attracted worldwide criticism – including from the United Nations, Japan, the United States, and the European Union – and an unprecedented joint statement calling for her release issued by ASEAN at their annual meeting of foreign ministers held in Cambodia in June 2003.[10]

General Than Shwe responded by dispatching his foreign minister and deputy foreign minister to Thailand, Japan, Malaysia, Indonesia, Singapore, China, Bangladesh, Pakistan, and India with a personal letter claiming that Suu Kyi and the NLD had been plotting an uprising and that Suu Kyi was encouraging armed ethnic rebel groups to take part.[11] While Great Britain persuaded the European Union to toughen sanctions against Burma – issuing a travel ban on Burma's leaders and their families, freezing the assets of 150 senior government officials, and tightening the arms embargo – Japan again froze its financial aid to Burma, and the United States Congress passed the Burmese Freedom and Democracy Bill. This Act, which came into effect in August 2003, bans specified Burmese imports into the United States, freezes the country's meager financial assets in U.S. banks, and places further visa restrictions on Burmese officials attempting to enter the United States. It is more than likely that without serious talks, the cycle of clashes between USDA and NLD supporters, arrests of Suu Kyi and the NLD, and rewarding the *Tatmadaw* with concessions for her release will continue in the foreseeable future.

Economic reform and international pressure for democracy

Burma's economic prospects will continue to remain poor for so long as the SPDC offers minor acts of good faith to bargain for international funding. Considerable infrastructure investment would be required from Burma's allies in Japan and Singapore if ASEAN were to pressure Burma to resist Chinese aid and strategic influence in the region.[12] Yet this would seem unlikely given that at the ASEAN summit held in Laos in November 2004, the member states pushed ahead with their proposals to incorporate China into a massive East Asian free trade bloc and regularly held East Asian summits that would include ASEAN, China, Japan, and South Korea. The Chinese government not only criticizes foreign interference in Rangoon's internal affairs, including the use of sanctions, it hosts visits by Burma's military leaders and promotes further co-operation between the People's Liberation Army and the *Tatmadaw*. Russia has also offered some infrastructure aid to Burma – its announcement in May 2002 that it will contribute US$150 million to the construction of a center for nuclear studies in Burma, including the design and building of a research nuclear reactor, laboratories, and support infrastructure, may in the future cause more trouble for Burma than good.

In the meantime, without the major international aid that has been denied to Burma by the IMF and the World Bank, the Kyat will remain overvalued and runaway inflation will prevent any improvement in Burma's foreign debt. Domestic private enterprise in Burma has been strangled and forced to revert to the black market, whose trade may be preventing a total financial collapse. Despite the passing of the Burmese Freedom and Democracy Act by the U.S. Congress, along with similar threats of further sanctions by the European Union following the arrest of Aung San Suu Kyi in 2003, Western trade sanctions remain effective symbolic measures that are relatively ineffective politically. Although the U.S. import ban forced the generals to switch to Euros as the currency for all importing and exporting business – thus creating a fourth tradable currency and further headaches for Burma's already troubled financial situation – exports to the United States from Burma, mainly textiles, were estimated to be worth only around $400 million per year in 2003.[13]

Despite the loss of jobs forcing many textile workers into poverty and prostitution, the generals have proven to be adept in adapting to isolationist policies and for much of their history have indeed welcomed them. Economic liberalization was, for them, only a relatively new experiment – primarily a means to gaining foreign currency – that could be withdrawn if it threatened their political stability. Hence the difficulty in their conceiving of sanctions as punitive measures designed to instigate political reform. Burma maintains alternative trade markets in China and India, its 1997 admission into ASEAN effectively secured its markets in Southeast Asia – particularly in Singapore and Thailand – and although it succumbed to pressure to forfeit its chance to chair the ASEAN summit in 2006, it still stands to benefit indirectly from the new ASEAN–China trade accord.

The generals' foreign direct investment strategies of the 1990s proved to be as expedient as their choice in trading partners. There was no evidence to suggest that long-term economic planning guided the approval of projects by the state-run Myanmar Investment Corporation (MIC), nor was there any evidence of foreign investment monies being distributed among the Burmese people. On the contrary, the *Tatmadaw*'s company, Union of Myanmar Economic Holdings (UMEH), whose finances are not publicly reported, operates an immense slush fund for their various endeavors.[14] Meanwhile, the SPDC blames foreigners for their economic woes,[15] continues to maintain faith in their own economic stewardship, and only occasionally replaces errant generals on the grounds of mismanagement.[16]

Despite their economic mismanagement and public displays of anti-corruption rhetoric, perhaps the *Tatmadaw*'s most reliable source of unreported income continues to be their drug tax. Ball claimed that in 1999 drugs provide by far the largest single source of export income for Burma, between US$700 million and US$1 billion annually in foreign currency for heroin exports alone, or about the same as the total of all other exports.[17]

Matthews notes that although it is impossible to verify statistically, Yawnghwe cited French estimates in 1998 to show that revenues from the export of narcotics may have provided the state or its co-opted agents with an annual profit of between US$2 and 8 billion.[18] Moreau claimed in 2001 that laundered narco-dollars account for as much as 50 percent of Burma's GDP.[19] By 1997, Burma's production of raw opium exceeded 2,500 tons, or more than double the yield in 1988 when the SLORC took power and assumed economic management of the country.[20]

Not suprisingly, some members of the SLORC–SPDC developed extensive business connections with drug lords and have benefited directly from drug trafficking since 1988, particularly following the ceasefire accommodations made with ethnic insurgent groups in northeast Burma. Working in co-operation with, and under the regulation of *Tatmadaw* units, the former insurgent groups were not only encouraged to increase their raw opium production but also to diversify into the manufacture of amphetamines and methamphetamines for the Thailand market.[21] To placate Western criticism over their lack of action taken against drug lords, their militias, and their trade, the SPDC has shown itself to be attacking the problem through a public program of eradication for the United Nations Office on Crime and Drugs (UNOCD), the U.S. government, and the world's press. While the generals opened their new anti-drugs museum, drug lords and local militias assisted by the *Tatmadaw* have continued to refine their lucrative business connections and trade in methamphetamines. Along with poor weather conditions, the booming trade in methamphetamines would seem to tarnish the allegedly successful eradication efforts of the SPDC as reported by UNOCD's annual *Opium Survey* and their figures for falling opium poppy cultivation in recent years.[22] Perhaps the close proximity of drug lords Lo Hsing-han and Khun Sa to the SPDC helped in co-ordinating the efforts required for diversifying production, as well as in securing facilities for laundering foreign currency.

While smuggling efforts continue through Yunnan and Thailand, and since most of Burma's heroin is smuggled into China through the Shan state – where most production takes place in areas under the control of various militias including the United Wa State Army (UWSA) – a great deal depends upon maintaining the Sino–Burmese relationship. Furthermore, because the Burmese national accounts simply do not reflect the US$2–3 billion worth of Chinese weaponry acquired by the *Tatmadaw*,[23] it appears that at least some of the *Tatmadaw*'s arms escalation has been financed with drug money. One could speculate, therefore, on the provisional nature of the *Tatmadaw*'s hardware and the spare parts required to maintain its operational capabilities should China apply further pressure on Burma to restrict drug smuggling into Yunnan. Yet the migration of Chinese into the Shan state makes the successful detection of smuggling more difficult and threatens the further spread of HIV-AIDS.

In early 2003, Burma failed to be certified by the U.S. State Department as being in compliance with anti-narcotics regulations, despite strong lobbying on their behalf by the Washington-based public relations firm, DCI Group. Because of rising discontent in Thailand towards drug dealers, in 2003 the Thai government ordered Thai police to clamp down on dealers of amphetamines and methamphetamines of Burmese origin, resulting in the death or arrest of large numbers of such dealers. Despite Burma's public relations efforts to curb production, however, opium remains a viable alternative to ethnic insurgent groups who have signed ceasefires with the government, should demand fall in the methamphetamines markets or demand, and prices, rise in the heroin markets.[24]

Aristotle believes that because the "middling element" in a regime is capable of overturning both democracies and oligarchies, they should not be neglected as they are in deviant regimes.[25] The middling element, or middle class, in Burma, however, comprises military officers and Chinese businessmen, all of whom stand to gain from maintaining the status quo. The SPDC clearly do not neglect the bulk of the regime's middle class and have created an "exclusive social order of privilege" with welfare, health, and educational facilities for active and retired officers and soldiers.[26] Regional commanders have also amassed great wealth through narcotics and other black-market trade. The "constructive engagement" argument used by Burma's ASEAN neighbors to justify any investment as being in the interests of promoting democracy and human rights through economic development and the growth of a more democratically minded middle class would, therefore, seem to be hollow in the case of Burma. Kyaw Yin Hlaing suggests that despite standing by Burma when the E.U. opposed its membership into the 2004 Asia–Europe Meeting (ASEM), ASEAN member states presently appear to lack a strategy for dealing with the junta should it fail to undertake political reforms demanded by the international community.[27]

Suu Kyi condemns foreign investment in Burma because it only enriches an already wealthy elite bent on monopolizing economic and political power.[28] While she has stated that her release, along with other members of the NLD, from incarceration in 2002 did not change her attitude towards sanctions, she is receptive to certain social development work and humanitarian aid directed towards the poor and disadvantaged.[29] She believes that a true policy of engagement should mean that countries engage the democratic forces as well as the *Tatmadaw*.

Much faith was placed in the possible ramifications of Khin Nyunt's "roadmap to democracy" announced in a speech delivered soon after he became prime minister in August 2003. Some saw this as a timely opening for the U.S. to re-engage Burma by reversing its sanctions policy.[30] Arguments can be offered on both sides of the sanctions debate – though morally symbolic, it is true that sanctions have not achieved their desired political effect. To date, there has been little to no indication of any realistic movements towards democratic structural change, by a "roadmap" or otherwise, and it may be too early to seize upon further announcements by the new cabinet to indicate any "tectonic shift" on the part of the SPDC given the distance they have placed between themselves and Khin Nyunt. A far more cogent moral imperative is the humanitarian crisis facing the country which justifies the provision of humanitarian aid directed towards those ends.

It is unclear what immediate effects the lifting of sanctions would have on the Burmese economy, or even whether many Western foreign investors would be clambering to return – the successes achieved by pro-democracy activists were not the only reason foreign investors pulled out of Burma in the 1990s.[31] It has been argued that returning to the so-called "two hands" policy or "carrot and stick" approach may be possible if the removal of sanctions, most particularly against infrastructure aid, is indeed wished for by the regime. While it would seem that this approach – lying between the extremes of isolationist sanctions and constructive engagement – at least provides the possibility of some middle ground for diplomatic maneuvering at the national level, it would require a co-ordinated effort on the part of the U.S., E.U., and Japan.[32] At the local level, a policy of "selective engagement," or better targeting of aid that promotes the growth of civil society, is also a reasonable objective.[33] Caution is warranted, however, since adequate safeguards to ensure the transparency and accountability of foreign capital inflows, for whatever purpose, are still lacking and, according to MacLean, a resurgence of nepotism and corruption accompanying foreign aid without safeguards could lead to the monopolization of goods and services giving non-state actors political legitimacy within ethnically, linguistically, and religiously divided nation states, thus contributing to state fragmentation in Burma.[34]

Change from the inside?

Aristotle believed that tyrannies could be destroyed, both from the outside and from the inside. When rule by the people opposes a tyranny, and the people back their intentions to destroy with men who have will and are capable, a tyranny will be destroyed from the outside.[35] Yet in the absence of a pre-emptive Iraq-like strike by the United States against Burma, perhaps the most worrisome threat to the preservation of the *Tatmadaw*'s regime would be described by Aristotle as that which comes from within: "Another mode [in which tyranny is destroyed] is from within itself, when those sharing [power] fall into factional conflict."[36]

Callahan believes that internal military dilemmas arising from the *Tatmadaw*'s state-building projects in the 1990s probably account as much for their unyielding behavior as their concerns about the NLD. Their two primary internal concerns, according to Callahan, are the appearance of a generation and experience gap in the officer corps and the tensions between Rangoon and regional warlord commanders. Discipline and morale are also low, reflecting the standards of mass recruitment, and private ethnic or drug armies, who retained their arms following ceasefire agreements, show little respect for authority.[37] Evidence of the generals' concern for maintaining discipline within their ranks can be gleaned from their occasional rotation of field commanders and the purging of senior SPDC members at various times since 1988.[38]

Marginalization of the military's political leaders is not uncommonly practiced among the generals and their treatment of Aung San is a case in point – Suu Kyi's presence has forced the generals to downplay the legacy of Aung San. Perhaps more important in terms of consolidating their power and independence in recent years was the leadership's decision to distance themselves from Ne Win and his daughter, Sandar. While there had been signs of this occurring, none were more revealing than the alleged failed attempted coup by Ne Win's three grandsons and son-in-law in March 2002. The plotters supposedly planned to coerce military commanders to kidnap the three top generals on Armed Forces Day, then take them to Ne Win to reorganize the junta and swear their allegiance. While Ne Win denied knowledge of the coup, and some observers saw the coup as a complete fabrication by the generals, both he and Sandar were placed under house arrest, the national police chief was dismissed, and the 83 officers and soldiers assigned to guard Ne Win were sentenced by a military tribunal to 15 years' imprisonment.

According to Maung Maung Gyi, under the rule of Burmese kings, offenses against the king, whether trivial words uttered against him or a serious conspiracy against the throne, were punishable by death.

> Moreover, if a person were declared implicated in treason, a usual charge for doing away with someone unwanted, his or her innocent relatives would be declared abettors and ordered to suffer the same fate. Hence when a person knew that the king was displeased with him either through personal resentment or ill advice he had to seek recourse to an open revolt or else a worse fate would befall him.
>
> (Maung Maung Gyi (1983): 24)

Ne Win's four relatives were found guilty of treason and sentenced to death by hanging in September 2002. The sentences were appealed and the appeals rejected, though it was possible that the sentences would be commuted to life imprisonment. Ne Win's death while under house arrest in December 2002 passed without ceremony, nor any domestic publication.

In August 2003, following the events since Suu Kyi's arrest in May 2003, the generals undertook a major reshuffling of cabinet positions. While Senior General Than Shwe remained head of state, chairman of the SPDC, and commander-in-chief of the armed forces, he made way for the more moderate – or at least less isolationist – Khin Nyunt to become prime minister. The move may have been undertaken in recognition of Khin Nyunt's superior ability to handle the international media and foreign diplomats on matters concerning Suu Kyi. However, the promotion of the hardliner Lt-General Soe Win to the position of Secretary-2 of the SPDC in February 2003 and to Secretary-1 following the cabinet reshuffle, as well as the naming of Shwe Mann as joint chief of staff in 2002, possibly to replace Maung Aye in the future, meant that Khin Nyunt would have to share power with Soe Win and Shwe Mann. Khin Nyunt's position as prime minister, therefore, was largely ceremonial for so long as the ruling council existed in its current form and, if he lost his role as director of military intelligence, he would have become a general without an army. In October 2004, he was charged with refusing to obey orders and corruption – a common justification during a purge – and placed under house arrest along with officers loyal to him. His intelligence apparatus was disbanded and he was replaced by Than Shwe's protégé, Soe Win. It seems that it may take the passing of the current generation of generals before factions within the *Tatmadaw* are allowed to thrive.

Institutions, power, and trust

Aristotle claims that reforming a regime is no less a task than to institute one from the beginning, just as unlearning something is no less a task than learning it from the beginning.[39] Forty years of autarchic military rule in Burma has made the people politically apathetic, fearful of reprisals, distrustful of the military-run institutions, and yet deeply wary of foreign influence and Western models of society. In 1996, Lee Kuan Yew correctly observed that there was only one effective instrument of government in Burma – the army.[40] The army remains the "dominant institution" in Burma today and, as Taylor says, "its grip over the media, the educational system and the bureaucracy is as firm as that of its predecessors."[41]

In 1990, Taylor claimed that the Burmese election results demonstrated mass rejection of the autarchic economic policies of the previous 26 years. He further claimed that the continuance of military rule, while a constitution is being written, would actually be a blessing for the civilians who will follow and that a civilian government would have a better chance of coping with the results of economic reform once the worst consequences of structural adjustment are over.[42] Taylor's faith in economic rationalism, it seems, has been trumped by the *Tatmadaw*'s lust for power. While such arguments reflect the empirical deficiencies of utilizing the political economy approach, adopting an institutionalist perspective of Burma's prospects for reform can produce an equally stunting effect:

> [O]ne wonders whether a western-style multi-party political system with its inescapably linked market economy, uniquely western notions

of individualism and related secular attitudes, as well as the infrastructure that it implies – the legal, administrative, and intellectual
baggage that are invariably invoked – are, in any case, in the best
interests of most of the people of Burma presently. That is to say, even
if a society such as Burma wishes to democratize (whatever that
means), its very short experience with, and total absence of, traditional institutions and conceptions even remotely resembling western-
style democracy as we know it (there is no equivalent indigenous
Burmese term for it) raises some serious infra-structural difficulties,
especially if an American version were imposed on Burma today.

(Aung Thwin, M. (2002): 498)

While the latter may fear that liberal democratic institutions and a
market economy may not lie in the best interests of the people, perhaps
it would be prudent to note that black-market trade is what currently prevents the total collapse of the Burmese economy. Nevertheless, currently
to impose a Western-style democratic political system upon Burma would
indeed strain the best interests of the people simply because the army has
been the dominant institution since 1962, when they began ruling like
Burmese kings, effectively concentrating all executive, legislative, and
judicial powers in themselves.[43] Yet Aristotle claims that existing regimes
can be assisted by introducing an arrangement which allows for the possibility that reforms may lead to what is best, most attainable, and most
fitting.[44] In other words, a better mixing of the oligarchic and the democratic elements within the Burmese regime can still occur within the
limitations imposed by Burma's severe institutional and infrastructural
deficiencies.

One of the greatest challenges to be faced in reforming the Burmese
regime, however, is not necessarily the absence of democratic political
institutions as such, but the people's trust in any political institutions at
all, and 40 years of military rule has only reinforced what Lucian Pye and
Maung Maung Gyi discovered and Gravers notes, namely: "[T]he traditional Burman concepts pertaining to power as personal attributes, rather
than attributes of systems, have been retained since independence....
Power in Burma is not merely concentrated within institutions, it is also
highly concentrated around a few persons."[45] Applying political and economic institutional analysis per se ignores the complex array of mores that
guide social relationships in Burma. As the case of East Timor shows,
attempts to rectify infrastructural shortfalls may be undertaken with international funding. However, Suu Kyi notes that if liberal democracy –
along with the basic institutions and practices that make for good governance – were to be established in Burma (let alone whether they are most
fitting), this would not provide the panacea to all of the country's ills.[46]
What most threatens a successful transition away from equating stability as
the maintenance of the status quo in Burma is the respect paid towards

personal power, which has only been magnified by the *Tatmadaw*'s running of all political and economic institutions for so long.

What passes as patron–client ties in one mind's eye may constitute nepotism in another, and at least in the present, bribes and blood ties may resonate more effectively for the average Burmese citizen than trusting in vague ideas about the merits of democratic institutions and the doctrine of the separation of powers. Yet patron–client ties which are backed by the brute force of reprisal could only intimidate the ruled and reinforce one of the chief desires on the part of a tyrant, that the ruled have only modest thoughts, "for a small-souled person will not conspire against anyone."[47] A long history of political opposition in Burma might suggest that spirited-ness is not a personal attribute that can be easily destroyed, nor that the Burmese people are particularly comfortable with the idea of enslave-ment. Spiritedness may, however, be suppressed, inciting people who cannot voice or act out their opposition openly without fear of reprisal to turn instead towards what Scott calls "everyday forms of peasant resis-tance."[48] The *Tatmadaw* have attempted to suppress Burmese spiritedness with impoverishment, draconian laws, fear, threats, and political rhetoric that allows any act to be justified on the grounds of national survival and fosters a communal paranoia of foreign influence. While their military power promises to inform their political agenda, the *Tatmadaw*'s political rhetoric will only succeed by maintaining the public's ignorance, and this provides one key to any possibility of reform.

According to Aristotle, the brutish mode of tyranny aims at making the ruled distrust one another, and tyranny cannot be overthrown until some persons are able to trust each other:

> [E]verything is done to make all as ignorant of one another as pos-sible, since knowledge tends to create trust of one another ... a tyranny will not be overthrown before some persons are able to trust each other – hence they make war on the respectable as being harmful to their rule not merely because they claim not to merit being ruled in the fashion of the master, but also because they are trustworthy, both among themselves and with respect to others, and will not denounce one another or others.
>
> (Aristotle, *Politics*, 1313b4–6, 1314a15–22)

While Fukuyama believes that social capital is often produced by hierar-chical sources of authority, including Buddhism and Confucianism, whose norms are "transmitted from one generation to the next through a process of socialization that involves much more habit than reason,"[49] Pye's analysis of Burmese social capital suggests that it is the socialization practices that reinforce the public's negative perceptions of power and trust. Addressing the problem of trust, therefore, is not a simple task, yet it may also not be an impossible one. Indeed, it has been argued that, following the ceasefires among ethnic insurgents, there has been a re-emergence of civil society networks – primarily religious or community development related – within and between ethnic nationality communities over the past decade which has been largely ignored owing to the focus on elite-level politics and the UN-brokered peace talks. While the most substantial constraint on the growth of civil society in Burma is "government distrust," according to South, the past five to ten years have seen a partial readjustment of state–society relations which may also be reflected in their need to reach some consensus-based position leading up to the National Convention.[50]

Yet democratic civil society, it would seem, also requires the rule of law and strong institutions in order to flourish. While it may be reasonable to argue for a "bottom up" approach to supplement any possible "top down" impetus for democratic reforms instigated by the elites, if the latter appears to be withheld indefinitely, this may also shape the character of the former – unless the minorities already consider themselves totally independent of mainstream Burmese civil society. While the average Burmese citizen may have little trust in the political and economic institutions of the government, in rules and regulations that can change on a whim, and in their Peace and Development Council representatives – at least at the higher division and township levels – the same may not be true for their various informal social and religious organizations. Naturally, one would also expect that the highest levels of trust the people have would be directed towards their immediate family, friends, and neighbors, rather than the majority of their fellow citizens. While it is difficult to see how fostering a change in the levels of trust people have in the system in general could occur without reforming the rule of law as it currently operates, therefore, social and religious organizations – at least those that have not been monopolized by the military – may play an important role in fostering the local norms required to sustain any just reforms introduced at the elite level.

The present study of Buddhist political rhetoric reveals that the *endoxa* on the subject may be coerced by politicians whose rhetoric is pitched towards a particular end. For both the *Tatmadaw* and the opposition, their final end is the preservation of the regime, either by maintaining stability through order or by improving stability through change. Since trust is lacking, at least among the Burman majority and in their formal institutions of governance, then political reformers must produce the right kind of rhetoric to amend this particular attribute, which, according to Aristotle, is also common to tyranny. Common sense would suggest that this means appealing to the social institutions that the Burman people place their trust in most – Buddhism and the *Sangha*. This is why Suu Kyi must present her ideas for democratic political reform, as far as possible, through the medium of Buddhist language and symbolism when addressing the majority Burman population:

Of the four Buddhist virtues conducive to the happiness of laymen, *saddha*, confidence in moral, spiritual and intellectual values, is the first. To instill such confidence, not by an appeal to the passions but through intellectual conviction, into a society which has long been wracked by distrust and uncertainty is the essence of the Burmese revolution for democracy.

(Aung San Suu Kyi (1991): 178)

Suu Kyi calls the Burmese struggle for democracy a "spiritual revolution" not only because unjust regulations make it impossible for it to be a political and social revolution but also because mistrust is so widespread that the people must be convinced that political change is needed and because this also requires a change in the values that they lived by before. A "revolution of the spirit" requires the development of new norms, based on a combination of traditional Buddhist values with modern political principles.[51] The people's *endoxa* on foreign ideas, and models of government, must also be addressed, and this is what Suu Kyi has attempted to do.

Reforming the Burmese regime indeed appears to be no lesser task than to institute one from the beginning. While it may appear drastic that the people must modify what they have learned from the beginning,[52] including the norms, mores, and socialization processes relative to the old regime, countless historical examples suggest that education and habituation relative to a new regime may be successfully undertaken and that some cultural traits, mores, and norms of behavior may not be as static as certain commentators claim. Perhaps the mass demonstrations in 1988 suggest not only that cultural traits may be more malleable than some believe but also that the modern Burmese do not fear anarchy more than tyranny.

Prudence assists the political expert in determining what laws are best and most fitting for reforming existing regimes.[53] The wholesale application of American-style democracy, for example, may not be the most fitting for Burma. Because a regime, according to Aristotle, comprises not only the arrangement and distribution of offices and the establishment of the authoritative element but also the end pursued by the partnership,[54] perhaps it is more important for political reformers to concentrate upon the ends that should be pursued in a reformed Burmese regime before advocating specific institutions which may or may not be the best or the most fitting. Given the differences in the mores between the people of America and the people of Burma, for example, it would not be fitting for Suu Kyi simply to replicate the political rhetoric of the *Federalist*. Her political rhetoric must present the new regime's ends in terms of Burmese culture in order that her message is favorably received. This message could include, for example, a basic respect for human rights. While the generals claim to respect the Universal Declaration of Human Rights, they state that the Eastern concept of human rights is not the same as the Western concept.[55] The SPDC, like Lee Kuan Yew, claims that respect for the individual would never take precedence over society. Suu Kyi, however, claims that democracy is based on respect for the individual,[56] and some observers claim that, based on her reliance on Buddhism in her writings, she would suggest that the Buddhist concept of the Middle Way would help avoid the extremes of individualism and collectivism.[57]

The generals' ends, on the other hand, revolve around power, and they play a constant game of balancing competing interests and claims against each other. Apart from fostering closer ties with the Chinese, Indians, and certain ASEAN member states in recent years – primarily for the acquisition of arms, to replenish foreign reserves, and to build regional moral legitimacy – their conduct in general reflects Burma's foreign policy since independence: neutralism – positively or negatively aligned non-action. Their economic policies remain shortsighted, along with their social, domestic, and foreign policies. Maintaining the preservation of the *Tatmadaw*'s political power is perhaps the only constant factor running through the SPDC's arguments for legitimacy and any policy, action, or institution – be it economic, social, domestic, foreign, or religious – which can be manipulated to keep the generals in power, will be used to do so.

Conclusion

Strauss believed that Xenophon's skepticism regarding the prospects of a benevolent tyrant is based not only on the absence of any reference to beneficent and happy tyrants who actually existed but also on the practical difficulties encountered when justice is equated with the legal. Being called a tyrant means that the tyrant has been unable to transform a defective title into a valid one, kingship. His lack of unquestioned authority requires a tyrannical government to be more oppressive and unstable, and no tyrant can dispense with a bodyguard which is more stable to him than to the city, enabling him to maintain his power against the wishes of the city.[58] Furthermore, the improvement of tyranny prescribed by Simonides would require a shift of part of the power from the mercenaries to the citizens, a move that would antagonize the mercenaries without providing the tyrant with any guarantee of support from the citizens. While such a shift is not absolutely impossible, its actualization is safe only in circumstances which man cannot create, or which no sensible man would create.[59]

Despite their kingly performance in recent years, Burma's generals have been unable to transform their defective title into a valid one. Their lack of unquestioned authority requires that they be more oppressive and unstable, enabling them to maintain their power against the wishes of the people, and any action or policy becomes justified if it helps to secure their power. The hopes of any faction-led changes arising from within the military would seem for the present to have been nipped in the bud upon Khin Nyunt's "early retirement," and replacement. The hardliners have shored up their base and now the "democratic process" lies solely in their hands, and in how they choose to define it – much will depend on whether power alone satisfies the generals and how important they regard international legitimacy.

Ultimately, any lasting improvements in justice and stability in Burma would require not only the successful resolution and securing of political arrangements for the ethnic minorities, but also a shift of part of the power from the army to the people – a move that would antagonize the army without providing the generals with any guarantee of support from the people. While such a shift of power was successfully undertaken in the Philippines to depose the Marcos regime in 1986, the Burmese lacked the organizational structure of social groups, an independent middle class, and the hierarchical equivalent of the Catholic Church to do it in 1988. And although the IMF created the circumstances leading to President Suharto's departure from office in Indonesia, Burma has already been ostracized from international funding and cannot as easily be pressured.[60] Further, unlike both of these cases, the *Tatmadaw* – like the People's Liberation Army in 1989 – did in fact open fire on their own people. Huntington believes that the better course for new democracies in dealing with the crimes of former authoritarian rulers is to adopt the least satisfactory alternative: "do not prosecute, do not punish, do not forgive, and, above all, do not forget."[61] For a shift in power from the army to the citizens to at least be possible, Suu Kyi must, and has, guaranteed not to hunt down the generals if power were ever to change hands in her direction. She believes that it should suffice that the people be told the truth.

Yet confidence building may be all that the current generation of generals, and especially the hardliners in charge, are prepared to commit themselves to in any dialogue with the NLD and the ethnic minorities, or with other opposition groups that follow for so long as the people recognize them, and not simply Ne Win alone, as being the ones most responsible for the tyrannical acts committed. While a shift of part of the generals' power to the people is not absolutely impossible, therefore, it would indeed seem that its safe actualization is highly improbable in the current circumstances. Since the generals cannot shift power without intimidating their own middle class, the *Tatmadaw*, nor would they sensibly wish to create the circumstances that could, in all probability, lead to their own downfall, improvements in the justice and stability in Burma are unlikely to eventuate any time soon. Lasting improvements in Burma would require circumstances that are beyond the generals' creation and control.

10 Conclusion

Modern political development theory suffers from deterministic tend-encies that were not present in classical comparative politics. In their quest to democratize the world, and because they assume that history is determined to move towards democracy, many political scientists no longer regard tyranny to be something other than mythical. Yet tyranny is still real, and its possibility should not be overlooked when it comes to classifying regimes. Studying the rhetoric of tyranny from an Aristotelian perspective allows us to understand the behavior of a regime's political leaders, to classify their speeches and actions accordingly, and to alert the people to how their leaders attempt to mold common opinions to conform to their enthymemes and, in so doing, legitimize their rule.

It is important that statesmen and policy-makers alike understand the national character of a regime and the character traits of the people that make up the regime. Hoping that democracy takes root in certain deviant regimes merely through the application of democratic institutions and procedures, without addressing the particular circumstances or the common opinions of the people, may prove to be as fruitless as hoping that a tyrant acquires virtue merely by performing a number of kingly duties – like consecrating pagodas. At times, tyrannical power may appear to be as lasting as the cultural traits of a people ruled in such a fashion, yet neither is inevitable or unchanging. Just as one tyrant's power cannot last forever, political culture is not a perfectly static thing but should be treated as something relative to the regime and to what the regime's leading figures look up to.

Political stability is important for the lasting preservation of any regime. Stability may be maintained by imposing order and resisting change, or it may be improved by moving the regime in just directions so as to prevent its degeneration into a worse form. Political stability should set the para-meters within which the regime's natural decay may be prevented by improvements in justice.

Moving towards justice in a tyrannical regime may occur if the tyrant moderates his behavior according to Aristotle's prescriptions. While a tyrant will always safeguard his power, these prescriptions serve both his interests as well as those of his people. Moving towards justice, for Aristotle, does not mean maintaining the status quo but working towards a better mixing of the democratic and oligarchic elements in a regime to improve its stability. Because the longevity of a regime is a sign of its justice, a tyrannical regime will always be more unstable and require more force than one that is not. An analysis of the justice, stability, and the rhetoric of benevolent despotism in two Asian regimes, Singapore and Burma, reveals that the character of each regime and the measures required to preserve their form may vary considerably by degree.

Singapore is somewhat of an anomaly when one attempts to describe the nature of its political multitude. The Europeans, according to Aristotle, were spirited but lacking in thought and art. Although they were free, they lacked ideas on political governance. Asians had souls rich in thought and art, but lacked spiritedness and remained ruled and enslaved. Singapore's culture is certainly rich in the thought of Lee Kuan Yew, but if spiritedness and freedom may be gauged by the degree of the people's participation in politics, then perhaps the multitude simply lack their own ideas on political governance and have deferred to their rulers. After all, the political and civil service elites are well educated in the British legal and administrative traditions. Yet if the people lack spiritedness, then we must question why the PAP would go to such lengths to secure their rule through the combination of harsh legislation and the liberal use of defamation suits. Indeed, a politically apathetic citizenry could more likely be the product of Lee's own creation. Choosing to rule the country, directly and indirectly, for well over 40 years as if he was still fighting an earlier struggle and suppressing all conceivable threats, no matter how remote, Lee created a political climate where intimidation and fear are subtly understood in everyday life. The traits revealed in this particular case could be labeled, if anything, "Singaporean values" – peculiar to the jurisdictional boundaries of courts in the city-state. Lee's rule and his ongoing legacy created a people who remain, effectively, as disconnected from politics today as they were under British rule in 1948.

Perhaps Lee's circumstances and behavior mirrored that of Pittacus of Mytilene, who was enrolled (along with Solon) among the "seven wise men" of Greece.[1] Lee provided a fine performance of kingly rule over Singapore, and this lengthened his tenure considerably. An application of rhetorical analysis reveals how, during a time of economic prosperity, Lee's peculiar interpretation of Confucian ethics led to the creation of a politically motivated understanding of "shared values" and the invention of the *endoxa* that they were particularly Asian values. Coupled with his survival rhetoric, this has enabled the PAP to draw the public's attention away from the fact that their participation in politics remains negligible, that restrictive legislation controls much of their lives, that criticism of the government is monitored and dealt with, and that elections in Singapore are not necessarily free and fair. Yet Lee's economic policies have made the people wealthy, and because of this, he cannot be labeled a common tyrant.

If the political regime's legitimacy rests largely upon Lee's paternal presence, then it is not inconceivable that Aristotle's "middling element," or the middle class, could gain in status to the extent required to overturn the ruling oligarchs in the future.[2] Yet the middling elements are also "least inclined either to avoid ruling or to wish to rule,"[3] and Lee Hsien Loong's appointment as Prime Minister ensures the continuation of his legacy.

While securing peace and stability may have provided early platforms for Lee's style of rule and for his survival rhetoric, for most of their tenure, Lee Kuan Yew and the PAP have grounded their legitimacy in Singapore's economic success. Whether the PAP will lose its legitimacy in times of economic hardship or, as Przeworski and Limongi suggest, that they could be overturned in times of economic crisis, has yet to be tested.[4] Perhaps, therefore, a younger generation, hardened by economic recession – if this were to occur – and exposed to alternative regimes abroad, could be prepared to influence the middling elements required for a proper mixing of the democratic with the oligarchic principles in Singapore, thus directing those who are more inclined to rule towards a higher standard of justice for the regime. Although since Singapore has been praised as the most economically competitive nation on earth, it is doubtful whether this standard of justice could be any higher than that which Adam Smith laid down in the *Wealth of Nations*. Future economic recessions could test the patience of a citizenry who have become accustomed to one of the highest standards of living in the world, just as it would test the foundations of any regime whose legitimacy relies primarily upon economic stewardship.

While the PAP may be concerned that Singapore's youth have no recollection of Lee's earlier struggles for independence, it should be noted that it was partly through the efforts of the Chinese youth, being influenced by events abroad, that Singaporeans were first awakened politically to the need for change, and it was with the support of the Chinese youth that Lee himself first came to power. Ultimately, the continuation of benevolent despotism in Singapore appears to rely far too much upon Lee's own paternal imprint, presence, and legacy, and upon the ignorance of the next generation of Singaporeans. A better informed citizenry facing economic hardship – should this ever occur – may demand just improvements in the regime, and it is not inconceivable that the next generation of PAP leaders may concede to their demands because it is in their own interests to do so. Because of these particular circumstances, Aristotle's advice on the longevity and preservation of such a regime should prove to be correct.

An Aristotelian analysis of Singapore seems to point in two different directions. On the one hand, that Aristotle could explain the soft authoritarianism of Singapore as a form of tyranny suggests a condemnation of Lee Kuan Yew's rule. On the other hand, that Aristotle would see Lee Kuan Yew's strategy as the more moderate way of preserving a tyranny suggests a modest endorsement of his rule as at least the most moderate form of tyranny. Perhaps Singapore is a dramatic illustration of where a very moderate form of tyranny is the best one could hope for in a regime whose leaders prize the virtue of economic freedom, as measured by the indicators of economic performance, above all else and whose people are willing to go along for the ride for so long as those indicators remain favorable. Of course, it is important to recognize that even a very moderate form of tyranny is still a tyranny, which inclines one to look for any opportunity for improvement. But until such an opportunity appears, Aristotelian prudence might dictate a modest accommodation with such a regime because the alternative could be worse. Burma, for example, is a nation where life is in fact worse, much worse.

An application of Aristotelian theory to Burma indicates that the *Tatmadaw*'s regime remains very much a common brutish tyranny. This is apparent despite their attempts to transform the regime into a more moderate and lasting one through adopting Aristotle's second mode of preservation, playing the kingly role and addressing the *endoxa* of the masses through their Buddhist political rhetoric. The *Tatmadaw*'s version of stability and order is inherently unstable, not only because it lacks political legitimacy, but because while it sets out to oppose the kind of individual freedoms fostered by Western liberalism, it effectively secures the rule of incumbents against any political change at all. Because the generals continue to act immoderately, visibly exercising excessive force on the one hand while appearing to act piously and benevolently on the other, one may reasonably condemn this regime.

Unlike the political multitude in Singapore who are comparatively wealthy, elements of the Burmese multitude remain spirited and the nation as a whole is certainly rich in Buddhist traditions. A successful transformation and preservation of their regime by rhetorical means, however, requires that the generals manipulate the common opinions on kingship and Buddhism to legitimize the safeguarding of their power. But a successful kingly performance relies largely upon their credibility in the eyes of the public. And in a country where Buddhism plays such a central role in the political culture of the people, their credibility has suffered. It is an open question whether the Burmese people would be more accepting of the generals' performance if they too were as wealthy as the citizens of Singapore.

Unlike Singapore, because of Aung San's assassination at an early age, Burma lacked a living political figure around which people could rally in times of trouble. Most Burmese political elites have tried to draw from Aung San's legacy to legitimize their own aspirations to rule – this may also continue for some time in Singapore when Lee passes on. Attempts to secure one's rule by tapping into the legacies of paternal figures, in the form of independence leaders, are common to both Singapore and Burma, along with Vietnam and many other Asian nations which, although they may possess documents establishing a rule of law and a constitutional framework for governing, often prize their political personalities above them.

Because the generals rule as common brutish tyrants, lasting improvements in Burma would require circumstances that are beyond their control. It may be too hopeful to believe that the generals could place themselves in harm's way by relinquishing their power to a civilian government. This supports theoretical criticism of the existence of a truly benevolent despot. While any blossoming of factions within the military may offer hope for future political change, the purge and consolidation of 2004 makes this possibility more unlikely in the foreseeable future. It is clear, however, that any future ruler would be faced with considerable problems were they to gain power, one of which is the general lack of trust that the people have in their institutions of government.

That personal power is respected more in Burma than the power embodied in various institutions of governance suggests that a transformation towards a more just regime would require a great deal of education, and time. The Burmese cannot trust in their political institutions until they trust each other, and just as ignorance maintains a tyranny, education is required to overcome one. It would seem reasonable that the basic social fabric in Burma, the norms, mores, and trust of the people, must be addressed before attempting to introduce the political and economic institutions of a liberal democracy because this will shape the character and functioning of the institutions themselves. And when these institutions are discussed, then perhaps it would be more sensible not to dismiss them as Western and, therefore, inappropriate, but to frame their discussion within the guidelines of flexibility and prudence. Statesmen should introduce the topic of universal ideas while taking into account the particular circumstances, the condition of trust, and the cultural beliefs of the people. Since knowledge creates trust, education with respect to improving justice in the arrangement of the regime should be of prime importance. Preceding this education could be another that alerts the people to the true nature of their ruler's political rhetoric.

Analyzing the rhetoric of benevolent despotism in Singapore and Burma produces some fundamental similarities between the rhetorical strategies undertaken by the leaders of both regimes. These point towards future research into the rhetoric of other harsh regimes. Common to the political rhetoric in both Burma and Singapore is a continual message of survival against threats, both internally and from abroad, whether real or invented. Emphasizing this theme strengthens the case made by the political elite for a nationalistic response built upon rallying around the leadership. It is only by constantly reinforcing this message that rulers may justify harsh and restrictive legislation and, on occasion, the exercise of power over a prolonged period of time.

A major attribute of this nationalistic cause accompanying the rhetoric of survival is the promotion of an allied form of political rhetoric which addresses that which is commonly understood as authoritative and revered by the people. A people's political culture comprises their common opinions. Central to some political cultures, and influential in most, is a religion or a system of ethics whose reverence may reflect that of a religion. Because the political elite must, in their political rhetoric, address the common opinions of the people, their enthymemes must include an appeal to this religion or ethical system in a manner that supports their own legitimacy.

While Lee Kuan Yew and the PAP, therefore, attempted to explain their regime's success in terms of Confucian thought, in Burma, the *Tatmadaw*'s need to address the Buddhist tradition arose as a consequence of a real rhetorical threat posed by Aung San Suu Kyi. Tyrants, however, are at a disadvantage when faced by a more credible challenger who also takes this into account because tyrants must use force, fear, and intimidation to hold onto their power. Appealing to Buddhist principles while using force, either in seizing power or in holding onto power, would transform persuasive rhetoric into mere sophistry. While all human governments require the use of force to some degree, to use brute force in the name of Buddhism equates Buddhism with power. This is why Aung San Suu Kyi's Buddhist rhetoric is more credible in the eyes of the public than either the *Tatmadaw*'s or her father's. This may also help to explain Aung San's position on religion and politics and why any references he made to Buddhism were subtle, rather than overt like the *Tatmadaw*'s.

Examining the rhetoric of political leaders helps us to understand their character and the character of their regime. An Aristotelian analysis of regimes serves to indicate that, while elections are important, they are not fundamental to the definition of a regime. Democratization theorists may promote democratic institutions unconditionally and in a deterministic fashion while ignoring cultural variations and the character of a people. It would be a facade to find democratic institutions where leaders rule more or less by decree. Investigating justice in the regime and discovering what particularly its leaders look up to are essential to improving the stability of the regime.

The conceptual framework of this book encourages future research on regimes to bridge the gap between theoretical generalization and area studies specificity. Adopting and synthesizing the political culture approach with classical political theory complements and enriches the comparative politics literature while rejecting its more deterministic elements. In order to perform a rhetorical analysis on other harsh regimes, one would first need to make inductive normative judgments in order to select appropriate case studies. Aristotle's classification of regimes, their attributes, and their means to preservation in the *Politics* serves as a guide for facilitating the early classification of regimes and the choice of case studies for rhetorical analysis. The *Politics* also informs our assessments of justice and stability in a regime.

Aristotle's *Rhetoric* guides our understanding of the basic elements of rhetorical persuasion and stresses the importance of the enthymeme. Two strategies common to the rhetoric of benevolent despotism are the presence of survival rhetoric and the formulation of enthymemes that address the common opinions, or *endoxa*, regarding a religion or authoritative ethical code. In order to select appropriate case studies, inductive judgments would be required to locate the presence of each, interpreted in a manner that serves to support a ruler's political legitimacy. Once the case studies are chosen, historical, cultural, and political research helps inform one of the *endoxa* while inductively developing enthymemes for rhetorical analysis. A design model utilizing content analysis may then serve to examine these enthymemes in the political rhetoric of the elite.

While compiling an exhaustive list of possible regimes that lend themselves to future research would itself require much inductive research, some preliminary observations may be made. Countries with strong religious traditions or authoritative ethical codes would appear to be the most likely candidates for a rhetorical study of benevolent despotism. Choosing case studies of benevolent despotism also requires one to focus upon tyrants that have attempted to follow the more moderate, and less brutish, path of self-preservation while seeking to legitimize their hold on power. If the aim of such an exercise is to identify and explain their kingly performance by rhetorical analysis, then one should shy away from common brutish tyrannies unless one discovers that the leaders of these tyrannies, like the Burmese generals, may be attempting to transform their regime into a more moderate or at least more lasting form.

Ideologically based tyrannies do not easily lend themselves to an examination of benevolent despotism because they may fall within the category of a common brutish tyranny. North Korea and China thus pose enthymematic difficulties because, while survival rhetoric may be discovered, they lack the religious or ethical *endoxa*. On the other hand, were China or North Korea to adopt the Confucian Asian values-style arguments of Singapore, rhetorical analysis could prove to be as fruitful as examining how an ideologically based, predominantly secular tyranny in the Middle East or Africa, for example, could turn to Islam to legitimize its rule.

Case studies may also be chosen regardless of the religion or source of ethical authority in each country. Some tyrannical leaders in Africa, for example, have found the Asian values arguments attractive and, presumably, could easily translate these sentiments into their own political interpretations of the religious *endoxa* in their own countries. Moreover, the fact that different countries professing the same religion may evidence radically different political conditions confirms the importance of examining the rhetorical element of addressing the *endoxa* in tyrannical regimes.

Analyzing the rhetoric of political leaders helps to reveal their desired ends, and hence the kind of justice they promote, without having to commit oneself to historically or politically predetermined paths of research, nor to be confined to the determinism and the analytical boundaries that plague and define modern comparative development theory. The case studies undertaken in this book serve to reinforce the usefulness of returning to Aristotelian theory to complement modern comparative political theory and offer a more substantial framework for analyzing certain types of regimes. Adopting an Aristotelian conceptual framework for examining tyranny and the rhetoric of tyrannical regimes allows us to understand modern, culturally specific examples of political rhetoric while also allowing us to draw general conclusions about the universal regularities of politics.

Appendix A

Methodology – Burma case study

Chapter 8 focuses upon the Buddhist political rhetoric of Aung San, Aung San Suu Kyi, and the *Tatmadaw* respectively. Content analysis of the speeches, political writings, biographical accounts, and the published works of Aung San and Aung San Suu Kyi, and the pronouncements, actions, and symbolism of the generals was conducted to show that the Burmese political elite have all engaged in Buddhist political rhetoric to support their claims to legitimacy. The methodology discussed below refers to the research conducted on the Buddhist political rhetoric of the *Tatmadaw*, the Burmese military elite's attempts to portray themselves as upholding and preserving Buddhist traditions.

Political rhetoric which appeals to the Buddhist political culture, whether by way of speeches or actions on the part of the military elite, as demonstrated through articles and photographs for example, is directed towards arousing some measure of support and legitimacy among the Burmese people. This research attempts to demonstrate how the military elite, in its various manifestations during times of crisis, have over the past 40 years used and still uses Buddhist ideas and concepts in their public speeches and publications as a rhetorical and political strategy. Content analysis directed towards this purpose not only illustrates how the generals have made use of Buddhist political rhetoric during times of crisis to support their own legitimacy and gain the popular support of the Burmese people, it also substantiates the thesis that the SPDC have been promoting Buddhism as part of a kingly duty normally attributed to the Burmese monarchy and shows that the generals have, over the past 15 years, increased their promotion of Buddhism and responded to Suu Kyi's Buddhist rhetoric with their own version.

The general hypothesis for this section of the study was that the military elite's use of Buddhist rhetoric in their political speeches and publications is more pronounced during times of political crisis. The specific hypothesis (H0) was that the military elite's use of Buddhist political rhetoric in their political speeches and publications increases before a political crisis. The dependent variable was Buddhist political rhetoric, as presented in state-owned newspapers, which is aimed at inferring legitimacy upon the regime by showing its concern for preserving the Buddhist traditions. Because the Burmese generals' use of such rhetoric should be most pronounced during times of political crisis, the independent variable was political crisis and instability.

This model proposed a causal relationship between the political crisis and the appearance of Buddhist political rhetoric in the state-owned media. Conforming to these hypotheses implies either that the military's behavior reflects some degree of control over the political event in question or that they had notice of the event and may have adjusted their rhetoric accordingly. It is assumed that force is required to produce relative stability since rhetoric alone is insufficient to do so, and a tyrant, while providing a kingly performance, safeguards his ability to use his power when necessary. It is proposed, therefore, that the tyrant uses rhetoric and power in tandem to produce stability.

The hypothesis was tested primarily by conducting a content analysis of samples taken from state-owned national newspapers published between 1962 and 2003. Because of the possible volume of source material which could have been examined for the rhetoric of the *Tatmadaw*, and in order to capture change over time, a time series design was incorporated with 11 periods of political crises selected according to historically significant political events. In addition, crisis periods were limited to 61 days and content analysis was conducted on the date designated for a significant event with samples limited to a period of 30 days preceding and 30 days following the significant event. This sample should, therefore, include periods of both crisis and relative stability.

Being a time series design using content analysis of a period covering over 40 years, the model's internal validity should have been strong. Crisis periods should be balanced by periods of relative stability, making one able to infer a valid causality between a political crisis and the use of Buddhist political rhetoric by the military elite. In a country that has experienced a long period of isolationism under authoritarian rule, the concept of political crisis may appear awkward and inappropriate. One could argue, for example, that Burma has experienced political crisis for as long as the military first seized power in 1962. To designate arbitrarily certain points in time as crisis periods may, therefore, appear to be an oversimplification of the general trend. Nevertheless, certain events have produced marked responses from the military in order to produce law and order, some normalcy to social life, and in general, a return to stability.

Eleven crisis periods in Burmese politics were chosen from a period spanning 41 years on the basis of the heightened tensions that existed throughout the country – both among the people and among the political elite. These dates represent major political events or significant changes in Burmese politics that either appear as a climax during a period of political instability or, if they pertain to an action planned by the government about which the public has been alerted, have the potential to create significant instability. For most of the events selected, the military had prior knowledge and time to pitch their rhetoric accordingly. In some cases, the outcome of the event, or the event itself, was one that the military could not have foreseen or chose to ignore. Significant events and the crisis periods surrounding them are marked by, *inter alia*, political unrest, civilian protests, military intervention, military coups, foreign influence, economic sanctions, and the release of political prisoners. The events chosen appear in Table A1.

Because the reasons behind a political crisis will vary on each occasion, and there are 11 crises selected in this design, one should proceed with caution. Some political crisis events should not reasonably be expected to provoke a reaction of the kind we are seeking. In addition, it may be argued that the military elite have in the past used economic stewardship and the suppression of insurgencies as adjunct arguments to support their legitimacy and have only relatively recently shelved these grounds in favor of returning to the traditional role of promoting themselves as protectors and preservers of Buddhist culture.

Table A1   Crisis periods in Burmese politics

Period	Date	Event
1	2 Mar. 1962	Prime Minister U Nu is replaced by General Ne Win in a *coup d'etat*. The *Tatmadaw* seize direct political control
2	2 Mar. 1974	A new constitution guaranteeing single-party socialist rule is adopted. Ne Win becomes president of the Socialist Republic of Burma
3	18 Sep. 1988	Widespread civilian protests against the military regime lead to harsh military crackdown and marshal law. The SLORC, composed almost entirely of *Tatmadaw* generals, ends the period of indirect constitutional rule since 1974
4	27 May 1990	National elections held, NLD wins over 80% of parliamentary seats (392 of 485) and 59.9% of popular vote. SLORC refuses to recognize the results
5	10 July 1995	Aung San Suu Kyi is released from five years of house arrest
6	23 May 1996	NLD convenes conference for all elected representatives from the 1990 elections for 21–25 May. Over 200 NLD delegates are arrested
7	15 Nov. 1997	SLORC renamed SPDC, reshuffling and purging of generals
8	22 Sep. 2000	Aung San Suu Kyi is again placed under house arrest
9	16 Jun. 2001	Some pro-democracy activists are released, some political parties allowed to reopen, including 18 of the 40 NLD offices in Rangoon
10	6 May 2002	Aung San Suu Kyi is released from a 19-month period of house arrest
11	30 May 2003	Aung San Suu Kyi is arrested following clashes with USDA supporters

One possible means of reducing the spuriousness and further validating the causality between the variables would be to re-examine the periods of crisis in order to remove, as far as possible, any other external influences upon the crisis itself. While Burma has been an inherently isolationist country for more than four decades, international events have had some impact on internal policy over the past 15 years. World reaction to the national elections of 1990, student protests of a recurring nature, Suu Kyi's popularity on the international stage, economic sanctions, international drug control efforts, and Burma's admission into the Association of Southeast Asian Nations have all impacted upon the military elite's internal policies. Although the generalizability of the research design is, therefore, limited to the case in question, the design's focus should remain strong because Buddhism is, more so than any other cultural influence, intricately linked to Burma's political culture.

Buddhist political rhetoric in state-owned newspapers takes on a variety of forms and appears in either written form – as speeches, articles, commentary, and symbolic text, or in visual form – as photographic evidence or artistic presentations. A brief and non-exclusive list of the measures for Buddhist political rhetoric used by the military elite appears in Table A2. Precise examples of each of the subvariables may be found in the Coding Sheet in Table A3.

Content analysis was conducted on the major state-owned newspapers which have been published daily in English under two different titles for almost the entire time series period being examined: the *Working People's Daily* – published from January 1964 to April 1993; and the *New Light of Myanmar* – published from April 1993 to the present. *The Nation* newspaper was sampled in order to cover the first significant event, in 1962. Originally an independent source, *The Nation* was published from August 1948 to May 1964. Political coverage in this paper became heavily censored under the Ne Win regime in 1962, which eventually banned all

Table A2 Buddhist political rhetoric

- Articles and editorials on Buddhist interpretation, Buddhism, and the military's role in preserving Buddhist culture
- Military donations (offertories) to the *Sangha* and military participation in religious celebrations and award ceremonies
- Public donations to the military for religious purposes and military donations to monasteries
- Coverage of the construction, renovation, or consecration of pagodas, Buddha images, and state-sponsored Buddhist education sites
- Coverage of the Shwedagon pagoda renovation project
- Coverage of visitations by the generals to the Pagan archeological zone
- Photographs of the *Tatmadaw's* involvement in preserving Buddhist traditions
- The appearance of religious text or Buddhist symbolism outside the text of the paper

---

Table A3 Coding sheet

ID #	Date	Source	Articles/editorials with references to the state preservation of Buddhist culture																										Nontext references to the state preservation of Buddhist culture					
			1			2			3			4			5			6			7			8			9			10			11		
			S	M	W	S	M	W	S	M	W	S	M	W	S	M	W	S	M	W	S	M	W	S	M	W	S	M	W	L	M	S	L	M	S

Source: *The Nation* (N); *The Working People's Daily* (W); *The New Light of Myanmar* (L)

Notes

1   References to official interpretation of Buddhist literature, history, or practices.

2   References to offerings of "soon" or alms and robes to the *Sangha* (monks) by government officials; accepting and making donations of money and provisions to monasteries, or nunneries, by government officials; government officials paying obeisance or homage to the *Sangha* or to shrines; government officials sharing merits and taking or receiving precepts from the *Sangha*.
    (Government officials include members of the *Tatmadaw* – Army, Navy, Air Force, police forces and their wives, ministers or members of government ministries.)

3   References to the attendance, or hosting, by government officials of monk novitiation and ordination ceremonies, re-ordination ceremonies, graduation ceremonies for monastic education courses, Sayadaw birthdays, final rites, paying respect to remains, donating monies for cremation rites, 'Waso' and Kathina robe-offering ceremonies, and ceremonies marking religious days of observance (e.g. full moon days – Kason, Thadinkyut, or Abhidhamma Day).

4   References to the presentation of awards to the *Sangha* and to religious associations by government officials.

5   References to state-sponsored religious education and religious-related education or involvement in Buddhist culture courses, *Dhamma* courses, Therevada missionary courses, Buddhist museums/houses of historical artifacts, and the construction of museums; government officials receiving donations for general religious cultural affairs; meetings to discuss religious affairs; establishment of trusts for Buddhist literature.

6   References to visitations to Pagan.

7   References to the Protection and Preservation of Cultural Heritage law, preservation of cultural objects, handing over of ancient cultural artifacts to the Ministry of Culture.

8   References to the inspection or participation by government officials in the construction, renovation, opening, consecration, enshrining, blessing, and pivot-fixing ceremonies of pagodas, stupas, shrines, Buddha images, monasteries, nunneries, ordination halls, monastic education schools, abbot training schools, Buddhist missionary centers, and structures or areas of religious significance, or to the Shwedagon Pagoda Preservation project; cash donation ceremonies – accepting donations and handing over monies for the construction or restoration of pagodas, shrines, structures, and buildings of religious significance.
    Ceremonies may include:
    • Enshrinement – sacred objects enshrined into reliquary of pagoda
    • Pivot-fixing on pagoda
    • Shwehtidaw hoisting on pagoda
    • Seinphudaw-fixing on pagoda
    • Sprinkling of scented water
    • Stake-driving ceremonies noting a new construction.

9   References to other state involvement in Buddhist activities.
    These may include:
    • State/government officials' visits to foreign Buddhist sites.
    • Government officials performing meritorious deeds (e.g. releasing fish or sparrows).
    • Accompanying foreign dignitaries to religious sites.
    • Accompanying or greeting Sayadaws to or from their pilgrimage, conference, or mission work.
    • Ceremonies denoting the transfer/conveying of religious/sacred relics between monasteries or between countries.
    • Accepting donations of Buddhist images.
    • Conducting robe-weaving competitions.
    • Conducting meetings to co-ordinate religious affairs policy, opening multireligious conferences.

10 Photographs of the military and government officials with Buddhist themes.

11 Religious text or symbolism outside the normal text of the paper.

For 1–9, S = Strong reference – majority of the text; M = Medium reference; W = Weak reference – minor mention.

For 10–11, L = Large size photograph, cartoon, or symbolism; M = Medium size; S = Small size.

independent newspapers later that year. It would have been desirable to enhance the research design further by incorporating elements of a quasi-experimental nature through performing the same content analysis on a non-state-owned newspaper or magazine. This would create a control group whereby further verification could have been inferred by the absence of the same Buddhist political rhetoric over the same period. In a tyrannical regime where freedom of speech is very much limited, however, freedom from propaganda was impossible to discover in any other sources of political information.

Data were collected using the Coding Sheet in Table A3. The dependent variable, Buddhist political rhetoric, was divided into 11 subvariables, for which a unit value was provided for the appearance of the variable. A system of weighting each subvariable could have enhanced the findings, yet this could also have obscured any change in the relative importance of subvariables over time. Totals of each variable per month were aggregated and 30-day totals constitute the total appearances for that variable in either the pre-crisis or the post-crisis period. Totals of the monthly aggregates of all subvariables were produced for each crisis period, along with the total of all variables in the pre-crisis and post-crisis periods and designated crisis date (61 days). These totals produce a time series comparison of Buddhist political rhetoric whereby pre-crisis periods can be compared with post-crisis periods across all 11 crisis periods. Figure B1 in Appendix B reflects the total of all subvariables for each 61-day period compared across time. A summary of the research design model may be found in Figure A1.

The external validity of the research design was supported by applying examples from Aristotle's analysis of rhetoric to all three groups of political elites. The external validity of the design may suffer from an overgeneralization of the importance of some of the rhetorical references to Buddhist ideas and religion where they are not warranted. Yet given the pragmatic nature of politics, particularly Burmese politics, it may be valid to highlight the rhetorical use of any references to Buddhism so long as they are analyzed within the context of the particular speech or written work, the enthymeme of the particular elite, and the political objectives underlying their rhetoric.

Variables:

Independent variable:

Dependent variable:

Measures:

Pre-crisis	Crisis (11 significant events)	Post-crisis
30 days	1962	30 days
30 days	1974	30 days
30 days	1988	30 days
30 days	1990	30 days
30 days	1995	30 days
30 days	1996	30 days
30 days	1997	30 days
30 days	2000	30 days
30 days	2001	30 days
30 days	2002	30 days
30 days	2003	30 days

Hypothesis:

H0: The military elite's use of Buddhist political rhetoric in their political speeches and publications increases before a political crisis.

Figure A1   Design model.

Note
2 state-owned national newspapers
The Working People's Daily (1964–93)
The New Light of Myanmar (1993–present)

1 Independent, heavily censored newspaper
The Nation (1948–64)

Appendix B

Findings – Burma case study

The *Tatmadaw* case study findings may be grouped into two sets of observations, those specifically addressing the hypotheses and those produced over the duration of the time series. It may be difficult to confirm that, on all occasions, the military's use of Buddhist political rhetoric becomes more pronounced during periods of political crisis. To reach a position where stability and crisis may be confidently viewed as distinct periods, and where more causality may be inferred between distinct crises and rhetoric, would require a far greater number of observations to be taken on either side of the period designated. While this was originally intended, a subsequent preference was to reduce the number of observations in the pre-crisis and post-crisis periods in favor of expanding the number of crisis periods, thus lengthening the overall time series. This has produced a number of revealing findings which are related to the military's overall tactics with respect to the application of rhetoric towards their kingly performance.

While the difference between pre-test and post-test results may not, on some occasions, have been that great, in all but two periods the specific hypothesis was found to be correct. Discounting the U Nu period, in the two periods where it was not correct, under Ne Win's rule in 1974 and during the mass demonstrations of 1988, there was either a stated or at least clearly understood government policy not to mix religion with politics and, therefore, not to use Buddhist rhetoric to legitimize rule. Alternatively, other political events simply overpowered the effectiveness of such rhetoric and dominated the media coverage.

Crisis periods during which the largest difference between pre-crisis and post-crisis results occurred may also correspond to periods in which the military exercised the greatest degree of control over the situation. Thus the SLORC's decision to reshuffle their hierarchy and transform themselves into the SPDC in 1997, and the SLORC's reaction to the NLD convention in 1996, were both periods where much notice was given and strategies could be planned leading up to the event. The spontaneous demonstrations of 1988, however, occurred during a period in which the military lacked control over the situation and over the activities of the

Sangha. The degree of the *Tatmadaw*'s control over a particular event may also have been somewhat diminished by the application of external pressures such as, for example, bargaining with United Nations intermediaries for a dialogue with the NLD in return for releasing political prisoners or making similar concessions in exchange for international funding.

When the results are analyzed and compared over the entire time-series period, certain key observations may be made. The first of these is the total absence of Buddhist political rhetoric under the Ne Win regime in 1974. Second, although newspapers may have remained independent under the U Nu government, U Nu was viewed by all as extremely devout, and his government's various policies embraced Buddhism and the *Sangha.* Coverage of the *Sangha*'s activities presents the Sayadaws as far more vocal in their protests, presenting petitions to Parliament and to U Thant – then Secretary General of the United Nations. Yet the media's coverage of U Nu himself and his religious activities are dwarfed in comparison with that of the SLORC–SPDC, a fact which suggests that while U Nu was not lacking in legitimacy, he was indeed devout and his faith, unlike the generals', was more or less accepted and perhaps more credible in the eyes of the people. And third, whereas the SLORC's rhetoric in the state-owned media remained minimal during the 1988 demonstrations, and mostly centered on winning over the *Sangha*'s support in helping control the people,[1] it also reflects a period during which Aung San Suu Kyi had only recently decided to enter politics. The SLORC's rhetoric, however, significantly increased leading up to the 1990 elections, perhaps also countering the threat of Suu Kyi.

In 1990, Suu Kyi was placed under house arrest and by 1995 her speeches and publications linking Buddhism and politics had become well known. SLORC's nation-building program began in 1993, and by 1995 when Suu Kyi was released, the state coverage of their Buddhist political rhetoric had reached staggering levels which have been fairly well maintained – though less than in 1995 – to the present day. The SPDC's Buddhist rhetoric increased noticeably again before Suu Kyi was re-released in 2002. Overall, this suggests that the SLORC–SPDC's rhetoric comes as a direct response to the threat posed by the presence and the Buddhist political rhetoric of Aung San Suu Kyi.

While the time-series results are revealing, some of the individual sub-variables are worth commenting upon. Prior to 1995, the generals paid relatively scant attention to attending or hosting religious ceremonies and observing holy days. By 1995, however, they had taken it upon themselves to do so in an official capacity, as well as to be seen publicly making offertories and donations to the *Sangha.* The very public nature of their acts of piety can be inferred by the fact that photographic coverage of the generals' religious activities in 1990 had remained generally small in size, though by 1995, both the volume and the size of photographic coverage had increased enormously.[2] Ten days prior to the NLD convention in

1996, for example, all of the top four senior SLORC generals were pictured presenting offertories to monks.[3] Again in 1997, prior to SLORC's transformation into the SPDC, four of the top five generals attended ceremonies for the conveying of Buddha images, paying homage to the images and offering alms to Sayadaws.[4]

In line with their kingly performance and their nation-building program, the generals' construction, renovation, and consecration of pagodas and Buddha images had also doubled by 1995, increasing again in 1996, and maintained a steady pace through to 2003. Again, ten days prior to the 1996 NLD conference, Chairman and Senior General Than Shwe was pictured placing a diamond bud atop a pagoda, and three days prior to the conference, the former Secretary-1 and Prime Minister, Lt.-General Khin Nyunt, also placed a diamond bud atop a pagoda and laid the foundation stone for the construction of a new pagoda.[5] Similar state coverage followed the release of Aung San Suu Kyi from house arrest in 2002.[6] In 1997, following SLORC's change of name, in another elaborate ceremony, Khin Nyunt, in his role as "Patron of the Leading Committee for Perpetual Renovation of the Shwedagon," laid a cornerstone of the northern stairway of the holiest of Buddhist sites in Rangoon, the Shwedagon pagoda.[7] The day following the government's Proclamation 1/97, constituting the SPDC, the state media announced the renovation of 287 pagodas and the excavation of another 890 pagoda sites "to be rebuilt with original style and taste of 11th century," along with the addresses at which cash donations would be received.[8] Since then the state has either constructed, or is in the process of constructing, new pagodas built with brick and concrete as well as bathroom tiles on top of ancient ruins, a 200 ft observation tower, hotel facilities along with a golf course, and a new palace in the middle of Pagan.[9]

While the state media often publishes articles by the Department of Religious Affairs and the Ministry of Information interpreting Buddhism and the religious significance of certain holy days or sacred Buddha images,[10] beginning sporadically in 1991–92, by 1995 religious messages were appearing regularly outside the normal text of state newspapers. These include Pre-Sabbath Reminders, whereby the government earned merit by reminding its people of keeping precepts on the Sabbath day, the days of the half and the full waxing and waning of the moon; the appearance of an alternative record of the date – in terms of the waxing and waning of the moon; and the appearance of proverbs and words of auspiciousness from the Mingala Sutta. The Mingala Sutta is the sermon given by the Lord Buddha containing the 38 rules for a beatific life.

In addition, since 20 September 1999, the Ministry of Information has published on the front page in the daily papers 138 of the 167 stanzas from the *Loka Niti* (guidance), a collection of proverbs for social conduct and social discipline, originally compiled by Minister Thiri Maha Saturinga Bala during King Thihaths's (Sihasu) reign in the fourteenth century and originally published as texts for use in monastic education.[11] Cartoons have also carried Buddhist themes or references to the state's successful efforts in preserving Buddhist tradition and culture.[12] And photographs often depict persons publicly greeting the generals with a *shekho* or *wai*, a custom adopted by the generals and encouraged among their subordinates since the late 1980s but which was normally reserved to show reverence towards monks or elderly relatives.

The generals' Buddhist rhetoric often disappears when foreign dignitaries visit the country and coverage is designated to issues of mutual interest, unless they are accompanied by the generals on tours of major religious sites like the Shwedagon. Criticism of Aung San Suu Kyi and the NLD, although recently reduced, was often placed in a sacrilegious context, both in text and in cartoons. This stood in marked contrast to earlier coverage when, for example, in 1990, photographs appeared of NLD candidates making offerings to the *Sangha* before the election.[13] In fact, for much of this period, there was a major reduction in the amount of Buddhist rhetoric produced by the generals because the focus was the election, and the generals, still under the direction of Ne Win, were reluctant to use Buddhism as a means of securing electoral popularity. This changed dramatically following the NLD's success at the polls, the popular attraction of Suu Kyi's Buddhist rhetoric, and the SLORC's response via its nation-building program.

While the findings are inconclusive with respect to the general thesis on the effect of the *Tatmadaw*'s Buddhist political rhetoric on political crisis and stability, they substantiate the thesis that the SLORC–SPDC have been promoting Buddhism, both as part of some kingly duty and in response to the Buddhist political rhetoric of Aung San Suu Kyi. They illustrate that the military elite have not only repeatedly, and increasingly, adopted this argument since the coup of 1988, and more emphatically since the early 1990s, but that they have come full circle since 1962 by actively promoting Buddhism as, if not the state religion, then at least the next closest thing to one. The summary findings of the content analysis conducted for the Burmese case study are shown in Table B1 and are illustrated graphically in Figure B1.

It appears that since the military's nation-building program began in 1993, the summary findings of 1995 and thereafter confirm that Ne Win's influence on the regime, at least in religious affairs, was forfeited to his younger progenies. Aware of the importance of respecting the commonly held opinions that make up the mass political culture, the generals wove this *endoxa* into their own legitimacy. In the process of doing so, they have blurred the truth upon which these common opinions should, for the most part, be grounded and created their own myth.

Table B1 Summary findings

Summary findings: Articles/editorials with references to the state preservation of Buddhist culture — Nontext references to the state preservation of Buddhist culture — Total

Period	Date	Source	1 S	1 M	1 W	2 S	2 M	2 W	3 S	3 M	3 W	4 S	4 M	4 W	5 S	5 M	5 W	6 S	6 M	6 W	7 S	7 M	7 W	8 S	8 M	8 W	9 S	9 M	9 W	10 L	10 M	10 S	11 L	11 M	11 S	Total
1	Pre-crisis	N																									4	2		1	1	1				9
	02 Mar. 62	N																																		0
	Post-crisis	N																									1	3		1						5
	Total	N																									5	5		2	1	1				14
2	Pre-crisis	W																																		0
	02 Mar. 74	W																																		0
	Post-crisis	W																																		0
	Total	W																																		0
3	Pre-crisis	W				7																														7
	18 Sep. 88	W																																		0
	Post-crisis	W				2			8		1																2	1				2				16
	Total	W				9			8		1																2	1				2				23
4	Pre-crisis	W				2						1					1							16		2	1	3		1	3	19				49
	27 May 90	W													1		1																			2
	Post-crisis	W																						15		2	6	6		1	1	3				34
	Total	W				2						1			1		2							31		4	7	9		2	4	22				85
5	Pre-crisis	L	2		2	9	1	6	4		1				3	5								39	3	2	17	2		3	12	96			30	237
	10 Jul. 95	L							2															1	1					2	1	3			1	11
	Post-crisis	L				11		25	13						3									33			2		2	7	10	63			30	199
	Total	L	2		2	20	1	31	19		1				6	5								73	4	2	19	2	2	12	23	163			61	447

Table B1 Summary findings *(cont.)*

Period	*Date*	*Source*	*Summary findings: Articles/editorials with references to the state preservation of Buddhist culture*																											*Nontext references to the state preservation of Buddhist culture*						*Total*
			1			2			3			4			5			6			7			8			9			10			11			
			S	M	W	S	M	W	S	M	W	S	M	W	S	M	W	S	M	W	S	M	W	S	M	W	S	M	W	L	M	S	L	M	S	
6	Pre-crisis	L	3		5	4	2		11	1	1	1			4									56	2	3	7		10	7	17	23	30			187
	23 May. 96	L				2																		1					1			2	1			7
	Post-crisis	L	2			1			5			1			2									34			5	1	30		9	12	30			132
	Total	L	5		5	7	2		16	1	1	2			6									91	2	3	12	1	41	7	26	37	61			326
7	Pre-crisis	L		1		18	11		43	1		1			4									14	8		9	1		9	50	32	30			232
	15 Nov. 97	L				1	1	3	4	1																				2	3	7	1			23
	Post-crisis	L	2	1		13	3		11															1						1	19	13	30			94
	Total	L	2	2		32	15	3	58	2		1			4									15	8		9	1		12	72	52	61			349
8	Pre-crisis	L	2	10		21	6	2							1			1			1			18	1		8			22	51		30	30		204
	22 Sep. 00	L																									1						1	1		3
	Post-crisis	L	1	7		15	3		3			1			3				1					22	3	3	4			10	42	12	30	30		190
	Total	L	3	17		36	9	2	3			1			4			1	1		1			40	4	3	13			32	93	12	61	61		397
9	Pre-crisis	L	1	1	2	9		4		1		4			3			1						16	1		2			13	40	9	30			137
	16 Jun. 01	L																															1			1
	Post-crisis	L		5	2	12	4	5	1			2			1	1								10	1	3				4	36	3	30			120
	Total	L	1	6	4	21	4	9	1	1		6			4	1		1						26	2	3	2			17	76	12	61			258
10	Pre-crisis	L		1		11	6	11	8						1									19	2	1	3			19	62	2	30			176
	06 May. 02	L					1		1																								1			3
	Post-crisis	L	1	5	1	8	8	4	5			2			6			1						17			7	1		15	54		30			165
	Total	L	1	6	1	19	15	15	14			2			7			1						36	2	1	10	1		34	116	2	61			344
11	Pre-crisis	L	2			16			9			7						3						11	2		3			17	42	7	30			149
	30 May. 03	L				1																		1							1		1			4
	Post Crisis	L	1			13						2			6									8			2			20	42	9	30			133
	Total	L	3			30			9			9			6			3						20	2		5			37	85	16	61			286

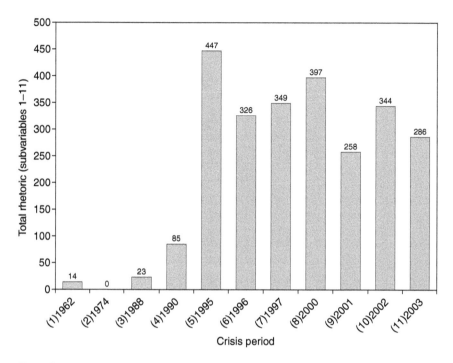

Figure B1   Buddhist political rhetoric of the *Tatmadaw*.

Notes

1 Introduction

1 President G. W. Bush (2005), "President Sworn-In to Second Term," The White House, Office of the Press Secretary, 20 January.

2 The intellectual crisis in comparative politics

1 Lichbach, M. and Zuckerman, A. (1998), *Comparative Politics: Rationality, Culture, and Structure*, Cambridge, UK: Cambridge University Press, p. ix.
2 Ibid.
3 Evans, P. (1995), in Kohli, A., Evans, P., Katzenstein, P., Przeworski, A., Hoeber Rudolph, S., Scott, J. C., and Skocpol, T., "The Role of Theory in Comparative Politics: A Symposium," *World Politics*, vol. 48, no. 1, October, 9.
4 See Wiarda, H. J. (ed.) (1991), "Comparative Politics: Past and Present," *New Directions in Comparative Politics*, Boulder: Westview Press; Geddes, B. (1991), "Paradigms and Sand Castles in the Comparative Politics of Developing Areas," in Crotty, W. (ed.), *Political Science: Looking to the Future. Volume Two: Comparative Politics, Policy, and International Relations*, Evanston: Northwestern University Press.
5 Almond, G. A. and Coleman, J. S. (eds) (1960), *The Politics of the Developing Areas*, Princeton, New Jersey: Princeton University Press.
6 Lipset, S. M. (1959), *Political Man: The Social Basis of Politics*, New York: Doubleday Anchor.
7 Rostow, W. W. (1960), *The Stages of Economic Growth*, New York: Cambridge University Press.
8 See Huntington, S. (1965), "Political Development and Political Decay," *World Politics*, vol. 17, no. 3, April, 387–388; Huntington, S. (1968), *Political Order in Changing Societies*, New Haven: Yale University Press; Huntington, S. (1971), "The Change to Change: Modernization, Development and Politics," *Comparative Politics*, vol. 3, no. 3, April, 282–322.
9 Przeworski, A. and Limongi, F. (1997), "Modernization: Theories and Facts," *World Politics*, vol. 49, January, 155–183.
10 Ibid., pp. 159–160.
11 Cardoso, F. and Faletto, E. (1979), *Dependency and Development in Latin America*, Berkeley: University of California Press.
12 See Almond, G. and Verba, S. (eds) (1963), *The Civic Culture: Political Attitudes and Democracy in Five Nations*, Princeton, New Jersey: Princeton University Press; Pye, L. and Verba, S. (1966), *Political Culture and Political Development*, Princeton, New Jersey: Princeton University Press.
13 Packenham, R. (1992), *The Dependency Movement: Scholarship and Politics in*

Development Studies, Cambridge, Massachusetts: Harvard University Press, pp. 82–109.

14 O'Donnell, G. (1973), *Modernization and Bureaucratic Authoritarianism*, Berkeley: Institute of International Studies, University of California.

15 See Diamond, L. (ed.) (1994), *Political Culture and Democracy in Developing Countries*, Boulder, Colorado: Lynne Reinner Publishers; Diamond, L. (1999), *Developing Democracy: Toward Consolidation*, Baltimore, Maryland: The Johns Hopkins University Press.

16 Almond, G. and Verba, S. (eds) (1989), *The Civic Culture Revisited*, Newbury Park, California: Sage Publications.

17 Diamond, L. (1994), p. 7; Diamond, L. (1999), p. 163.

18 Almond, G. (1989), pp. 27–28.

19 Easton, D. (1965a), *A System Analysis of Political Life*, New York: John Wiley and Sons.

20 Almond, G. (1989), p. 28.

21 Alagappa, M. (ed.) (1995), *Political Legitimacy in Southeast Asia: The Quest for Moral Authority*, Stanford, California: Stanford University Press, pp. 4–7.

22 Ibid.

23 Diamond, L. (1999), p. 161; Inglehart, R. (1990), *Culture Shift in Advanced Industrial Society*, Princeton, New Jersey: Princeton University Press, p. 45; Inglehart, R. (1988), "The Renaissance of Political Culture," *American Political Science Review*, vol. 82, no. 4, 1203–1230.

24 See Pye, L. (1959), *The Spirit of Burmese Politics: A Preliminary Survey of a Politics of Fear and Charisma*, Political Development paper C/59–11, Cambridge, Massachusetts: Center for International Studies, Massachusetts Institute of Technology; Pye, L. (1962), *Politics, Personality, and Nation Building: Burma's Search for Identity*, Cambridge, Massachusetts: Massachusetts Institute of Technology.

25 Pye, L. (1985), *Asian Power and Politics: The Cultural Dimensions of Authority*, Cambridge, Massachusetts: Harvard University Press.

26 Ibid., p. vii.

27 Ibid.

28 Ibid., pp. vii–viii.

29 Huntington, S. (1991), *The Third Wave: Democratization in the Late Twentieth Century*, Norman: University of Oklahoma Press.

30 Diamond, L. (2000), "Is Pakistan the (Reverse) Wave of the Future?" *Journal of Democracy*, July, vol. 11, no. 3, 94–95; Diamond, L. (1999), pp. 10–12.

31 Fukuyama, F. (1992a), "Asia's Soft-Authoritarian Alternative," *New Perspectives Quarterly*, Spring, 60.

32 Fukuyama, F. (1995), "The Primacy of Culture," *Journal of Democracy*, vol. 6, no. 1, 11.

33 Fukuyama, F. (1992a), p. 60.

34 Ibid.

35 Ibid.

36 Diamond, L. (2000), pp. 96–97.

37 Fukuyama, F. (1995), pp. 7–9.

38 Ibid., p. 12.

39 Ibid., p. 13.

40 Diamond, L. (1994), p. 9; Diamond, L. (1999), pp. 164–165.

41 Diamond, L. (1999), p. 8.

42 Diamond, L. (1994), pp. 9–10; Diamond, L. (1999), p. 165.

43 Diamond, L. (1994), pp. 9–10; Diamond, L. (1999), p. 165.

44 Diamond, L. (1999), p. 2.

45 Diamond, L. (2000), pp. 91–92.

46 Ibid., p. 91.
47 Ibid., p. 92.
48 Ibid.
49 Hewison, K. (1997), "Power, Opposition and Democratisation," in Hewison, K. (ed.), *Political Change in Thailand*, London: Routledge, p. 2.
50 Ibid., p. 73.
51 Diamond, L. (1999), p. 166.
52 Ibid.
53 Fukuyama, F. (1989), "The End of History?" *The National Interest*, no. 16, Summer, 4.
54 Fukuyama, F. (1999), "Second Thoughts, The Last Man in a Bottle," *The National Interest*, Summer, 17–19.
55 Ibid., p. 27.
56 Fukuyama, F. (2005), "The End of History Fifteen Years Later," 2004–2005 Lecture Series, 8 February 2005, The John M. Olin Center for Inquiry into the Theory and Practice of Democracy, University of Chicago.
57 Ibid.; also see Fukuyama, F. (2004), *State-Building: Governance and World Order in the 21st Century*, Ithaca, New York: Cornell University Press.
58 Fukuyama, F. (2004), pp. 5, 21–42, 93, 96–99.
59 Fukuyama, F. (2004), pp. 104–118; Fukuyama, F. (2005).
60 Fukuyama, F. (1999), p. 22.
61 Ibid.
62 Fukuyama, F. (1992b), *The End of History and the Last Man*, New York: Avon Books, p. 204.
63 Fukuyama, F. (1989), p. 16.
64 Strauss, L. (1988), "Restatement on Xenophon's *Hiero*," *What is Political Philosophy? and Other Studies*, Chicago: University of Chicago Press, p. 128.
65 Ibid., p. 129.
66 Fukuyama, F. (2005).
67 Strauss, L. (1988), p. 129.
68 Ibid.
69 Fukuyama, F. (1999), p. 33.
70 Fukuyama, F. (2002b), "How to Regulate Science," *The Public Interest*, no. 146, Winter, pp. 3–22.
71 Fukuyama, F. (2005).
72 Wade, N. (2002), "A Dim View of a 'Posthuman Future,'" *New York Times*, 2 April.
73 Wilson, E. O. (1999), "Responses to Fukuyama," *The National Interest*, Summer, 37.
74 Fukuyama, F. (1999), p. 21.
75 Geertz, C. (1973), "Thick Description: Toward an Interpretive Theory of Culture," *The Interpretation of Cultures*, New York: Basic Books, p. 5.
76 Ibid., p. 7.
77 Ibid., p. 9.
78 Ibid., p. 13.
79 Ibid.
80 Ibid., p. 14.
81 Ibid., p. 15.
82 Ibid.
83 Ibid., p. 16.
84 Ibid., p. 21.
85 Ibid.
86 Ibid., p. 23.

87　Parochial universalism, a concept proposed by Brantly Womack, seems to articulate well the ethnographer's awkward predicament.
88　Geertz, C. (1973), p. 26.
89　Ibid., p. 29.
90　Geertz, C. (1973), "The Impact of the Concept of Culture on the Concept of Man," *The Interpretation of Cultures*, p. 40.
91　Ibid.
92　Ibid., p. 41.
93　Ibid., p. 42.
94　Ibid., p. 43.
95　Ibid., pp. 43–44.
96　Ibid., p. 49.
97　Geertz, C. (1973), "Notes on the Balinese Cockfight," *The Interpretation of Cultures*, p. 450.
98　Ibid.
99　Ibid., p. 451 (n. 41).
100　Ibid., p. 453.
101　Aung Thwin, M. (2002), "Parochial Universalism, Democracy *Jihad* and the Orientalist Image of Burma: The New Evangelism," *Pacific Affairs*, vol. 74, no. 4, Winter, 487.
102　Ibid., p. 489.
103　Ibid., p. 497.
104　Ibid.
105　Ibid., pp. 485–493.
106　Ibid., p. 486.
107　Ibid., p. 494.
108　Ibid., pp. 494–496.
109　Aung San Suu Kyi (1991), "In Quest for Democracy," *Freedom from Fear*, New York: Viking Press, p. 175.
110　Huntington, S. (1993), "The Clash of Civilizations?" *Foreign Affairs*, vol. 72, no. 3, Summer, 29.
111　Fukuyama, F. (2002a), "Has History Restarted Since September 11?" The Nineteenth Annual John Bonython Lecture, Melbourne, 8 August 2002.
112　Fukuyama, F. (2005).
113　Fukuyama, F. (2002c), *Our Posthuman Future*, New York: Farrar, Straus and Giroux, p. 128.
114　Ibid.
115　Ibid.
116　Zakaria, F. (1994), "Culture Is Destiny, A Conversation with Lee Kuan Yew," *Foreign Affairs*, vol. 73, no. 2, Mar.–Apr., 117.
117　Fukuyama, F. (2002c), p. 128.
118　Aristotle, *The Politics*, trans. Carnes Lord (1984), Chicago: University of Chicago Press, 1327b23–38.
119　Lord, C. (1991), "Aristotle's Anthropology," in Lord, C. and O'Connor, D. K. (eds), *Essays on the Foundations of Aristotelian Political Science*, Berkeley: University of California Press, p. 52.
120　Ibid., p. 59.
121　Ibid., p. 72.
122　See Pye, L. (1975), *Political Science and Area Studies, Rivals or Partners?* Bloomington, Indiana: Indiana University Press.
123　Scott, J. C. (1985), *Weapons of the Weak: Everyday Forms of Peasant Resistance*, New Haven: Yale University Press.
124　Scott, J. C. (1990), *Domination and the Arts of Resistance: Hidden Transcripts*, New Haven: Yale University Press.

125 Scott, J. C. (1998b), *Seeing Like a State*, New Haven: Yale University Press, p. 322.
126 "Metis," Lindemans, M. (ed.), *Encyclopedia Mythica*. Online. Available at: www.pantheon.org/articles/m/metis.html (accessed 15 May 2005); see also Smith, W. (ed.) (1873), *A Dictionary of Greek and Roman Biography and Mythology*, London: John Murray, reprinted in William Smith and Chris Stray (eds) (2005), New York: Palgrave Macmillan. Online. Available at: www.perseus.tufts.edu/cgi-bin/ptext?doc=Perseus%3Atext%3A1999.04. 0104%3Aid%3Dmetis1 (accessed 15 May 2005).
127 Scott, J. C. (1998b), p. 313.
128 Ibid., p. 320.
129 Ibid., p. 323.
130 Ibid., p. 324.
131 Ibid., p. 327.
132 Ibid.
133 Ibid.
134 Ibid., p. 329.
135 Ibid., p. 316.
136 Ibid., pp. 331–332; Oakeshott, M. (1962), "Rationalism in Politics," *Rationalism in Politics and Other Essays*, New York: Basic Books, p. 31.
137 Scott, J. C. (1998b), p. 340.
138 Ibid.
139 Ibid., p. 340.
140 Ibid., pp. 340–341.
141 Ibid., p. 341.
142 Ibid.
143 Ibid., p. 357.
144 Ibid.
145 Ibid.
146 Ibid., p. 332.
147 Strauss, L. (1953), p. 193.
148 Hegel, George Wilhelm Friedrich, *The Philosophy of History*, trans. J. Sibree, C. J. Friedrich and Charles Hegel (1956), New York: Dover.
149 For a similar discussion of the difference between the modern and classical understanding of regimes, see Winborne, W. (2001), "Modernization and Modernity: Thomas Hobbes, Adam Smith, and Political Development," unpublished doctoral dissertation, Department of Political Science, Northern Illinois University, esp. pp. 24–25.
150 *Politics*, 1286b19–22.
151 It is not my purpose here to address the debate on what Aristotle may or may not have regarded as the best regime, particularly because he leaves the question open. Clifford Bates, for example, argues that Aristotle's best regime, both practically and theoretically, was a virtuous democracy limited by the rule of law. While his argument is interesting and, unlike modern democratic theorists, it is not an argument of legitimacy, his solution remains highly conditioned upon the existence of a virtuous *demos* who can deliberate, as a group, better than the few who are wise. While this may remain possible, perhaps Aristotle was also aware of how improbable it was. Bates cites Hobbes's criticism of Aristotle for promoting democracy as the best regime and Algernon Sydney's citing of Aristotle as supporting modern republican government. In dismissing Strauss's belief that the gentleman is more open to philosophy than the *demos*, Bates also exhibits a misplaced Victorian sense of "gentleman" which tarnishes the possibility of their co-existence, at least at the practical level. See Bates, C. (2003), *Aristotle's Best Regime: Kingship,*

Democracy, and the Rule of Law, Baton Rouge: Louisiana State University Press, esp. pp. 153, 160 (n. 10), 161–162 (n. 12), 175, 179–180, 211 (n. 11).

152 See Easton, D. (1965b), *A Framework for Political Analysis,* Englewood Cliffs: Prentice Hall; Easton, D. (1965a), *A Systems Analysis of Political Life,* New York: John Wiley and Sons.

153 See Rueschemeyer, D., Stephens, E., and Stephens, J. (1992), *Capitalist Development and Democracy,* Chicago: University of Chicago Press.

154 See Przeworski, A. (1992), *Democracy and the Market: Political and Economic Reforms in Eastern Europe and Latin America (Studies in Rationality and Social Change),* Cambridge, UK: Cambridge University Press.

155 See Evans, P., Rueschemeyer, D., and Skocpol, T. (1985), *Bringing the State Back In,* Cambridge, UK: Cambridge University Press.

156 Strauss, L. (1953), *Natural Right and History,* Chicago: University of Chicago Press, pp. 190–191.

157 Ibid.

158 Ibid., p. 191.

159 Ibid., p. 192.

160 See "Survey Methodology" in Freedom House (2004), *Freedom in the World 2004: The Annual Survey of Political Rights and Civil Liberties,* New York, New York. Online. Available at: www.freedomhouse.org/research/freeworld/ 2004/methodology.htm (accessed 15 May 2005); Freedom House (2004), *Freedom in the World 2004: The Annual Survey of Political Rights and Civil Liberties,* Lanham: Rowman and Littlefield; Freedom House (2005), *Freedom in the World 2005: Table of Independent Countries Comparative Measures of Freedom,* New York, New York. Online. Available at: freedomhouse.org/research/freeworld/2005/table2005.pdf (accessed 8 May 2005). In their 2005 survey, Singapore scored 5 points for political rights and 4 points for civil liberties and was classified as "partly free," while Burma scored 7 points (the lowest) for both political rights and civil liberties and was classified "not free" (Freedom House, [2005], Ibid.).

161 Aung Thwin, M. (2002), p. 497; also see Sahlins, M. (1983), "Other Times, Other Places: The Anthropology of Today," *American Anthropologist,* vol. 85, no. 3, September, 517–544.

162 Putnam, R. (1993), *Making Democracy Work,* Princeton, New Jersey: Princeton University Press, p. 167.

163 Ibid.

164 Putnam, R. (1995), "Bowling Alone: America's Declining Social Capital," *Journal of Democracy,* vol. 6, no 1, January, 67.

165 Coleman, J. (1988), "Social Capital in the Creation of Human Capital," *American Journal of Sociology* (Supplement), 94, s95–s120; Putnam, R. (2000), *Bowling Alone,* New York: Touchstone, pp. 19–20.

166 See Pye, L., (2001), "Civility, Social Capital and Civil Society: Three Powerful Concepts for Explaining Asia," in Rotberg, R. (ed.), *Patterns of Social Capital, Stability and Change in Historical Perspective,* Cambridge, UK: Cambridge University Press.

167 Fukuyama, F. (2001), "Social Capital, Civil Society and Development," *Third World Quarterly,* vol. 22, no. 1, p. 7.

168 Ibid.

169 Putnam, R. (1993), p. 11.

170 Almond, G. (1989), in Almond G. and Verba, S. (eds), *The Civic Culture Revisited,* Newbury Park, CA: Sage Publications, p. 4.

171 Smith, Adam, *An Inquiry into the Nature and Causes of the Wealth of Nations,* in R. H. Campbell and A. S. Skinner (eds) (1981), Indianapolis: Liberty Fund, p. 25.

172 *Wealth of Nations*, pp. 26–27.
173 *Wealth of Nations*, p. 26.
174 Smith, Adam, *The Theory of Moral Sentiments*, in D. D. Raphael and A. L. Macfie (eds) (1984), Indianapolis: Liberty Fund, p. 9.
175 Aristotle, *Nicomachean Ethics*, trans. Hippocrates G. Apostle (1984), Iowa: The Peripatetic Press, 1160a12.
176 Walzer, M. (1980), "Civility and Civic Virtue in Contemporary America," *Radical Principles*, New York: Basic Books.
177 Putnam, R. (1995), p. 3.
178 *Ethics*, 1161b11–1162a4.
179 Putnam, R. (1995).
180 Almond, G. (1989), pp. 5–6; Putnam, R. (1993), p. 11.
181 Zakaria, F. (2003), *The Future of Freedom: Illiberal Democracy at Home and Abroad*, New York: Norton, p. 158.
182 Ibid., p. 156.
183 Ibid., p. 158.
184 Ibid., p. 256.
185 Putnam, R. (2000), pp. 174–180.
186 Putnam, R. (1995), p. 73.
187 See Pye, L. (2001) for an example of this approach.
188 Pye, L., (2001), p. 377; see also Strauss, L. (1953), p. 105; Strauss, L. (1964), *The City and Man*, Chicago: University of Chicago Press, p. 100; Plato, *The Republic*, trans. Allan Bloom (1968), New York: Basic Books, 409c–d.
189 Strauss, L. (1988), p.113.

3 The political science of tyranny

1 This is not wholly a new phenomenon. Over 50 years ago in the wake of World War II, Strauss noted "It is no accident that present-day political science has failed to grasp tyranny as what it really is. Our political science is haunted by the belief that 'value judgments' are inadmissible in scientific considerations, and to call a regime tyrannical clearly amounts to pronouncing a 'value judgment.' The political scientist who accepts this view of science will speak of the mass-state, of dictatorship, of totalitarianism, of authoritarianism, and so on, and as a citizen he may wholeheartedly condemn these things; but as a political scientist he is forced to reject the notion of tyranny as 'mythical.'" Strauss, L. (1963), "On Tyranny," reprinted in V. Gourevitch and M. Roth (eds) (1991), *On Tyranny*, New York: The Free Press, p. 23. This article was originally published in 1948 and revised in 1954.
2 See Collier, D. and Levitsky, S. (1997), "Democracy with Adjectives," *World Politics*, vol. 49, April, 430–451; Schedler, A. (2002), "The Menu of Manipulation," *Journal of Democracy*, vol. 13, no. 2, April, 36–50; Levitsky, S. and Way, L. A. (2002), "The Rise of Competitive Authoritarianism," *Journal of Democracy*, vol. 13, no. 2, April, 51–65; Lord, C. (2003), *The Modern Prince*, New Haven: Yale University Press, pp. 96–105.
3 Collier, D. and Levitsky, S. (1997), p. 451.
4 Boesche, R. (1996), *Theories of Tyranny from Plato to Arendt*, University Park, Pennsylvania: Pennsylvania State University Press, p. 456.
5 Ibid.
6 Ibid., p. 457.
7 Ibid., pp. 456–457.
8 Lilla believes that "Academic political science, which once considered the categorization and study of different regime types one of its main tasks, no longer does. Daunted by the variety of types and their rapid transformations, and

perhaps also worried about appearing judgmental or racist, political scientists today have retreated to formal 'models' or statistical studies of the phantom 'processes' of democratization and economic modernization. Tyranny as such is simply not an issue or a recognized term of analysis." Lilla, M. (2002), "The New Age of Tyranny," *The New York Review of Books*, vol. 49, no. 16, 24 October, p. 29.

9 Strauss, L. (1988), "Restatement on Xenophon's *Hiero*," *What Is Political Philosophy? and Other Studies*, Chicago: University of Chicago Press, p. 96. An earlier version of this article was published in 1954.

10 Ibid; Xenophon, *Memorabilia*, trans. E.C. Marchant (1992), Cambridge, Massachusetts: Harvard University Press, Loeb, I, 1.11–15; Plato, *Theaetetus*, trans. John McDowell (1973), Oxford: Clarendon Press, 180c5–183c4. Compare with Thomas Hobbes on Man as Matter in Motion (Hobbes, Thomas, *Leviathan*, R. Tuck (ed.), [1996], revised student edition, Cambridge, UK: Cambridge University Press, Introduction).

11 *Memorabilia*, I, 1.16.

12 Cicero, *The Republic*, in *De Re Publica, De Legibus*, trans. C. W. Keyes (1928), Cambridge, Massachusetts: Harvard University Press, Loeb, II, xxvii, 49.

13 Ibid., II, xxvi, 47.

14 Ibid, II, xxvi, 47–48.

15 Lilla, M. (2002), op. cit., p. 28.

16 Ibid.

17 Ibid., p. 29.

18 Aristotle, *Nicomachean Ethics*, trans. Hippocrates G. Apostle (1984), Iowa: The Peripatetic Press, 1160b.

19 *Memorabilia*, IV, 6.12.

20 Strauss, L. (1963), p. 68; Aristotle, *Politics*, trans. Carnes Lord (1984), Chicago: University of Chicago Press, 1295a1–24.

21 Strauss, L. (1963), Ibid.

22 Ibid., p. 69.

23 *Politics*, 1285a30–1285b3.

24 For example, Pittacus was elected by the Mytilenaens to defend them against the exiles headed by Antimenides and the poet Alcaeus (*Politics*, 1285a34–41). Aristotle also includes magistrates and ambassadors elected for long periods of time, or a single person with authority over the greatest offices (*Politics*, 1310b15–23). For a modern example, Carnes Lord calls Lee Kuan Yew the leader of an "autocratic democracy" (Lord, C. [2003], pp. 96–105).

25 Strauss, L. (1963), p. 24.

26 Ibid., p. 25.

27 *Politics*, 1313a40–1313b6.

28 Ibid., 1314a31, my italics.

29 Ibid., 1310b3.

30 Ibid., 1310b10–13.

31 Xenophon, *Hiero* or *Tyrannicus*, trans. Marvin Kendrick in Strauss, L. (1963), "On Tyranny," reprinted in V. Gourevitch and M. Roth (eds) (1991), p. 20.

32 *Politics*, 1314a34–40.

33 Ibid., 1314a40–1315a30.

34 Ibid., 1313a17–33, 1315b4–1315b7.

35 Aristotle, "The Constitution of Athens," trans. J. M. Moore (1975), *Aristotle and Xenophon on Democracy and Oligarchy*, Berkeley: University of California Press, XV–XVI.

36 Ibid.

37 Ibid.

38 Strauss, L. (1988), p. 110; Strauss, L. (1963), pp. 70–71.

39 *Politics*, 1130b30–1131a9.

40 Diamond, L. (1994), p. 9.
41 Strauss, L. (1988), p. 106.
42 Machiavelli, Niccolo, *Discourses on Livy*, trans. Harvey C. Mansfield and Nathan Tarcov (1996), Chicago: University of Chicago Press, I, 2.
43 *Discourses*, I, 9–10.
44 Ibid., I, 10; Machiavelli, Niccolo, *The Prince*, trans. Leo Paul S. de Alvarez (1980), Dallas: University of Dallas Press, XIX, 115–121.
45 *Politics*, 1315b8–10.
46 *Discourses*, III, 21, 2–3.
47 Ibid., III, 21, 3.
48 Ibid., III, 21, 3–4.
49 Ibid., III, 21, 4
50 *Prince*, XV, 93.
51 Ibid.
52 Ibid.
53 Ibid.
54 *Discourses*, III, 21, 3.
55 Ibid., I, 2.
56 *Politics*, 1272b29–32.
57 Ibid., 1303b14–15.
58 Ibid., 1314a12–14.
59 Ibid., 1281a8–10.
60 Huntington, S. (1991).
61 Fukuyama, F. (1992a).
62 *Politics*, 1310a29–31.
63 Ibid., 1310a26–28.
64 Ibid., 1310a30–34.
65 Ibid., 1310a12–35.
66 Ibid., 1310a17–18.
67 Ibid., 1314a39–40.
68 Ludwig, A. (2002), *King of the Mountain: The Nature of Political Leadership*, Lexington: University of Kentucky Press, pp. 285–290, esp. p. 286. Note that for convenience I have combined Ludwig's separate categories for leaders who are "visionaries" (among which he includes Stalin and Hitler – 21 years average rule), "tyrants" (14 years), and "authoritarian" (11 years) into one category of tyrants in order to emphasize the monarchy–tyranny–democracy comparison.
69 Lord, C. (1981), "The Intention of Aristotle's Rhetoric," *Hermes*, no. 109, 326–339, reprinted in E.A. Schiappa (ed.) (1994), *Landmark Essays on Classical Greek Rhetoric*, Davis, California: Hemagoras Press.
70 Aristotle, *On Rhetoric: A Theory of Civic Discourse*, trans. George A. Kennedy (1991), New York: Oxford University Press, 1355b.
71 Arnhart, L. (1990), "The Deliberative Rhetoric of the Federalist," *The Political Science Reviewer*, vol. 19, Spring, 56.
72 Ibid., p. 57.
73 *Politics*, 1311a1–4.
74 Arnhart, L. (1990), pp. 56–57.
75 Lord, C. (1981), p. 334.
76 Ibid., p. 338.
77 Diamond, L. (1994), p. 7; Diamond, L. (1999), p. 163.
78 Almond, G. (1989), p. 28.
79 Diamond, L. (1999), p. 163.
80 See Pye, L. (1965) in Diamond, L. (1999), p. 163.
81 Arnhart, L. (1990), p. 55.
82 Diamond, L. (1999), p. 173.

83 Ibid., pp. 173–174.
84 Arnhart, L. (1990), p. 59.
85 Arnhart, L. (1982), *Aristotle on Political Reasoning: A Commentary on the Rhetoric*, DeKalb, Illinois: Northern Illinois University Press, p. 187.
86 Cicero, *Laws* (1928), II, xxvii, 69; Cicero, *The Republic* (1928), II, xiv, 27; Cicero, *Laws*, trans. J. G. Zetzel (1999), *On the Commonwealth and On the Laws*, Cambridge, UK: Cambridge University Press, II, 26.
87 *Discourses*, I, 11, 3–4.
88 Ibid., I, 13, 1; I, 56.
89 Hume, David (1779), "Dialogues Concerning Natural Religion," reprinted in A. Flew (ed.) (2000), *David Hume: Writings on Religion*, Peru, Illinois: Open Court.
90 See Smith, D. (1965), *Religion and Politics in Burma*, Princeton, New Jersey: Princeton University Press, pp. 318–319.
91 Edelman, M. (1964), *The Symbolic Uses of Politics*, Urbana, Illinois: University of Illinois Press; Edelman, M. (1971), *Politics as Symbolic Action: Mass Arousal and Quiescence*, Institute for Research on Poverty monograph series, Chicago: Markham Publishing.

4 Tyranny in Singapore?

1 Khong, Cho Oon (1995), "Singapore: Political Legitimacy through Managing Conformity," in M. Alagappa (ed.), *Political Legitimacy in Southeast Asia*, Stanford, California: Stanford University Press, p. 112.
2 Ibid.
3 Singh, Daljit and Arasu, V. T. (eds) (1984), *Singapore: An Illustrated History 1941–1984*, Singapore: Ministry of Culture, Information Division, pp. 226, 252.
4 *Politics*, 1311a13–14.
5 Scott claims that "The PAP sought to supersede the older forms of settlement that were the most politically opaque and resistant to PAP control. Thus local Malay kampung areas of the city as well as the poorer Chinese areas dominated by local clan associations were explicitly targeted for dispersal. The obliteration of the old neighborhoods and the re-creation of a newly designed urban space were tailor-made to make the disaggregated population beholden to the PAP. There is also no doubt that they were resettled in a way designed to maximize the surveillance and monopolistic political control of the PAP. The ruling party rehoused Singapore and in so doing designed a more directly legible and more easily dominated population." Scott, J. C. (1998), "Freedom and Freehold: Space, People and State Simplification in Southeast Asia," in D. Kelly and A. Reid (eds), *Asian Freedoms*, Cambridge, UK: Cambridge University Press, pp. 58–59.
6 *Politics*, 1318a22–23.
7 Khong, Cho Oon (1995), p. 114.
8 *Politics*, 1313a41–1313b4.
9 Ibid., 1313b12–13.
10 Khong, Cho Oon (1995), p. 118.
11 Ibid., p. 119.
12 Ibid., p. 122.
13 See Gordon, U. (2000), "Machiavelli's Tiger: Lee Kuan Yew and Singapore's Authoritarian Regime," *Viewpoint*, March, Israel: Tel-Aviv University, Department of Political Science.
14 *Discourses*, II, 58.
15 See Lee Kuan Yew (1998), *The Singapore Story: Memoirs of Lee Kuan Yew*, Singapore: Prentice Hall.
16 Gordon, U. (2000).

17 *Discourses*, III, 9.
18 Winborne, W. (2001), "Modernization and Modernity: Thomas Hobbes, Adam Smith, and Political Development," unpublished doctoral dissertation, Department of Political Science, Northern Illinois University, pp. 28, 63, 75–111.
19 *Politics*, 1313b20 and 29.
20 Ibid., p. 264, n. 109.
21 Ibid., 1314a15–29.
22 Ibid., 1314a35–40.
23 Ibid., 1314b1–8.
24 Ibid., 1314b13–15. Singapore's defense spending is pegged to its large GDP, and cannot exceed 6 per cent of GDP. In 1998, Singapore spent US\$4.3b on defense, making it the largest defense budget in ASEAN and the highest expenditure per capita in the Asia-Pacific region (Tan Tai Yong (2001), p. 277). In 2004, the defense budget accounted for 28 percent of government operating expenditures and 5.4 percent (est.) of GDP, or US\$5.94b (U.S. Department of State, Bureau of East Asian and Pacific Affairs (2005), *Singapore Profile*, Washington, D.C. April).
25 Xenophon, *Hiero*, 11 (3), in Strauss, L. (1963), *On Tyranny*, reprinted in V. Gourevitch and M. Roth (eds) (1991), *On Tyranny*, New York: The Free Press, pp. 19–20.
26 *Politics*, 1314b22–23.
27 Ibid.
28 *Politics*, 1314b23–24, 1315a21–22.
29 See Glenn, G. (1992), "Cyrus' Corruption of Aristocracy," in J. Murley, R. Stone, and W. Braithwaite (eds), *Law and Philosophy: The Practice of Theory. Essays in Honor of George Anastaplo*, Athens, Ohio: Ohio University Press.
30 Xenophon, *Cyropaedia*, trans. Walter Miller (1989), Cambridge, Massachusetts: Harvard University Press, Loeb, VIII, 1, 1; VIII, 1, 44; VIII, 2, 9.
31 *Politics*, 1314b18–19.
32 Ibid., 1314b25–27.
33 Ibid., 1314b27–36.
34 Ibid., 1314b37–38.
35 *Hiero*, 5 (3), p. 12.
36 Ibid., 11 (2), p. 19.
37 *Politics*, 1315a2–6.
38 Khong, Cho Oon (1995), p. 128.
39 See *Politics*, 1315a15–16.
40 Ibid., 1315a20–22.
41 Ibid., 1315a31–34.
42 Ibid., 1315a41–1315b1.
43 Ibid., 1315b4 and 7.

5 The rhetoric of Asian values

1 Khong, Cho Oon (1995), "Singapore: Political Legitimacy through Managing Conformity," in M. Alagappa (ed.), *Political Legitimacy in Southeast Asia*, Stanford, California: Stanford University Press, p. 124.
2 Ibid., p. 123. For details on Jeyaretnam's campaign and subsequent trials in Parliament see Lydgate, C. (2003), *Lee's Law: How Singapore Crushes Dissent*, Melbourne: Scribe Publications.
3 Loh Kah Seng (1998), "Within the Singapore Story: The Use and Narrative of History in Singapore," *Crossroads*, vol. 12, no. 2, 3–5.
4 Chua Beng Huat (1995), *Communitarian Ideology and Democracy in Singapore*, London: Routledge, p. 22, in Loh Kah Seng (1998), p. 15.

5   Loh Kah Seng (1998), p. 4.
6   Englehart, N. (2000), "Rights and Culture in the Asian Values Argument: The Rise and Fall of Confucian Ethics in Singapore," *Human Rights Quarterly*, vol. 22, no. 2, May, 554–555.
7   See Tu Wei-Ming (1984), "Confucian Ethics and the Entrepreneurial Spirit in East Asia," in Tu Wei-Ming (ed.), *Confucian Ethics Today: The Singapore Challenge*, Curriculum Development Institute of Singapore, Singapore: Federal Publications, pp. 65–99; Tu Wei-Ming (1991), *The Triadic Chord: Confucian Ethics, Industrial East Asia, and Max Weber: Proceedings of the 1987 Singapore Conference on Confucian Ethics and the Modernization of Industrial East Asia*, Singapore: Institute of East Asian Philosophies, National University of Singapore.
8   Khong, Cho Oon (1995), p. 125.
9   Ibid.; Englehart, N. (2000), p. 561.
10 Khong, Cho Oon (1995), p. 126.
11 Kong, L. (2002), "In Search of Permanent Homes: Singapore's House Churches and the Politics of Space," *Urban Studies*, vol. 39, no. 9, 1573–1586.
12 Zakaria, F. (1994), "Culture Is Destiny, A Conversation with Lee Kuan Yew," *Foreign Affairs*, vol. 73, no. 2, Mar.–Apr., 112.
13 Ibid.
14 Lee Kuan Yew (2000), *From Third World to First, The Singapore Story: 1965–2000*, New York: HarperCollins, p. 488.
15 Zakaria, F. (1994), p. 112.
16 Ibid.
17 Zakaria, F. (1994), p. 126.
18 Ibid., p. 118.
19 Ibid., p. 119.
20 Roy, D. (1994), "Singapore, China, and the 'Soft Authoritarian' Challenge," *Asian Survey*, vol. 34, no. 3, March, 235–238.
21 Lee Kuan Yew (2000), p. 495.
22 Zakaria, F. (1994), p. 125.
23 Ibid., p. 126.
24 Ibid.
25 Goh Chok Tong (1994), "Moral Values: The Foundation of a Vibrant State," National Day rally address given on 21 August 1994, Singapore, published as "Social Values, Singapore Style," *Current History*, vol. 93. December, pp. 417–422.
26 Kim Dae Jung (1994), "Is Culture Destiny? The Myths of Asia's Anti-Democratic Values," *Foreign Affairs*, Nov.–Dec., 190.
27 Ibid.
28 De Bary, Wm. T. (2000), *Asian Values and Human Rights*, Cambridge, Massachusetts: Harvard University Press, pp. 8–9.
29 *Politics*, 1314b38–1315a2.
30 Gordon, U. (2000), "Machiavelli's Tiger: Lee Kuan Yew and Singapore's Authoritarian Regime," *Viewpoint*, March, Israel: Tel-Aviv University, Department of Political Science, p. 2.
31 Ibid., 5.
32 *Discourses*, I, 12.
33 Gordon, U. (2000), p. 6.
34 Ibid., p. 5.
35 Cotton, J. (1993), "Political Innovation in Singapore: The Presidency, the Leadership, and the Party," in Garry Rodan (ed.), *Singapore Changes Guard: Social, Political, and Economic Directions in the 1990's*, Melbourne: Longman Press, p. 13.
36 Lee Kuan Yew (2000), pp. 151–153.

37 Ibid., p. 153.
38 Tu Wei-Ming. (1984), "Confucian Ethics and the Entrepreneurial Spirit in East Asia," op cit., p. 79.
39 Hsu Cho-Yun, "Discussion with Members of Parliament," in Tu Wei-Ming (ed.) (1984), *Confucian Ethics Today*, p. 149.
40 Tu Wei-Ming (1984), "Conversation with the Ministers," in Tu Wei-Ming (ed.), *Confucian Ethics Today*, pp. 163–197, esp. p. 168.
41 Ibid.
42 Xenophon, *Cyropaedia*, trans. Walter Miller (1989), Cambridge, Massachusetts: Harvard University Press, Loeb.
43 Lee Kuan Yew in Han Fook Kwang, Warren Fernandez, and Sumiko Tan (eds) (1998), *Lee Kuan Yew: The Man And His Ideas*, Singapore: The Straits Times Press, Times Editions, p. 229.
44 Englehart, N. (2000), pp. 556–557.
45 In April 2001, then Deputy Prime Minister Lee Hsien Loong launched a similar national campaign to discourage Singaporeans from speaking "Singlish" and to become even more proficient in English because it was the language of globalization and the Internet (Hussain Mutalib [2002], "The Socio-Economic Dimension in Singapore's Quest for Security and Stability," *Pacific Affairs*, vol. 75, no. 1, Spring, 49).
46 De Bary, Wm. T. (2000), p. 3.
47 Ibid., pp. 3–4.
48 Pye, L. (2000), "Civility, Social Capital and Civil Society: Three Powerful Concepts for Explaining Asia," in Robert Rotberg (ed.), *Patterns of Social Capital, Stability and Change in Historical Perspective*, Cambridge, UK: Cambridge University Press, p. 389.
49 De Bary, Wm. T. (2000), pp. 3–4.
50 Pye, L. (2000), p. 388.
51 De Bary, Wm. T. (2000), p. 5.
52 Ibid., p. 6.
53 Ibid., p. 7.
54 Ibid., pp. 90, 95.
55 Ibid., p. 90.
56 Ibid., p. 15.
57 Ibid., p. 7; also see Summer Twiss (1997), "A Constructive Framework for Discussing Confucianism and Human Rights," and Tu Wei-Ming (1997), "Epilogue: Human Rights as a Confucian Moral Discourse," in Wm. Theodore De Bary and Tu Weiming (eds), *Confucianism and Human Rights*, New York: Columbia University Press, pp. 27–53, 297–307.
58 De Bary, Wm. T. (2000), pp. 7–8.
59 Ibid.
60 Ibid., p. 16.
61 Kim Dae Jung (1994), p. 191.
62 De Bary, Wm. T. (2000), p. 95.
63 Kim Dae Jung (1994), pp. 191–192.
64 Ibid.
65 Ibid., p. 193.
66 Ibid., p. 194.
67 Emmerson, D. (1995), "Singapore and the Asian Values Debate," *Journal of Democracy*, vol. 6, no. 4, 96–100.
68 Sen, A. (1999), "Democracy as a Universal Value," *Journal of Democracy*, vol. 10, no. 3; see also Sen, A. (1997), "Human Rights and Asian Values," Morgenthau Memorial Lecture, Carnegie Council on Ethics and International Affairs, New York, also in *The New Republic*, 14–21 July 1997.

69 Jones, E. (1994), "Asia's Fate: A Response to the Singapore School," *The National Interest*, vol. 35, Spring, 21.
70 H.H. The XIV Dalai Lama of Tibet (1993b), "Human Rights and Universal Responsibility," in *United Nations World Conference on Human Rights*, Vienna, Austria, 1993, New York: United Nations.
71 Jones, E. (1994), p. 22.
72 United Nations (1993a), "Bangkok Declaration of Asian States," adopted at the United Nations World Conference on Human Rights, Regional Meeting for Asia in Bangkok on 29 March–2 April 1993, New York: United Nations.
73 Ibid.
74 Ibid.
75 ASEAN (1993), "Joint Communique," 26th ASEAN Ministerial Meeting, Singapore, 23–24 July 1993, Singapore: ASEAN.
76 *Ethics*, 1137b 13–14.
77 Huntington, S. (1993), "The Clash of Civilizations?" *Foreign Affairs*, vol. 72, no. 3, 40–41.
78 Morsink, J. (1999), *The Universal Declaration of Human Rights: Origins, Drafting, and Intent*, Philadelphia: University of Pennsylvania Press, p. xiii.
79 Ibid., pp. 252–258, 281–328.
80 Chuan Leekpai, "Opening Statement," in United Nations (1993a), United Nations World Conference on Human Rights, Regional Meeting for Asia, Bangkok, 29 March–2 April, 1993, New York: United Nations.
81 Morsink, J., op. cit., pp. 252–258.
82 Cassin, R., in Morsink, J., Ibid., p. 255.
83 Malik, C., in Morsink, J., Ibid.
84 Ibid., p. 256.
85 *Ethics*, 1155a19–21, 1161b5–7.
86 Ibid., 1155a21–22.
87 Ibid., 1135a5.
88 See Kung, H. and Kuschel K. J. (eds) (1993), *A Global Ethic, The Declaration of the Parliament of the World's Religions*, New York: Continuum.
89 H.H. The XIV Dalai Lama of Tibet (1993), op. cit.
90 United Nations (1948), *Universal Declaration of Human Rights*, New York: United Nations, Article 29(1), my emphasis added.
91 Bangkok Declaration, Article 1.
92 Ibid., Articles 3, 4, 5, 6, 7, and 8.
93 Ibid., Articles 12 and 13.
94 *Universal Declaration*, Preamble.
95 Bangkok Declaration, Article 27.
96 *Universal Declaration*, Preamble.
97 Tosh, J. (1991), *The Pursuit of History*, second edition, New York: Longman, p. 27, in Loh Kah Seng (1998), p. 7.
98 Loh Kah Seng (1998), p. 7.
99 Ibid., p. 2.
100 Lee Hsien Loong, "Why we need National Education," *Straits Times*, 20 May 1998, 29, in Loh Kah Seng (1998), 2.
101 Loh Kah Seng (1998), 3.
102 Ibid., p. 7.
103 Ibid.
104 Lee Kuan Yew (1980), "History is Not Made the Way it is Written," *Speeches: A Bimonthly Selection of Ministerial Speeches*, Singapore: Information Division, Ministry of Culture, vol. 3, no. 8, 3–12.
105 Lianhe Zaobao (ed.) (1995), *Lee Kuan Yew*, Singapore: Sony, CD-ROM.

106 Loh Kah Seng (1998), p. 7.
107 Ibid.
108 Ibid., pp. 8–9.
109 Ibid.
110 Ibid., p. 9.
111 Ibid., pp. 9, 15.
112 Ibid., pp. 5–6.
113 Lee Hsien Loong in "Telling the Singapore Story," *Straits Times*, 20 May 1997, 29, in Loh Kah Seng, Ibid., p. 6.
114 Lee Hsien Loong in "Program Based on Verifiable Facts: BG Lee," *Straits Times*, 19 May 1997, 26, in Loh Kah Seng, Ibid., p. 6.
115 Loh Kah Seng, Ibid.
116 Ibid.
117 Lee Hsien Loong in "Telling the Singapore Story," op cit.
118 Loh Kah Seng, op. cit., p. 17.
119 See Tu Wei-Ming (1984), "Confucian Ethics and the Entrepreneurial Spirit in East Asia," op. cit.; Tu Wei-Ming (1991); Englehart, N. (2000), p. 558.
120 French, H. (1996), "Africa Looks East for a New Model," *New York Times*, 4 February, 4:1, in De Bary, Wm. T. (2000), p. 3. De Bary remarks, "When authoritarian regimes in far-off Africa declare themselves cousin to similar states in Asia, it cannot be that they spring from the same ethnic or cultural roots but that a common cause is defined negatively in resistance to certain Western democratic values that they see as needlessly complicating the task of economic development." (De Bary, Wm. Theodore (2000), p. 4)
121 Mutalib, H. (2002), "The Socio-Economic Dimension in Singapore's Quest for Security and Stability," *Pacific Affairs*, vol. 75, no. 1, Spring, 46–47.
122 Loh Kah Seng, op. cit., p. 17.

6 Stability and justice in Singapore

1 *Politics*, 1323b40–43.
2 Ibid., 1329a21–24.
3 Ibid., 1325a22–32.
4 *Ethics*, 1095a15–1096a11.
5 *Politics*, 1272b29–32.
6 *Ethics*, 1134b19–21, 1134b28–30.
7 *Politics*, 1295a25–31.
8 Roy, D. (1994), "Singapore, China, and the 'Soft Authoritarian' Challenge," *Asian Survey*, vol. 34, no. 3, 235–236.
9 Jiang Zemin in "Party Chief on Seven Hot Issues," *Beijing Review*, 22–28 March 1993, p. 8, in Roy, D., Ibid., p. 236.
10 Roy, D., Ibid., p. 238.
11 Aung Thwin, for example, writes "If anything, it was more a vote for economic change after thirty years of the 'Burmese Way to Socialism,' than an unequivocal plea for democracy." (Aung Thwin, M. (2002), "Parochial Universalism, Democracy *Jihad* and the Orientalist Image of Burma: The New Evangelism," *Pacific Affairs*, vol. 74, no. 4, Winter, pp. 496–497).
12 Roy, D. (1994), p. 232.
13 Ibid., p. 233.
14 Ibid., p. 234.
15 Baker, M. (2002), "Squeaky-clean Singapore Eases up on Gum Control," *The Age*, 21 November 2002, Melbourne.
16 Ibid.; see also Logartha, M. (2004), "Oh behave, Singapore: It's now okay to be naughty in the Lion City – the government approves," *Business Traveller*

Magazine, March. Online. Available at: www.yawningbread.org/apdx_2004/ imp-140.htm (accessed 15 May 2005).

17 Roy, D. (1994), p. 234.
18 *Internal Security Act* (1963), Singapore, s. 8 (1) (a) and s. 8 (1) (b).
19 Ibid., s. 8 (1)–(2).
20 Ibid., s. 8 (1)–(5).
21 See "Singapore to Raise Public Awareness About Internal Security Act," Agence France Press, 12 April 2002.
22 Manikas, P. and Jennings, K. (2001), *The Political Process and the 2001 Parliamentary Elections in Singapore*, Washington, D.C.: National Democratic Institute for International Affairs, p. 9.
23 Hamilton, A. (1998), "A Man Who Never Gave In: The nation's last political prisoner speaks out," *Asiaweek*, 11 December; Teo Soh Lung (1998), "Introduction: Petition to Repeal the Internal Security Act," 6 December.
24 Lee Kuan Yew (2000), *From Third World to First, The Singapore Story: 1965–2000*, New York: HarperCollins, p. 488. Both the *Universal Declaration of Human Rights* (Article 9) and the *International Covenant on Civil and Political Rights* (Article 9) declare that "No one shall be subjected to arbitrary arrest, detention or exile." Singapore has not ratified the *International Covenant on Civil or Political Rights* nor the *International Covenant on Economic, Social and Cultural Rights*, both of which were adopted by the United Nations General Assembly in 1966 and ratified by 35 states ten years later.
25 See "Singapore Government Press Statement on Further Arrests under the Internal Security Act," Singapore Government Press Release, Media Relations Division, Ministry of Information, Ministry of Home Affairs, 19 September 2002.
26 *Straits Times*, 2 December 2002.
27 *The Constitution of the United States*, Article I, s. 9, Penguin, 1995.
28 Lincoln, Abraham, "To Erastus Corning and Others," 12 June 1863, in Fehrenbacher, D. (ed.) (1989), *Lincoln, Speeches and Writings 1859–1865*, New York: The Library of America, p. 460.
29 Roy, D. (1994), p. 234.
30 Manikas, P. and Jennings, K. (2001), p. 12.
31 Ibid., p. 10.
32 Huxley, T. (2002), "Singapore in 2001," *Asian Survey*, vol. 42, no. 1, Jan.–Feb., 161–162.
33 See Mutalib, H. (2002), "The Socio-Economic Dimension in Singapore's Quest for Security and Stability," *Pacific Affairs*, vol. 75, no. 1, Spring, 49.
34 Rodan, G. (2005), "Singapore in 2004: Long-Awaited Leadership Transition," *Asian Survey*, vol. 45, no.1, Jan.–Feb., 140–141.
35 Manikas, P. and Jennings, K. (2001), pp. 11–12.
36 Ibid., p. 9.
37 Lee Kuan Yew, in Bell, D. (1997), "A Communitarian Critique of Authoritarianism: The Case of Singapore," *Political Theory*, vol. 25, no.1; Gordon, U. (2000), "Machiavelli's Tiger: Lee Kuan Yew and Singapore's Authoritarian Regime," *Viewpoint*, March, Israel: Tel-Aviv University, Department of Political Science.
38 Gomez, J. (1999), "Politics and Law in Singapore," in Kevin Y. L. Tan (ed.), *The Singapore Legal System*, second edition, Singapore: Singapore University Press; Gordon (2000), Ibid.
39 Roy, D. (1994), p. 235.
40 Case, W. (2003), "Singapore in 2002," *Asian Survey*, vol. 43, no. 1, Jan.–Feb., 168.
41 Lee Kuan Yew in "Answering Questions at a Discussion Organized by the

Institute of International Relations of France, Paris on 23 May 1990," in Lianhe Zaobao (ed.) (1991), *Lee Kuan Yew on China and Hong Kong after Tiananmen*, Singapore: Lianhe Zaobao, p. 78.

42 Lee Kuan Yew in Richardson, M. (2001), "Proposed Electoral Changes Are Rejected: Singaporean Leaders Dismiss Reform Calls," *International Herald Tribune*, 13 November 2001, p. 6.

43 Richardson, M. (2001), Ibid., p. 9.

44 Ibid., p. 6.

45 Manikas, P. and Jennings, K. (2001), pp. 2, 18.

46 *Politics*, 1315a6–7.

47 Lee Kuan Yew (2000), p. 130.

48 Manikas, P. and Jennings, K. (2001), p. 8.

49 Lee Kuan Yew (2000), p. 130.

50 Ibid., p. 128.

51 Tang Liang Hong (1998), "Legal Terrorism in Singapore." Online. Available at: members.ozemail.com.au/-tangtalk/legalter.html (accessed 15 May 2005).

52 Manikas, P. and Jennings, K. (2001), p. 8.

53 In 1986, Jeyaretnam was disqualified from Parliament for five years and prohibited from practicing law because of alleged irregularities concerning the collection of party funds. He successfully appealed to the Privy Council in England, which was then Singapore's final court of appeal, who ruled that he and his co-defendant had been "publicly disgraced for offenses of which they were not guilty." The government, however, refused to remove the convictions (Judge Paul Bentley [1997], "The Politics of Defamation in Singapore," *The Provincial Judges' Journal*, Autumn, Canada; also see Lydgate, C. [2003], *Lee's Law: How Singapore Crushes Dissent*, Melbourne: Scribe Publications).

54 Judge Paul Bentley (1997), Ibid.

55 Manikas, P. and Jennings, K. (2001), p. 10.

56 See Gordon, U. (2000).

57 Lee Kuan Yew in *Associated Press*, Singapore, 13 June 1995; *New Light of Myanmar*, Rangoon, 14 June 1995.

58 *New York Times*, 29 August 2002.

59 Gomez, J. (1999), op. cit.

60 Manikas, P. and Jennings, K. (2001), p. 5.

61 Huxley, T. (2002), pp. 159–160; Burton, J. (2001), "Why Bother Voting? The Government Is Almost Unopposed," *The Economist*, 1 November.

62 Huxley, T. (2002), p. 162.

63 Lee Kuan Yew (2000), p. 133.

64 Manikas, P. and Jennings, K. (2001), p. 13.

65 Ibid., p. 3.

66 Chee Soon Juan in Nadel, A. (1997), "Singapore's Voice of Reason," *South China Morning Post*, 1 March.

67 Tan Tai Yong (2001), "Singapore: Civil–Military Fusion," in Alagappa, M. (ed.), *Coercion and Governance: The Declining Political Role of the Military in Asia*, Stanford, California: Stanford University Press, p. 278.

68 Goh Chok Tong in *Far Eastern Economic Review*, 13 January 1983; Tan Tai Yong (2001), p. 280.

69 Concerning the arrests, *Straits Times* reported "Whatever qualms some Singaporeans or foreigners may have had before about the use of the Internal Security Act to detain people without trial, few would entertain such qualms now," *Straits Times*, 21 September, 2002; Case, W. (2003), pp. 171–172.

70 Tan Tai Yong (2001), pp. 289, 276.

71 Mutalib, H. (2002), p. 47. In 1999, Singapore spent 24.9 percent of the total government budget on defense.
72 See Fukuyama, F. (1992a), "Asia's Soft-Authoritarian Alternative," *New Perspectives Quarterly*, vol. 9, no. 2, Spring, 60; Fukuyama, F. (1998), "Asian Values and the Asian Crisis," *Commentary*, vol. 105, no. 2.
73 Lee Kuan Yew (2000), p. 347.
74 Lee Kuan Yew in *Time*, 16 March 1998; Milner, A. (1999), "What's Happened to Asian Values?" in Goodman, D. and Segal, G. (eds), *Beyond the Asia Crisis*, London: Routledge.
75 Lee Kuan Yew (2000), p. 348.
76 Ibid.
77 Lee Kuan Yew in "Asia Will Rise Again," *Forbes*, 23 March 1998, p. 114; also in Milner, A. (1999), op. cit.
78 Case believes that, owing to Singapore's loss of world semiconductor sales, the Economic Development Board has begun to invest heavily in new industries, one of which is biotechnology. Although an ethics committee has been established, the government has approved "some of the most liberal stem-cell research guidelines in the world," *Far Eastern Economic Review*, 11 July 2002; Case, W. (2003), p. 169.
79 Case, W. (2003), Ibid., p. 173; see also *BBC NEWS*, "Port of Singapore Faces New Rival," 14 May 2002.
80 Huxley, T. (2002), p. 156.
81 Ibid., p. 157; Burton, J. (2001), op. cit.
82 Rodan, G. (2005), p. 142.
83 Case, W. (2003), p. 168.
84 Rodan, G. op. cit., p. 143.
85 Ibid., pp. 142–143.
86 Case, W. op. cit., p. 169.
87 In January 2001, for example, the "top 20 percent of households had an average income which was 21 times that of the lowest 20 percent last year, up from 11.4 times a decade ago," *Straits Times*, 10 February 2001; Mutalib, H. (2002), p. 51.
88 Huxley, T. (2002), p. 158.
89 *Politics*, 1318b9–20.
90 Ibid., 1318b21–25, see p. 265, n. 14.
91 Zakaria, F. (2003), p. 156.
92 Ibid.
93 Ibid.
94 See Kong, L. (2002), "In Search of Permanent Homes: Singapore's House Churches and the Politics of Space," *Urban Studies*, vol. 39, no. 9; Winborne, W., "Modernization and Modernity: Thomas Hobbes, Adam Smith, and Political Development," unpublished doctoral dissertation, Department of Political Science, Northern Illinois University, 2001, pp. 93–95.
95 Case, W. op. cit., p. 169.
96 Rodan, G. op. cit., p. 143.
97 *Politics*, 1289a5–6.
98 Ibid., 1289a3–4.
99 Ibid., 1289a4–5.
100 Huntington, S. in Diamond, L., Plattner, M., Yunhan Chu and Hung-mao Tien (eds) (1997), *Consolidating the Third Wave Democracies*, Baltimore, Maryland: Johns Hopkins University Press, p.13.
101 BBC News Online, "Lee Kuan Yew Staying on at 80," 16 September 2003.

7 Tyranny in Burma

1 *Politics*, 1295a7–24.
2 Ibid., 1295a17–24.
3 Ibid., 1310b14–15.
4 Ibid., 1310b33.
5 Ibid., 1312b8–10, 1312b39–40.
6 Ibid., 1311a1–3.
7 Burmese refers to both the people of Burma and the predominant language spoken in Burma, while Burman refers to the ethnic majority of Burma. The Burmese therefore include both Burmans and non-Burmans (the ethnic minorities comprising, among others, the Shans, Karens, Kachin, Chin, Rakhine, Naga, Lahu, Akha, Pao, Kayan, Karenni, Mon, Wa, and Palaung). In 1988, SLORC changed the name of the country to Myanmar, being a closer transliteration of the country's name in the Burmese language.
8 Seekins, D. (2002), *The Disorder in Order: The Army State in Burma since 1962*, Bangkok: White Lotus Press, p. 210.
9 Smith, M. (1993), *Burma, Insurgency and the Politics of Ethnicity*, Oxford: Zed Books, p. 124.
10 Ibid., p. 178.
11 Ibid., p. 179.
12 Ibid.
13 Seekins, D. (2002), p. 39.
14 Smith, M. (1993), p. 179.
15 Ibid.
16 Ibid.; Director of Information (1960), *Is Trust Vindicated? The Chronicle of a Trust, Striving and Triumph, Being an Account of the Accomplishments of the Government of the Union of Burma: November 1, 1958–February 6, 1960*. Rangoon.
17 Smith, M. (1993), Ibid.
18 Huntington, S. (1968), *Political Order in Changing Societies*, New Haven: Yale University Press, pp. 217–218.
19 Trager, F. (1963), "The Failure of U Nu and the Return of the Armed Forces in Burma," *Review of Politics*, 25 July, 320–321.
20 BBC, "Former Burma Dictator Ne Win dies," *BBC NEWS*, 5 December 2002; "U Ne Win, Ex-Strongman of Burma, Dies at 91," *New York Times*, Associated Press, 5 December 2002; "Ex-Dictator Ne Win's Remains Scattered," *New York Times*, Associated Press, 6 December 2002; "Disgraced Former Myanmar Military Ruler Ne Win Dies," Reuters, 5 December 2002.
21 *Politics*, 1313a34–38.
22 Pye, L. (2001), "Civility, Social Capital, and Civil Society: Three Powerful Concepts for Explaining Asia," in Rotberg, R. (ed.), *Patterns of Social Capital, Stability and Change in Historical Perspective*, Cambridge, UK: Cambridge University Press, pp. 386–387.
23 Pye, L. (1962), *Politics, Personality, and Nation Building: Burma's Search for Identity*, New Haven: Yale University Press, pp. 203, 292.
24 Huntington, S. (1968), pp. 29–30.
25 Pye, L. (2001), p. 387.
26 Ibid.
27 Ibid.
28 *Politics*, 1313b12–16.
29 Ibid., 1313b16–18.
30 See also Gravers, M. (1999), *Nationalism as Political Paranoia in Burma*, London: Curzon Press, p. 140.
31 Aung San Suu Kyi (1997a), *Letters from Burma*, New York: Penguin, p. 185.

32   Lord notes that the Cypselids were the family of Periander of Corinth, and the temple of Olymia Zeus at Athens was begun by Pisistratus (*Politics*, p. 264, n. 108).

33   GDP per capita is a little over $200 per year.

34   Chirot notes that demonetization was ostensibly used to strike at insurgents and black marketeers operating along the Thai and Chinese border. Yet since neither group traded in Kyat because it had long been unconvertible, the demonetization hit ordinary Burmese the hardest. The 35 and 75 Kyat notes were introduced in the mid-1980s because they were said to be, according to Ne Win's numerological superstitions, luckier than the 50 and 100 Kyat notes, and the 75 Kyat note was introduced on Ne Win's 75th birthday. The 35 and 75 Kyat notes were replaced with 45 and 90 Kyat notes because nine was Ne Win's lucky number (Chirot, D. [1994], *Modern Tyrants: The Power and Prevalence of Evil in Our Age*, New York: The Free Press, p. 336).

35   Burma became the first country to be banned from the International Labor Organization (ILO) after the publication of an ILO report in 2001, compiled with the co-operation of the SPDC (Agence France Press, "ILO Mission to Verify Junta's Promises on Forced Labour in Burma," September 2002, in Clark, A. [2003], "Burma in 2002," *Asian Survey*, vol. 43, no. 1, Jan.–Feb., 128).

36   *Politics*, 1311a12, 1313b28–29.

37   Ibid., 1311a12–14.

38   Ibid., 1314a25–26.

39   Ibid., 1314a31–32.

40   Ibid., 1314a34–37.

41   Smith, M. (1993), pp. 46–47.

42   Aung San (1947b) "Bogyoke Aung San's Address at the Convention Held at the Jubilee Hall, Rangoon on the 23rd May, 1947," in Silverstein, J. (ed.) (1993), *The Political Legacy of Aung San*, Ithaca, New York: Cornell University Press, Southeast Asia Program Series, no. 11, p. 156.

43   Aung San (1947d), "The Aung San Letter," *The Nation*, 2 March 1962, Rangoon. This letter, written on 2 July 1947 by Aung San, implied statehood and was published on the front page of *The Nation* on the same day that Ne Win led a military coup against U Nu's government.

44   For a detailed account of Burma's postindependence insurgency conflicts, see Smith, M. (1993).

45   See Selth, A. (2002), *Burma's Armed Forces: Power Without Glory*, Norwalk, Connecticut: Eastbridge; Selth, A. (1998), "The Armed Forces and Military Rule in Burma," in Rotberg, R. (ed.), *Burma, Prospects for a Democratic Future*, Washington, D.C.: Brookings Institution Press; Selth, A. (1996), *Transforming the Tatmadaw: The Burmese Armed Forces Since 1988*, Strategic and Defence Studies Centre (SDSC), Australian National University, Canberra; Selth, A. (1997a), *Burma's Intelligence Apparatus*, Working Paper no. 308, SDSC, Canberra; Selth, A. (1997b), *Burma's Defence Expenditure and Arms Industries*, Working Paper no. 309, SDSC, Canberra; Selth, A. (1997c), *The Burma Navy*, Working Paper no. 313, SDSC, Canberra; Selth, A. (1997d), *The Burma Air Force*, Working Paper no. 315, SDSC, Canberra; Selth, A. (1999), *Burma and Weapons of Mass Destruction*, Working Paper no. 334, SDSC, Canberra.

46   Mya Maung (1992), *Totalitarianism in Burma: Prospects for Economic Development*, New York: Paragon House, p. 169.

47   Moncrief, J. (2002), "Shan Struggle Set to Continue," *The Irrawaddy*, vol. 10, no. 2, Feb.–Mar.; "Shan Army Forced to Desert Base," *Bangkok Post*, 4 October 2003, Bangkok; "Troops Mass to Attack Shan Army," *Bangkok Post*, 22 June 2003, Bangkok; "Shan Army Denies Ambushing Junta Troops," *Bangkok Post*, 24 January 2003, Bangkok; "Burma Army Moves in on Shan Bases," *Bangkok*

Post, 6 February 2002, Bangkok; "Shan Rebels Headed for Junta Bases," *Bangkok Post*, 7 March 2001, Bangkok.

48 Mason, M. (1998), "Foreign Direct Investment in Burma," in Rotberg, R. (ed.), *Burma, Prospects for a Democratic Future*, op. cit., pp. 209–210.

49 Ibid., p. 210.

50 Ibid.

51 Ibid.

52 For a flattering account of the unique economic system which arose under Ne Win's autarchic policies, see Schumacher, E. F. (1974), *Small is Beautiful*, London: Sphere Books, Abacus edition. For a more critical account, see Mya Maung (1992), op. cit.

53 Aung San described his "New Democracy" as somewhere betwixt and between capitalism and socialism. For details see Aung San (1947b), pp. 153–155.

54 Trade between China and Burma was worth over US$600 million in 2002, of which 80 percent were imports and 20 percent exports (Clark, A. [2003], p. 131).

55 Seekins, D. (1999), "The North Wind and the Sun: Japan's Response to the Political Crisis in Burma, 1988–1998," *The Journal of Burma Studies*, vol. 4, 9.

56 Ibid., pp. 22–23.

57 Fairclough, G. (1996a), "Enter at Own Risk," *Far Eastern Economic Review*, 15 August, p. 65.

58 Selth, A. (2000), *Burma's Secret Military Partners*, Strategic and Defence Studies Centre, Research School of Pacific and Asian Studies, Australian National University, Canberra, p. 31. See also Kean, L. and Bernstein, D. (1998), "Burma–Singapore Axis: Globalizing the Heroin Trade," *CAQ Magazine (Covert Action Quarterly)*, no. 64, Spring. Online. Available at: www.singapore-window.org/804caq9.htm (accessed 15 May 2005).

59 Selth, A. (2000), Ibid.

60 Ibid.

61 Ibid., pp. 28–37.

62 Ibid., p. 32.

63 Ibid., p. 38.

64 Ibid. See also Kean, L. and Bernstein, D. (1998), op. cit.

65 Aung San Suu Kyi (1997b), *The Voice of Hope, Conversations with Alan Clements*, New York: Seven Stories Press, p. 97.

66 *Straits Times*, 12 June 1996, Singapore; *New Light of Myanmar*, 15 June 1996, Rangoon.

67 Brandon, J. (1998), "The State's Role in Education in Burma," in Rotberg, R. (ed.), *Burma, Prospects for a Democratic Future*, op. cit., p. 234.

68 Although the local Burmese currency is the Kyat, business is also conducted using Foreign Exchange Certificates (FECs), along the lines of a similar second currency formerly adopted by the People's Republic of China. Before the United States imposed a ban on Burmese imports in August 2003, U.S. dollars were readily accepted for most trade, their use being either discouraged or encouraged depending upon the government's concern for inflation or attracting foreign investment. The black market traded in all three forms of currency, including FECs which were devalued by the authorities in 2001 from a 1:1 peg to the U.S. dollar, thus creating a tradable third currency in Burma. In August 2003, the Burmese government instructed all government organizations and private business to use Euros for importing and exporting goods. While the official exchange rate was 6 Kyat to US$1, on the black market the Kyat fell to its then lowest level in May 2002, trading at K1,200:US$1, rising to K820:US$1 after Suu Kyi's release, then falling again

to K1,060:US$1 by the end of August 2002. By late 2002, it was K900:US$1 and in August 2003, following the announcement of a U.S. ban on Burmese imports, it fell to 1,100 as dealers sought the greenback, then settled to 1,030. By October 2003, the Kyat was again trading at 910 to US$1. Burma's inflation rate rose from 34.5 percent in 2001 to a high of 58.1 percent in 2002 before slowing to 24.9 percent in 2003 and 9.0 percent in 2004. Inflation was expected to rise again to 17.5 percent in 2005 and 27.5 percent in 2006 (*Independent*, London, 13 May 2002; *BBC*, 27 August 2002; BBC, "Burma Favors Euros Over Dollars," *BBC NEWS*, 15 August 2003, available online at news.bbc.co.uk.go/pr/fr/-/1/hi/business/3154885.stm; *The Irrawaddy*, 27 October 2003; *Daily Times*, 28 October 2003; Clark, A. [2003], pp. 129–130; IMF [2005], *World Economic Outlook: Globalization and External Imbalances*, World Economic and Financial Surveys, Washington, D.C., April 2005, available online at: www.imf.org/external/pubs/ft/weo/2005/01/index.htm [Accessed 9 May 2005], p. 218).

69 Crispin, S. (1998), "Burma's Economy Edges towards Collapse," *Far Eastern Economic Review*, 27 August.
70 See "Trouble Ahead for Burma," *The Nation*, 25 February 1998, Bangkok.
71 See Przeworski, A. (1992), *Democracy and the Market: Political and Economic Reforms in Eastern Europe and Latin America (Studies in Rationality and Social Change)*, Cambridge, UK: Cambridge University Press. It could be argued that because the sincerity for liberalization on the part of the SPDC was lacking, Burma could be a good case study for testing Przeworski's model.
72 Aung Thwin maintains that economic growth in Burma over the past decade, as evidenced in GDP growth rates, forced the NLD into talks with the government (Aung Thwin, M. [2002], "Parochial Universalism, Democracy *Jihad* and the Orientalist Image of Burma: The New Evangelism," *Pacific Affairs*, vol. 74, no. 4, Winter, 501). Suu Kyi, on the other hand, notes "the reason why it seems that Burma has developed economically" in recent years is perhaps because they "started from less than zero, and it's very easy to show progress from that point" (Aung San Suu Kyi [1997b], p. 97).
73 Callahan, M. (2001), "Burma: Soldiers as State Builders," in Alagappa, M. (ed.), *Coercion and Governance: The Declining Role of the Military in Asia*, Stanford, California: Stanford University Press, p. 428.
74 See Lieberman, V. (1984), *Burmese Administrative Cycles: Anarchy and Conquest, c.1580–1760*, Princeton, New Jersey: Princeton University Press; Taylor, R. (1987), *The State in Burma*, Honolulu: University of Hawaii Press.
75 Aung Thwin, M. (1985), *Pagan, The Origins of Modern Burma*, Honolulu: University of Hawaii Press.
76 Smith, D. (1965), *Religion and Politics in Burma*, Princeton, New Jersey: Princeton University Press, p. 23.
77 Pye, L. (1962), *Politics, Personality, and Nation Building: Burma's Search for Identity*, New Haven: Yale University Press, p. 75.
78 Houtman, G. (1999), *Mental Culture in Burmese Crisis Politics: Aung San Suu Kyi and the National League for Democracy*, Tokyo: Institute for the Study of Languages and Cultures of Asia and Africa, Tokyo University of Foreign Studies, Monograph Series no. 33, p. 160; see also Smith, M. (2001), "Burmese Politics after 1988: An Era of New and Uncertain Change," in Taylor, R. (ed.), *Burma: Political Economy under Militray Rule*, New York: Palgrave, p. 21.
79 Interview with Daw May Kyi Win, 22 April 1999.
80 Reynolds, F. (1972), "The Two Wheels of Dhamma: A Study of Early Buddhism," in Obeyesekere, G., Reynolds, F., and Smith, B., *The Two Wheels of Dhamma*, Chambersburg, Pennsylvania: American Academy of Religion, AAR Studies in Religion, no. 3, p. 15.

81   Ibid.
82   Ibid., pp. 15–16.
83   Ibid., p. 17.
84   Ibid.
85   Ibid., pp. 17–18.
86   Ibid., p. 18.
87   Ibid.
88   Ibid., pp. 18–22.
89   Ibid., p. 18.
90   Ibid.
91   Ibid., pp. 13, 20.
92   Ibid., pp. 20, 21.
93   Ibid., p. 21.
94   Ibid., p. 22.
95   Gravers, M. (1999), *Nationalism as Political Paranoia in Burma*, London: Curzon Press, pp. 16–17.
96   Reynolds, F. (1972), p. 22.
97   Ibid., p. 23.
98   Ibid., pp. 26–27.
99   Ibid., pp. 27–28.
100 Ibid., p. 29.
101 Ibid.
102 Ibid., p. 30.
103 Maung Maung Gyi (1983), *Burmese Political Values*, New York: Praeger, p. 21; see also Aung San Suu Kyi (1991), *Freedom from Fear and Other Writings*, London: Viking Press, pp. 170–173.
104 Maung Maung Gyi (1983), pp. 21–22.
105 Ibid., p. 57; Aung San Suu Kyi (1991), pp. 170–173.
106 Maung Maung Gyi (1983), p. 22.
107 Ibid., p. 23.
108 Smith, D. (1965), p. 27.
109 Pye, L. (1962), p. 75.
110 Maung Maung Gyi (1983), p. 32.
111 Ibid., p. 25.
112 Ibid., p. 26.
113 Ibid.
114 Ibid.
115 Ibid., p. 27.
116 Minredeippa was elected king in 1628, for example, because the ministers feared that the kingdom would be in turmoil if they had waited for one of the king's brothers to claim the throne (Maung Maung Gyi [1983], p. 64).
117 Ibid., pp. 33–34.
118 Ibid., p. 28.
119 Smith, D. (1965), pp. 22–23.
120 Pye, L. (1985), *Asian Power and Politics: The Cultural Dimensions of Authority*, Cambridge, Massachusetts: Harvard University Press, p. 97.
121 Maung Maung Gyi (1983), p. 29.
122 Ibid.
123 Ibid., p. 28.
124 Pye, L. (1962), p. 146; see also *The Nation*, 22 February 1959, Rangoon.
125 Pye, L. (1962), Ibid.
126 Department of the Myanmar Language Commission (1993), *Myanmar–English Dictionary*, Rangoon: Ministry of Education, Union of Myanmar, p. 615.
127 Ibid., p. 604.

128 Houtman (1999), pp. 161, 170.
129 For a more elaborate account of Buddhism and its historical relation to Burmese society and politics, see Spiro, M. (1982), *Buddhism and Society: A Great Tradition and Its Burmese Vicissitudes*, Berkeley: University of California Press; Smith, D. (1965), op. cit.; Sarkisyanz, E. (1965), *Buddhist Backgrounds of the Burmese Revolution*, The Hague: Martinus Nijhoff; Mendelson, E. M. (1975), *Sangha and State in Burma: A Study of Monastic Sectarianism and Leadership*, Ithaca, New York: Cornell University Press. See also Spiro, M. (1967), *Burmese Supernaturalism*, Institute for the Study of Human Issues, Philadelphia: Prentice-Hall. For a general account of the political relevance and influence of Buddhism on social and economic issues, see Reynolds, F. (1972), op. cit.
130 Pye, L. (1987), p. 97; Cady, J. (1958), *A History of Modern Burma*, Ithaca, New York: Cornell University Press, pp. 3–38.
131 Smith, D. (1965), p. 22; Gravers, M. (1999), pp. 15–16.
132 For a commentary on the extensive scale of Burma's drug trade, see Ball, D. (1999), *Burma and Drugs: The Regime's Complicity in the Global Drug Trade*, Working Paper no. 336, July, Strategic and Defence Studies Centre, Australian National University, Canberra.
133 See for example, Pe Maung Tin and Luce, G. H., trans. (1923); Leach, E. R. (1965); Reid, A. (1983); Aung Thwin, M. (1983), (1985), (1998), (2002); Taylor, R. (1987); Lieberman, V. (1984); Maung Maung Gyi (1983); Silverstein, J. (1998a), (1998b); Scott, J. C. (1998a), and Houtman, G. (1999).
134 The town of Pagan lies in the northern heartland of Burma, along the Irrawaddy River. It served as the former capital and throne of the kingdom.

8 Buddhist political rhetoric

1 See Houtman, G. (1999), *Mental Culture in Burmese Crisis Politics: Aung San Suu Kyi and the National League for Democracy*, Tokyo: Institute for the Study of Languages and Cultures of Asia and Africa, Tokyo University of Foreign Studies, Monograph Series no. 33, pp. 26–27. Martyr's Day is celebrated annually on 19 July, commemorating the death of Aung San and his cabinet.
2 Naw, A. (2001), *Aung San and the Struggle for Burmese Independence*, Bangkok: Silkworm Books, p. 7.
3 Dagon Taya in Mya Sein (1962), "Into the Mainstream of History," in Maung Maung (ed.), *Aung San of Burma*, The Hague, Netherlands: Martinus Nijhoff; Naw, A. (2001), p. 21; compare with Aung San Suu Kyi (1984), p. 7.
4 Thakin, meaning "lord" or "master," was commonly used when addressing British residents. When used to address members of the organization it signified a reversal of their roles under British rule. Von der Mehden believes that while it is difficult to characterize the *thakin* ideology, the party was nationalist but tinged with various shades of Marxism, and its main basis was correctly described by Dr Ba Maw as a "spirit of revolt." (Von Der Mehden, F. [1963], *Religion and Nationalism in Southeast Asia*, Madison: University of Wisconsin Press, p. 80).
5 Aung San (1946), *Burma's Challenge, 1946*, 15 July, Rangoon, in Silverstein, J. (ed.) (1993), *The Political Legacy of Aung San*, revised edition, Ithaca, New York: Cornell University Press, Southeast Asia Program (SEAP) Series, no. 11, p. 75.
6 U Nu in Naw, A. (2001), p. 41.
7 Cady, J. (1960), *A History of Modern Burma*, Ithaca, New York: Cornell University Press, p. 416; Naw, A. (2001), p. 52.
8 Ba Maw (1968), *Breakthrough in Burma: Memoirs of a Revolution, 1936–1946*, New Haven: Yale University Press, p. 65; Naw, A. (2001), p. 62.

9 See Aung San (1945b), "The Resistance Movement," address delivered at the meeting of the East and West Association held on 29 August 1945 at the city hall of Rangoon, in Silverstein, J. (ed.) (1993), p. 83; Naw, A. (2001), pp. 62–66. Some authors prefer to claim that he was "literally kidnapped" (see Houtman, G. [1999], p. 19).

10 Won Z. Yoon (1973), *Japan's Scheme for the Liberation of Burma: The Role of the Minami kikan and the Thirty Comrades*, Athens, Ohio: Ohio University Press, Center for International Studies, Papers in International Studies, Southeast Asia Series, no. 27, p. 6; Naw, A. (2001), pp. 68–69.

11 Naw, A. (2001), pp. 63–66.

12 Aung San Suu Kyi (1984), *Aung San of Burma*, St. Lucia, Brisbane: University of Queensland Press, p. 18; Aung San Suu Kyi (1991), *Freedom from Fear and Other Writings*, London: Viking Press, p. 14.

13 Aung San Suu Kyi (1997b), *The Voice of Hope: Conversations with Alan Clements*, New York: Seven Stories Press, p. 106.

14 Naw, A. (2001), p. 81.

15 Ibid., p. 76.

16 Ibid., pp. 81, 88.

17 Gravers, M. (1999), *Nationalism as Political Paranoia in Burma*, London: Curzon Press, pp. 43–47.

18 Ibid., p. 46.

19 Naw, A. (2001), p. 118.

20 Ibid.

21 Ibid., p. 124.

22 Ibid., pp. 174–176.

23 Ibid., p. 171.

24 Aung San (1947a), *The Burma Review*, 13 January 1947, p. 7, in Naw, A. (2001), p. 187.

25 Naw, A. (2001), p. 11.

26 Ibid., p. 12; Thein Swe, Bo (ed.) (1951), *Bogyoke Aung San Attopati [Biography of Aung San]*, Rangoon: Amyotha Pon-ngeik-taik, p. 34.

27 Aung San Suu Kyi (1984), pp. 6–7; Aung San Suu Kyi (1991), p. 7.

28 Ibid. (1984), pp. 3–4; Ibid. (1991), p. 5.

29 Silverstein, J. (ed.) (1993), "Introduction," pp. 7–8.

30 One such example is Aung San's 1941 treatise *Blue Print for Burma* (reprinted in Silverstein, J. [1993], pp. 19–22). Aung Thwin adopts Dr Maung Maung's (Ne Win's personal biographer) and the *Tatmadaw*'s interpretation of *Blue Print for Burma* to show that Aung San supported Nazi Germany, endorsed fascism, and generally authoritarian rule (Aung Thwin, M. [1998], p. 157). Silverstein's account of Aung San's intentions when writing *Blue Print for Burma*, on the other hand, suggests that it was written to appease his Japanese advisors shortly after arriving in Japan, and when his essay is read together with the total body of his writings and speeches of both the war and postwar periods, it is clear that the ideas in *Blue Print for Burma* were not central to his thought (Silverstein, J. [1998b], p. 196). While scholars will continue to debate this point, one thing that should become apparent is that Aung San himself was not politically naïve. In this respect, Aung Thwin's account of Aung San as a political opportunist holds a great deal of substance, even though history was unable to judge the merits of his ultimate intentions.

31 Ibid., p. 5.

32 Silverstein, J. (1998a), "The Evolution and Salience of Burma's National Political Culture," in Rotberg, R. (ed.), *Burma, Prospects for a Democratic Future*, Washington, D.C.: Brookings Institution Press, pp. 11–32; Silverstein, J. (1998b), "The Idea of Freedom in Burma and the Political Thought of Daw

Aung San Suu Kyi," in Kelly, D. and Reid, A. (eds), *Asian Freedoms*. Cambridge, UK: Cambridge University Press, pp. 187–204.
33 Maung Maung (ed.) (1962), op. cit.
34 Silverstein, J. (ed.) (1993), p. 5. One possible way to understand Silverstein's position may be that he selectively interpreted Aung San's speeches as neutral with respect to Buddhism because he wished to oppose Ne Win's own attempts at a Buddhist interpretation of Aung San to legitimize his *Burmese Way to Socialism*. Published in 1962, Ne Win's *Burmese Way to Socialism* was an attempt to integrate socialist political and economic thought with Buddhism and Burmese nationalism. The first edition of Silverstein's compilation was published in 1972, and whereas the new Constitution, which was sold under the name of the *Burmese Way to Socialism*, was not ratified by national referendum until 1974, it had already been composed by Ne Win in 1968. Yet Silverstein chose not to amend his original claim in the second edition, published in 1993.
35 Ibid., p. 96.
36 Ibid., p. 6.
37 Ibid; Aung San (1947c), "Summary and Quotations from Aung San's Concluding Speech to AFPFL Convention, May 23, 1947," *New Times of Burma*, 24 May 1947, Rangoon, in Silverstein, J. (ed.) (1993), p. 71.
38 Silverstein, J. (ed.) (1993), p. 6.
39 Gravers, M. (1999), p. 41.
40 Ibid.
41 Silverstein, J. (ed.) (1993), p. 6.
42 Ibid.
43 Von der Mehden, F. (1963), p. 81.
44 Aung San (1940), *New Burma*, 10 May 1940 in Von der Mehden, F. (1963), p. 81.
45 Aung San (1945a), "Defense of Burma," n.p., "Confidential," January 1945, p. 11, in Von der Mehden, F. (1963), p. 81; "Defence of Burma, January 30, 1945," Defence Services Historical Research Institute, Rangoon, in Silverstein, J. (ed.) (1993), p. 27.
46 Anti Fascist People's Freedom League (AFPFL), *The New Burma in the New World*, in Von der Mehden, F. (1963), pp. 81–82.
47 Von der Mehden, F. (1963), p. 82.
48 Aung San Suu Kyi (1984), p. 7; Aung San Suu Kyi (1991), p. 8.
49 Ibid. (1984), p. 13; Ibid. (1991), p. 11.
50 Ibid. (1991), p. 200.
51 Ibid. (1984), p. 7; Ibid. (1991), p. 8.
52 Houtman, G. (1999), p. 15.
53 Ibid., p. 225; see also Maung Maung Gyi (1983), *Burmese Political Values*. Praeger: New York, p. 25.
54 Houtman, G. (1999), p. 225.
55 Ibid., pp. 218–219.
56 Ibid., p. 213.
57 Aung San Suu Kyi (1984), p. 21; Aung San Suu Kyi (1991), p. 16.
58 Houtman, G., (1999), p. 243.
59 Ibid., p. 19. Houtman also overlooks Aung San's alleged personal involvement in a civilian murder and the war crimes committed by his Burma Independence Army against the Karen while working with the Japanese in 1942.
60 Aung San Suu Kyi (1997b), p. 79.
61 Aung San Suu Kyi (1984), p. 36.
62 Houtman, G. (1999), p. 257.
63 Silverstein, J. (ed.) (1993), p. 95.
64 Aung San Suu Kyi (1991), p. 183.

65 Houtman, G. (1999), pp. 36, 221.
66 Houtman claims that "for Aung San, 'secular' means *loki* and calls forth its opposite 'transcendental' *lokuttara*, which is associated with the highest forms of mental culture in Buddhism. The former he regarded as a social goal involving social means, whereas the latter he regarded as an individual quest based on individual means. My view [Houtman's] is that in his designation of politics as 'secular', Aung San was primarily concerned with one kind of secularity from another – he argued against certain prevalent interpretations of politics which linked it to low forms of magic. He was against interference in politics by certain kinds of 'contaminated' Buddhism, as opposed to the higher forms of Buddhist practice with social implications, such as *byama-so taya* mental culture, which he admired and observed as the most vital component in the politics of a socialist society, indeed, as *representing* socialism." (Houtman, G. [1999], p. 246).
67 Gravers, M. (1999), p. 41.
68 Smith, D. (1965), *Religion and Politics in Burma*, Princeton, New Jersey: Princeton University Press, p. 118.
69 Silverstein, J. (ed.) (1993), p. 5.
70 Houtman, G. (1999), pp. 167, 297.
71 Aung San Suu Kyi (1997b), p. 107.
72 Houtman, G. (1999), p. 244, my italics.
73 Ibid., pp. 161, 170.
74 Von der Mehden, F. (1963), p. 81.
75 Houtman, G. (1999), pp. 219–220.
76 Aung San Suu Kyi (1991), (1993), (1995), (1997a), (1997b), (1998).
77 Gravers, M. (1999), p. 77.
78 Kane describes well her appeal: "[Aung San] left a legacy of love, respect and disappointed hope that his family members might at some time draw upon should they choose to do so. Senior leaders of the pro-democracy movement of the 1980's were quite aware of the value of this inheritance and keen to harness it. . . . Her complete lack of experience in politics, Burmese or any other, was no barrier and probably even an advantage, for it meant an absence of the political taint carried by many of the other opposition leaders, most of whom had served under Ne Win. . . . To truly realize her inheritance, she had to show that she was something *more* than her father's daughter. . . . She has mentally prepared herself for the assumption of her father's legacy" (Kane, J. [2001], *The Politics of Moral Capital*, New York: Cambridge University Press, pp. 152–153).
79 Aung San Suu Kyi (1991), "Speech to a Mass Rally at the Shwedagon Pagoda," *Freedom from Fear*, p. 198.
80 Ibid., pp. 199–200.
81 Aung San Suu Kyi (1997a), *Letters from Burma*, London: Penguin, pp. 160–161.
82 According to Kane, "In a still predominantly peasant country like Burma, direct communication with people is essential, and Suu Kyi proved to have a gift for making emotional contact. Her speeches were short and to the point, and people responded eagerly to her lucidity and directness. Her capacity to convert crowds of people into admirers and supporters set in motion a swift cycle of accumulation that swept her rapidly into the leadership, symbolical and actual, of the nation" (Kane, J. [2001], p. 166).
83 Ibid., p. 167.
84 Ibid.
85 Aung San Suu Kyi (1997b), p. 92; Pandita, Sayadaw U. (1993), *In This Very Life: The Liberation Teachings of the Buddha*, 2nd edition., Boston: Wisdom Publications.

86   Aung San Suu Kyi (1993), "Towards a True Refuge," Eighth Joyce Pearce Memorial Lecture, delivered by Dr Michael Aris on 19 May 1993 at Oxford University.

87   Aung San Suu Kyi (1997b), p. 85.

88   Aung San Suu Kyi, "The True Meaning of Boh," in Aung San Suu Kyi (1991), p. 191.

89   Aung San Suu Kyi (1997b), p. 37; Aung San Suu Kyi (1998), "Heavenly Abodes and Human Development," 11th Pope Paul VI Memorial Lecture, delivered by Dr Michael Aris on 3 November 1997 at the Royal Institution of Great Britain, London, see *Bangkok Post*, 4 January 1998, Bangkok.

90   Aung San Suu Kyi (1997b), p. 158.

91   Aung San Suu Kyi (1997a), pp. 199–200.

92   Ibid., p. 199.

93   Ibid., pp. 200–201.

94   Ibid., p. 201.

95   Aung San Suu Kyi (1997b), p. 187.

96   Ibid., pp. 187–188.

97   Ibid., pp. 28, 85.

98   Reynolds, F. (1972), p. 29.

99   Ibid., pp. 29–30.

100   Mya Maung claims that by the end of 1988, her Shwedagon pagoda speech along with her many subsequent campaign speeches had established Suu Kyi as the only legitimate *min laung*. Her status was further enhanced by fragmentation among the other opposition leaders as well as their former ties to the military. Mya Maung (1992), pp. 144–146.

101   Myint Zan (1997), "Position of Power and Notions of Empowerment: Comparing the Views of Lee Kuan Yew and Aung San Suu Kyi on Human Rights and Governance," *Newcastle Law Review*, vol. 2, no. 2, pp. 66–68.

102   Houtman, G. (1999), p. 343.

103   Aung San Suu Kyi (1997b), pp. 172–173.

104   *Politics*, 1295a7–24.

105   Cicero, *Laws*, in *De Re Publica, De Legibus*, trans. C. W. Keyes (1928), Cambridge, Massachusetts: Harvard University Press, Loeb, II, vii, viii, x, xi, xii, xxvii; Cicero, *Laws*, in *On the Commonwealth and On the Laws*, trans. J. G. Zetzel (1999), Cambridge, UK: Cambridge University Press, II, 26, 30; Cicero, *The Republic*, in *De Re Publica, De Legibus*, trans. C. W. Keyes (1928), II, xiv, 27.

106   *Politics*, 1314b38–1315a2.

107   Naw, A. (2001), pp. 17–18; Collis, M. S. (1938), *Trials in Burma*, London: Faber and Faber, pp. 208–210.

108   Naw, A. (2001), pp. 221–222.

109   Ibid., p. 19.

110   Ibid., p. 89.

111   Gravers, M. (1999), p. 56.

112   Ibid., p. 55; See Spiro, M. (1982), *Buddhism and Society: A Great Tradition and Its Burmese Vicissitudes*, Berkeley: University of California Press, p. 385.

113   Chirot, D. (1994), pp. 327–328.

114   Smith, D. (1965), pp. 25–26; *Guardian*, 18 August 1961, Rangoon.

115   Chirot, D. (1994), p. 327.

116   Gravers, M. (1999), p. 57.

117   Chirot, D. (1994), p. 332.

118   Lintner, B. (1989), *Outrage: Burma's Struggle for Democracy*, Hong Kong: Review Publishing Co; Chirot, D. (1994), p. 332.

119   Gravers, M. (1999), p. 62.

120   Burma Socialist Programme Party (1963), *The System of Correlation of Man and*

His Environment, Rangoon: BSPP, Union of Burma, pp. 36, 38–39; Seekins, D. (2002), *The Disorder in Order: The Army State in Burma Since 1962*, Bangkok: White Lotus Press, p. 46.
121 Seekins, D. (2002), Ibid.
122 Ibid.
123 Chirot, D. (1994), p. 309.
124 Deutsche Press-Agentur, "Burma's Ex-Strongman Ne Win Hosts Luncheon for 99 Senior Monks," 21 March 2001, in *Burma News Update*, no. 132, 4 April 2001.
125 Mya Maung (1992), p. 184.
126 Ibid.
127 Ibid., p. 186.
128 Chirot, D. (1994), p. 309.
129 *Politics*, 1285a2–1285a16, 1285b26–27; see also Chapter 7 above.
130 Ibid.
131 Steinberg, D. (1997), "The Union Solidarity and Development Association," *Burma Debate*, vol. 4, no. 1, Jan.–Feb., p. 3; Kane, J. (2001), p. 168.
132 Gravers, M. (1999), p. 86.
133 Ibid., p. 132.
134 Philp, J. and Mercer, D. (2002), "Politicised Pagodas and Veiled Resistance: Contested Urban Space in Burma," *Urban Studies*, vol. 39, no. 9, August, 1592.
135 Ibid.
136 Houtman, G. (1999), p. 27.
137 Ibid.
138 See Ibid., pp. 180–181.
139 Aung Thwin, M. (1998), pp. 157–158.
140 Reynolds, F. (1972), pp. 27–29.
141 Edelman, M. (1964), p. 190.
142 Gravers, M. (1999), p. 91.
143 Gravers notes that before it was finished, Ne Win too appealed to Buddhist cosmology, kingship, and perhaps attempted to accumulate merit when he raised the spire on his own pagoda (Maha Vizeya) constructed behind the Shwedagon (Gravers, M. [1999], p. 62; see also Philp, J. and Mercer, D. [2002], pp. 1602–1605).
144 Gravers, M. (1999), p. 107.
145 Philp, J. and Mercer, D. (2002), p. 1602.
146 Ibid., pp. 1597, 1600.
147 Ibid.
148 Ibid., p. 1598.
149 Ibid., pp. 1592, 1599.
150 Ibid., p. 1600.
151 Aung Zaw, "Burma's Generals Beyond Reason," *Bangkok Post*, 10 September 2000, Bangkok.
152 *Politics*, 1314b38–1315a2. Silliness (*abelteria*) in this context means excessive behavior. *Abelteria* translates to "silliness, stupidity, fatuity;" "Though he should not display a foolish religiosity," see Liddel and Scott (1940), *A Greek–English Lexicon*, Oxford: Clarendon Press; The Perseus Digital Library, Tufts University. Online. Available at: www.perseus.tufts.edu/cgi-bin/ptext?doc=Perseus:text:1999.01.0058:book=5:section=1315a (accessed 15 May 2005).
153 *Discourses*, I, 11, 3–4; I, 13, 1; I, 56.
154 Philp, J. and Mercer, D. (2002), p. 1591.
155 *Prince*, XVIII, 108.

9 Stability and justice in Burma

1 *Politics*, 1314a35–36.
2 See "NLD Vice Chairman, U Tin Oo in response to Thailand's Defence Minister, Chavalit," *Irrawaddy*, 17 September 2001.
3 Aung San Suu Kyi (1997b), *The Voice of Hope: Conversations with Alan Clements*, New York: Seven Stories Press, p. 39.
4 See Amnesty International (2004), *Myanmar: The Administration Of Justice – Grave And Abiding Concerns*, report issued 1 April 2004; Assistance Association for Political Prisoners (AAPP), Mae Sot, Thailand, data available online.
5 In November 2004 over 30 political prisoners were released from prisons in Rangoon, Mandalay, and Western Burma, including several senior NLD members along with the 1988 pro-democracy protests' student leader Min Ko Naing as part of a "good cop" move that hoped to distance the junta from Khin Nyunt's disbanded National Intelligence Bureau. Their release was part of 9,000 prisoners to be freed, announced in the weeks leading up to an ASEAN summit in Laos.
6 See *Far Eastern Economic Review*, 4–10 May 2001; Allen Clark (2003), "Burma in 2002: A Year of Transition," *Asian Survey*, vol. 43, no. 1, Jan./Feb., 127–134, esp. 132; Reuters, 13 May 2002.
7 Xinhua News Agency, "South Korea, Japan seal deals with Junta," 9 July 2002.
8 BBC, "Burma moves to stifle protest," *BBC NEWS*, 2 June 2003; BBC, "Protests mark Burma anniversary," *BBC NEWS*, 8 August 2003.
9 BBC, "Burma's Suu Kyi attacks junta," *BBC NEWS*, 23 April 2003.
10 ASEAN (2003), "Joint Communique" of the 36th ASEAN Ministerial Meeting held on 16–17 June 2003 in Phnom Penh, Clause 18.
11 BBC, "Burma defends Suu Kyi custody," *BBC NEWS*, 13 July 2003.
12 China is assisting Burma in building three hydropower plants and its third international airfield, Hanthawady International Airport, in the Bago division. Mandalay airfield is now Southeast Asia's longest runway and is capable of handling military transports. China helped fund its construction and also funded the building of a deep sea port at Tilowa – facing the Indian Ocean – which may be capable of handling Chinese nuclear submarines in the future, along with a highway connecting the port to Yunnan province.
13 BBC, "Mixed feelings over Burma sanctions," *BBC NEWS*, 16 July 2003.
14 Callahan, M. (2001), "Burma: Soldiers as State Builders," in Muthiah Alagappa (ed.), *Coercion and Governance: The Declining Role of the Military in Asia*, Stanford, California: Stanford University Press, p. 426.
15 For example, the SPDC seemed to concur with the former Malaysian Prime Minister Dr. Mahathir's claims that Asia's financial crisis was instigated by George Soros as a conspiracy to topple Asian currencies (*New Light of Myanmar*, 11 November 1997).
16 The two generals responsible for overseeing foreign investment approvals, then Secretary-3 and the former head of UMEH, Win Myint, and then Deputy Prime Minister and head of the MIC, Tin Hla, were sacked for corruption in a purge of seven senior generals in late 2001.
17 Ball, D. (1999), *Burma and Drugs: The Regime's Complicity in the Global Drug Trade*, Working Paper no. 336, July, Strategic and Defence Studies Centre, Australian National University, Canberra, p. 3. See also Kean, L. and Bernstein, D. (1998), "Burma–Singapore Axis: Globalizing the Heroin Trade," *CAQ Magazine (CovertAction Quarterly)*, no. 64, Spring.
18 Matthews, B. (1999), "Burma/Myanmar: Government, *La Mode* – From SLORC to SPDC: A Change of Public Dress-Up and Manner?" *The Round Table*, No. 349, p. 88, n. 45; Chao-Tzang Yawnghwe (1998), *Burma, the Heroin Trade, and Canada*, National Consultative Conference on Burma, April, Ottawa.

19 Moreau, R. (2001), "Transplanted Trouble: The Burmese Drug Syndicates, *Newsweek International*, 16 July 2001, p. 43.

20 Ball, D. (1999), pp. 2–3.

21 Ibid., p. 2.

22 The UNOCD's annual Opium Survey is carried out under the supervision and implementation of the Myanmar Central Committee for Drug Abuse Control (CCDAC). The survey states that it "was not designed to monitor or validate the results of the eradication campaigns carried out by the Myanmar Government" (UNODC (2005), *Myanmar Opium Survey 2005*, New York: United Nations, p. 37). The UNODC claims that opium poppy cultivation in Myanmar has decreased by 75 percent since 1998, including a decrease of 26 percent from 2004–05, 29 percent from 2003–04, and 24 percent from 2002–03 (UNODC, *Myanmar Opium Survey 2003; 2004; 2005*). The survey is undertaken using a combination of satellite remote sensing and field surveys of sample villages randomly selected from a database of villages provided by the Myanmar Forest Department. The results are then extrapolated to the entire country using area estimation formulae. This haphazard methodology produces a national estimate which is rightly open to criticism. Villages can disappear from the Department's listing, for example, and access to others may not be possible. In the case of a disappearing village, survey staff will simply include another village on the Department's list in order to keep the stratification structure of their sample intact. And yet the composition of the database itself appears to remain beyond question. Also in the 2005 survey, no satellite images were acquired for the North Shan State region (see UNODC (2005), Ibid., pp. 43, 45–46).

23 In particular, there is no meaningful change in Burma's budget deficit over the years corresponding to the general arms build-up that reflects the weapons purchases.

24 See also Yawnghwe, Chao Tzang, "Shan State Politics: The Opium-Heroin Factor," Paper presented at the Conference *Drugs and Conflicts in Burma (Myanmar)*, Transnational Institute, Amsterdam, 13–16 December 2003; Jelsma, M., Kramer, T. and Vervest, P. (eds) (2003), *Drugs and Conflict in Burma (Myanmar): Dilemmas for Policy Responses*, Debate Papers, December 2003, No. 9, Amsterdam: Transnational Institute; ALTSEAN-Burma (2004), *A Failing Grade: Burma's Drug Eradication Efforts*, Bangkok: Alternative ASEAN Network on Burma, November 2004; Jelsma, M., Kramer, T. and Vervest, P. (eds) (2005), *Trouble in the Triangle: Opium and Conflict in Burma*, Chiang Mai: Silkworm Books.

25 *Politics*, 1309b18–34.

26 See Callahan, M. (2001), p. 424; also see Andrew Selth (2002), *Burma's Armed Forces: Power Without Glory*, Norwalk, Connecticut: EastBridge, pp. 259–268.

27 Kyaw Yin Hlaing (2005), "Myanmar in 2004: Another Year of Uncertainty," *Asian Survey*, vol. 45, no. 1, Jan.–Feb., 178–179.

28 Aung San Suu Kyi (1997c), "Commencement Address" delivered on her behalf by Dr Michael Aris at the American University Upon Receiving Honorary Doctor of Laws Degree, 26 January 1997, Washington, D.C.

29 Allen Clark (2003), p. 129.

30 Badgley, J. (ed.) (2004), *Reconciling Burma/Myanmar: Essays on U.S. Relations with Burma*, NBR Analysis, Seattle: The National Bureau of Asian Research.

31 McCarthy, S. (2000), "Ten Years of Chaos in Burma: Foreign Investment and Economic Liberalization under the SLORC–SPDC, 1988–1998," *Pacific Affairs*, vol. 73, no. 2, Summer, 233–262.

32 See Kurlantzick, J. (2002), "Can Burma Reform?" *Foreign Affairs*, vol. 81, no. 6, Nov.–Dec., 134–135; Bert, W. (2004), "Burma, China and the U.S.A.," *Pacific Affairs*, vol. 77, no. 2, Summer, 279.

33 South, A. (2004), "Political Transition in Myanmar: A New Model for Democratization," *Contemporary Southeast Asia*, vol. 26, no. 2, 254.

34 MacLean, K. (2004), "Reconfiguring the Debate on Engagement: Burmese Exiles and the Changing Politics of Aid," *Critical Asian Studies*, vol. 36, no. 3, 342–343.

35 *Politics*, 1312a40–1312b8.

36 Ibid., 1312b8–9.

37 Callahan, M. (2001), pp. 426–427.

38 Most noticeably at the inception of the SPDC in 1997, yet perhaps also at the death of the hardliner and main rival to Kyin Nyunt, Secretary-2 Tin Oo, along with several senior officers in a helicopter crash in February 2001. In November 2001, Secretary-3 Win Myint, along with Deputy Prime Minister Tin Hla and five other senior officers were sacked, and in October 2004 Prime Minister Khin Nyunt himself was sacked.

39 *Politics*, 1289a3–5.

40 Lee remarked, "The civil service, in the sense that we have it in Singapore, it does not exist. If a minister there wanted something it was the army which carried out his wishes. The general calls up his brigadier and says: Get the unit moved there, clean that road. And they called the troops up, and the whole quarters moved. And the next time you go there, all the roads were cleaned up. Who cleaned up? The army did" (Lee Kuan Yew, *Straits Times*, 12 June 1996).

41 Taylor, R. (ed.) (2001), *Burma: Political Economy under Military Rule*, New York: Palgrave, p. 13.

42 Taylor, R. (1990), "Burmese army and the 'national interest,'" *Bangkok Post*, 16 June 1990, Bangkok; *Working People's Daily*, 20 June 1990, Rangoon, p. 7.

43 Maung Maung Gyi (1983), pp. 34–35.

44 *Politics*, 1289a5–6.

45 Gravers, M. (1999), *Nationalism as Political Paranoia in Burma*, London: Curzon Press, pp. 69, 134.

46 Aung San Suu Kyi (1997c), op. cit.

47 *Politics*, 1314a16–17.

48 See Scott, J. C. (1985), *Weapons of the Weak: Everyday Forms of Peasant Resistance*, New Haven: Yale University Press; Scott, J. C. (1990), *Domination and the Arts of Resistance: Hidden Transcripts*, New Haven: Yale University Press; Philp, J. and Mercer, D. (2002), "Politicised Pagodas and Veiled Resistance: Contested Urban Space in Burma," *Urban Studies*, vol. 39, no. 9, 1587–1610.

49 Fukuyama, F. (2001), "Social Capital, Civil Society and Development," *Third World Quarterly*, vol. 22, no. 1, 16.

50 South, A. (2004), p. 253. An analogy could be made here to the "civil society" forged along the lines of the "spirit of Panglong" at the Panglong conference in 1947.

51 Aung San Suu Kyi (1997b), pp. 74–76.

52 *Politics*, 1289a3–5.

53 Ibid., 1289a3–14.

54 Ibid., 1289a15–17.

55 Aung San Suu Kyi (1991), pp. 171–172.

56 Ibid., p. 173.

57 Myint Zan (1997), p. 63.

58 Strauss, L. (1963), p. 75.

59 Strauss, L. (1988), p. 107.

60 See Taylor, R. (2001).

61 Huntington, S. (1991), *The Third Wave: Democratization in the Late Twentieth Century*, Norman, Oklahoma: University of Oklahoma Press, p. 231; Huntington, S. (1995), "Reforming Civil–Military Relations," *Journal of Democracy*, vol. 6, no. 4, 15–16.

10 Conclusion

1 *Politics*, 1274b18, n. 106.
2 Ibid., 1309b18–34.
3 Ibid., 1295b12–13.
4 Przeworski, A. and Limongi, F. (1997), "Modernization: Theories and Facts," *World Politics*, vol. 49, no. 2, 155–183.

Appendix B

1 *New Light of Myanmar*, 13, 14 August 1988, Rangoon.
2 For example, see "SLORC Chairman Senior General Than Shwe continues up-country visit with pilgrimage to religious centers," *New Light of Myanmar*, 9 August 1995, Rangoon.
3 *New Light of Myanmar*, 11 May 1996, Rangoon.
4 See "With State Patronage, Religion, Culture and Traditions Flourish," *New Light of Myanmar*, 20 and 22 October 1997, Rangoon.
5 *New Light of Myanmar*, 18 May 1996, Rangoon.
6 *New Light of Myanmar*, 14 May 2002, Rangoon.
7 *New Light of Myanmar*, 12th Waxing of Nadaw, 12 December 1997, Rangoon; see also *New Light of Myanmar*, 27 October 1997, Rangoon.
8 *New Light of Myanmar*, 16 November 1997, Rangoon.
9 See "Burma rebuilding risks Pagan jewel," *BBC NEWS*, 4 June 2005.
10 See for example, *Working People's Daily*, 30 July 1988, 24 June 1990, Rangoon; *New Light of Myanmar*, 1 and 2 May 1996, 16 and 17 June 1996, 11 and 17 September 2000, and 11 October 2000, Rangoon.
11 *New Light of Myanmar*, 17 September 2000, Rangoon.
12 See *New Light of Myanmar*, 25 October 1998, 13 and 15 July 1999, and 15 September 1999, Rangoon; see also Philp, J. and Mercer, D. (2002), "Politicised Pagodas and Veiled Resistance: Contested Urban Space in Burma," *Urban Studies*, vol. 39, no. 9, pp. 1596, 1600, 1604, 1605.
13 *New Light of Myanmar*, 1 May 1990, Rangoon.

Bibliography

General sources

Ajami, F. (1993). "The Summoning," *Foreign Affairs*, vol. 72, no. 4, Sep.–Oct., pp. 2–9.

Alagappa, M. (ed.) (1995). *Political Legitimacy in Southeast Asia: The Quest for Moral Authority*, Stanford, California: Stanford University Press.

—— (ed.) (2001). *Coercion and Governance: The Declining Role of the Military in Asia*, Stanford, California: Stanford University Press.

Almond, G. A. and Coleman, J. S. (eds) (1960). *The Politics of the Developing Areas*, Princeton, New Jersey: Princeton University Press.

—— and Verba, S. (eds) (1963). *The Civic Culture: Political Attitudes and Democracy in Five Nations*, Princeton, New Jersey: Princeton University Press.

—— and Verba, S. (eds) (1989). *The Civic Culture Revisited*, Newbury Park, California: Sage Publications.

ALTSEAN-Burma (2004). *A Failing Grade: Burma's Drug Eradication Efforts*, Bangkok: Alternative ASEAN Network on Burma, November.

Amnesty International (2004). *Myanmar: The Administration Of Justice – Grave And Abiding Concerns*, report issued 1 April 2004. Online. Available at: web. amnesty.org/library/Index/ENGASA160012004?open&of=ENG-MMR (accessed 15 May 2005).

Anti Fascist People's Freedom League (AFPFL) (1945). *The New Burma in the New World*, Rangoon: Nay Win Kyi Press.

Aristotle. *The Politics*, trans. Carnes Lord (1984). Chicago: University of Chicago Press.

—— *Nicomachean Ethics*, trans. Hippocrates G. Apostle (1984). Iowa: The Peripatetic Press.

—— *Metaphysics*, trans. Hugh Tredennick (1947). Cambridge, Massachusetts: Harvard University Press, Loeb.

—— "The Constitution of Athens," trans. J. M. Moore (1975). *Aristotle and Xenophon on Democracy and Oligarchy*, Berkeley: University of California Press.

—— *On Rhetoric: A Theory of Civic Discourse*, trans. George A. Kennedy (1991). New York: Oxford University Press.

Arnhart, L. (1982). *Aristotle on Political Reasoning: A Commentary on the Rhetoric*, DeKalb, Illinois: Northern Illinois University Press.

—— (1990). "The Deliberative Rhetoric of the Federalist," *The Political Science Reviewer*, 19, Spring, pp. 49–86.

Assistance Association for Political Prisoners (AAPP), Mae Sot, Thailand. Online. Available at: www.aappb.net/data.html (accessed 15 May 2005).

Association of Southeast Asian Nations (ASEAN) (1993). "Joint Communique" of the 26th ASEAN Ministerial Meeting held on 23–24 July 1993 in Singapore.

—— (2003). "Joint Communique" of the 36th ASEAN Ministerial Meeting held on 16–17 June 2003 in Phnom Penh, Clause 18. Online. Available at: www. aseansec.org/14833.htm (accessed 15 May 2005).

Aung San (1940). *New Burma*, 10 May 1940, in Von der Mehden, F. (1963), *Religion and Nationalism in Southeast Asia*, Madison: University of Wisconsin Press, p. 81.

—— (1941). "Blue Print for Burma," Tokyo, in the *Guardian*, March 1947, Rangoon, pp. 33–35, reprinted in Silverstein, J. (ed.) (1993), *The Political Legacy of Aung San*, revised edition, Ithaca, New York: Cornell University Press, Southeast Asia Program (SEAP) Series, no. 11, pp. 19–22.

—— (1945a). "Defence of Burma, January 30, 1945," Defence Services Historical Research Institute, Rangoon, in Silverstein, J. (ed.) (1993), pp. 23–27.

—— (1945b). "The Resistance Movement," address delivered at the meeting of the East and West Association held on 29 August 1945 at the city hall of Rangoon, in Silverstein, J. (ed.) (1993), pp. 77–93.

—— (1946). *Burma's Challenge, 1946*, 15 July, Rangoon, in Silverstein, J. (ed.) (1993), pp. 74–161.

—— (1947a). *The Burma Review*, 13 January 1947, p. 7, in Naw, A. (2001), p. 187.

—— (1947b). "Bogyoke Aung San's Address at the Convention Held at the Jubilee Hall, Rangoon on the 23rd May, 1947," in Silverstein, J. (ed.) (1993), pp. 151–161.

—— (1947c). "Summary and Quotations from Aung San's Concluding Speech to AFPFL Convention, May 23, 1947," *New Times of Burma*, 24 May 1947, Rangoon, in Silverstein, J. (ed.) (1993), pp. 70–71.

—— (1947d). "The Aung San Letter," 2 July 1947, in *The Nation*, 2 March 1962, Rangoon, p. 1.

Aung San Suu Kyi (1984). *Aung San of Burma*, St. Lucia, Brisbane: University of Queensland Press.

—— (1991). *Freedom from Fear and Other Writings*, London: Viking Press.

—— (1993). "Towards a True Refuge," Eighth Joyce Pearce Memorial Lecture, Refugee Studies Programme, University of Oxford, delivered by Dr Michael Aris on 19 May 1993 at the University of Oxford. Online. Available at: www. burmainfo.org/assk/DASSK_1993_TowardsATrueRefuge.html (accessed 15 May 2005).

—— (1997a). *Letters from Burma*, London: Penguin.

—— (1997b). *The Voice of Hope: Conversations with Alan Clements*, New York: Seven Stories Press.

—— (1997c). "Commencement Address" delivered on her behalf by Dr Michael Aris at the American University Upon Receiving Honorary Doctor of Laws Degree, 26 January 1997, Washington, D.C.. Online. Available at: www.uscampaignforburma.org/assk/auaddress1.html (accessed 15 May 2005).

—— (1998). "Heavenly Abodes and Human Development," 11th Pope Paul VI Memorial Lecture delivered by Dr Michael Aris on 3 November 1997 at the Royal Institution of Great Britain, London. Reprinted in *Bangkok Post*, Bangkok, 4 January 1998. Online. Available at: www.burmainfo.org/assk/DASSK_1997_ HeavenlyAbodesHumanDevelopment.html (accessed 15 May 2005).

Aung Than (1964). *Aung Than Ai Aung San* (Aung Than on Aung San). Rangoon.

Aung Thwin, M. (1983). "Athi, Kyun-Taw, Hpaya-Kyun: Varieties of Commendation and Dependence in Pre-Colonial Burma," in Reid, A. (ed.), *Slavery, Bondage, and Dependency in Southeast Asia,* New York: St. Martin's Press, pp 64–89.

—— (1985). *Pagan, The Origins of Modern Burma,* Honolulu: University of Hawaii Press.

—— (1998). *Myth and History in the Historiography of Early Burma,* Athens, Ohio: Ohio University Center for International Studies.

—— (2002). "Parochial Universalism, Democracy Jihad and the Orientalist Image of Burma: The New Evangelism," *Pacific Affairs,* vol. 74, no. 4, Winter, pp. 483–505.

Aung Zaw (2000). "Burma's Generals Beyond Reason," *Bangkok Post,* Bangkok, 10 September 2000.

—— (2003). "Burma's Emperors: Wearing New Clothes," *The Irrawaddy,* vol. 11, no. 7, 27 October 2003. Online. Available at: www.irrawaddy.org/aviewer. asp?a=3102&z=5 (accessed 15 May 2005).

Ba Maw (1968). *Breakthrough in Burma: Memoirs of a Revolution, 1936–1946,* New Haven: Yale University Press.

Badgley, J. (ed.) (2004). *Reconciling Burma/Myanmar: Essays on U.S. Relations with Burma,* NBR Analysis, Seattle: The National Bureau of Asian Research.

Baker, M. (2002). "Squeaky-clean Singapore eases up on gum control," *The Age,* Melbourne, 21 November 2002.

Ball, D. (1999). *Burma and Drugs: The Regime's Complicity in the Global Drug Trade,* Strategic and Defence Studies Centre, Working Paper 336, July, Canberra: Australian National University.

Bates, C. (2003). *Aristotle's Best Regime: Kingship, Democracy, and the Rule of Law,* Baton Rouge: Louisiana State University Press.

Bell, D. (1997). "A Communitarian Critique of Authoritarianism: The Case of Singapore," *Political Theory,* vol. 25, no. 1, February, pp. 6–32.

Bentley, Justice P. (1997). "The Politics of Defamation in Singapore," *The Provincial Judges' Journal,* Canada, Autumn. Online. Available at: www.singapore-window.org/80217can.htm (accessed 15 May 2005).

Bert, W. (2004). "Burma, China and the U.S.A.," *Pacific Affairs,* vol. 77, no. 2, Summer, p. 279.

Boesche, R. (1996). *Theories of Tyranny from Plato to Arendt,* University Park, Pennsylvania: Pennsylvania State University Press.

Burma Socialist Programme Party (BSPP) (1963). *The System of Correlation of Man and His Environment: The Philosophy of the Burma Socialist Programme Party,* Rangoon: BSPP, Union of Burma. Online. Available at: www.ibiblio.org/obl/docs/System-of-correlation.htm (accessed 15 May 2005).

Burton, J. (2001). "Why Bother Voting? The Government is Almost Unopposed," *The Economist,* 1 November 2001.

Bush, President G. W. (2005). "President Sworn-In to Second Term," The White House, Office of the Press Secretary, 20 January 2005. Online. Available at: www.whitehouse.gov/news/releases/2005/01/print/20050120–1.html (accessed 15 May 2005).

Cady, J. (1958). *A History of Modern Burma,* Ithaca, New York: Cornell University Press.

Callahan, M. (2001). "Burma: Soldiers as State Builders," in Alagappa, M. (ed.),

Coercion and Governance: The Declining Role of the Military in Asia, Stanford, California: Stanford University Press, pp. 413–429.

Cardoso, F. and Faletto, E. (1979). *Dependency and Development in Latin America*, Berkeley: University of California Press.

Case, W. (2003). "Singapore in 2002," *Asian Survey*, vol. 43, no. 1, Jan.–Feb., pp. 167–173.

Chirot, D. (1994). *Modern Tyrants: The Power and Prevalence of Evil in Our Age*, New York: The Free Press.

Chua Beng Huat (1995). *Communitarian Ideology and Democracy in Singapore*, London: Routledge.

Chuan Leekpai (1993). "Opening Statement," in United Nations, "Bangkok Declaration of Asian States," United Nations World Conference on Human Rights, Regional Meeting for Asia, Bangkok, 29 March–2 April 1993, New York: United Nations.

Churchill, W. (1947) "Burma Independence Bill," *Parliamentary Debates, House of Commons*, 5th Series, no. 443, 5 November 1947.

Cicero. *Laws*, trans. C. W. Keyes (1928). *De Re Publica, De Legibus*, Cambridge, Massachusetts: Harvard University Press, Loeb

—— *The Republic*, trans. C. W. Keyes (1928). *De Re Publica, De Legibus*, Cambridge, Massachusetts: Harvard University Press, Loeb.

—— *Laws*, trans. J. G. Zetzel (1999). *On the Commonwealth and On the Laws*, Cambridge, UK: Cambridge University Press.

Clark, A. L. (2003). "Burma in 2002," *Asian Survey*, vol. 43, no. 1, Jan.–Feb., pp. 127–134.

Coleman, J. (1988). "Social Capital in the Creation of Human Capital," *American Journal of Sociology*, Supplement, vol. 94, s95–s120.

Collier, D. and Levitsky, S. (1997). "Democracy with Adjectives," *World Politics*, vol. 49, no. 3, April, pp. 430–451.

Collis, M. S. (1938). *Trials in Burma*, London: Faber and Faber.

Constitution of the United States (1995). New York: Penguin.

Cotton, J. (1993). "Political Innovation in Singapore: The Presidency, the Leadership, and the Party," in Garry Rodan (ed.), *Singapore Changes Guard: Social, Political, and Economic Directions in the 1990's*, Melbourne: Longman Cheshire, pp. 3–15.

Crampton, T. (2001). "Aid Linked to Junta's Talks With Opposition: Japan Rewards Burma For Political Opening," *International Herald Tribune*, 26 April. Online. Available at: www.iht.com/articles/2001/04/26/burma_ed3_.php (accessed 15 May 2005).

Crispin, S. (1998). "Burma's Economy Edges Towards Collapse," *Far Eastern Economic Review*, vol. 161, no. 35, 27 August 1998, pp. 56–58.

—— and Lintner, B. (2001). "Something for Nothing," *Far Eastern Economic Review*, vol. 164, no. 18, 10 May 2001, pp. 28–29.

Crotty, W. (ed.) (1991). *Political Science: Looking to the Future. Volume Two: Comparative Politics, Policy, and International Relations*, Evanston: Northwestern University Press.

De Bary, Wm. T. (2000). *Asian Values and Human Rights*, Cambridge, Massachusetts: Harvard University Press.

—— and Tu Weiming (eds) (1997). *Confucianism and Human Rights*, New York: Columbia University Press.

Department of the Myanmar Language Commission (1993). *Myanmar–English Dictionary*, Rangoon: Ministry of Education, Union of Myanmar.

Diamond, L. (ed.) (1994). *Political Culture and Democracy in Developing Countries*, Boulder, Colorado: Lynne Reinner Publishers.

—— (1999). *Developing Democracy: Toward Consolidation*, Baltimore, Maryland: Johns Hopkins University Press.

—— Plattner, M., Yunhan Chu, and Hung-mao Tien (eds) (1997). *Consolidating the Third Wave Democracies*, Baltimore, Maryland: Johns Hopkins University Press.

—— (2000). "Is Pakistan the (Reverse) Wave of the Future?" *Journal of Democracy*, vol. 11, no. 3, July, pp. 91–106.

Director of Information (1960). *Is Trust Vindicated? The Chronicle of a Trust, Striving and Triumph, Being an Account of the Accomplishments of the Government of the Union of Burma: November 1, 1958–February 6, 1960*. Rangoon.

Dreifus, C. (1996). "The Passion of Suu Kyi," *New York Times Magazine*, interview with Aung San Suu Kyi, 7 January 1996, pp. 31–37.

Easton, D. (1965a). *A System Analysis of Political Life*, New York: John Wiley and Sons.

—— (1965b). *A Framework for Political Analysis*, Englewood Cliffs: Prentice Hall.

Edelman, M. (1964). *The Symbolic Uses of Politics*, Urbana, Illinois: University of Illinois Press.

—— (1971). *Politics as Symbolic Action: Mass Arousal and Quiescence*, Monograph Series, Institute for Research on Poverty, Chicago: Markham Publishing.

Emmerson, D. K. (1995). "Singapore and the Asian Values Debate," *Journal of Democracy*, vol. 6, no. 4, October, pp. 95–105.

Englehart, N. (2000). "Rights and Culture in the Asian Values Argument: The Rise and Fall of Confucian Ethics in Singapore," *Human Rights Quarterly*, vol. 22, no. 2, May, pp. 548–568.

Evans, P., Rueschemeyer, D., and Skocpol, T. (1985). *Bringing the State Back In*, Cambridge, UK: Cambridge University Press.

—— (1995). In Kohli, A., Evans, P., Katzenstein, P., Przeworski, A., Hoeber Rudolph, S., Scott, J. C., and Skocpol, T. (1995), "The Role of Theory in Comparative Politics: A Symposium," *World Politics*, vol. 48, no. 1, October, pp. 1–49.

Fairclough, G. (1996a). "Enter at Own Risk," *Far Eastern Economic Review*, vol. 159, no. 33, 15 August 1996, pp. 62–65.

—— (1996b). "Troubled Waters: International Oil Firms in Middle of Burma Battle," *Far Eastern Economic Review*, vol. 159, no. 33, 15 August 1996, p. 66.

—— (1996c). "Good Connections: Firms Linked to Junta Draw Lion's Share of Business," *Far Eastern Economic Review*, vol. 159, no. 33, 15 August 1996, pp. 66–67.

Freedom House (2004). *Freedom in the World 2004: The Annual Survey of Political Rights and Civil Liberties*, New York, New York. Online. Available at: www.freedomhouse.org/research/freeworld/2004/methodology.htm (accessed 15 May 2005).

—— (2004). *Freedom in the World 2004: The Annual Survey of Political Rights and Civil Liberties*, Lanham: Rowman and Littlefield.

—— (2005). *Freedom in the World 2005: Table of Independent Countries Comparative Measures of Freedom*, New York, New York. Online. Available at: reedomhouse.org/research/freeworld/2005/table2005.pdf (accessed 8 May 2005).

French, H. (1996). "Africa Looks East for a New Model," *New York Times*, New York, 4 February 1996.

Fukuyama, F. (1989). "The End of History?" *The National Interest*, no. 16, Summer, pp. 3–18.

—— (1992a). "Asia's Soft-Authoritarian Alternative," *New Perspectives Quarterly*, vol. 9, no. 2, Spring, pp. 60–61.

—— (1992b). *The End of History and the Last Man*, New York: Avon Books.

—— (1995). "The Primacy of Culture," *Journal of Democracy*, vol. 6, no. 1, pp. 7–14.

—— (1998). "Asian Values and the Asian Crisis," *Commentary*, vol. 105, no. 2, February, pp. 23–27.

—— (1999). "Second Thoughts, The Last Man in a Bottle," *The National Interest*, 56, Summer, pp. 16–33.

—— (2001). "Social Capital, Civil Society and Development," *Third World Quarterly*, vol. 22, no. 1, pp. 7–20.

—— (2002a). "Has History Restarted Since September 11?" The Nineteenth Annual John Bonython Lecture, Melbourne, 8 August. Online. Available at: www.cis.org.au/events/jbl/jbl02.htm.

—— (2002b). "How to Regulate Science," *The Public Interest*, no. 146, Winter, pp. 3–22.

—— (2002c). *Our Posthuman Future*, New York: Farrar, Straus and Giroux.

—— (2004). *State-Building: Governance and World Order in the 21st Century*, Ithaca: Cornell University Press.

—— (2005). "The End of History Fifteen Years Later," The John M. Olin Center for Inquiry into the Theory and Practice of Democracy, University of Chicago, 2004–2005 Lecture Series, 8 February 2005.

Geddes, B. (1991). "Paradigms and Sand Castles in the Comparative Politics of Developing Areas," in Crotty, W. (ed.), *Political Science: Looking to the Future. Volume Two: Comparative Politics, Policy, and International Relations*, Evanston: Northwestern University Press.

Geertz, C. (1973). *The Interpretation of Cultures: Selected Essays*, New York: Basic Books.

Glenn, G. (1992). "Cyrus' Corruption of Aristocracy," in Murley, J., Stone, R., and Braithwaite, W. (eds), *Law and Philosophy: The Practice of Theory. Essays in Honor of George Anastaplo*, Athens, Ohio: Ohio University Press.

Goh Chok Tong (1993). "Drop the Stick, Grow with the Chinese," *International Herald Tribune*, 21 May 1993. Online. Available at: www.iht.com/articles/1993/05/21/edgoh.php (accessed 15 May 2005).

—— (1994). "Moral Values: The Foundation of a Vibrant State," National Day rally address given on 21 August 1994, Singapore, published as "Social Values, Singapore Style," *Current History*, vol. 93, December, pp. 417–422.

Gomez, J. (1999). "Politics and Law in Singapore," in Tan, Kevin Y. L. (ed.), *The Singapore Legal System*, second edition, Singapore: Singapore University Press.

Gordon, U. (2000). "Machiavelli's Tiger: Lee Kuan Yew and Singapore's Authoritarian Regime," *Viewpoint*, March, Israel: Tel-Aviv University, Department of Political Science. Online. Available at: www.singapore-window.org/sw00/000614ug.htm (accessed 15 May 2005).

Gourevitch, V. and Roth M. (eds) (1991). *On Tyranny*, New York: The Free Press.

Gravers, M. (1999). *Nationalism as Political Paranoia in Burma*, London: Curzon Press.

H.H. The XIV Dalai Lama of Tibet (1993). "Human Rights and Universal Responsibility," in United Nations, *United Nations World Conference on Human Rights*, Vienna, Austria. New York: United Nations.

Hamilton, A. (1998). "A Man Who Never Gave In: The nation's last political prisoner speaks out," *Asiaweek*, 11 December. Online. Available at: www.asiaweek.com/asiaweek/98/1211/nat5.html (accessed 15 May 2005).

Han Fook Kwang, Fernandez, W., and Sumiko Tan (1998). *Lee Kuan Yew: The Man And His Ideas*, Singapore: The Straits Times Press, Times Editions.

Hegel, George Wilhelm Friedrich. *The Philosophy of History*, trans. J. Sibree, C. J. Friedrich, and Charles Hegel (1956), New York: Dover.

Hewison, K. (1997). "Power, Opposition and Democratisation," in Hewison, K. (ed.), *Political Change in Thailand*, London: Routledge.

Hobbes, Thomas. *Leviathan*, Tuck, R. (ed.) (1996). Revised student edition, Cambridge, UK: Cambridge University Press.

Houtman, G. (1999). *Mental Culture in Burmese Crisis Politics: Aung San Suu Kyi and the National League for Democracy*, Monograph Series no. 33, Tokyo: Institute for the Study of Languages and Cultures of Asia and Africa, Tokyo University of Foreign Studies.

Hsu Cho-Yun (1984). "Discussion with Members of Parliament," in Tu Wei-Ming, *Confucian Ethics Today*, Curriculum Development Institute of Singapore, Singapore: Federal Publications.

Hume, David. "Dialogues Concerning Natural Religion," in Flew, A. (ed.) (2000), *David Hume: Writings on Religion*, Peru, Illinois: Open Court.

Huntington, S. (1965). "Political Development and Political Decay," *World Politics*, vol. 17, no. 3, April, pp. 386–430.

—— (1968). *Political Order in Changing Societies*, New Haven: Yale University Press.

—— (1971). "The Change to Change: Modernization, Development and Politics," *Comparative Politics*, vol. 3, no. 3, April, pp. 283–322.

—— (1991). *The Third Wave: Democratization in the Late Twentieth Century*, Norman: University of Oklahoma Press.

—— (1993). "The Clash of Civilizations?" *Foreign Affairs*, vol. 72, no. 3, Summer, pp. 22–49.

—— (1995). "Reforming Civil–Military Relations," *Journal of Democracy*, vol. 6, no. 4, October, pp. 9–17.

—— (1996). *The Clash of Civilizations and the Remaking of World Order*, New York: Simon and Schuster.

Huxley, T. (2002). "Singapore in 2001," *Asian Survey*, vol. 42, no. 1, Jan.–Feb., pp. 156–164.

Ibrahim, Anwar (1996). *The Asian Renaissance*, Singapore: Times Books International.

Inglehart, R. (1988). "The Renaissance of Political Culture," *American Political Science Review*, vol. 82, no. 4, pp. 1203–1230.

—— (1990). *Culture Shift in Advanced Industrial Society*, Princeton, New Jersey: Princeton University Press.

Internal Security Act (1963). Singapore. Online. Available at: http://agcvldb4.agc.gov.sg/ (accessed 15 May 2005).

International Monetary Fund (2005). *World Economic Outlook: Globalization and External Imbalances*, World Economic and Financial Surveys, Washington, D.C., April 2005. Online. Available at: www.imf.org/external/pubs/ft/weo/2005/01/index.htm (accessed 9 May 2005).

Jelsma, M., Kramer, T., and Vervest, P. (eds) (2003). *Drugs and Conflict in Burma (Myanmar): Dilemmas for Policy Responses*, Debate Papers, December, No. 9, Amsterdam: Transnational Institute.

——— (eds) (2005). *Trouble in the Triangle: Opium and Conflict in Burma*, Chiang Mai: Silkworm Books.

Jones, E. (1994). "Asia's Fate, A Response to the Singapore School," *The National Interest*, vol. 35, Spring, pp. 18–28.

Jones, S. (1996). "Regional Institutions for Protecting Human Rights in Asia," *Australian Journal of International Affairs*, vol. 50, no. 3, pp. 269–277.

Kagan, R. (2003). *Of Paradise and Power: America vs. Europe in the New World Order*, New York: Knopf.

Kane, J. (2001). *The Politics of Moral Capital*, New York: Cambridge University Press.

Kean, L. and Bernstein, D. (1998), "Burma–Singapore Axis: Globalizing the Heroin Trade", *CAQ Magazine (CovertAction Quarterly)*, no. 64, Spring. Online. Available at: www.singapore-window.org/804caq9.htm (accessed 15 May 2005).

Kelly, D. and Reid, A. (eds) (1998). *Asian Freedoms*. Cambridge: Cambridge University Press.

Khong, Cho Oon (1995). "Singapore: Political Legitimacy through Managing Conformity," in Alagappa, M. (ed.), *Political Legitimacy in Southeast Asia: The Quest for Moral Authority*, Stanford, California: Stanford University Press, pp. 108–135.

Kim Dae Jung (1994). "Is Culture Destiny? The Myth of Asia's Anti-Democratic Values," *Foreign Affairs*, vol. 73, no. 6, Nov.–Dec., pp. 189–194.

Kong, L. (2002). "In Search of Permanent Homes: Singapore's House Churches and the Politics of Space," *Urban Studies*, vol. 39, no. 9, pp. 1573–1586.

Kung, H. and Kuschel, K. J. (eds.) (1993). *A Global Ethic, The Declaration of the Parliament of the World's Religions*, New York: Continuum.

Kurlantzick, J. (2002). "Can Burma Reform?" *Foreign Affairs*, vol. 81, no. 6, Nov.–Dec., pp. 134–135.

Kyaw Yin Hlaing (2005). "Myanmar in 2004: Another Year of Uncertainty," *Asian Survey*, vol. 45, no. 1, Jan.–Feb., pp. 174–179.

Leach, E. R. (1959). "Hydraulic Society in Ceylon," *Past and Present*, vol. 15, 2–25.

——— (1965). *Political Systems of Highland Burma: A Study of Kachin Social Structure*, Boston: Beacon Press.

Lee Hsien Loong (1998). "Why we need National Education," *Straits Times*, 20 May 1998, p. 29.

Lee Kuan Yew. (1980). "History is Not Made the Way it is Written," in *Speeches: A Bimonthly Selection of Ministerial Speeches*, Singapore: Information Division, Ministry of Culture, vol. 3, no. 8, pp. 3–12.

——— "Address to the Singapore Press Club," *Reuters*, 8 June 1996; also in *New Light of Myanmar*, Rangoon, 15 June 1996.

——— *Straits Times*, Singapore, 12 June 1996.

——— "Myanmar opposition must face reality: SM Lee," *New Light of Myanmar*, Rangoon, 19 June 1996, p. 3.

——— (1998). *The Singapore Story: Memoirs of Lee Kuan Yew*, Singapore: Prentice Hall.

——— *Time*, 16 March 1998.

——— "Asia Will Rise Again," *Forbes*, 23 March 1998.

——— (2000). *From Third World to First, The Singapore Story: 1965–2000*, New York: HarperCollins.

Levitsky, S. and Way, L. A. (2002). "The Rise of Competitive Authoritarianism," *Journal of Democracy*, vol. 13, no. 2, April, pp. 51–65.

Lichbach, M. and Zuckerman, A. (1998). *Comparative Politics: Rationality, Culture, and Structure*, Cambridge, UK: Cambridge University Press.

Liddel and Scott (1940), *A Greek–English Lexicon*, Oxford: Clarendon Press; The Perseus Digital Library, Tufts University. Online. Available at: www.perseus. tufts.edu (accessed 15 May 2005).

Lieberman, V. (1984). *Burmese Administrative Cycles: Anarchy and Conquest, c. 1580–1760*, New Jersey: Princeton University Press.

Lilla, M. (2002). "The New Age of Tyranny," *The New York Review of Books*, vol. 49, no. 16, 24 October, pp. 28–29.

Lincoln, Abraham. "To Erastus Corning and Others," 12 June 1863, in Fehrenbacher, D. (ed.) (1989), *Lincoln, Speeches and Writings 1859–1865*, New York: The Library of America, pp. 454–463.

Lindemans, M. (ed.). *Encyclopedia Mythica*. Online. Available at: www.pantheon.org (accessed 15 May 2005).

Lintner, B. (1989). *Outrage: Burma's Struggle for Democracy*, Hong Kong: Review Publishing Co.

Lipset, S. M. (1959). *Political Man: The Social Basis of Politics*, New York: Doubleday Anchor.

Logartha, M. (2004). "Oh behave, Singapore: It's now okay to be naughty in the Lion City – the government approves," *Business Traveller Magazine*, March. Online. Available at: www.yawningbread.org/apdx_2004/imp-140.htm (accessed 15 May 2005).

Loh Kah Seng (1998). "Within the Singapore Story: The Use and Narrative of History in Singapore," *Crossroads*, vol. 12, no. 2, pp. 1–21.

Lord, C. (1981). "The Intention of Aristotle's Rhetoric," *Hermes*, 109, pp. 326–339, reprinted in E. A. Schiappa (ed.) (1994), *Landmark Essays on Classical Greek Rhetoric*, Davis, California: Hemagoras Press.

—— (1991). "Aristotle's Anthropology," in Lord, C. and O'Connor, D. K. (eds), *Essays on the Foundations of Aristotelian Political Science*, Berkeley: University of California Press, pp. 49–73.

—— (2003). *The Modern Prince: What Leaders Need to Know Now*, New Haven: Yale University Press.

Ludwig, A. (2002). *King of the Mountain: The Nature of Political Leadership*, Lexington: The University of Kentucky Press.

Lydgate, C. (2003). *Lee's Law: How Singapore Crushes Dissent*, Melbourne: Scribe Publications.

McCarthy, S. (2000). "Ten Years of Chaos in Burma: Foreign Investment and Economic Liberalization under the SLORC–SPDC, 1988–1998," *Pacific Affairs*, vol. 73, no. 2, Summer, pp. 233–262.

Machiavelli, Niccolo. *Discourses on Livy*, trans. Harvey C. Mansfield and Nathan Tarcov (1996), Chicago: University of Chicago Press.

—— *The Prince*, trans. Leo Paul S. de Alvarez (1980). Dallas: University of Dallas Press.

MacLean, K. (2004). "Reconfiguring the Debate on Engagement: Burmese Exiles and the Changing Politics of Aid," *Critical Asian Studies*, vol. 36, no. 3, pp. 323–354.

Manikas, P. and Jennings, K. (2001). *The Political Process and the 2001 Parliamentary Elections in Singapore*, Washington, D.C.: National Democratic Institute for International Affairs. Online. Available at: www.accessdemocracy.org/library/ 1326_sgp_2001parlelect.pdf (accessed 15 May 2005).

Mason, M. (1998). "Foreign Direct Investment in Burma," in Rotberg, R. (ed.), *Burma, Prospects for a Democratic Future*, Washington, D.C.: Brookings Institution Press, pp. 209–232.

Matthews, B. (1999). "Burma/Myanmar: Government, *La Mode* – From SLORC to SPDC: A Change of Public Dress-Up and Manner?" *The Round Table*, No. 349, pp. 77–96.

Maung Maung (ed.) (1962). *Aung San of Burma*, The Hague, The Netherlands: Martinus Nijhoff.

Maung Maung Gyi (1983). *Burmese Political Values*, New York: Praeger.

Mauzy, D. (1997). "The Human Rights and 'Asian Values' Debate in Southeast Asia: Trying to Classify the Key Issues," *The Pacific Review*, vol. 10, no. 2, pp. 210–236.

Mendelson, E. M. (1975). *Sangha and State in Burma: A Study of Monastic Sectarianism and Leadership*, Ithaca, New York: Cornell University Press.

Milner, A. (1999). "What's Happened to Asian Values?" in Goodman, D. and Segal, G. (eds), *Beyond the Asia Crisis*, London: Routledge. Online. Available at: www.anu.edu.au/asianstudies/values.html (accessed 15 May 2005).

Moncrief, J. (2002). "Shan Struggle Set to Continue," *The Irrawaddy*, vol. 10, no. 2, Feb.–Mar. Online. Available at: www.irrawaddy.org/database/2002/vol10.2/cover5.html (accessed 15 May 2005).

Moreau, R. (2001). "Transplanted Trouble: The Burmese Drug Syndicates," *Newsweek International*, 16 July, p. 43.

Morsink, J. (1999). *The Universal Declaration of Human Rights: Origins, Drafting, and Intent*, Philadelphia: University of Pennsylvania Press.

Mutalib. H. (2002). "The Socio-economic Dimension in Singapore's Quest for Security and Stability," *Pacific Affairs*, vol. 75, no. 1, Spring, pp. 39–56.

Mya Maung (1992). *Totalitarianism in Burma: Prospects for Economic Development*, New York: Paragon House.

—— (1997). "Burma's Economic Performance under Military Rule: An Assessment," *Asian Survey*, vol. 37, no. 6, pp. 503–524.

Mya Sein (1962). "Into the Mainstream of History," in Maung Maung (ed.), *Aung San of Burma*, The Hague, The Netherlands: Martinus Nijhoff.

Myanmar Investment Commission (1996). *Report on Direct Foreign Investments*, February, Rangoon.

Mydans, S. (2002). "A Coup Plot Gone Awry, or a Burmese Comic Opera?" *New York Times*, 8 July, New York.

Myint Zan (1997). "Position of Power and Notions of Empowerment: Comparing the Views of Lee Kuan Yew and Aung San Suu Kyi on Human Rights and Governance," *Newcastle Law Review*, vol. 2, no. 2, pp. 49–69.

Nadel, A. (1997). "Singapore's Voice of Reason," *South China Morning Post*, 1 March 1997.

Naw, A. (2001). *Aung San and the Struggle for Burmese Independence*, Bangkok: Silkworm Books.

O'Donnell, Guillermo (1973). *Modernization and Bureaucratic Authoritarianism*, Berkeley: University of California, Institute of International Studies.

Oakeshott, M. (1962). "Rationalism in Politics," *Rationalism in Politics and Other Essays*, New York: Basic Books.

Packenham, R. (1992). *The Dependency Movement: Scholarship and Politics in Development Studies*, Cambridge, Massachusetts: Harvard University Press.

Pandita, Sayadaw U. (1993). *In This Very Life: The Liberation Teachings of the Buddha*, second edition, Boston: Wisdom Publications.

Pe Maung Tin and Luce, G. H. (trans.) (1923). *The Glass Palace Chronicle of the*

Kings of Burma, Oxford: Oxford University Press, reprinted in (1960), Rangoon: Burma Research Society.

Philp, J. and Mercer, D. (2002). "Politicised Pagodas and Veiled Resistance: Contested Urban Space in Burma," *Urban Studies*, vol. 39, no. 9, pp. 1587–1610.

Plato. *The Republic*, trans. Allan Bloom (1968), New York: Basic Books.

—— *Theaetetus*, trans. John McDowell (1973), Oxford: Clarendon Press.

Przeworski, A. (1992). *Democracy and the Market: Political and Economic Reforms in Eastern Europe and Latin America (Studies in Rationality and Social Change)*, Cambridge, UK: Cambridge University Press.

—— and Limongi, F. (1997). "Modernization: Theories and Facts," *World Politics*, vol. 49, no. 2, January, pp. 155–183.

Putnam, R. (1993). *Making Democracy Work*, New Jersey: Princeton University Press.

—— (1995). "Bowling Alone: America's Declining Social Capital," *Journal of Democracy*, vol. 6, no. 1, January, pp. 65–78.

—— (2000). *Bowling Alone*, New York: Touchstone.

Pye, L. (1959). *The Spirit of Burmese Politics: A Preliminary Survey of a Politics of Fear and Charisma*, Political Development paper C/59–11, Center for International Studies, Massachusetts Institute of Technology, Cambridge, Massachusetts.

—— (1962). *Politics, Personality, and Nation Building: Burma's Search for Identity*, Cambridge, Massachusetts: Massachusetts Institute of Technology.

—— (1975). *Political Science and Area Studies, Rivals or Partners?* Bloomington: Indiana University Press.

—— (1985). *Asian Power and Politics: The Cultural Dimensions of Authority*, Cambridge, Massachusetts: Harvard University Press.

—— (2001). "Civility, Social Capital and Civil Society: Three Powerful Concepts for Explaining Asia," in Rotberg, R. (ed.), *Patterns of Social Capital, Stability and Change in Historical Perspective*, Cambridge, UK: Cambridge University Press, pp. 375–394.

—— and Verba, S. (1966). *Political Culture and Political Development*, New Jersey: Princeton University Press.

Reid, A. (1983). "Introduction: Slavery and Bondage in Southeast Asian History," in Reid, A. (ed.), *Slavery, Bondage and Dependency in Southeast Asia*, New York: St. Martin's Press, pp. 1–43.

Remmer, K. (1997). "Theoretical Decay and Theoretical Development: The Resurgence of Institutional Analysis," *World Politics*, vol. 50, October, pp. 34–61.

Reynolds, F. (1972). "The Two Wheels of Dhamma: A Study of Early Buddhism," in Obeyesekere, G., Reynolds, F., and Smith, B. (eds), *The Two Wheels of Dhamma: Essays on the Theravada Tradition in India and Ceylon*, AAR Studies in Religion, no. 3, Chambersburg, Pennsylvania: American Academy of Religion, pp. 6–30.

Richardson, M. (2001). "Proposed Electoral Changes are Rejected: Singaporean Leaders Dismiss Reform Calls," *International Herald Tribune*, 13 November. Online. Available at: www.iht.com/articles/2001/11/13/a6_24.php (accessed 15 May 2005).

Rodan, G. (ed.) (1993). *Singapore Changes Guard: Social, Political, and Economic Directions in the 1990's*, Melbourne: Longman Cheshire.

—— (1993). "Preserving the One-Party State in Contemporary Singapore," in Kevin Hewison, Richard Robison, and Garry Rodan (eds), *Southeast Asia in the 1990s: Authoritarianism, Democracy and Capitalism*, St. Leonard, NSW: Allen and Unwin.

—— (2005). "Singapore in 2004: Long-Awaited Leadership Transition," *Asian Survey*, vol. 45, no.1, Jan.–Feb., pp. 140–145.

Rostow, W. W. (1960). *The Stages of Economic Growth*, New York: Cambridge University Press.

Rotberg, R. (ed.) (1998). *Burma, Prospects for a Democratic Future*, Washington, D.C.: Brookings Institution Press.

—— (ed.) (2001). *Patterns of Social Capital, Stability and Change in Historical Perspective*, Cambridge, UK: Cambridge University Press.

Roy, D. (1994). "Singapore, China, and the 'Soft Authoritarian' Challenge," *Asian Survey*, vol. 34, no. 3, pp. 231–242.

Rueschemeyer, D., Stephens, E., and Stephens, J. (1992). *Capitalist Development and Democracy*, Chicago: University of Chicago Press.

Safire, W. (2002). "Bloomberg News Humbled," *New York Times*, 29 August 2002.

Sahlins, M. (1983). "Other Times, Other Places: The Anthropology of Today," *American Anthropologist*, vol. 85, no. 3, September, pp. 517–544.

Sarkisyanz, E. (1965). *Buddhist Backgrounds of the Burmese Revolution*, The Hague: Martinus Nijhoff.

Saywell, T. and Plott, D. (2002). "Re-Imagining Singapore," *Far Eastern Economic Review*, vol. 165, no. 27, 11 July 2002, pp. 44–48.

Schedler, A. (2002). "The Menu of Manipulation," *Journal of Democracy*, vol. 13, no. 2, April, pp. 36–50.

Schiappa, E. A. (ed.) (1994). *Landmark Essays on Classical Greek Rhetoric*, Davis, California: Hemagoras Press.

Schumacher, E. F. (1974). *Small is Beautiful*, London: Sphere Books, Abacus edition.

Scott, J. C. (1985). *Weapons of the Weak: Everyday Forms of Peasant Resistance*, New Haven, Connecticut: Yale University Press.

—— (1990). *Domination and the Arts of Resistance: Hidden Transcripts*, New Haven, Connecticut: Yale University Press.

—— (1998a). "Freedom and Freehold: Space, People and State Simplification in Southeast Asia," in Kelly, D. and Reid, A. (eds), *Asian Freedoms*, Cambridge, UK: Cambridge University Press, pp. 37–64.

—— (1998b). *Seeing Like a State*, New Haven, Connecticut: Yale University Press.

Seekins, D. (1999). "The North Wind and the Sun: Japan's Response to the Political Crisis in Burma, 1988–1998," *Journal of Burma Studies*, vol. 4, pp. 1–34.

—— (2002). *The Disorder in Order: The Army State in Burma Since 1962*, Bangkok: White Lotus Press.

Selth, A. (1996). *Transforming the Tatmadaw: The Burmese Armed Forces Since 1988*, Strategic and Defence Studies Centre, Australian National University, Canberra.

—— (1997a). *Burma's Intelligence Apparatus*, Working Paper 308, Strategic and Defence Studies Centre, Australian National University, Canberra.

—— (1997b). *Burma's Defence Expenditure and Arms Industries*, Working Paper 309, Strategic and Defence Studies Centre, Australian National University, Canberra.

—— (1997c). *The Burma Navy*, Working Paper 313, Strategic and Defence Studies Centre, Australian National University, Canberra.

—— (1997d). *The Burma Air Force*, Working Paper 315, Strategic and Defence Studies Centre, Australian National University, Canberra.

—— (1998). "The Armed Forces and Military Rule in Burma," in Rotberg, R. (ed.), *Burma, Prospects for a Democratic Future*, Washington, D.C.: Brookings Institution Press, pp. 87–108.

—— (1999). *Burma and Weapons of Mass Destruction*, Working Paper 334, Strategic and Defence Studies Centre, Australian National University, Canberra.

—— (2000). *Burma's Secret Military Partners*, Strategic and Defence Studies Centre, and Research School of Pacific and Asian Studies, Australian National University, Canberra.

—— (2002). *Burma's Armed Forces: Power Without Glory*, Norwalk, Connecticut: East-Bridge.

Sen, A. (1997). "Human Rights and Asian Values," Sixteenth Morgenthau Memorial Lecture on Ethics and Foreign Policy, Carnegie Council on Ethics and International Affairs, New York. Also in *The New Republic*, 14–21 July 1997.

—— (1999). "Democracy as a Universal Value," *Journal of Democracy*, vol. 10, no. 3, July, pp. 3–17.

Silverstein, J. (ed.) (1993). *The Political Legacy of Aung San*, revised edition, Southeast Asia Program Series, 11, Ithaca, New York: Cornell University Press.

—— (1998a). "The Evolution and Salience of Burma's National Political Culture," in Rotberg, R. (ed.), *Burma, Prospects for a Democratic Future*, Washington, D.C.: Brookings Institution Press, pp. 11–32.

—— (1998b). "The Idea of Freedom in Burma and the Political Thought of Daw Aung San Suu Kyi," in Kelly, D. and Reid, A. (eds), *Asian Freedoms*, Cambridge, UK: Cambridge University Press, pp. 187–204.

Singapore Government (2002). "Singapore Government Press Statement on Further Arrests under the Internal Security Act," *Press Release*, 19 September 2002, Singapore: Media Relations Division, Ministry of Information, Ministry of Home Affairs.

Singh, Daljit and Arasu, V. T. (eds) (1984). *Singapore: An Illustrated History 1941–1984*, Singapore: Ministry of Culture, Information Division.

SLORC (1996). "Law No. 5/96" (7 June), in *New Light of Myanmar*, Rangoon, 8 June 1996.

Smith, Adam. *An Inquiry into the Nature and Causes of the Wealth of Nations*, in R. H. Campbell and A. S. Skinner (eds) (1981), Indianapolis: Liberty Fund.

—— *The Theory of Moral Sentiments*, in D. D. Raphael and A. L. Macfie (eds) (1984), Indianapolis: Liberty Fund.

Smith, D. (1965). *Religion and Politics in Burma*, New Jersey: Princeton University Press.

Smith, M. (1993). *Burma, Insurgency and the Politics of Ethnicity*, Oxford: Zed Books.

—— (2001). "Burmese Politics After 1988: An Era of New and Uncertain Change," in Taylor, R. (ed.), *Burma: Political Economy under Military Rule*, New York: Palgrave.

Smith, P. and Browning, P. (1983). "The Citizen Soldier: Singapore Stresses Security as an Arm of Nation Building," *Far Eastern Economic Review*, vol. 119, no. 2, 13 January, pp. 26–29.

Smith, W. (ed.) (1873). *A Dictionary of Greek and Roman Biography and Mythology*. London: John Murray, reprinted in William Smith and Chris Stray (eds) (2005), New York: Palgrave Macmillan.

South, A. (2004). "Political Transition in Myanmar: A New Model for Democratization," *Contemporary Southeast Asia*, vol. 26, no. 2, p. 254.

Spiro, M. (1967). *Burmese Supernaturalism*, Institute for the Study of Human Issues, Philadelphia: Prentice-Hall.

—— (1982). *Buddhism and Society: A Great Tradition and Its Burmese Vicissitudes*, Berkeley: University of California Press.

Steinberg, D. (1997). "The Union Solidarity and Development Association," *Burma Debate*, vol. 4, no. 1, Jan.–Feb.

—— (2001a). "Burma Has Done Nothing to Deserve Japan's Aid Reward," *International Herald Tribune*, 28 April. Online. Available at: www.iht.com/articles/2001/04/28/edstein_ed2_.php (accessed 15 May 2005).

—— (2001b). *Burma: The State of Myanmar*, Washington, D.C.: Georgetown University Press.

Strauss, L. (1953). *Natural Right and History*, Chicago: University of Chicago Press.

—— (1963). "On Tyranny," reprinted in Gourevitch, V. and Roth, M. (eds) (1991), *On Tyranny*, New York: The Free Press.

—— (1964). *The City and Man*, Chicago: University of Chicago Press.

—— (1988). "Restatement on Xenophon's *Hiero*," in *What is Political Philosophy? And Other Studies*, Chicago: University of Chicago Press, pp. 95–133.

Tan, Kevin Y. L. (ed.) (1999). *The Singapore Legal System*, second edition, Singapore: Singapore University Press

Tan Tai Yong (2001). "Singapore: Civil–Military Fusion," in Alagappa, M. (ed.), *Coercion and Governance: The Declining Role of the Military in Asia*, Stanford, California: Stanford University Press, pp. 276–293.

Tang Liang Hong (1998). "Legal Terrorism in Singapore." Online. Available at: members.ozemail.com.au/-tangtalk/legalter.html (accessed 15 May 2005).

Taylor, R. (1987). *The State in Burma*, Honolulu: University of Hawaii Press.

—— (1990). "Burmese army and the 'national interest,'" *Bangkok Post*, Bangkok, 16 June 1990, also in *Working People's Daily*, Rangoon, 20 June 1990, p. 7.

—— (ed.). (2001). *Burma: Political Economy under Military Rule*, New York: Palgrave.

Teo Soh Lung (1998). "Introduction: Petition to Repeal the Internal Security Act," 6 December. Online. Available at: www.sfdonline.org/sfd/Link%20Pages/Link%20Folders/Human%20Rights/repealisa.html (accessed 15 May 2005).

Thein Swe, Bo (ed.) (1951). *Bogyoke Aung San Attopatt* (Biography of Aung San), Rangoon: Amyotha Pon-ngeik-taik.

Tint Lwin (1990). "The Buddha's Instruction in Kingly Duties," *Working People's Daily*, Rangoon, 24 June 1990, p. 7.

Tosh, J. (1991). *The Pursuit of History*, second edition, New York: Longman.

Trager, F. (1963). "The Failure of U Nu and the Return of the Armed Forces in Burma," *Review of Politics*, vol. 25, no. 3, July, pp. 309–328.

Tu Wei-Ming (ed.) (1984). *Confucian Ethics Today: The Singapore Challenge*, Curriculum Development Institute of Singapore, Singapore: Federal Publications.

—— (ed.) (1991). *The Triadic Chord: Confucian Ethics, Industrial East Asia, and Max Weber: Proceedings of the 1987 Singapore Conference on Confucian Ethics and the Modernization of Industrial East Asia*, Singapore: Institute of East Asian Philosophies, National University of Singapore.

—— (1997). "Epilogue: Human Rights as a Confucian Moral Discourse," in De Bary, Wm. T. and Tu Weiming (eds), *Confucianism and Human Rights*, New York: Columbia University Press, pp. 297–307.

Tun Pe (1949). *Sun Over Burma*, Rangoon: Raskia Ranjani Press.

Twiss, S. (1997). "A Constructive Framework for Discussing Confucianism and Human Rights," in De Bary, Wm. T. and Tu Weiming (eds), *Confucianism and Human Rights*, New York: Columbia University Press, pp. 27–53.

United Nations (1993a). "United Nations World Conference on Human Rights,

Regional Meeting for Asia," Bangkok, 29 March–2 April 1993, New York: United Nations.

—— (1993b). "United Nations World Conference on Human Rights," Vienna, Austria, 1993, New York: United Nations.

—— (1948). *Universal Declaration of Human Rights*, New York: United Nations.

United Nations Office on Crime and Drugs (UNODC) (2005). *Myanmar Opium Survey 2005*, New York: United Nations, November.

U.S. Department of Commerce (1995). *Country Commercial Guides–Burma*, August, Washington, D.C.

U.S. Department of State, Bureau of East Asian and Pacific Affairs (2005). *Singapore Profile*, Washington, D.C., April. Online. Available at: www.state.gov/r/pa/ei/bgn/2798.htm (accessed 8 May 2005).

Vatikiotis, M., Plott, D., and Saywell, T. (2002). "Building a Whole New Mindset," Interview: Lee Hsien Loong, *Far Eastern Economic Review*, vol. 165, no. 27, 11 July, pp. 49–50.

Von der Mehden, F. (1963). *Religion and Nationalism in Southeast Asia*, Madison: University of Wisconsin Press.

Wade, N. (2002). "A Dim View of a 'Posthuman Future,'" *New York Times*, New York, 2 April.

Walzer, M. (1980). *Radical Principles: Reflections of an Unreconstructed Democrat*, New York: Basic Books.

Wiarda, H. J. (ed.) (1991). "Comparative Politics: Past and Present," *New Directions in Comparative Politics*, Boulder: Westview Press.

Wilson, E. O. (1999). "Responses to Fukuyama," *The National Interest*, 56, Summer, pp. 35–37.

Winborne, W. (2001). "Modernization and Modernity: Thomas Hobbes, Adam Smith, and Political Development," unpublished doctoral dissertation, Northern Illinois University.

Wise, D. (ed.) (1997). "Burma," *Asia 1997 Yearbook*, Hong Kong: Far Eastern Economic Review, pp. 130–137.

Won Z. Yoon (1973). *Japan's Scheme for the Liberation of Burma: The Role of the Minami kikan and the Thirty Comrades*, Center for International Studies, Papers in International Studies Southeast Asia Series, 27, Athens, Ohio: Ohio University Press.

Xenophon. *Cyropaedia*, trans. Walter Miller (1989). Cambridge, Massachusetts: Harvard University Press, Loeb.

—— *Hiero* or *Tyrannicus*, trans. Marvin Kendrick in Strauss, L. (1963), "On Tyranny," reprinted in Gourevitch, V. and Roth, M. (eds) (1991), *On Tyranny*, New York: The Free Press.

—— *Memorabilia*, trans. E. C. Marchant (1992). Cambridge, Massachusetts: Harvard University Press, Loeb.

Yawnghwe, Chao-Tzang (1998). *Burma, the Heroin Trade, and Canada*, National Consultative Conference on Burma, Ottawa, April.

—— (2003). "Shan State Politics: The Opium-Heroin Factor," Paper presented at the Conference *Drugs and Conflict in Burma (Myanmar)*, Transnational Institute, Amsterdam, 13–16 December.

Zakaria, F. (1994). "Culture is Destiny, A Conversation with Lee Kuan Yew," *Foreign Affairs*, vol. 73, no. 2, Mar.–Apr., pp. 109–126.

—— (1997). "The Rise of Illiberal Democracy," *Foreign Affairs*, vol. 76, no. 6, 22–43.

—— (2003). *The Future of Freedom: Illiberal Democracy at Home and Abroad*, New York: Norton.

Zaobao L. (ed.) (1991). *Lee Kuan Yew on China and Hong Kong after Tiananmen*, Singapore: Lianhe Zaobao.

—— (1995). *Lee Kuan Yew*, Singapore: Sony, CD-ROM.

Zarny Win (2001). "More NLD Offices Allowed to Re-open," *Irrawaddy*, 23 October. Online. Available at: www.irrawaddy.org/aviewer.asp?a=3453&z=21 (accessed 15 May 2005).

Media sources

The Age. "Squeaky-clean Singapore eases up on gum control," 21 November 2002, Melbourne.

Agence France Press. "Talks at Standstill as Restrictions on NLD," 18 & 22 November 2001, in *Burma News Update*, no. 147, 27 November 2001. Online. Available at: www.burmaproject.org/burmanewsupdate/index147.html (accessed 15 May 2005).

—— "Singapore to raise public awareness about Internal Security Act," 12 April 2002. Online. Available at: www.singapore-window.org/sw02/020413a1.htm (accessed 15 May 2005).

—— "ILO Mission to Verify Junta's Promises on Forced Labour in Burma," September 2002.

Asiaweek. "A Man Who Never Gave In: The nation's last political prisoner speaks out," 11 December 1998. Online. Available at: www.asiaweek.com/asiaweek/98/1211/nat5.html (accessed 15 May 2005).

Associated Foreign Press. "Support Grows in US Congress for Sanctions Against Burma," 5 June 2003, Washington, D.C.

Associated Press. 13 June 1995, Singapore.

Bangkok Post. "Burmese army and the 'national interest,'" 16 June 1990, Bangkok.

—— "Burma's Generals Beyond Reason," 10 September 2000, Bangkok.

—— "Shan Rebels Headed for Junta Bases," 7 March 2001, Bangkok.

—— "Burma Army Moves in on Shan Bases," 6 February 2002, Bangkok.

—— "Shan Army Denies Ambushing Junta Troops," 24 January 2003, Bangkok.

—— "Troops Mass to Attack Shan Army," 22 June 2003, Bangkok.

—— "Shan Army Forced to Desert Base," 4 October 2003, Bangkok.

BBC. "Port of Singapore faces new rival," *BBC NEWS*, 14 May 2002. Online. Available at: news.bbc.co.uk/1/hi/business/1986486.stm (accessed 15 May 2005).

—— "Burma's currency hits record low," *BBC NEWS*, 27 August 2002. Online. Available at: news.bbc.co.uk/2/hi/business/2219746.stm (accessed 15 May 2005).

—— "Burmese 'coup plotters' jailed," *BBC NEWS*, 15 September 2002. Online. Available at: news.bbc.co.uk/2/hi/world/asia-pacific/2259751.stm (accessed 15 May 2005).

—— "Burmese ex-leader's relatives face death," *BBC NEWS*, 26 September 2002. Online. Available at: news.bbc.co.uk/2/hi/world/asia-pacific/2281363.stm (accessed 15 May 2005).

—— "Former Burma Dictator Ne Win dies," *BBC NEWS*, 5 December 2002. Online. Available at: news.bbc.co.uk/2/hi/asia-pacific/2544975.stm (accessed 15 May 2005).

—— "Obituary: Ne Win," *BBC NEWS*, 5 December 2002. Online. Available at: news.bbc.co.uk/2/hi/asia-pacific/1581413.stm (accessed 15 May 2005).

—— "Burma's Suu Kyi attacks junta," *BBC NEWS*, 23 April 2003. Online. Available at: news.bbc.co.uk/go/pr/fr/-/1/hi/world/asia-pacific/2969327.stm (accessed 15 May 2005).

—— "Burma moves to stifle protest," *BBC NEWS*, 2 June 2003. Online. Available at: news.bbc.co.uk/go/pr/fr/-/2/hi/asia-pacific/2955410.stm (accessed 15 May 2005).

—— "Hardliners winning Burma debate," *BBC NEWS*, 2 June 2003. Online. Available at: news.bbc.co.uk/go/pr/fr/-/2/hi/asia-pacific/2956002.stm (accessed 15 May 2005).

—— "Asean calls for Suu Kyi release," *BBC NEWS*, 17 June 2003. Online. Available at: news.bbc.co.uk/go/pr/fr/-/2/hi/asia-pacific/2992550.stm (accessed 15 May 2005).

—— "Do sanctions against Burma work?" *BBC NEWS*, 20 June 2003. Online. Available at: news.bbc.co.uk/1/hi/world/asia-pacific/3006908.stm (accessed 15 May 2005).

—— "Japan freezes aid to Burma," *BBC NEWS*, 25 June 2003. Online. Available at: news.bbc.co.uk/1/hi/world/asia-pacific/3019732.stm (accessed 15 May 2005).

—— "Burma defends Suu Kyi custody," *BBC NEWS*, 13 July 2003. Online. Available at: news.bbc.co.uk/1/hi/world/asia-pacific/3062655.stm (accessed 15 May 2005).

—— "US approves Burma sanctions," *BBC NEWS*, 16 July 2003. Online. Available at: news.bbc.co.uk/1/hi/world/asia-pacific/3069841.stm (accessed 15 May 2005).

—— "Mixed feelings over Burma sanctions," *BBC NEWS*, 16 July 2003. Online. Available at: news.bbc.co.uk/1/hi/world/asia-pacific/3073053.stm (accessed 15 May 2005).

—— "Bush approves Burma sanctions," *BBC NEWS*, 29 July 2003. Online. Available at: news.bbc.co.uk/1/hi/world/asia-pacific/3105489.stm (accessed 15 May 2005).

—— "Protests mark Burma anniversary," *BBC NEWS*, 8 August 2003. Online. Available at: news.bbc.co.uk/1/hi/world/asia-pacific/3134123.stm (accessed 15 May 2005).

—— "Burma favors euros over dollars," *BBC NEWS*, 15 August 2003. Online. Available at: news.bbc.co.uk/1/hi/business/3154885.stm (accessed 15 May 2005).

—— "China slams Burma sanctions," *BBC NEWS*, 20 August 2003. Online. Available at: news.bbc.co.uk/1/hi/world/asia-pacific/3166785.stm (accessed 15 May 2005).

—— "Cabinet reshuffle in Burma," *BBC NEWS*, 25 August 2003. Online. Available at: news.bbc.co.uk/1/hi/world/asia-pacific/3180339.stm (accessed 15 May 2005).

—— "Lee Kuan Yew Staying on at 80," *BBC NEWS*, 16 September 2003. Online. Available at: news.bbc.co.uk/1/hi/world/asia-pacific/3112220.stm (accessed 15 May 2005).

—— "Burma rebuilding risks Pagan jewel," *BBC News*, 4 June 2005. Online. Available at: news.bbc.co.uk/1/hi/world/asia-pacific/4606759.stm# (accessed 5 June 2005).

Burma News Update. "Japanese Reward Regime for Talking," no. 134, 9 May 2001.

Online. Available at: www.burmaproject.org/burmanewsupdate/index134.html (accessed 15 May 2005).

—— "Few Signs of a Real Dialogue," no. 143, 22 September 2001. Online. Available at: www.burmaproject.org/burmanewsupdate/index143.html (accessed 15 May 2005).

—— "NLD says No Improvement in Political System," no. 146, 1 November 2001. Online. Available at: www.burmaproject.org/burmanewsupdate/index146.html (accessed 15 May 2005).

The Burma Review. 13 January 1947, Rangoon.

Daily Times. Associated Foreign Press. "Economic Chaos Grips Myanmar as Sanctions Bite," 28 October 2003. Online. Available at: www.dailytimes.com.pk/?page=story_18–8-2003_pg4_12 (accessed 15 May 2005).

Deutsche Press-Agentur. "Burma's Ex-Strongman Ne Win Hosts Luncheon for 99 Senior Monks," 21 March 2001, in *Burma News Update*, no. 132, 4 April 2001. Online. Available at: www.burmaproject.org/burmanewsupdate/index132.html (accessed 15 May 2005).

The Economist. "Why Bother Voting? The Government is Almost Unopposed," 1 November 2001.

Forbes. "Asia Will Rise Again," 23 March 1998.

Guardian. 18 August 1961, Rangoon.

Independent. "Plummeting Kyat Revived," 13 May 2002, London, in *Burma News Update*, no. 153, 21 May 2002. Online. Available at: www.burmaproject.org/burmanewsupdate/index153.html (accessed 15 May 2005).

International Herald Tribune. "Aid Linked to Junta's Talks With Opposition: Japan Rewards Burma For Political Opening," 26 April 2001. Online. Available at: www.iht.com/articles/2001/04/26/burma_ed3_.php (accessed 15 May 2005).

—— "Burma Has Done Nothing to Deserve Japan's Aid Reward," 28 April 2001. Online. Available at: www.iht.com/articles/2001/04/28/edstein_ed2_.php (accessed 15 May 2005).

—— "Proposed Electoral Changes are Rejected: Singaporean Leaders Dismiss Reform Calls," 13 November. Online. Available at: www.iht.com/articles/2001/11/13/a6_24.php (accessed 15 May 2005).

—— "Drop the Stick, Grow with the Chinese," 21 May 1993. Online. Available at: www.iht.com/articles/1993/05/21/edgoh.php (accessed 15 May 2005).

The Irrawaddy. "NLD Vice Chairman, U Tin Oo in response to Thailand's Defense Minister, Chavalit," 17 September 2001.

—— "More NLD Offices Allowed to Re-open," 23 October 2001. Online. Available at: www.irrawaddy.org/aviewer.asp?a=3453&z=21 (accessed 15 May 2005).

—— "Shan Struggle Set to Continue," vol. 10, no. 2, Feb.–Mar. 2002. Online. Available at: www.irrawaddy.org/database/2002/vol10.2/cover5.html (accessed 15 May 2005).

—— "Burma's Emperors: Wearing New Clothes," vol. 11, no. 7, 27 October 2003. Online. Available at: www.irrawaddy.org/aviewer.asp?a=3102&z=5 (accessed 15 May 2005).

The Nation. 22 February 1959, Rangoon.

—— "Trouble Ahead for Burma," 25 February 1998, Bangkok.

New Burma. 10 May 1940, Rangoon.

New Light of Myanmar. 13 August 1988, Rangoon.

—— 14 August 1988, Rangoon.

—— 1 May 1990, Rangoon.

—— 14 June 1995, Rangoon.

—— "SLORC Chairman Senior General Than Shwe continues up-country visit with pilgrimage to religious centers," 9 August 1995, Rangoon.

—— 1 May 1996, Rangoon.

—— 2 May 1996, Rangoon.

—— 11 May 1996, Rangoon.

—— 18 May 1996, Rangoon.

—— "Law No. 5/96," 8 June 1996, Rangoon.

—— "West Simplistic on Myanmar, says Singapore's Elder Statesman Lee Kuan Yew," 14 June 1996, Rangoon, p. 5.

—— "Burma: Aung San Suu Kyi Better Off as Symbol," 15 June 1996, Rangoon, p. 3.

—— "Address to the Singapore Press Club," 15 June 1996, Rangoon.

—— 16 June 1996, Rangoon.

—— 17 June 1996, Rangoon.

—— "Myanmar opposition must face reality: SM Lee," 19 June 1996, Rangoon, p. 3.

—— "West told to mind its own business," 20 June 1996, Rangoon, p. 5.

—— "With State patronage, religion, culture and traditions flourish," 20 and 22 October 1997, Rangoon.

—— 27 October 1997, Rangoon.

—— "About an American Sonuttho," 11 November 1997, Rangoon, p. 5.

—— "Ancient pagodas in Bagan under renovation," 16 November 1997, Rangoon.

—— 12th Waxing of Nadaw, 12 December 1997, Rangoon.

—— 25 October 1998, Rangoon.

—— 13 July 1999, Rangoon.

—— 15 July 1999, Rangoon.

—— 15 September 1999, Rangoon.

—— 11 September 2000, Rangoon.

—— "Clarification on 'Loka Niti,'" Ministry of Information, 17 September 2000, Rangoon, p. 5.

—— 11 October 2000, Rangoon.

—— 14 May 2002, Rangoon.

New York Times. "Africa Looks East for a New Model," 4 February 1996, New York.

—— "A Dim View of a 'Posthuman Future,'" 2 April 2002, New York.

—— "A Coup Plot Gone Awry, or a Burmese Comic Opera?" 8 July 2002, New York.

—— "Bloomberg News Humbled," 29 August 2002, New York.

—— Associated Press. "U Ne Win, Ex-Strongman of Burma, Dies at 91," 5 December 2002, New York.

—— Associated Press. "Ex-Dictator Ne Win's Remains Scattered," 6 December 2002, New York.

New York Times Magazine. "The Passion of Suu Kyi," interview with Aung San Suu Kyi, 7 January 1996, New York, pp. 31–37.

Newsweek. "Meth Labs Shift to Heroin as Prices Soar," 16 July 2001, *Sydney Morning Herald,* 3 July 2001, *Bangkok Post,* 11 January 2001, in *Burma News Update,* no. 139, 17 July 2001. Online. Available at: burmaproject.org/burmanewsupdate/index139.html (accessed 15 May 2005).

Reuters. "Address to the Singapore Press Club," 8 June 1996.

—— "Senior Officers Purged for Corruption," 17 November 2001, Associated Press, 18 November 2001, in *Burma News Update*, no. 147, 27 November 2001. Online. Available at: www.burmaproject.org/burmanewsupdate/index147.html (accessed 15 May 2005).

—— "Japan Moves Forward With ODA," 13 May 2002, *Asahi Shimbun*, 14 May 2002, in *Burma News Update*, no. 153, 21 May 2002. Online. Available at: www.burmaproject.org/burmanewsupdate/index153.html (accessed 15 May 2005).

—— "Disgraced Former Myanmar Military Ruler Ne Win Dies," 5 December 2002.

South China Morning Post. "Singapore's Voice of Reason," 1 March 1997, Hong Kong.

Straits Times. 12 June 1996, Singapore.

—— "Program Based on Verifiable Facts: BG Lee," 19 May 1997, Singapore.

—— "Telling the Singapore Story," 20 May 1997, Singapore.

—— "Why we need National Education," 20 May 1998, Singapore, p. 29.

—— 10 February 2001, Singapore.

—— 12 February 2002, Singapore.

—— 21 September 2002, Singapore.

—— 2 December 2002, Singapore.

—— "S'pore GDP down worse than expected 4.3%," 10 July 2003, Singapore.

Time. 16 March 1998.

Working People's Daily. 30 July 1988, Rangoon.

—— "Burmese army and the 'national interest,'" 20 June 1990, Rangoon, p. 7.

—— "The Buddha's instruction in kingly duties," 24 June 1990, Rangoon, p. 7.

Xinhua News Agency. "South Korea, Japan seal deals with Junta," 9 July 2002, *Myanmar Times*, 1–7 July 2002, *Xinhua News Agency*, 3 July 2002, in *Burma News Update*, no. 155, 12 July 2002. Online. Available at: www.burmaproject.org/burmanewsupdate/index155.html (accessed 15 May 2005).

Index